The Complete Sewing Course

...stitch darts...

...join bra pieces...

...add lace...

The Complete Sewing Course

Edited by
DEBORAH EVANS

GALLERY BOOKS
An Imprint of W. H. Smith Publishers Inc.
112 Madison Avenue
New York City 10016

This edition published in 1990 by
Gallery Books,
An imprint of W.H. Smith Publishers, Inc.
112 Madison Avenue,
New York, New York 10016

First published in Great Britain in 1989
by The Hamlyn Publishing Group Limited

ISBN 0 8317 1587 1

Produced by Mandarin Offset
Printed in Hong Kong

Contents

Introduction

The Complete Sewing Course, with its clear illustrations and straighforward instructions, guides you through the various techniques and methods of sewing, from the basics of handling and cutting out fabric to advanced techniques such as tailoring and making slipcovers. If you are taking up sewing for the first time, Chapter 1 will introduce you to the special equipment you may need. It also offers guidance on how to arrange an efficient sewing room, tips on pressing and handling fabrics, and advice on buying dressmaking patterns, and instructions for preparing fabric for cutting out.

Chapter 2 introduces you to the techniques of hand sewing – both functional and decorative, including a selection of the most useful embroidery stitches. It also includes a simple project which gives you the opportunity to practice these skills. The projects are a particularly useful feature of the book; there are ten in all, providing a useful starting point for both dressmaking and home decorating projects.

The third chapter looks at the sewing machine and how to make the best use of it. Chapter 4 then guides you through the different techniques that help to give home-sewn clothes, furnishings, and accessories an individual touch.

For most people, of course, dressmaking is an important part of sewing as a hobby. Chapter 5 takes you through its basic principles, beginning with the crucial aspect of insuring a perfect fit when using printed paper patterns and going on to describe some of the most frequently used methods of construction. Although commercial patterns include instructions, these often presuppose a knowledge of dressmaking. The detailed instructions given in this chapter are intended to supplement pattern instructions and help you to achieve a professional finish.

Professional techniques are developed further in the following chapter; there is advice on working with tricky fabrics, such as leather, silk, and lace, as well as details of special methods of construction for making hard-wearing children's clothes and tailored garments for adults.

If your main interest lies in home decorating, you will find plenty of practical ideas and guidance in chapter 7. Detailed instructions for making bed linen and tablecloths, curtains and draperies, shades and slipcovers will help you to save money while creating furnishings to enhance your surroundings.

1 Before you start

Before you start learning to sew, decide on a suitable corner to set up as a sewing place. You need a cheerful, comfortable, neatly organized sewing area where you can keep your sewing machine and sewing supplies. The ideal place, of course, is a room where you can leave the machine open, the ironing board up, and the work spread out when you have to stop. But most people have to compromise and find a corner where they can.

Much, of course, depends on the space available and the time you spend in sewing. If you sew in the evening you may be able to find a place in the dining room where you can work while the rest of the household is busy in the living room or elsewhere – watching television or doing homework. You could fit a large closet with your sewing and pressing equipment, and the dining table could double as your cutting table. A spare bedroom can be set up as a permanent workroom, which need be straightened up only when guests come to stay. If you have a light and modern utility room that is large enough, you could make that your sewing studio. Make sure you can sit comfortably, with both feet squarely on the floor.

Whatever the space you have found for your sewing corner, you can, with skillful planning, arrange your sewing equipment and tools for long sewing sessions.

SEWING AND PRESSING
You will need a sturdy table for the sewing machine, if it does not have its own cabinet. Make sure the sewing machine cannot slip around and will not cause vibrations. Nearby, arrange places for pins, scissors, spools of thread, bobbins, sewing machine accessories and maintenance equipment, tape measure and so on. These should be within reach as you sit at the machine. Use a stool or straight chair without arms so that you can move your own arms and body freely as you work.

For pressing, you will need a good ironing board and steam iron. Use a stool of a suitable height if you prefer not to stand.

Of course, you will need good lighting in both these areas: place the sewing machine near a window if possible, so that you have the benefit of natural daylight. The light on your machine is focused on the stitching area, but you will need a floor or table lamp nearby, as well as a good level of general lighting throughout the room for reading instructions, cutting out and pressing.

If you have a dress form, place it near the sewing machine so that it is convenient for fitting your garments. For fitting clothes on yourself, you will need a full-length mirror so that you can inspect the fit as you try them on during construction. Fix an inexpensive sheet of mirrored glass to the wall or the back of the door.

Keep a wastebasket bin handy for scraps and threads. If you keep your working area neat as you go along, you will find that you can clean up quickly when you have finished sewing.

LAYOUT AND CUTTING AREA
You will need a smooth working surface, preferably measuring at least 60 by 30 inches. A ping pong table is satisfactory, particularly since it folds away. If you have storage room, use a sheet of chipboard or plywood, with neatly smoothed edges. Stand it on a smaller table or trestles. If you plan to use a dining table, protect it with heavy brown paper, a vinyl cloth or a table pad.

STORAGE AREA
In an ideal world, the storage area is close to the sewing area – preferably folding away into a vast built-in closet. But in reality there are limitations. Try to store everything together and close to where you work. If you have to bring the iron and ironing board from the kitchen, a work basket from the living room, patterns and books from the hall closet and bundles of fabric from the top of the bedroom closet, you will be reluctant to start new projects.

The storage area should be near the sewing area. The amount of space needed will depend on your sewing supplies and tools and the kind of sewing you do. You may need two or three drawers in a chest for fabrics: consider storing them in plastic crates on shelves so that you can bring them out to the table easily. Use clear plastic bags to store remnants of fabric, interfacings, trimmings, and so on. Store patterns in large brown envelopes, clearly marked with the number of the pattern and the pattern pieces. This will save having to crush delicate sheets of tissue into the small envelopes they are supplied in. Keep the original packet in the large envelope for reference, or cut it open and glue it to the outside of the envelope.

A sewing basket or sewing box is ideal for the smaller items, such as scissors, thimbles, pin cushion, tape measure and notions. It is easier to keep needles and spools of thread in a set of trays – cutlery trays are ideal.

All your pressing equipment should be stored together in a bag or box so that it is readily accessible when you are sewing.

Plan the wiring. There are several pieces of essential electrical equipment, and you must be careful to avoid trailing wires across the room. Position pressing and sewing areas close to electric sockets.

For home decorating, particularly curtains and bed linen, you could take a tip from the professionals. They work on a large board (preferably plywood), padded with blankets, tightly covered with a sheet, standing it on trestles at a convenient height. It can be used as a pressing table and is ideal for cutting, marking, basting and hand finishing.

It is important to have somewhere to hang up work in progress and to hang lengths of fabric that you may buy to make up later. You should have several padded hangers and a rail to hang them on so that garments will not get crushed. As soon as the darts in a garment are basted or shaped seams are stitched, hang it on a padded hanger if you have to stop work, rather than folding it and putting it away. This will keep the fabric free of creases and save you time later because you will not have to

press the garment before you start working on it the following day.

When considering closet and shelf space, don't forget to plan wall storage space. You can make use of the wall behind a work table for hanging items – on a wire grid or pegboard. Scissors, pincushions and tape measure can hang from hooks, and small trays can be added to hold pins, needles, and markers.

SIZING UP THE SEWING ROOM

If you can furnish your sewing room from scratch, plan work surfaces and storage for maximum comfort. The plan and diagram show how much space you will need to arrange the furniture and suggests convenient heights for working areas and storage. Of course, you may have to use pieces of furniture that you already have, but the dimensions here are ideal targets. If you are tall, short, large, or small, adjust the proportions to suit your size.

The cutting table is higher than the average dining table; it's the same height as a kitchen work surface, which saves bending when stretching across. Note the toe-space at base of the cupboard beneath the cutting table: this will make it more comfortable to stand close to the edge. If possible, make room to walk all around the table.

It is often easier to sew on a small, free-standing table, although a table against the wall may be a more convenient arrangement. Make sure there is room to move your chair back so you are free to get up and go to the cutting table and ironing board.

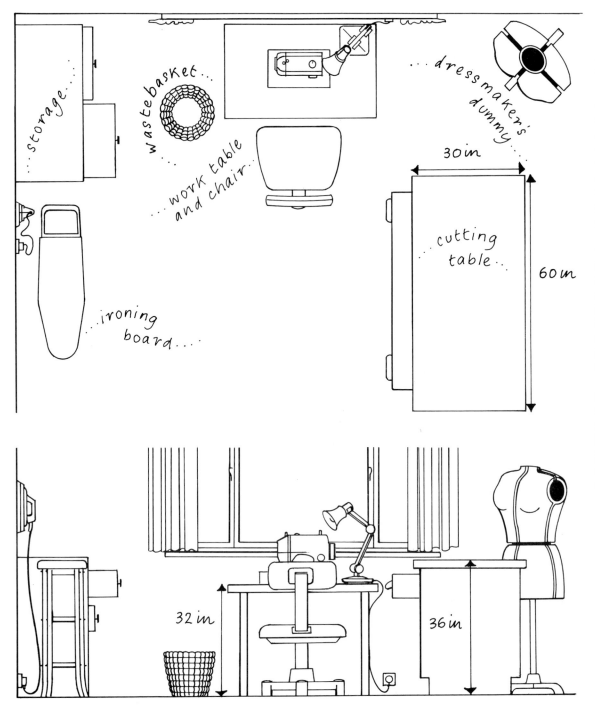

storage ... wastebasket ... work table and chair ... dressmaker's dummy ... ironing board ... 30 in ... cutting table ... 60 in ... 32 in ... 36 in

Equipment and supplies

Keep a small reference section with your sewing equipment: this sewing book, your sewing machine handbook, special stitch guides and pattern books, your collection of dressmaking patterns, a folder or scrap book for clippings and fashion features from newspapers and magazines, envelopes for swatches of fabric and wallcovering, a notebook and sketch pad, and graph paper for drawing plans and patterns.

THE SEWING ROOM
Good lighting, flexible work space, and plenty of storage all add up to a perfect sewing room (opposite). The drapery rod fitted to the top of the wall is a convenient way to provide hanging space for those dressmaking projects and draperies that need to be left to "drop".

STORE IT AWAY
If you can arrange your sewing equipment in trays on a lightweight cart, this will enable you to move it to other parts of the room. The cart can be wheeled to one side, into a cupboard or out of the room, when your sewing space gets taken over by dinner guests or visiting relatives.

Your most important piece of equipment is your sewing machine. It may be a sophisticated, up-to-the minute model, or one you and your family have relied on for years. However old, it must be reliable, and produce regular, even stitches. You should practice using it on a wide range of fabrics, so that you are confident in your ability.

An iron is also vital: to give homemade garments, furnishings, and accessories a smart, professional finish, you have to press your work at every stage, to set the stitches into the fabric and give a crisp finish to seams and edges. In order to use your iron efficiently, you will need a good ironing board. There are also more specialized pieces of ironing equipment, to press awkward corners, such as sleeves and other enclosed seams.

Besides a good sewing machine and iron, your place to sew should have many small tools and sewing accessories. Some items, such as screwdrivers, oil, stitch ripper, special-purpose feet, and spare bobbins are supplied with your machine, but you may want to add to these.

Good quality scissors, which will cut a wide range of fabrics, are vital. Keep your sewing scissors with your sewing equipment, and don't allow them to be used for other household activities – paper cutting, for example, is notorious for blunting the blades. It is useful to have smaller scissors, as well as the pair you use for cutting out, to trim seams, and to clip into seam allowances accurately.

Even if you do not plan to do much hand sewing, you will still need a selection of needles: hems are

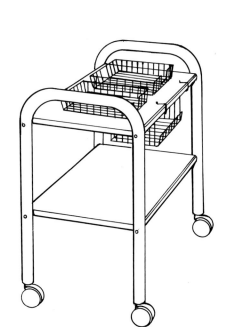

almost invariably sewn by hand, and many parts of the garment – buttons, buttonholes, and strengthening stitches such as arrowheads – are also finished by hand. You will also have to baste some seams and other finishes, such as facings, during fitting and before stitching by machine. Plenty of pins are essential during cutting out and assembling sewing projects.

Most of the other items you require for professional results are for marking the fabric, either before cutting out or during sewing. It is worthwhile investing in a range of marking equipment, so that you have the appropriate items at hand, whatever fabrics you are working with.

Buy good quality tools and supplies, and look after them. Store them so that you can find what you want when you need it. You will be rewarded with good service, convenience, and satisfying sewing results. The list below is essential for advanced sewing. Build up your supplies as you need them – put them on your Christmas list and watch for new sewing aids which may appear on notions counters.

FABRICS AND NOTIONS
Good-quality fabrics are the main ingredient of any sewing project, and a careful choice will not only help to give a good result, but will also ensure that your work is distinctive and exclusive.

When buying fabrics for dressmaking, consider the pattern you plan to use at the same time; and conversely, if it is a fabric that catches your eye first, make sure you can find a suitable pattern before going ahead.

For home furnishings, you may prefer to go to a store specializing in furnishing fabrics. Most manufacturers have their own showrooms, and some will sell to the public.

Unusual sewing notions – ribbons, lace trims, ready-made embroidered motifs – are also distinctive touches, so check the stocks in local stores, and watch for specialist suppliers. And keep an eye on the trimmings counter: you may spot unusual ribbons, buttons, or appliqué motifs which could add a special finesse to your work.

Special interfacings are also invaluable for a good finish: patterns give details of quantities and types of interfacing, but you will often find that you have to buy more than you need, so store any leftovers for future sewing projects.

Store remnants carefully: clear plastic bags make it easy to see what you have, and keep fabrics and notions pristine.

EQUIPMENT CHECKLIST

- **Thread** Buy sewing threads of the appropriate type and color as you need them for new projects. Leftover thread can be used for mending and basting. However, it is a good idea to keep on hand a large spool of white basting thread and some cotton-wrapped polyester in a few basic colors.

- **Hand-sewing needles** Buy good quality steel needles and keep them in the package to prevent rust. Needles are available in various lengths and sizes, to suit different types of stitch and fabric, and with different-sized eyes to suit the thread you are using. You will certainly need *sharps* for general hand sewing; and you may wish also to have some *betweens*, which, being short, are ideal for fine running stitches, as in quilting. For basting, long needles such as *milliner's, straws,* or *darners* are useful. *Ballpoint* needles should be used for sewing knits. Various embroidery needles, such as *crewel* (also good for general sewing) and *tapestry*, can be purchased as required.

- **Upholstery needles** are curved, for stitching into a cushioned surface.

- **Machine needles** Keep an assortment of different sizes, weights and points on hand. Most needles are now sized according to both European and American systems. In addition, they are classified according to type. A widely used European classification is 130/705, which bears additional letters designating the needle type. General purpose, or universal, needles (H) and ballpoint needles (SUK), for sewing knits, are available in sizes 70–100 (US 9–16). There is also a very fine size 60 (US 7) and a very heavy 110 (US 18) universal needle, which are less widely available. Leather (HLL) and jeans (H-J) needles (the latter for sewing denim) come in sizes 90–100 (US 13–16); a fine stretch needle (H–S) has a special antistatic coating ideal for silky knits.

- **Bodkin** Have one for threading cord, ribbon, or elastic into casing and for forming a thread shank for buttons.

- **Pins** Select fine, slender dressmaking pins with needle-like points and smooth blades. Always keep them separate from household pins, since they will become bent and blunt if used for purposes other than sewing. A magnet is useful for collecting pins at the end of the sewing session.

- **Tape measure** Select a tape measure with metal tips, 60 inches (150 cm) long.

- **Gauges** Keep several 6-inch sewing and knitting gauges for measuring short distances. Some gauges have a useful pointed end, which you can use to turn out corners after stitching lapels and other shaped items.

- **Rulers** Have one 18-inch ruler and a yardstick for measuring and positioning fabric grainlines when laying out patterns, and a folding ruler or retractable steel tape for measuring when making curtains and draperies. Use French curves or a flexible ruler for enlarging graph patterns and cutting your own patterns.

- **Skirt marker** Invaluable for measuring and marking hems.

- **Thimbles** Make sure that thimbles fit well, and use one for all hand sewing.

- **Scissors and shears** You will need the following: bent-handled dressmaker's shears with 6- or 7-inch blades for cutting out; light trimmers for trimming seams and cutting out small items; small embroidery scissors for cutting threads and buttonholes; pinking shears for finishing seams on non-fraying fabrics.

- **Pressing equipment** You will need a steam iron, sleeveboard, seamboard, ironing board, pressing mitt and tailor's ham, three kinds of pressing cloth, sponge, paintbrush, clothes brush and pressing pad. See page 24 for information on how to use this equipment.

- **Pincushion** Use for pins and needles.

- **Extra bobbins** Keep a good supply on hand for your machine. Always have one bobbin wound with black thread and one with white, ready to use in mending.

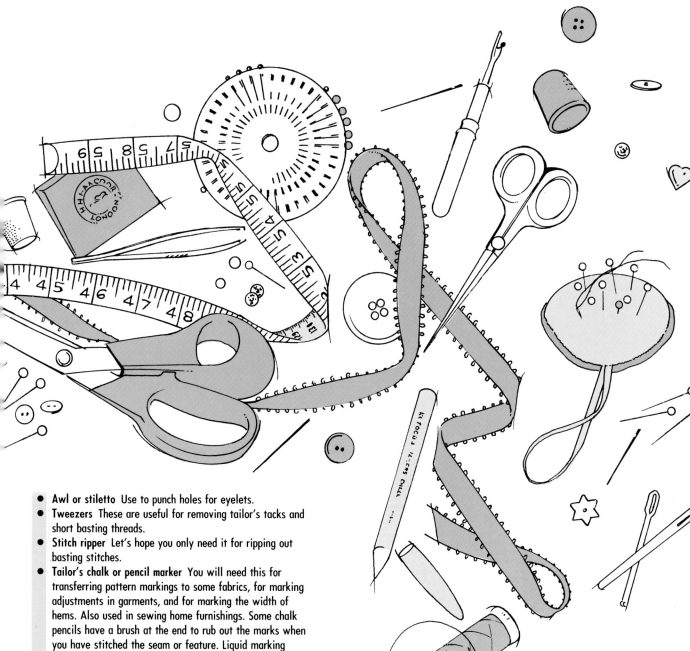

- **Awl or stiletto** Use to punch holes for eyelets.
- **Tweezers** These are useful for removing tailor's tacks and short basting threads.
- **Stitch ripper** Let's hope you only need it for ripping out basting stitches.
- **Tailor's chalk or pencil marker** You will need this for transferring pattern markings to some fabrics, for marking adjustments in garments, and for marking the width of hems. Also used in sewing home furnishings. Some chalk pencils have a brush at the end to rub out the marks when you have stitched the seam or feature. Liquid marking pencils are also useful; the marks either disappear in a few days or wash out with water.
- **Tracing wheel and dressmaker's tracing paper** These are useful for transferring pattern markings on interfacing, mounting and some fabrics. Also called dressmaker's carbonpaper, it is also useful for marking decorative motifs.
- **Embroidery hoops** You will need different sizes, according to the project.
- **Beeswax** Keep a piece on hand for waxing thread before sewing on heavy buttons. It strengthens the thread and prevents twisting and fraying.
- **Basic notions** Keep an assortment of snap fasteners, hooks and eyes, elastic, seam tape, straight seam binding, and bias binding.
- **Buttons** Keep several cards of pearl buttons of various sizes, for new projects and mending jobs. Also, keep a box for buttons that you remove from discarded clothes. They may always come in handy.
- **Darning egg** Traditionally used to hold socks in shape while darning, and useful for other mending jobs.

The sewing machine

You may already have a sewing machine, but buying a sewing machine (or replacing an old one) may be your first step in taking up sewing as a hobby. It is important to practice using the machine, and to try out techniques on remnants before tackling a project.

BUYING A SEWING MACHINE

Sewing machines are not cheap, so it is worthwhile going to a large store and trying out several models before making a decision. You will find that there is a wide choice – the factors that affect your buying decision are your budget and the number of decorative stitches and other special features you think you will need (see below).

Sit at the machine and try out all the features it offers, using a variety of different fabrics. Always bear in mind the type of sewing you plan to do.

You may consider spending more and buying an overlock machine: the bobbin is replaced by one or more extra spools of thread on top of the machine. The fast, easy finish for raw edges is a particularly useful feature.

CARING FOR YOUR MACHINE

Sewing machines need a minimum of care and maintenance. Your dealer will advise you on having the machine serviced and cleaned, but it is up to you to keep it free from dust and fluff and to oil it when necessary.

You will be supplied with one or more stiff brushes for clearing the fluff, and a plastic bottle of sewing machine oil. Always clear fluff and dust from the machine before oiling. If you use the machine constantly, it should be oiled every day. If you use it moderately, oil it every week or two. If you have not used the machine for some time, oil it the day before you use it. Always clear fluff and oil the machine if you are going to put it away for more than a couple of weeks.

Your sewing machine handbook will give details of where the machine should be oiled – some do not need any oiling. Apply a drop or two of oil at each oiling point; never flood the machine. Run the machine slowly, without thread, for a couple of minutes after oiling to allow the oil to work in, then remove the excess from around the needle position with clean muslin. Polish the take-up lever, the thread guides, and the area around the needle and presser foot.

The only other maintenance problem you may have is that from time to time the light bulb will blow. Consult your handbook for instructions on the type of bulb required and how to fit it.

CLEARING DUST AND FLUFF
Remove the needle, foot, and needle plate to gain access to the bobbin mechanism. Use a stiff brush to clear out the fluff and dust from the mechanism.

Oil the machine, if appropriate, before re-fitting the cover plate.

...clear fluff...

...oil if necessary...

WHAT ARE YOUR NEEDS?

- How much can you afford to spend on the machine?
- Do you want a portable machine, which is easy to carry around, or do you have the space for a machine built into a cabinet?
- How many different decorative stitches do you plan to use?
- How easy is the machine to operate? Is it easy to change to different stitches, is bobbin winding simple?
- Do you need a free arm, for stitching sleeve seams and intricate accessories?
- Does the control pedal feel comfortable, and is it easy to control the speed of the machine?
- Can you see the work easily, without bending or hunching over the machine?
- Consider a machine with a horizontal bobbin position, which allows the thread to unwind without dragging, and is particularly useful if you are using nylon or metallic thread.

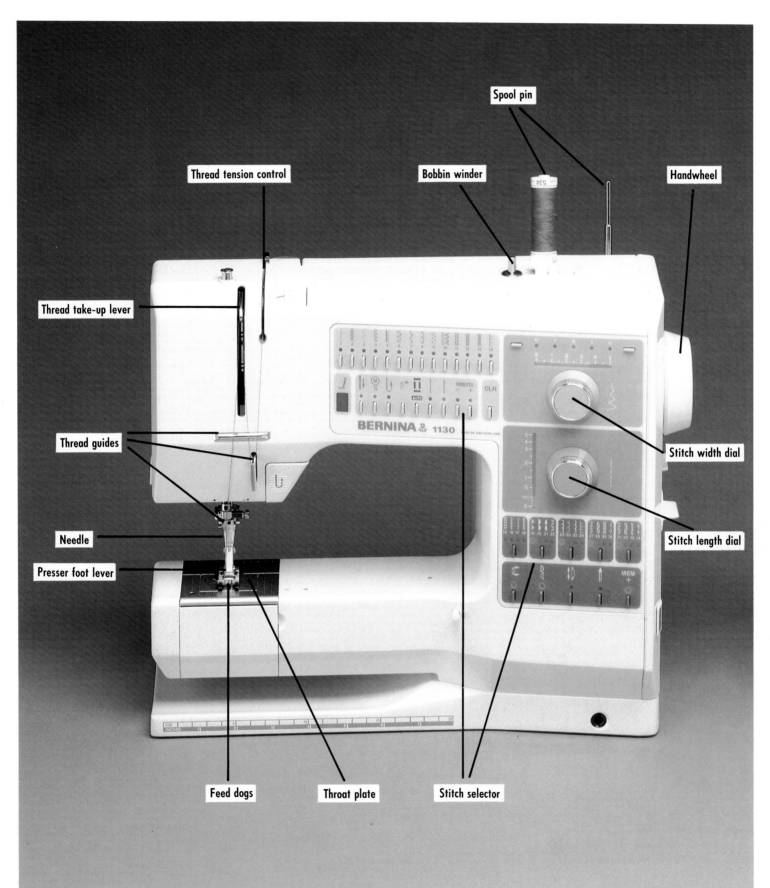

Spool pin

Bobbin winder

Handwheel

Thread tension control

Thread take-up lever

Thread guides

Needle

Presser foot lever

Stitch width dial

Stitch length dial

BERNINA 1130

Feed dogs

Throat plate

Stitch selector

STARTING TO SEW

The first step is to wind some thread onto the bobbin then thread the machine and you are ready to sew. The most versatile thread to choose is cotton-wrapped polyester, which has the strength of a synthetic along with the resistance to high iron temperatures of pure cotton. Otherwise, choose a mercerized cotton or silk thread for sewing natural-fiber fabrics and a synthetic thread for synthetic fabrics.

You will have to test that the tension, needle, and thread you have selected are suitable for the fabric; you may need to make some minor adjustments.

CHANGING THE NEEDLE

You may need to change the needle, either to suit the type of fabric you are stitching or because the one in the machine is bent, blunt, or out of set. Using a damaged needle will give poor results – you may not be able to stitch with it at all, and it may damage your machine if you use it. Unscrew the needle clamp and remove the needle. Slip the new needle in place (normally with the flat edge of the shank facing back, but this may vary from one machine to another). Tighten the screw again.

WINDING THE BOBBIN

Sewing machines are supplied with several extra bobbins, so that you can keep frequently-used colors and threads ready-wound. Position the bobbin on the bobbin-winder spindle. With most machines, you have to take the thread around the upper tension device, and wind it a few times around the bobbin by hand. Then disengage the handwheel according to the instructions in the handbook. Take care not to over-fill the bobbin if your machine does not stop automatically.

Set the bobbin into the mechanism under the throat plate and loop the thread around it. The diagrams show a typical machine – but check your handbook. Pull a couple of inches of thread free of the bobbin, and replace the slide plate.

THREADING THE MACHINE

Your machine handbook will explain how to thread the machine: it is simply a question of taking the thread around various devices that control the tension and adjust the amount of free thread, so that the stitch can be formed. After threading, draw the bobbin thread through the hole in the throat plate before starting to sew.

NEEDLES AND THREADS

Type	Size		Thread	Fabric
General purpose (type 130/705H)	60	7	Very fine	Sheer fabrics such as batiste, voile, chiffon, silk, very light synthetics
	70	9	Fine	Georgette, lingerie tricot, lace, hosiery, organdy, light synthetic fabrics
	80	11	Medium	Cotton, light woolens, silk, taffeta, velvet, poplin, synthetics
	90	13	Medium/thick	Woolens, piqué, flannel, heavy linen, light canvas, synthetics
	100	16	Thick	Coat and suit fabrics, furnishing fabrics, canvas
	110	18		Extra-heavy fabrics
Ballpoint (type 130/705H–S)	70	9	Fine	Sheer knits
	80	11	Medium	Medium-sheer knits, jersey, nylon, underwear
	90	14	Medium	Knitted garments, double knits, active sportswear
Stretch (type 130/705S)	75	10	Synthetic	Synthetic knits needle has antistatic finish good for silks and silky polyesters
	90	13	Synthetic	Heavy knits in synthetic fibers
Jeans (type 130/705J)	90/100	13/16	Heavy	Tightly woven fabric such as denim and canvas
Leather point (type 130/705HLL)	90/100	13/16	Heavy	Special cutting point for leather and suede prevents splitting and tearing
Twin needles	2.7		Medium-fine	For decorative work, such as pin-tucks and double rows of embroidery or topstitching

Always check that the take-up lever is at its highest point when threading. Do not skip any of the thread guides – they help to control tension and prevent loops of thread from getting caught or knotted up.

ADJUSTING THE STITCH

The elements you need to adjust to get the stitch you need are: the thread tension, the bobbin tension, the stitch length, and the stitch width. For decorative stitches there are extra adjustments. You may also have to change the foot.

PRESSURE

With some machines, you have to adjust the pressure of the presser foot to suit the fabric. This is done by means of a screw at the top of the machine or a pressure dial on the front. The pressure should be heavy enough to prevent the fabric from creeping sideways and light enough to carry the fabric without marking it.

Generally, heavy fabrics require heavy pressure and lightweight fabrics require light pressure. Surface finish must also be considered: soft fabrics require less pressure than crisp ones.

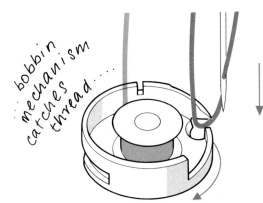

bobbin mechanism catches thread....

....and draws it around....

....to form a stitch....

....right tension....

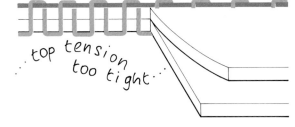

....top tension too tight....

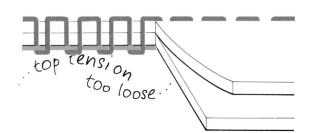

....top tension too loose....

MAKING A STITCH

At the beginning of the stitch the needle is drawn fully out of the fabric. As the needle descends and rises again, the upper thread forms a loop. This is caught by the point of the bobbin mechanism. The thread is drawn around the bobbin, and the loop is enlarged and slips under the bobbin. As the needle continues to rise, the bobbin thread is drawn up into the fabric.

THE RIGHT TENSION

The tension of the threads has to be controlled to make sure they lock evenly into each other. The upper tension controls the thread in the needle and the lower tension controls the bobbin thread. The tensions must be balanced so the threads are drawn into the fabric to the same degree. Your machine should be set to the right tension. Make a test line of stitching and check that it is even.

Normally, adjustments can be made by the top tension only. If the lower thread shows on the top of the sample stitching, the upper tension is too strong – turn it to a lower graduation on the scale. If the upper thread shows on the underside, the upper tension is too loose – turn up the tension.

For some threads, you may need to adjust the bobbin tension: this is done with a screw in the bobbin mechanism. Consult your sewing machine handbook. Turn the bobbin tension back to its original tension when you revert to using an ordinary thread.

USING A ROLLED HEM FOOT

This foot rolls the fabric to give a narrow folded edge under the needle as you stitch. A hem allowance of about ¼ inch is normally required. Guide the fabric into the foot with your right hand as you stitch. Some fabrics are easier to handle than others, so experiment to see whether the rolled hem foot is right for the fabric you have in mind. Loosely woven and slippery fabrics are not generally suitable, so you will have to allow extra hem allowance if you cannot make a rolled hem in this way.

ROLLER FOOT

Some machines are supplied with a roller foot, which is designed to be used with difficult fabrics which tend to stick, or slip about as you stitch such as vinyl-coated cottons, synthetic leather and slippery synthetic fabrics. The roller foot is also particularly useful with bulky fabrics, which tend to get stuck under an ordinary foot.

...rolled hem foot....

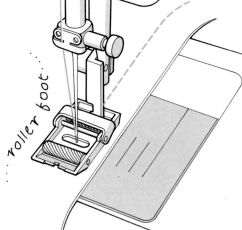

...roller foot...

EXTRA ACCESSORIES

Most machines are supplied with a range of special-purpose feet – for example for stitching cording and zippers, for using with hard-to-handle fabrics, and so on. Check your sewing machine handbook for instructions on using the different feet, and try them all out.

Some accessories, such as rufflers and stitch disks, are extras, which you need not buy at the same time as you buy the machine.

PRACTICE MAKES PERFECT

Every machine has its own characteristics, with different methods of changing stitch, different controls for tension, and so on. It is essential to familiarize yourself with the way in which your machine works, and the various adjustments before setting out to make a garment or home furnishing accessory.

Make up a series of samplers, using different threads, stitches, and fabrics, to see how your machine reacts to various treatments. Zig-zag stitch widths and spacing, in particular, take a little getting used to, and the way in which a machine adjusts from one type of stitch to another.

Of course, different embroidery stitches also vary from one machine to another, so run through each stitch, to gauge the different ways you can add decorative touches. This will give you ideas for planning machine-embroidered items, as well as helping you to develop your sewing skills.

FAULT FINDER

Fault	Cause
Irregular feeding	Pressure too light Needle throat plate wrongly fitted Feed dog clogged with dirt and fluff Unsuitable foot or stitch length
Uneven stitching	Pressure too light
Puckering	Upper and or lower tension too strong Stitch too long, thread too thick Thread not drawn up correctly
Skipped stitches	Out-of-set or bent needle Needle coated with dressing from fabric Machine not correctly threaded Sewing foot and needle not suitable for fabric Thread too coarse, too stiff, or of poor or uneven quality Thread not wound evenly on bobbin or bobbin wrongly inserted
Motor does not run	Check that machine is switched on, foot control is connected and, with air foot control, that the tube is clear

Fault	Cause
Seam pulls to side	Bent needle
Fabric fibers snag	Blunt or unsuitable needle
Upper thread breaks	Wrong needle, poor quality, bent or not properly fitted Upper tension too tight Thread not suitable for work Machine incorrectly threaded Machine needs cleaning
Lower thread breaks	Thread not wound evenly on the bobbin, or not drawn up correctly Lower tension too strong
Needle caught in fabric	Turn off the power. Free the needle by turning the handwheel by hand, raising it backward and forward. Raise needle to its highest point and check that all threads are freed from the throat plate. Replace needle if necessary
Machine is noisy	Needle is blunt or bent Bobbin mechanism is not oiled, or is clogged with fluff

...straight stitch...

...zig-zag...

...over edge zig-zag...

...align hem edge...

...zipper/cording foot....

GUIDING THE FABRIC THROUGH THE MACHINE

Use the markings on the machine throat plate and the width of the foot as a guide for stitching, to ensure even spacing from the edge of the fabric where possible.

For straight stitching, guide the fabric with two fingers held in front of the foot. The feed dogs, underneath the foot, carry the fabric through the machine, so no extra guidance should be necessary. The center of the foot should be aligned with any seamline marking on the fabric, and the edge of the fabric should be aligned with the appropriate mark on the throat plate.

When using the zig-zag stitch, note that the needle moves from side to side: check which side it is on when you position the fabric. Again, the center of the foot aligns with the center of the stitch. When zig-zag stitching over the edge of fabric, check that the fabric does not catch in the throat plate as you stitch. The raw edge of the fabric should align with the end of the slot in the presser foot. When stitching a deep hem or other topstitched seam in an item, find a suitable part of the foot to align with an existing fold or seamline.

ZIPPER/CORDING FOOT

This foot is essential when you need to position a line of stitching close to a bulky trim, such as cording or a zipper. The foot can be adjusted to either the left-hand or right-hand side of the needle so that you can stitch down each side of a zipper. It may also be necessary to adjust the foot when stitching awkward seams, in slipcovers, for example. Normally, the foot should be set to the left-hand side of the needle.

Introduction to fabrics

Napped fabrics have hair-like fibers lying in one direction. This effect is achieved during the finishing of the fabric, by brushing the surface to raise the fibers.

When buying fabrics, either for dressmaking or for home decorating, you must choose one that is of a suitable fiber (either natural or synthetic) and a suitable weave. It is these two considerations that determine the "hand" of the fabric.

FIBERS AND YARNS

The fibers that make up fabrics are spun into yarns and woven on various types of looms, or knitted by machine to make knit fabrics. The way the fibers are spun has a great effect on the texture of the fabric: looped and bouclé yarns, for example, produce textured fabrics, and some methods of spinning produce extra stretch.

The natural fibers are cotton, linen, ramie, silk and wool. Cotton is probably the easiest fiber to work with and is a good choice for a beginner. It is available in a wide choice of weights and weaves, from fine lawn to heavy upholstery fabrics.

Linen, like cotton, comes from a plant, and is fairly easy to handle. Yarns often have a slightly slubbed finish, which may make them slightly more tricky to deal with.

Ramie is a flaxlike fiber often used for dressmaking fabrics.

Silk is a strong fiber, which can be spun into very fine yarns, for very fine fabrics. However, you will also find heavier silks, for both tailored garments and home decorating.

Wool has more natural "give" than other natural fibers, particularly after spinning. For this reason, it is often used for knitted fabrics, where the stretch of the fabric is used in the construction of the garment. Garments made from woven wool fabrics should be lined, to prevent their stretching out of shape (particularly around the "seat" of a skirt or pair of pants, and at knees and elbows).

Synthetic fibers include acrylic, modacrylic, nylon, polyester and several types of rayon. Most are spun and woven to imitate natural fibers, so that, for example, rayon acetate is used to imitate silk. Different manufacturers have their own "ingredients" for man-made fibers, and give them different names.

Always try to find out the exact fiber content of a fabric when buying, and check washing instructions. For ironing and pressing, see the note on page 25.

WEAVES AND KNITS

The weave or knit of a fabric also affects the "hand". Woven fabrics are constructed on a loom, with vertical and horizontal threads (warp and weft). The way the threads interweave affects the appearance of the fabric, and can make patterns on the surface, even if only one type and shade of yarn is used.

Knitted fabrics may be constructed from a single yarn, as in hand knitting, on a circular or flat-bed machine. This gives a very elastic fabric, and the patterns are as varied as those produced by hand knitting – plain knit, rib, jacquard, etc. Double knits are made from two threads and two sets of needles, producing a fabric with a smooth finish on both sides. These knits are known as weft knits.

Warp knits are constructed on flat-bed machines. Multiple yarns run vertically down the fabric, and are manipulated into interlocking loops. Warp knits are generally firmer and flatter than weft knits. The most important point when choosing knitted fabrics is to know how much they will stretch, and to test how they handle before starting to sew.

FINISHES AND PATTERNS

Many fabrics are given special finishes to improve wear, make them crease resistant or stain resistant, and so on. In some cases, this may affect the way they handle – for example, with vinyl-coated cottons.

As well as considering the fiber and weave or knit, you must choose a pattern that suits the item you are making. For example, vertical stripes are difficult to work with if you are making a closely fitted garment, with a lot of darts and seams. Patterns always give suggestions for types of fabric and designs to choose.

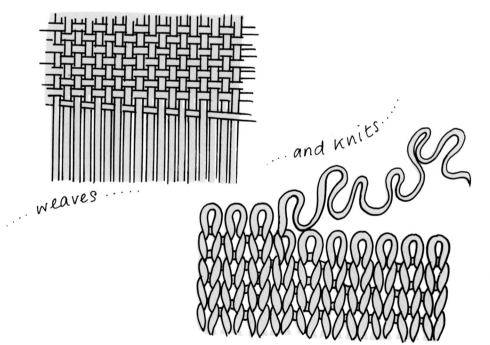

...and knits...

....weaves.....

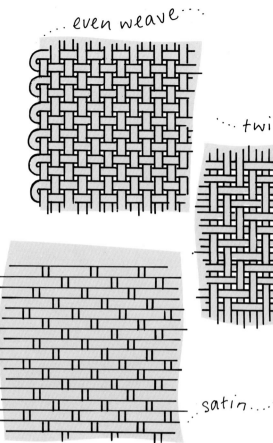

... even weave ...

... twill ...

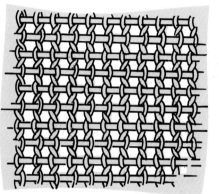

.. pile ...

... leno ...

satin ....

TYPES OF WEAVE

Plain weaves are the simplest and most common: the weft threads pass alternately over and under successive vertical threads. Muslin and taffeta are examples.

Twill weaves are more closely woven, and give a diagonal rib on the face of the fabric. Gaberdine is an example. A common variation is the herringbone or flamestitch effect.

Satin weave is made by floating one set of threads over several of the opposite threads, to give a smooth, lustrous finish, as in cotton sateen.

Leno weave is a porous, open-looking weave, used to produce a lightweight, gauze-like fabric.

Jacquard weave is an intricate weave, with a pattern produced by varying the type of weave as in damask and brocade.

Dobby weave is a simpler weave than jacquard, but still produces a small geometric pattern.

Double cloth weave is made with more than one set of yarns, so that different colors appear on each side of the fabric.

Pile weaves, such as velvet and corduroy, have a third set of threads interwoven between the warp and weft threads which are cut to form a dense, fur-like surface.

... plain knit ....

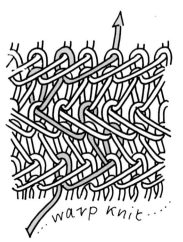

... warp knit ....

TYPES OF KNIT

With a plain knit, which is often made up in a tubular piece, yarns run across the fabric.

A warp knit is made up from several yarns, running down the fabric, but twisted and looped to make a firm knit.

A raschel knit is made from rows of plain knit, like chain stitch, which interlock with insertion yarns to form a lace-like or looped surface pattern.

CHOOSING FABRICS

- **CASUAL WEAR**
  Flannel, denim, sailcloth, cotton, wool, corduroy, stretch fabrics, and knits.
- **SHIRTS AND BLOUSES**
  Broadcloth, madras cotton, cotton-wool mixtures, denim, chambray, seersucker, polished cotton, silk, voile, chiffon, etc.
- **DRESSES FOR DAYWEAR**
  Cotton and blends (including poplin, gingham, batiste, piqué, seersucker), fine wool, wool or synthetic crêpe, linen, silk, pinwale, corduroy, velveteen, gabardine, jersey, cotton/wool mixtures (Viyella), etc
  For softer styles: very fine wool and wool crêpe, soft silk, voile, chiffon, lace, etc.
- **DRESSES FOR EVENING**
  Silk, satin, moiré, taffeta, brocade, Lurex and metallic fabrics, lace, chiffon, net, voile, velvet, velveteen, organdy, etc.
- **SUITS AND SKIRTS**
  Linen, wool, seersucker, heavy cottons, tweed, gabardine, worsted, corduroy, velvet, silk, synthetic blends.
- **COATS**
  Wool broadcloth, flannel, camel, vicuña, corduroy, velveteen, fur fabric, jersey coating, worsted, tweed, gabardine, cotton drill, vinyl.

FIBERS AND WEAVES

- **BABY CLOTHES**
  Stretch terry cloth, brushed cotton and wool-cotton blends, fine lawns, woven synthetic fabrics (easy care).
- **CHILDREN'S WEAR**
  Woven cotton and drill, pinwale corduroy, brushed cotton, synthetic fabrics for easy care.
- **DRAPERIES**
  Furnishing cotton (including glazed cotton and cotton sateen), velvet, silk (for a grand effect).
- **SLIPCOVERS**
  Heavy furnishing cotton, cotton-linen mixture.

- **Top, left to right:** slubbed silk, viscose-nylon lace, polyester-cotton with metallic thread, synthetic lining fabric, printed polyester knit, printed polyester crêpe de chine.
- **Center, left to right:** color-woven polyester-cotton, viscosepolyester linen effect, trellis weave furnishing cotton, cotton terry cloth, glazed furnishing cotton, felt.
- **Bottom left to right:** polyester-wool twill weave, wool knit, color- and pattern-woven furnishing fabric in cotton-viscose-polyester, cotton-linen blend, polyester moiré furnishing fabric, cotton velvet.

Pressing as you sew

Pressing often seems to be an unnecessary interruption to your work. But it is very important to remember that pressing is an integral part of sewing. After stitching seams, darts, tucks, facings, and hems, you must press them. You must also press garment sections before joining them. Pressing beds stitches into the fabric, flattens seams, and shapes the item you are making. Some seams can never be made to lie well if they are not pressed as soon as they are stitched: at a later stage in the construction they may become inaccessible. You must get into the habit of pressing as you go to give everything you make a professional finish.

PRESSING EQUIPMENT

Collect pressing equipment together and arrange it conveniently, near the sewing machine. You will need most of the following items:

Iron. The most important piece of equipment is a reliable iron. Use one with a dependable thermostat, so that you know it is at the right temperature for delicate fabrics. A steam/spray iron will provide enough moisture for most pressing jobs. Keep the sole plate clean, and if you live in a hard-water area, use distilled water to prevent deposits from forming on the iron.

Ironing board. A sturdy board that you can easily adjust to several heights is the next requirement. Make sure that your board has a smooth, clean, padded surface. A heat-reflective cover makes the best use of the heat of the iron.

Sleeveboard. This small ironing board, which stands on the ironing board, is used for pressing sleeves, seams, and all fine details. The ironing board supports the weight of the item being pressed, and prevents unfinished areas from stretching or wrinkling.

Seamboard. This board, which is used like a sleeveboard, is for pressing seams open on facings and at points. It is used mainly for worsteds and other fabrics with a hard finish.

Seam roll. This is similar in function to a seamboard, but is in the form of a firmly padded cushion, and is suitable for a greater variety of fabrics.

Pressing mitt. This is essential for pressing darts,

sleeve board

seam board

pressing pad

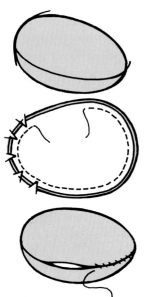

TAILOR'S HAM

To make your own pressing ham, use ½ yard of cotton drill. Wash it to shrink. Make an egg-shaped paper pattern, about 14 inches long and 10 inches wide at the widest point. Use the pattern to cut two pieces of drill. Pin together and stitch, taking ½ inch seams and leaving a 5 inch long opening in one side. Backstitch at each end of the stitching. Fill with clean, sifted silver sand or sawdust, packing the filling firmly into the cover. Turn under raw edges at opening and overcast together by hand.

When extra moisture is required, if the iron does not have a spray, use a hand-held plastic plant spray, full of clean water.

PRESSING PRINCIPLES

- The main difference between pressing and ironing is that in pressing there is little motion of the iron when it is in contact with the fabric. In ironing, you slide the iron over the fabric, with the fabric grain, to remove creases and restore the shape of an item that has been laundered.
- When pressing, correct temperature is even more important than when ironing. Always test the fabric for pressing. If necessary, make a seam or dart in a scrap of the same fabric and press it to see how much heat and moisture the fabric requires. Yard goods do not always come with washing instructions like those normally supplied with ready-made clothing.
- Position the item to be pressed on the board, making sure the fabric is as straight and smooth as possible.

- Always use both hands when lifting your sewing to and from the ironing board.
- Always press on the wrong side to guard against shine.
- Use a press cloth on all fabrics, except cottons and linens. Place it between the iron and the fabric.
- Place the iron lightly in position and allow the steam to penetrate the fabric. Use minimum pressure on the iron, and press in the direction of the fabric grain. This helps to retain the shape. Lift the iron to move to another section.
- Do not over press. It will take the life out of the fabric and cause shine. Overpressing results when you use too hot an iron, leave it in one place too long, use an inadequate press cloth, apply too much moisture, or press too frequently.

the top of set-in sleeves, and curved seams on garments or slipcovers, for example, where the shape and fit must be preserved. Place the pressing mitt on the narrower end of the sleeveboard.

Tailor's ham. This is used on the ironing board for pressing and shaping curved seams, darts, collars, and lapels on tailored garments. You can buy one in some notions departments, or make your own (see opposite).

Pressing cloths. You will need several different pressing cloths (also called press cloths) to suit various kinds of fabric. Use a firmly woven, starch-free cloth or a special chemically treated pressing cloth for heavy fabrics; use a double thickness of soft muslin or cheesecloth for pressing medium and lightweight fabrics; and use wool woven interlining for top pressing on all fabrics. A special transparent pressing cloth allows you to check that the fabric is smooth and interfacing correctly positioned. You will also need a yard of good-quality muslin for moistening cottons and linens when pressing. Moisten it by dipping it in clean water and wringing it out. Place it over the area to be pressed. When pressing silks, woolens, and delicate fabrics, place a dry pressing cloth on the area to be pressed, then cover it with a moistened cloth to provide low, even moisture.

Brown paper. Keep some stiff brown paper with your pressing equipment to use when pressing seams and facings on certain fabrics. To prevent a ridged imprint of the seam allowance from appearing on the main fabric, slip the paper between the seam allowance and the fabric.

Wooden pounding block. Use this to flatten the edges of faced lapels and collars, hems, facings and pleats on tailored garments or furnishings made of heavy or bulky fabrics. Steam the area first, then quickly apply the pounding block. After a little practice you will be able to judge the amount of pressure needed.

Sponge and camelhair brush. Use these to moisten the seams of woolens.

Clothes-brush. Use this for brushing napped fabrics after pressing.

Pressing pad. This is used when pressing monograms, lace, raised decorative stitching, corded quilting and so on. To make a pad, take three or four thicknesses of wool interlining about 20 inches long by 14 inches wide, and stitch them to a backing of drill. To use the pad, place it on the ironing board with the layers of wool interlining right side up.

Hand steamer. This optional extra, which resembles a small steam iron, is useful for applying a concentrated amount of steam to places that need it, such as hems and seams in heavy fabrics. It can be used without a pressing cloth, even on the right side of the fabric.

PRESSING DIFFERENT FABRICS

The texture and thickness of the fiber and the weave of the fabric determine how it should be pressed. Always set the dial to the right fabric.

Nylon, polyester, acrylic and most other synthetic fibers require little heat. Set the dial to the lowest setting. Press on the wrong side, using a thin press cloth. The iron will not steam at this low temperature. If extra moisture is required, place a single thickness of moist, soft muslin over the dry pressing cloth.

Rayon also requires a low heat, but slightly more than nylon. Press on the wrong side, using a thin pressing cloth. Generally, steam from the iron will supply sufficient moisture. If you need more moisture, place a single thickness of moist, soft muslin over the thin, dry pressing cloth.

Silk needs slightly more heat than rayon. But too hot an iron will weaken the fiber and discolor pastels and white silk. Press on the wrong side and use a thin pressing cloth for lightweight silk. If you need added moisture on thick seams, place a single thickness of moist, soft muslin over the thin, dry pressing cloth. On medium- and heavy-weight silks, use a double thickness of moist muslin over the thin, dry pressing cloth for extra moisture.

Lightweight cotton requires slightly more heat than silk. Press on the wrong side. You may place the iron directly on the fabric unless you are using a dark color. To provide uniform moisture on seams, cover with moist soft muslin. Press until dry.

Wool requires more heat than lightweight cotton. Press on the wrong side using a heavy pressing cloth or a double thickness of muslin, covered with moist muslin. Do not press until dry. If you are working with a napped fabric, brush it with a clothes-brush, while there is still a moist steam, to raise the nap.

Linen and heavy cotton require a very hot iron. Press on the wrong side. You may place the iron directly on linen unless it is a dark color. Use a thin pressing cloth covered with damp, soft muslin to prevent shine on thick seams and dark colors.

Blended fabrics should be pressed at the appropriate setting for the more delicate fiber.

Crêpe weaves may present a problem, since they tend to shrink when damp and stretch when under pressure. Use a pressing pad and soft muslin or wool pressing cloth to retain the crinkles in the fabric. Set the iron temperature according to the fiber content.

VELVET AND VELVETEEN
Do not press these, or bring the iron in contact with the fabrics, as you will flatten the pile. Steam them instead. Stand the iron on its heel and place a damp cotton towel over the sole plate. Hold the wrong side of the velvet close to the towel and move it back and forth to allow the steam to penetrate the fabric.

You can also steam velvet and velveteen on a velvet board, which has fine fiber needles, or you can use a wool-faced pressing pad for steaming. Place the velvet face down on the board or pad. Hold the steam iron close to the fabric — not on it — and brush the fabric lightly to distribute the steam. Press seams open with finger tips, then steam the fabric by holding the iron close to it. Do not handle the velvet until it is dry.

PRESSING CONSTRUCTION DETAILS

There are a few basic techniques for pressing particular seams and stitching, which are adapted for pressing all stages of construction.

Always remove pins and basting stitches before pressing. Pins damage the fabric and the sole plate of the iron; basting stitches leave an imprint and are not so easy to remove after pressing. If you have to press prior to stitching, use fine thread and diagonal basting.

When pressing a section of a garment for the first time, press the whole piece, not just the area around the seam or dart. In many cases there is a slight shrinkage even with pre-shrunk fabrics.

Always use a sleeveboard, seamboard, pressing mitt or tailor's ham when pressing small details.

... pressing plain seams ...

... French seam ...

... pressing darts ...

... curved ...

PLAIN SEAM

Press the seam in the same position as it was stitched, using a pressing cloth if necessary.

Open out the seam, wrong side up, over the sleeveboard. Use your fingers and the point of the iron to open out the seam.

Press the seam open, using a pressing cloth between the iron and fabric. For heavy fabrics, place a strip of brown paper under the seam allowance to prevent the imprint of the edge of the fabric from showing on the right side.

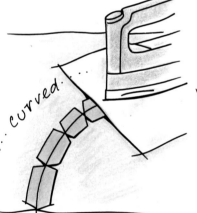

CURVED SEAM

A curved seam must be graded before it is pressed. See seam grading, page 51. Then place the curved seam over the curve of a pressing mitt on the end of a sleeveboard, or over the curve of a tailor's ham. Open and press as for a plain seam.

FRENCH SEAM

After stitching the first stage of a French seam, press as for a plain seam in the position it was stitched. Use a pressing cloth, as the seam is stitched on the right side of the fabric. Press the seam open with the point of the iron in the usual way, then trim seam allowance. Turn seam to wrong side and fold sharply on the first line of stitching. Press again. Stitch the second stage of the seam, then press the stitching and fold back on itself again, before pressing for the final time.

DARTS AND TUCKS

Press the dart flat, as it was stitched, pressing the crease only as far as the point of the stitching.

Place the dart over the curve of a pressing mitt, which has been placed on the small end of a sleeveboard, or over the curve of a tailor's ham. Darts are pressed toward the center of a skirt front and back, blouse front and back; and downward at the underarm and elbow.

Turn dart in the appropriate direction, and, if the fabric is heavy, slip a piece of brown paper under the dart to prevent an imprint on the right side. Press toward the point of the dart, and then press the entire section, using a pressing cloth.

Press tucks in the same way: they are normally pressed toward the center if they are on the inside of a garment, and outward or downward if they are on the outside of an item.

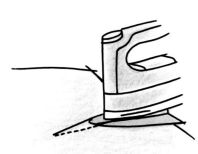

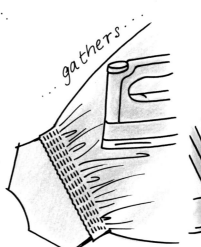

CURVED DARTS

After pressing as stitched, slash darts at waistline to relieve strain. Position the top half of the dart over a pressing mitt on the end of the ironing board as for ordinary darts. Repeat for the lower half of the dart. Use the appropriate pressing cloth and moisture.

DARTS IN HEAVY FABRICS

Darts in heavy fabrics are slashed and pressed open to reduce bulk. After pressing the dart flat, as stitched, place the dart over the curve of a pressing mitt or tailor's ham. Open the dart with the point of the iron.

Place a strip of brown paper under each side of the dart, cover with the correct pressing cloth and moist cloth where necessary. Press the dart open.

USING A POUNDING BLOCK

Use a pounding block to press faced lapels and collars on tailored suits and coats that are made of heavy or bulky fabrics. Stand the iron on its heel and cover with a piece of damp terry cloth. Hold the facing in front of the cloth and allow the steam to penetrate the fabric. Then quickly pound the finished edge of the garment with the wooden block. This will force out the steam and leave a flat edge without a shine.

GATHERS

Press from the wrong side, moving the point of the iron in toward the stitching. Lift the iron, move along and repeat. Since the gathers are usually made in soft fabric, a pressing cloth is not usually necessary (and would make the job more tricky).

HEMS

Hems should not be visible on the right side of the finished garment. Besides marking, folding, and finishing the hem properly (see page 100) you must press it carefully. First mark and fold up the hem, then baste the hem in position ¼ inch from the fold. Position the garment, wrong side up, over the end of the ironing board. Cover with the correct pressing cloth and apply the moisture required by the fabric. Do not slide the iron: lift it from one section to the next, pressing lightly and forcing steam through the pressing cloth to form a sharp crease at the fold.

When pressing bulky fabrics, use a wooden pounding block.

If you want a softer hemline, particularly on double knits and woolens, press the hem very lightly so that you do not flatten the fold.

NECKLINE FACING SEAMS

Press the seam in the same position as stitched, after trimming the seam allowance, clipping corners and curves, and notching where necessary.

Slip the facing over the seamboard, so that the seam lies along the top of it. Apply moisture with a sponge or paintbrush. Carefully control the heat of the iron so that you can press without a pressing cloth in this step.

On the curve of the neckline, press just a small portion at a time. Lift the garment with both hands to move it.

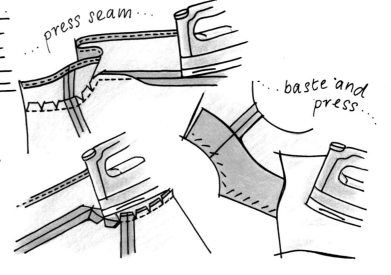

Turn the facing to the underside, roll it under slightly at stitching line, and baste. On silks and woolens use silk thread and diagonal basting to hold the facing securely in place. Press on the underside, using an appropriate pressing cloth and moisture.

Introduction to patterns

For most of the items you make, you will need some sort of pattern. In dressmaking, a wide range of tissue paper patterns is available, from fabric shops and department stores. The patterns tell you how much fabric is required, what notions you need for fastenings and decoration, how to lay out the pattern pieces on the fabric, and how to construct the garment. You may find that more than one size is given on each paper pattern, which may appear confusing, but actually gives you some flexibility in cutting garments to fit exactly if you are not a standard size.

You may also find graph patterns for clothes in books and magazines (there are some in this book). These patterns usually have to be cut out in paper so that you can cut out the garment in the same way as a ready-made pattern. Instructions for doing this are given on page 33. You may also use an existing garment as a pattern: again, cut out your own pattern pieces following the garment as a guide, and use them like a ready-made pattern.

The pattern has markings, indicating special features like darts, positions of openings and fastenings, and where to match the edges of the fabric to stitch seams. These markings are transferred from the pattern to the fabric before removing the paper pattern; you will find instructions for this on pages 30 – 31.

For home decorating, you may find ready-made tissue patterns or graph patterns, or you may have to work without a pattern, when making cushions, draperies and slipcovers, for example. See pages 176–246 for home furnishings without patterns.

You cannot try on a pattern, as you can a ready-made garment, and you may not yet have the skills of an experienced dressmaker, so consider the following points when choosing a pattern.

KNOW YOUR SIZE

There are different types of pattern, cut to suit different figure types and sizes. Measure yourself carefully and consult the pattern manufacturer's chart before buying a pattern. The measurements you should consider are given on page 110. Pattern sizes tend to be smaller than the same size in ready-to-wear clothing; for example, a pattern size 12 is equivalent to a 10 in ready-to-wear.

Small adjustments to fit can be made during construction of a garment, but you may have to adjust the pattern before cutting out, to make major alterations, to allow for a high bustline or broad shoulders, for example. Techniques for adjusting patterns are given on page 112. Select patterns according to your bust measurement, and make adjustments where needed for other measurements.

However, if your bust is larger in proportion to all other measurements, take your chest measurement (page 110) and compare it to the bust size. If the difference is 4 inches or more, buy your pattern one size smaller than the bust measurement and enlarge it at the bust. The smaller size will give a better fit around the shoulders and armholes. For skirts and pants, select the pattern according to the hip measurement – it is easier to adjust the waist.

All the patterns are based on actual body measurements, and include an allowance for ease. So a coat or jacket pattern will have more ease (and larger pattern pieces) than a close fitting garment.

FIGURE TYPE

Patterns are also proportioned according to figure type. The chart below explains the figure types that you may find, though not all patterns are available for all figure types. Try to be objective and

---

TYPES OF PATTERN

Young Junior/Teen	Size 5/6 to 15/16	Designed for developing teen or preteen figure 5'1"–5'3"
Junior Petite	Size 3jp to 13jp	Designed for a well-developed figure, 5'–5'1", with shorter waist than a Junior
Junior	Size 5 to 15	Designed for the well-developed figure, 5'4"–5'5", slightly more short-waisted than a Miss
Miss Petite	Size 6mp to 16mp	Designed for a well-proportioned figure, 5'2"–5'4", with a slightly shorter and larger waist than a Miss
Miss	Size 6 to 20	Designed for the average, well developed figure, 5'5"–5'6" tall
Half-size	Size 10½ to 24½	Designed for a fully developed figure, 5'2"–5'3", with relatively narrow shoulders and large waist
Woman	Size 38 to 52	Designed for a full figure, 5'5"–5'6" tall
Maternity	Size 6 to 16	Designed for a figure of Miss's height, in fifth month of pregnancy, but with ease to accommodate ninth month

be prepared to alter the pattern further if you are not a standard figure type.

SEWING SKILLS

When choosing a pattern, you must consider your own skills, and the features of the pattern. Start with simple shapes which do not rely on complicated fitting for their style. Avoid garments that demand difficult-to-handle fabrics and items with intricate openings, if you do not have much experience. If you progress from simple patterns to more complicated ones, you can practice your skills and build up confidence. If you choose a difficult pattern before you have mastered simple techniques you will not get good results.

Many manufacturers group their patterns according to ease of sewing, so look for patterns marked "easy", or similar to start with.

YOUR BUDGET AND LIFESTYLE

Some people take up sewing as an economy measure in order to save money on the cost of clothes. Others make their own clothes because they can't get a good fit from ready-made ranges, and others sew because they want to add their own design touches to their wardrobe. Be prepared to spend money on good fabrics if you are after professional results. It is worthwhile checking to see how much fabric is needed, and what types of fabric are recommended before buying a pattern – you may find that the cost of making it is more than you expected.

The style of pattern you choose should also suit your lifestyle. There is no point in spending time and money making clothes that will hang at the back of your closet for months on end. To make the most of your work, consider its suitability and purpose. Can the garment be worn all the year round? Will it be fashionable for more than one season? Will it mix with other clothes in your wardrobe, and do you have suitable accessories?

GARMENT STYLE

Of course, your figure type also affects the style of garment you choose. Look at yourself and your measurements objectively. Decide which points you want to emphasize and which you want to disguise. For example, you may want to emphasize a trim waistline or choose a garment which will draw attention away from large hips. Choose the same style of garments in pattern form as you would choose if you were buying a ready-made garment. You probably know from your existing wardrobe which shapes suit you – and what you feel most comfortable in.

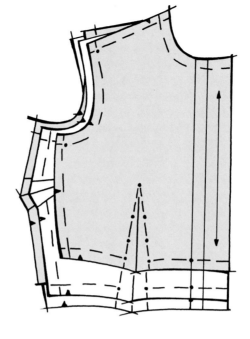

PATTERN PROPORTIONS
By laying four front bodice pieces, designed for different figure types, on top of each other, you can see how the proportions vary. In this case, size 12 has been used for the Girls', Misses' and Miss Petite patterns. The Half size is 11½.

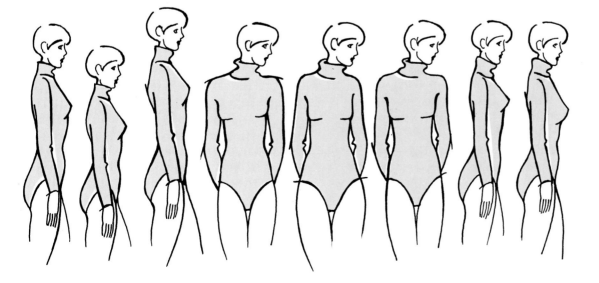

RECOGNIZING YOUR FIGURE TYPE
Each of the figures shown here is a size 12, but you can see that the silhouettes and proportions vary considerably. Decide which figure "defects" you have, and be ready to adjust patterns to give a better fit. Of course, you may have to make more than one adjustment, to suit a tall figure with a high bust, for example.

Marking the fabric

Pattern markings may be transferred to the fabric before, during, or after cutting out. If you are not using a pattern, mark the fabric with dressmaker's chalk. This is available in blocks or pencils, and there are also some fiber-tipped markers on the market, which use easily washable inks.

Some markings are transferred to the edge of the fabric as you cut out the pattern pieces. These are marked as printed or inward-cut notches on the pattern pieces, and are cut as outward notches on the edge of the fabric pattern piece. If the fabric frays easily, notches can be marked with tailor's tacks or chalk. Single and double notches are used to avoid confusion when assembling a garment. Notches on adjacent pattern pieces are matched when you come to stitch seams.

Markings on the pattern such as dots, triangles, and squares indicate the positions for darts, openings, buttonholes, tucks, and similar features on a garment. They are marked with tailor's tacks, chalk or a tracing wheel and dressmaker's carbon paper.

A tracing wheel is a small spiked wheel on the end of a handle. You position the paper on or under the fabric to be marked and run the wheel along the line to be marked, and the color from the paper is transferred onto the fabric. The paper is available in white and several colors.

If you are working with a pattern – either a tissue pattern or one enlarged from a graph pattern – leave it pinned in position until you have transferred all these marks. Use tailor's tacks, chalk, or chalked thread in different colors for different types of mark so that you can find them easily during construction.

CUTTING OUTWARD NOTCHES

Cut out the pattern, following the cutting line, until you reach a notch. Use a small pair of scissors to clip outward and back to the cutting line, following the printed notch on the pattern if there is one.

TAILOR'S TACKS

Use a double length of thread about 24 inches in length and in a color contrasting with the fabric. Do not knot the end. You can use ordinary sewing thread, but some dressmakers prefer embroidery or darning thread because it is soft and clings to the fabric. At the point to be marked, take a small stitch through the pattern and double thickness of fabric, leaving a ¾ inch thread end.

Take a backstitch in the same place and leave a loop a little shorter than the thread end. Continue to the next point to be marked, if it is not more than about 4 inches from the first. Cut through the threads between the tailor's tacks. If the tack is through a double layer of fabric, ease the layers apart and snip the threads, leaving a tuft of thread in each layer.

FOLDLINE MARKINGS

To mark a foldline on a single layer of fabric, make a line of basting stitches along the fold. On a double layer of fabric cut a piece of thread over twice the length of the line to be marked and use it double. Baste through the two layers of fabric along the line to be marked, taking small stitches, about 2 inches apart and leaving a loop between the stitches. Cut the loops between the stitches, then pull the layers of fabric apart and snip the threads, leaving lines of tufts down the foldline.

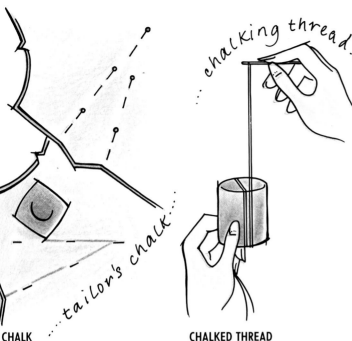

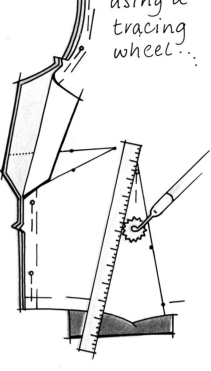

CHALK

Tailor's or dressmaker's chalk may be used when there is no danger of damaging the fabric. Because it rubs off easily, use it when the construction is to be done immediately. Always mark the wrong side of the fabric – fold it with right sides inward when cutting a double layer of fabric.

Place a pin through the double thickness of fabric to one side of the point to be marked. Bring the point of the pin back through the fabric to the other side of the point to be marked. Mark the fabric over the pins on one side, then turn it over to mark the back of the other side of the other piece of fabric.

CHALKED THREAD

Chalked thread can be used to mark foldlines, dart stitching lines, pocket positions, and so on. Use a double thread about 12 inches long. Do not knot the end. Pull the thread around a square of tailor's chalk several times so that it is well coated. Take a stitch in the fabric at each point to be marked through both thicknesses of fabric and pattern where appropriate. Draw the thread right through the fabric, and it will leave a tiny chalk deposit in each layer of fabric. Rechalk the thread frequently.

TRACING WHEEL AND DRESSMAKER'S CARBON

To mark through a pattern on a single layer of fabric, place the fabric, right side up, on a flat surface, with the pattern pinned on top. Slip a piece of dressmaker's carbon paper, right side up, under the fabric, beneath the feature on the pattern. Run the tracing wheel over the feature on the pattern, and carbon marks will be left on the wrong side of the fabric.

With a double layer of fabric, leave the pattern in place and mark the wrong side of the top layer of fabric with chalk. With the two layers of fabric pinned together, right sides facing, position a piece of the paper, right side up, under the fabric as before. Slip a second piece of the paper, right side down, between the pattern and the fabric. Trace the feature, following the pattern marking, and it will be transferred to the fabric.

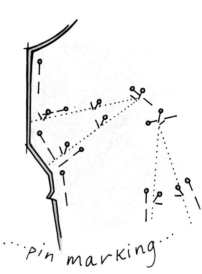

MARKING WITH PINS

Stick a pin into the fabric, through the pattern, where appropriate, at the point to be marked. Push it right into the fabric, so that the head is against the top layer. Turn the fabric over and push a second pin through at the same point from the other side. When the layers of fabric (and pattern) are pulled apart, one pin is left in each layer of fabric.

RULES FOR MARKING FABRIC

- When marking with tailor's tacks, use fine threads for fine fabrics. Also, use fine needles, to avoid damaging the fabric. Do not use chalk or tracing wheel and dressmaker's carbon for marking fine or delicate fabrics: the marks may be tricky to remove.
- Always cut notches outward to avoid problems with seam allowances fraying. Trim off the notches when you trim the seam allowances.
- Work on a flat surface, keeping the fabric smooth and straight as you work.
- If you are working on a polished table, cover it with cardboard to prevent the fabric from slipping and to protect the table from needles, pins, and the tracing wheel.
- Mark on the wrong side of the fabric, so that it will not show if it does not wash out immediately, and so that you can see the marks during construction.
- Do not use tailor's chalk or pins to mark fabric unless you are going to assemble the item immediately: these marks rub off easily or slip out of place.
- When using dressmaker's carbon, use white where possible. If you use a color, choose one near the color of the fabric with just sufficient contrast to make visible marks. Use small pieces of the paper and move them from one section to another as you work across the fabric.

Preparing to cut out

If you are not sure whether to shrink washable fabrics, make a test: cut a swatch on the true lengthwise and crosswise grain of the fabric and make a note of the exact length and width. Shrink the swatch as described on the right, press and measure again. If the swatch is smaller than the original size, you will have to shrink the fabric.

Before you can start to sew, you have to do some cutting out. And before you cut out, you have to prepare the fabric. Start by examining the fabric to check which is the right and wrong side, and to familiarize yourself with any pattern repeat on printed and self-patterned fabrics. Make sure that patterned or checked fabrics are printed "on grain" – that is the lengthwise direction of the pattern corresponds to the lengthwise grain of the fabric.

PREPARING THE FABRIC

If the fabric is crushed or there is a crease where the fabric has been folded and stored, press well. Then straighten the ends of the fabric, and check that the lengthwise grain runs at right angles to the crosswise grain. If the grain lines do not run true to the markings on the pattern piece, the item will not

hang as it should. You may also need to shrink the fabric.

It often helps to apply moisture to a fabric when straightening it, so bear the following points in mind.

Cottons and linens. Use a damp sponge to moisten the fabric, then pull gently on the bias.

Woolens. Place a wet sheet over the fabric and leave it long enough to moisten the wool (two or three hours). Take care that the fabric lies flat and there are no creases in either the fabric or the sheet. Pull gently to straighten.

SHRINKING FABRIC

Most fabrics are pre-shrunk; information to that effect usually appears on the descriptive label or on the selvage (the edge of the fabric, finished during manufacture). Look for the labels "pre-shrunk" or "Sanforized". If one of them is used it means that the fabric is guaranteed not to shrink more than 1 inch per 1 yard; if you fail to find any information, ask the sales staff. Fabrics that have not been pre-shrunk must be shrunk before cutting, except wool crêpe and silk crêpe.

Before shrinking a fabric, snip or clip the fabric every 2 to 3 inches along each selvage. If the selvage is not cut, it will draw up in the shrinking process.

Cottons, linens, and washable fabrics. Open out the fabric to its full width, and make deep folds of about 18 inches on the crosswise grain. Place the fabric in a basin of water and let it soak for an hour. Drain the water from the bowl, then press the water out with your hands. (Do not wring, spin, or twist the fabric.) Hang the fabric lengthwise over a line. Make sure that it is straight and smooth. Remove as much water as you can with a towel. Before the fabric is completely dry, press it on the wrong side, gliding the iron with the lengthwise grain. Press out the center fold. Use the same method for shrinking woven interfacings and waistbanding for use in washable garments.

Woolens. Fold the fabric lengthwise on the straight grain, and place it between the folds of a wet sheet. Fold on the crosswise grain in deep folds. Avoid forming wrinkles in the fabric and sheet. Cover the folded sheet with a towel so that the top section will not dry out, and leave for eight or ten hours. Then remove the sheet, and spread the fabric on a flat surface to dry. Be sure that the grains are straight. When dry, press on the wrong side with a pressing cloth or cheesecloth between the fabric and iron. Press out the center fold.

STRAIGHTENING THE ENDS

To straighten the end of the fabric, find the crosswise grain as follows:

Snip through the selvage at the longer edge and use your fingers or tweezers to get hold of a thread.

Pull it gently, allowing the fabric to gather onto the thread.

Cut the fabric along the line of the pulled thread. When you reach the gathers, ease them flat and pull and cut again.

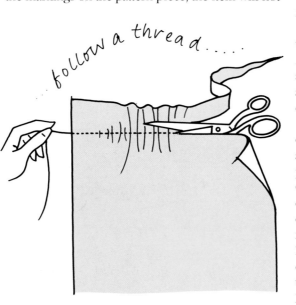

follow a thread.....

STRAIGHTENING THE GRAIN

In the manufacturing process, during weaving, finishing, printing or rolling, some fabrics are pulled off grain, and you must straighten them before cutting out. To see whether this is necessary, place the fabric on a flat surface and fold it with selvages together. Pin the edges together along the straightened end. If the fabric lies flat, the crosswise and lengthwise grains are at right angles and the grain is straight.

Gently pull the fabric on the true bias, gradually working down the full length of the fabric. Steam pressing also helps to straighten some fabrics.

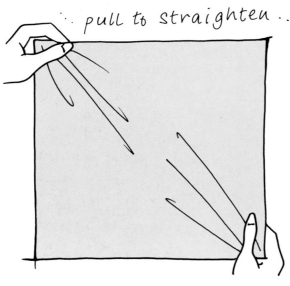

... pull to straighten ...

USING GRAPH PATTERNS

Graph patterns are given in some books and magazines. They are a way of giving you a pattern to follow without having to print a full-size pattern piece. The pieces that you need to make the item are printed on a background grid of squares, each square on the grid representing a given measurement. In order to enlarge the pattern to full size, you need paper marked with a grid of the correct size. Cross section paper, which is available from art supply stores, can be used for this. It is marked with 1-inch squares and comes in large sheets (normally 17 by 22 inches); several can be taped together, if necessary, for large pattern pieces. Or you can use dressmaker's pattern paper. This is marked with small numbers placed at 1-inch intervals (used in drafting original patterns). To use it for enlarging, draw a grid through the numbers at 1- or 2-inch intervals, as required.

For drawing curved lines in the patterns, you may find a French curve or a flexible curve useful. These can be bought at art supply stores.

Check the scale of the graph pattern – this should be indicated, "Each square represents 2 inches" or the appropriate measurement. Then mark out the area represented by the graph pattern on the sheet

...use a table top....

of pattern paper. Following the pattern, mark the outline on the pattern paper. If there are any extra markings, transfer these to the enlarged pattern.

Pin the pattern pieces in place on the fabric, adjusting positions to give the best use of the fabric. You may be given a pattern layout to make this easier. Be sure to make a note of how many times each piece should be cut out, and whether any of them have to be placed on a fold.

SPECIAL FINISHES

Fabrics such as glazed chintz, polished cotton, vinyl, and those with a crease-resistant finish cannot be straightened because of their finish. Square off the crosswise grain with a ruler. Place the fabric flat on a table with the selvage parallel to the side of the table. Lay a ruler across the cut end so that it forms a right angle with the selvage (parallel to the end of the table). Draw a chalk line, and cut on this line. Use only the lengthwise grain as a guide when cutting out. These fabrics will hang satisfactorily, since they will not lose their shape in wearing, hanging, or pressing.

ENLARGING A GRAPH PATTERN

Starting at one corner of one pattern piece on the graph pattern, find the corresponding point on the area marked out on the dressmaker's graph paper. Make a series of crosses on the graph paper corresponding to the outline of the pattern piece. Make a cross every time an outline changes direction.

With curved and straight, angled lines, make a cross every time the outline crosses a grid line. When you have worked all the way around the pattern, you should come back to the starting point. If you don't, you have made a mistake, and should go back, checking the position of each cross. Finally join up all the crosses to give the finished outline.

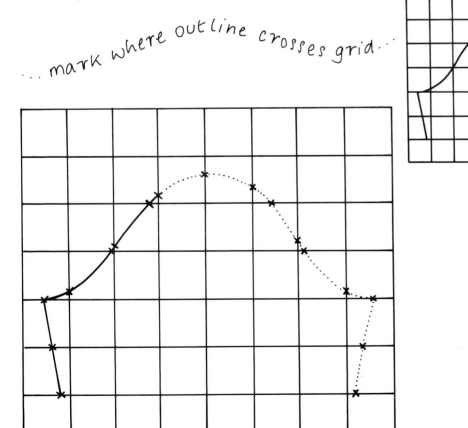

...mark where outline crosses grid...

2 Hand sewing

Although you will probably stitch most of your work on the machine, there are certain hand techniques that you must master. Some stitches are functional, others purely decorative. Hand-sewn embroidery gives an individual touch to a garment or accessory, and has the advantage that you can carry around work in progress and pick it up at a quiet moment in the day, without having to set up your sewing area.

NEEDLES

The right choice of needle and thread for the fabric you are sewing will make light work of the job. The size of the needle refers to its diameter: the smaller the diameter of the needle, the larger the number, from 1 to 24 for very fine tapestry needles. Needles are also made in different proportions, to suit different uses, which are reflected in their names. For example, if you are running long, even basting stitches through thick fabric you will want a long needle with a small eye. The same type of needle, a *sharp*, is used for sewing slipstitch in fine fabrics. For most plain hand sewing, use *betweens*, which are shorter, and therefore easier to work with when making short, even stitches. *Embroidery needles*, such as *crewel*, *tapestry*, *chenille*, and *beading needles* are all intended for decorative stitching, using heavier threads than the small-eyed sharps or betweens. For fine embroidery, use the longest small-eyed needles, known as *milliner's* or *straws*.

For darning, use the longest long-eyed needles, *darners*.

The sharpness also varies, according to the type of fabric to be sewn. Tapestry needles and ball-point sewing needles have rounded points so that they do not split the weave or fibers as you sew.

THREADS

For most hand sewing you will be using ordinary sewing threads, such as mercerized cotton, polyester, and cotton-wrapped polyester, all of which come in several different weights. Quilting thread (cotton or polyester-cotton) is especially useful for hand sewing, since it does not tangle or untwist. Buttonhole twist is a heavy thread used for topstitching as well as hand-worked buttonholes. Silk thread is ideal for sewing silk fabrics.

There are also several different types of embroidery thread, including six-strand floss; pearl cotton, which has a twisted appearance and comes in several weights; and brilliant embroidery cotton, also called *coton à broder*. All of these have a sheen. Matte embroidery cotton is a rather thick, dull-finish thread.

SEWING BY HAND

Choose an appropriate needle and thread for the fabric (and decorative effect where required) and use a thimble. This may feel awkward and uncomfortable to start with, but once you are used to it, a thimble will make work faster and better, as well as protecting your finger. Find one that fits snugly – they are available in sizes 6 to 12 (small to large) and are made in metal and plastic. Wear it on the middle finger of your right hand, and use it to direct and force the needle through the fabric.

As you pull the thread through the fabric, you may find that the remaining supply of thread tends to twist and kink. Some threads twist more readily than others – for example, buttonhole twist. And some hand stitches, such as fine overcasting, tend to cause greater twisting and kinking than straight running stitches. To remove excessive twisting without unthreading the needle, simply hold the thread end and draw the needle down to the fabric. Then let go of the thread end and slide the needle back along the thread to the sewing position. This pushes the extra twist to the end of the thread.

Waxing the thread makes it easier to draw through certain fibers, and helps to prevent kinking. You can either draw the thread several times over a block of wax, or run it through a special wax holder, available at notions counters.

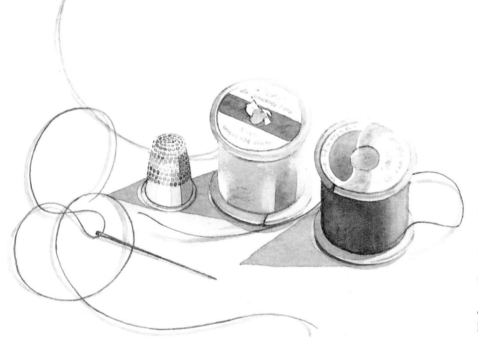

...roll thread......

...use a backstitch...

...or loop thread under needle...

FASTENING THREADS

In some situations, you can fasten the end of the thread by knotting, and in other places you will have to take a couple of backstitches. Backstitches are also used for finishing lines of stitching.

To knot the thread, hold the end between the thumb and forefinger of the left hand. Use the right hand to bring the thread over and around the tip of the finger, crossing it over the end of the thread. Hold the longer thread taut, and push the left thumb towards the finger tip, rolling it around the loop. Slip the loop off the finger tip and at the same time pull against the longer thread held in the right hand to set the knot.

To fasten a line of basting, take one short backstitch. This makes it easy to remove the stitching.

To fasten a line of fine hand stitching, bring the needle through to the underside of the fabric. Take one backstitch, catching only a single thread in the fabric; pull the needle through, leaving a small loop in the thread. Take another small backstitch, then pass the needle through the thread loop of the first stitch and set the knot close to the fabric. Repeat if greater security is needed.

Use the same technique to start threads if a knot would not be suitable.

TEMPORARY STITCHES

Before assembling any work with the final lines of stitching, and while constructing facings and shapings, you must hold the layers of fabric together temporarily. This leaves you free to concentrate on even stitching, without worrying about the layers of fabric slipping around. The traditional method of doing this, essential with tailored and intricately shaped items, is by hand basting. When hand sewing, and when stitching long, straight, or gently curved seams, pin basting is a useful short cut. Short seams can be machine-basted. These last two techniques are described in Chapter 3, page 46.

For hand basting, use a long, slender needle and a single strand of thread, not more than 30 inches long and in a contrasting colour so that it is easy to see. "Basting" thread is soft and lightly twisted. Silk thread does not mark the fabric as it is drawn through or leave a mark after pressing; use it for fine fabrics when basting on the right side, for example to hold the finished edge of a facing in place when pressing. A special water-soluble glue can be used to baste washable fabrics; test first.

When basting, lay out the pieces of fabric to be joined on a flat surface such as a table or a lap pad. Pin at each end, at the center and at any marked points such as notches. Then space out pins between, working out from the center, without distorting or easing the fabric. Place the pins at right angles to the seam, with heads to the seam edge.

Knot the end of the thread and baste by hand using one of the methods illustrated, then finish with a couple of backstitches. Remove basting after the seam has been stitched.

If you do not feel the need to use a thimble, and find them uncomfortable, try this test. Take a piece of heavy cotton or denim and make a few hand stitches through several layers of fabric. You will soon feel the need for the protection of a thimble.

HINTS FOR EASY THREADING

- Cut the thread with sharp scissors at an angle. Avoid breaking or biting it, for then you will have trouble threading it through the needle eye.
- Use a short thread. For finishing and embroidery stitches, use a length less than 24 inches. Use a longer thread for basting, and an appropriate length for gathering. A thread that is too long will tangle and weaken from being pulled through the fabric. And it will make your arm tired from pulling the thread through.

- Use a single thread for most sewing. A double thread helps to speed up sewing when attaching buttons and fasteners, for example.
- Hold the needle in the left hand and the end of the thread tightly in the right hand. Pass the thread through the eye and with the same motion grasp the needle with the right thumb and index finger. Use the left hand to draw the thread end, pulling it through so that it hangs half way down the remaining supply of thread.

- Note that you may have to reverse the direction of working if you are left-handed.

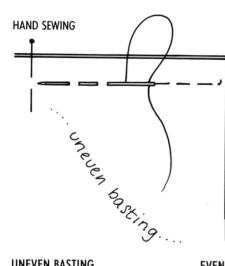
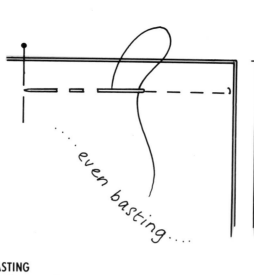

uneven basting....

even basting....

diagonal basting....

UNEVEN BASTING

This may be used to baste any seam, but its main use is to mark the stitching line for topstitching zippers, seams, and facings.

Working from right to left, make a short stitch on the underside of the fabric, about 1/16 to 1/4 inch, and a long stitch on the top side, about 1/4 to 3/8 inch.

EVEN BASTING

This is used to join side seams, stitched with the grain, and is a better method for basting smooth fabrics than uneven basting. It is also better for seams that need control, such as set-in sleeves.

Working from right to left, take long, even running stitches (see opposite). Slip several on the needle before pulling it through.

DIAGONAL BASTING

This is used to hold layers of fabric together for pressing, rather than when stitching seams. It is a technique used mainly for facings around scallops, collars, lapels, and other curved edges. It is usually done with silk thread. In tailoring it is also used to hold interfacings and underlinings against the fabric during assembly.

Working from right to left, and with the needle point toward you, take a short stitch at right angles to the edge, through all layers of fabric. The stitch length should measure from 1/4 to 3/8 inch, depending on the thickness of the fabric. Take the next stitch in the same way, placing it 1/8 to 1/4 inch to the left of the first. This makes a row of diagonal stitches on the upper side and a row of stitches at right angles to the edge on the underside of the fabric.

SLIP BASTING

This is used to match patterns and to join intricate curved sections.

Press under the seam allowance on one half of the seam. Lap the folded edge over the adjoining section, matching the pattern carefully. Pin in place at right angles to the seamline, with pin heads toward seam. Insert the needle, from the wrong side, up through the three thicknesses of fabric near the folded edge. Pull through. Then take the needle back through the single layer of fabric, directly opposite the previous stitch. Bring the needle back up through the three thicknesses of fabric near the folded edge. The stitch should measure between 1/4 and 5/8 inch, depending on the pattern and the angle of the seam.

A long stitch appears on the underside and a short stitch under the folded edge. To stitch, fold fabric over, flatten out stitches, and stitch through the center of the short basting stitches.

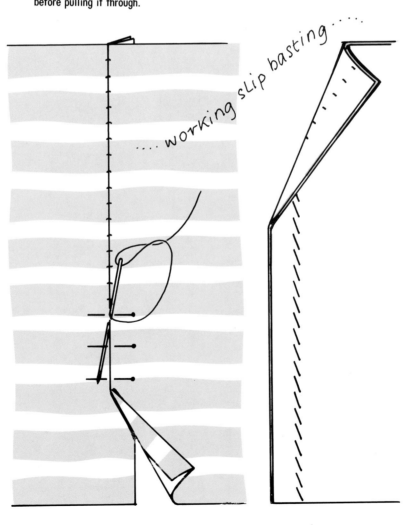

....working slip basting....

Hand stitches

Hand sewing is an essential part of some projects – for example decorative table linen or a child's christening gown. It is also useful in dressmaking for getting an accurate fit, for sewing awkward seams, and to ensure a good drape in some home furnishings, particularly draperies and shades.

Hemming is an important part of most items, and hand-sewn hems give a good finish, particularly with crisp fabrics. There are also certain features, such as arrowheads and thread loops, that give a professional finish when accurately sewn.

Always practice hand stitches on a scrap of the fabric you are using before going ahead. You can choose from a wide range of needles and threads, to suit the weave and fiber of the fabric, and the type of stitch. For construction stitching, use cotton-wrapped polyester or other sewing thread to suit the fabric in a color to match. For decorative stitching, choose cotton or silk embroidery floss, wool, or other decorative thread to suit.

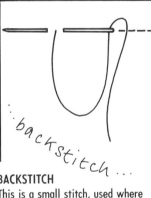

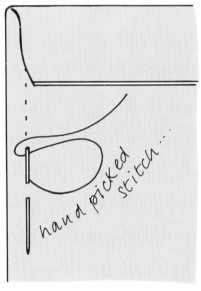

RUNNING STITCH

This is used for seams, tucks, mending and gathering stitch and other decorative and delicate sewing. Use a medium-to-long needle (a sharp or straw, size 6 to 8) and cotton-wrapped polyester or other thread to match the fabric.

Work from right to left, with the fabric edge between the thumb and index finger of the left hand. Weave the point of the needle in and out of the fabric five or six times before pulling the thread through, making even stitches, ⅛ to ½ inch long, as appropriate. Do not pull the thread tight.

BACKSTITCH

This is a small stitch, used where topstitching by machine would be too harsh – for example, in the final stitching of the zipper in sheer, delicate fabrics or fine woolens. It is also used in other areas of dressmaking, where machine stitching would be difficult, and in mending split seams.

Even backstitch shows as a solid line. Work toward yourself, or from right to left. Bring the needle up through the fabric. Insert it a stitch length behind, or to the right of, the point where the thread comes out, and bring the needle forward and out the same distance beyond the backstitch. Angle the needle very slightly, to avoid catching the thread under the fabric. Stitches are anything from ⅛ inch upward, depending on the fabric.

Half backstitch looks like running stitch. It is made in the same way as backstitch, but the thread is carried twice the stitch length forward under the fabric.

When the backstitches are much shorter than the total stitch length, this is known as prickstitch.

HAND PICKED STITCH

This stitch is similar to backstitch, but no stitching shows on the wrong side. It is used to add a tailored look to collars, cuffs, lapels, pockets, and topstitched seams on coats, suits, and tailored dresses. Mark the line of the stitching with tacking stitches, positioning it ½ to 1 inch from the seamline. Use a gauge to measure the distance as you baste. Use buttonhole twist.

Work towards you, bringing the needle up through the interfacing and top layer of fabric. Insert it a couple of fabric threads behind where it came out through the top layer of fabric and interfacing only. Bring the needle out ⅜ inch from the backstitch. Do not draw thread taut – the stitch should sit on the surface. Remove basting as you work.

SLIPSTITCH

This is an almost invisible stitch, used when an edge is turned under, as in hems, bias binding, curved seams, top facings, linings, and so on.

Work from right to left, with the hem fold between the thumb and forefinger of the left hand. Bring the needle up through the fold. Take a stitch into the fabric directly opposite and barely outside the fold, catching only one thread of the fabric; then slip the needle through the fold for the length of the stitch, normally about ¼ to ⅜ inch. Make the stitches shorter if the stitching is subject to strain. Do not pull the threads taut.

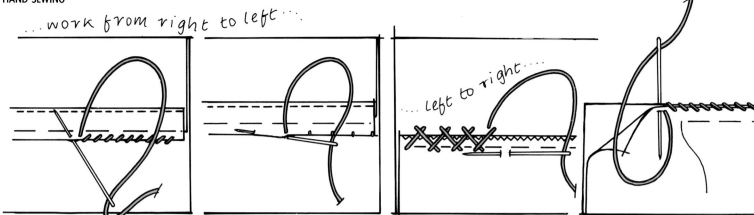

... work from right to left ...

... left to right ....

HEMMING STITCH

This is a popular stitch for finishing hems, particularly where the edge of the hem is bound with bias or seam binding. Baste the hem in place.

Work toward you, or from right to left, with the hem edge between the thumb and index finger of the left hand. Bring the needle up through the edge of the hem and take a stitch in the fabric over the hem edge, taking only a single thread of the fabric. Then bring the needle out through the hem edge. The stitch should be invisible on the right side.

BLIND HEMMING

This is the most frequently used hemming stitch. Baste the hem in place.

Work toward you, or from right to left, with the hem fold between the thumb and index finger of the left hand. Bring the needle up through the hem edge. Directly opposite and barely outside the hem, take a stitch, catching only one thread of the fabric. Then direct the needle diagonally up through the hem edge. Space the stitches about 1/4 to 3/8 inch apart. Do not pull the thread taut. This is similar to slipstitch, but the thread does not run inside the fold of the fabric or hem binding.

HERRINGBONE STITCH

This is used for hemming, for fixing interfacing in place, for certain techniques used in finishing lining, and as a decorative stitch. Baste the edge to be stitched in place.

Work from LEFT to RIGHT with the needle pointing to the left. Hold the hem edge in the left hand. Make a stitch in the hem or facing, catching one or two threads in the top layer of fabric. Then take the needle up and to the right, and make a stitch barely outside the edge, catching only a single thread of the under layer of fabric. Then take the next stitch down and to the right, working along in a zig-zag fashion, with the thread crossing between the stitches.

WHIP STITCH

Use this stitch to join lace, insertion and ribbon. Use a short fine needle and fine thread, and baste the edges to be joined.

Make small stitches over and over the edge of the seam, about 1/16 inch apart.

Overcasting is a similar stitch, which is used to finish edges of seams by hand, where it would be difficult to use a machine stitch. Overcasting is usually done over a single layer of fabric, rather than two edges, as in whip stitch and is worked from left to right.

BLANKET STITCH

This was originally used for edging blankets, but is now more often used to decorate children's clothes, lingerie, and fine linens. It is also used for hand appliqué. Baste the edge to be sewn. Take two backstitches on the underside of the fold, bringing the needle to the right side of the fabric.

Work from right to left, with the edge of the fabric toward you and the needle pointing toward you. Hold the thread down with the thumb and insert the needle through the fabric from the right side. Then bring it out from under the edge of the fabric and over the thread. Pull the thread toward you to tighten, but not tauten the stitch. The stitches may be evenly spaced, grouped, angled, or varied in length.

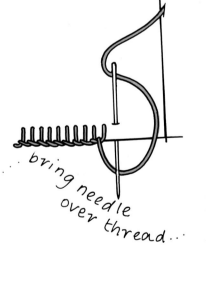

... bring needle over thread ...

BUTTONHOLE STITCH

This stitch looks similar to blanket stitch, but there is an extra knot on the edge of the fabric. For buttonholes, the stitches should be about 1/16 to 1/8 inch long and very closely spaced. The stitch can also be used as a decorative finish.

Work from right to left, with the edge being finished away from you. With the right side of the fabric up, bring the edge over the first finger of the left hand. Take two backstitches at the edge to fasten the thread. Bring the thread to the left and then around to the right to form a loop on the edge where the stitch will be made. Insert the point of the needle from the underside up through the fabric, keeping both sides of the thread loop under the needle. Holding the loop with the left thumb, pull the needle up through the fabric, then away from

you, to place the "purl" of the stitch on the edge of the fabric. Keep the stitches as even as possible.

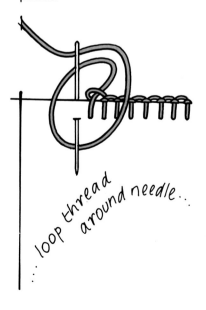

... loop thread around needle ...

Mainly for decoration

Most of the embroidery stitches described here should be sewn with heavier thread than you would use for constructing a garment or finishing the hem. Patterns in books and magazines will give suggestions for suitable fabrics and yarns. It is always a good idea to follow patterns for embroidery, as you would for dressmaking, until you have some experience and can go on to develop your own designs. As with the more functional stitches, always try them out on a scrap of the fabric you are using, so that you can check that you are using a thread that is the right weight for the effect you wish to achieve. You can also judge how to control the tension of the thread as you sew by making a few practice stitches to ensure a smooth, and not puckered, finish.

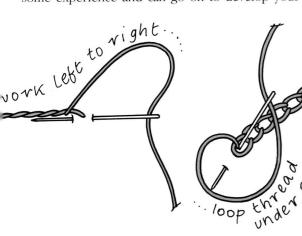

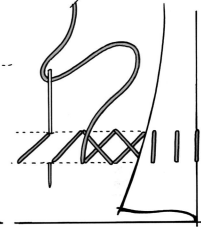

STEM STITCH
This stitch, also known as outline stitch, is a bolder form of backstitch. Lightly mark the line of the stitching on the fabric.

Work from right to left, with the needle pointing to the left. Bring the needle up through the fabric and make a small backstitch about 1/16-inch long. Take the next stitch about 1/8 to 1/4 inch further on, and take another backstitch, slightly shorter than the stitch on the top, angling the needle to make a twisted rope effect.

CHAIN STITCH
This is a bold embroidery outline stitch. Start by knotting the thread. Work from right to left. Bring the needle up through the fabric and hold the thread against the fabric with the left hand. Form a loop of thread, and insert the needle close to the point where the thread came out. Bring it out over the thread just a stitch length away, so that the loop is held in position. For subsequent stitches, insert the needle inside the last loop, to form a chain. Do not pull taut.

CROSS STITCH
This is one of the oldest decorative stitches. It is often used in needlepoint, and is also used on household linens, blouses, children's clothes, and so on. Mark the fabric with an iron-on transfer, lines of even basting, or follow the weave of the fabric: a gingham check or evenweave linen, for example. If using a woven fabric, simply count the threads for each stitch (counted thread work).

Work from left to right, with the needle pointed toward you. Bring the needle up through the fabric to the right side of the lower left corner of the cross, leaving a thread about 1/2 inch long. Catch that thread under the stitches as they are made, to fasten it. Carry the thread diagonally to the right, insert the needle in the upper right corner, and bring it out at the lower left corner of the next cross. A diagonal stitch will appear on the right side, and a straight, vertical stitch on the wrong side. When you reach the end of the row, work back the opposite way to form crosses.

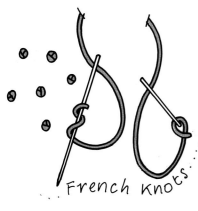

FRENCH KNOT
This is a familiar embroidery stitch, used in the middle of flowers, or grouped to make a pattern. Start by knotting the end of the thread.

Bring the needle up through the fabric where you want to make the knot. Hold the needle over the point where the thread comes out, and wrap the thread once or twice around the needle. Keep the thread tightly wrapped around the point of the needle, and insert the point back into the fabric at the point where it came out. Pull through, to hold the knot against the fabric.

LAZY DAISY
This stitch, also known as detached chain stitch, is used to form a daisy petal.

Bring the needle up through the fabric at the central end of the petal. Make a loop with the thread and hold it in place on the fabric. Insert the needle close to where it came out of the fabric, then bring it out at the opposite end, just inside the loop. Make a tiny stitch over the loop, and bring the needle out again at the central end of the next petal. Do not draw taut.

ROUMANIAN STITCH

This stitch gives a firm finish over relatively large areas. Bring the needle up through the fabric at one side of the area to be embroidered. Take a stitch across the area, then bring the needle back through the fabric half way across, to one side of the previous stitch. Take a small stitch over the previous stitch to hold it in place. Then bring the needle back up through the fabric close to the starting point. Continue working across the fabric, forming a rib down the center of the motif.

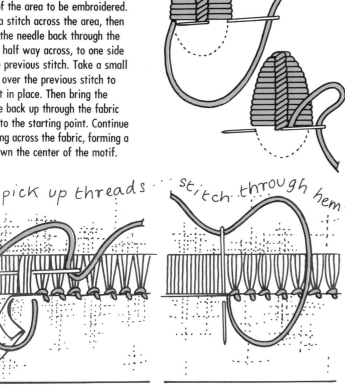

SATIN STITCH

Solid shapes can be filled with straight, parallel stitches, worked close together. For best results, work at a slight angle to the edges of the shape.

Long and short stitch is similar to satin stitch and is used to fill larger areas. Begin by working across the top edge of the motif, alternating the length of the stitches. On following rows, work stitches of the same length, taking the needle down into the ends of the first ones. Taper the stitches to fit.

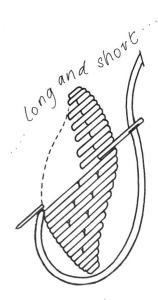

long and short

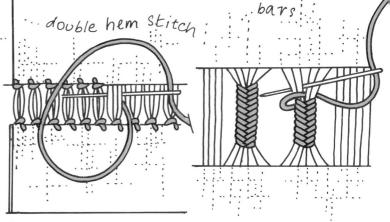

pick up threads · stitch through hem · double hem stitch · bars

DRAWN THREAD HEMS

Work this stitch in fine, evenly woven fabrics for decorative effect in table linen and christening gowns, for example. It is also known as hemstitching. The edge to be hemmed must be cut on the lengthwise or crosswise grain of the fabric – cut by following a thread in the fabric. Take a seam allowance of the depth of the hem plus ¼ inch. Draw three or four threads from the fabric parallel to the hem

measuring twice the depth of the hem plus ¼ inch from the raw edge.

Turn under ¼ inch, then the hem allowance, so that it is just inside the drawn threads. Baste in place and press. Stitch with a fine sewing thread, working from the wrong side. Work from right to left. Knot the end of the thread and bring it up through the fold of the hem. Slide the needle under several threads of the fabric; loop the thread to the

left under the point of the needle. Pull the thread through and draw up the stitch tightly by pulling the thread toward you. Then take a stitch in the edge of the hem fold, catching only a single thread of fabric. Repeat the stitch along the edge, grouping the fabric threads evenly.

For double hemstitching, turn the work and make matching stitches on the opposite edge.

DRAWN THREAD BARS

To give a firmer, bolder effect in drawn thread work, draw out at least four threads of the fabric. Working along the drawn thread area, grouping the cross threads in sets of four. Use a needle and thread to weave over and under pairs of cross threads, to create bars of drawn threads.

alternate stitches

FAGGOTING

This technique is used to make a decorative seam between sections in blouses, dresses, lingerie etc.

Fold under the seam allowance on the cut edges to be joined. Press and finish raw edge. Baste the edges to heavy paper for support, leaving a slight gap between them.

Stitch using pearl cotton or other suitable thread, slightly heavier than you would use for an ordinary seam. Knot the thread and bring the needle up through the fabric fold.

Carry the thread diagonally across the opening, and take the needle up through the fabric fold on the opposite side. Pull through and pass the needle under the thread, diagonally across the opening, and up through the fabric on the opposite side. Continue alternating the stitches across the opening. Fasten the thread on the underside, remove the basted paper, and press.

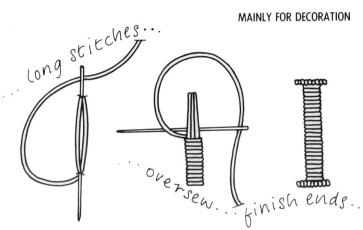

DARNING BY HAND
Use a darning ball to darn socks and a small embroidery hoop for flat work. Use a fine needle, and do not knot the end of the thread.

Make small running stitches, beginning and ending about ¼ inch beyond the edge of the hole, working back and forth, running threads over the hole, parallel with lines of stitching. Then work across the threads, weaving alternately over and under in parallel lines.

BAR TACKS
These are used to prevent splitting at the end of a fly opening, and to strengthen the ends of pockets, particularly in shorts and slacks. They are also used to hold belt carriers in place. They can also be made by machine.

Make two or three long stitches, the length of the bar tack. Then make small overhand stitches across the threads and through the fabric. Finish with tiny bar tacks stitched across the ends.

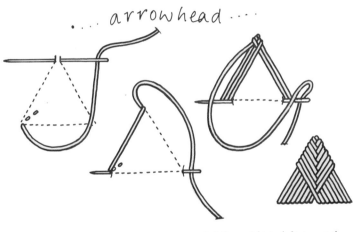

ARROWHEAD
This is used in tailored suits as a decorative and secure finish at the ends of pockets and top of pleats. Mark the triangular shape of the arrowhead with chalk or thread. Use buttonhole twist thread.

Make two small stitches to secure, bringing the needle out at the bottom left-hand corner of the triangle. At the upper corner, take a stitch from right to left. Insert the needle at the bottom right corner and bring it out at the bottom left corner, just inside the first thread.

Repeat the procedure, positioning each stitch just inside the last, until the triangle is completely filled in with interwoven stitches.

CROW'S FEET
This is used in the same place as an arrowhead. Mark a triangle with slightly curved, concave sides. Use buttonhole twist.

Start with two small stitches, bringing the needle out at the bottom left-hand corner. At the upper corner, take a tiny stitch from right to left. Take another tiny stitch, diagonally upward to the right across the bottom right-hand corner, and then move to the bottom left-hand corner, taking another diagonal stitch down and to the right.

Repeat, taking each successive stitch just inside the last one across each corner, and a little longer each time, following the lines of the triangle. Continue until the triangle is filled in with interwoven stitches.

SEAMS BY HAND
For most types of straight seam, running stitch or backstitch is used. Use the same technique as for machine seams (see page 46), and don't forget to press the seam during construction (see page 24). For a plain seam, the layers of fabric to be joined are laid on top or each other, right sides facing and with the raw edges matching. After pinning or basting the layers of fabric, stitch the seam, placing the line of stitching ⅝ inch from the edge of the fabric. The seam is then pressed. Of course, in many cases you will want to use a decorative stitch: make a lapped seam so that you can work the stitching from the right side.

Table linen

Fine linen and carefully worked embroidery make this delightful table cloth an accessory to treasure. Pale, delicate colors give a fresh, summery feeling – work the embroidery in pure white for a more formal effect.

Matching napkins have been embroidered with initials: you can use the initials of your family's first names or embroider the first letter of your surname for a matching set using a different colour for each napkin.

FINISHED SIZES
Tablecloth, 50 inches square.
Napkins, 13 inches square.

YOU WILL NEED
1⅞ yds of 54 inch wide white linen
Dressmaker's carbon paper
Matching sewing thread
White and pale green stranded
    embroidery floss
Tracing paper

TO CUT OUT
From fabric cut one piece 54 inches square. For each napkin cut out a piece of fabric 13½ inches square.

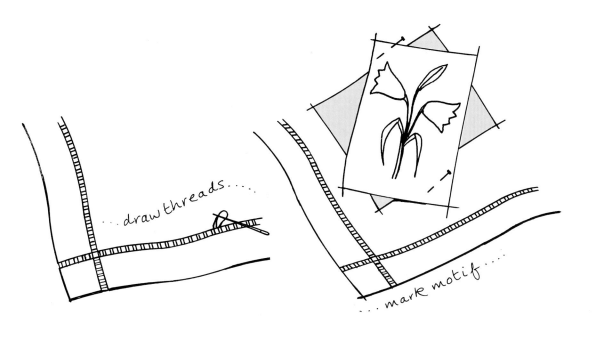

...drawthreads....

...mark motif....

TO MAKE TABLECLOTH

1 Measure in for 2 inches all around tablecloth. Withdraw four threads on all edges at this position.
2 Turn under a double 1 inch wide hem – up to withdrawn threads – mitering the corners neatly.
3 Using white sewing thread, work hemstitch (see page 40) all around the outer edge, catching in hem edge.
4 Trace the design. Pin tracing diagonally on corner of tablecloth, 4 inches from corner point. Slide dressmaker's carbon between tracing and fabric, shiny side down; mark over design.
5 Using three strands of white embroidery floss, work outer petals and front sections of leaves in satin stitch (see page 40). Work remainder of flowers and leaves in stem stitch (see page 39), used as a filling stitch to give texture. Work the bud in satin stitch, using two strands of white mixed with two strands of green. Work over the base of petals with a single strand of green.

TO MAKE NAPKINS

1 Turn under a double ¼ inch-wide hem all around, forming neat corners; pin and stitch hem.
2 Trace the chosen letter from diagram. Mark in the corner of the napkin in the same way as for tablecloth.
3 Using three strands of white embroidery floss work the outline of letter in stem stitch (see page 39), then satin stitch (see page 40) over each letter.

PATTERN DESIGN

Scale: 1 square represents 5 cm (2 inches)

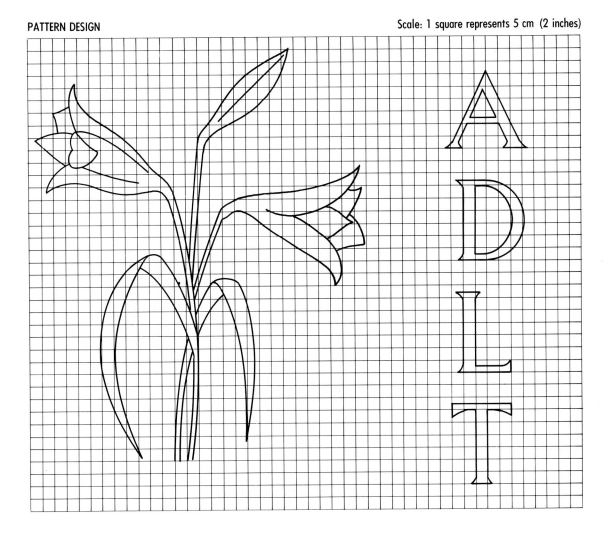

3 Machine sewing

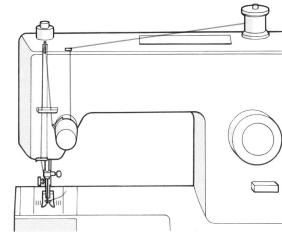

When you have familiarized yourself with the various parts of the machine (see page 15), prepared your fabric, and cut out your pattern (see page 30), you are ready to start sewing.

Your handbook will give instructions on how to thread, but before you can start you must pull the bobbin thread through the throat plate. Practice stitching before you start to make a garment, using a sample of the fabric.

THREADING THE NEEDLE
Thread the needle with the take-up lever at its highest point. Use a needle threader, if you like, to draw the thread through the needle (normally from front to back).

DRAWING UP THE BOBBIN THREAD
Hold the needle thread in the left hand. Turn the handwheel toward you until the needle goes down into the machine and up again, and the take-up lever returns to its highest point. Pull the needle thread so the bobbin thread follows and forms a large loop.

Pull out the loop with your finger. Place both the needle and bobbin threads under the presser foot and lay them diagonally to the right.

...hold thread...

...turn handwheel...

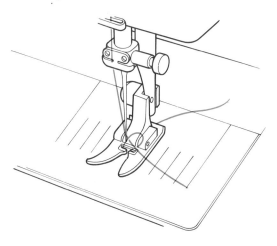

STITCH LENGTH FOR STRAIGHT STITCHING
Adjust the length of the stitch to suit the type of fabric.
Delicate fabrics require a short, fine stitch.
Heavy fabrics require a long, heavy stitch.
For topstitching, using the same thread as you used for the seams, adjust the stitch length to slightly longer than it was for the seams.
Curved seams require a shorter stitch than used for straight seams. For example, if you are using a 12 stitch length for straight seams, use a 15 stitch for curves to give the seam greater elasticity and strength.
Bias and **semi-bias cut seams** also require a short stitch since they must have more elasticity than seams following the lengthwise or crosswise grain of the fabric.
Bound buttonholes and pockets are made with a short stitch to ensure strength and durability.
To ease fullness at the top of a sleeve, at the elbow of long sleeves, or at the waistline, use a slightly longer stitch.

STRAIGHT STITCHING
Correct posture at the machine enables you to work comfortably and produce good results. Sit back on the chair or stool, squarely in front of the needle. Do not lean against the chair back, instead, bring your body forward slightly. Place both feet flat on the floor, with the right foot forward over the foot control.

Position the bulk of the fabric to the left of the needle and the seam edge to the right. Place the left hand lightly on top of the fabric so that your fingers can control it. Make sure that the weight of your left arm is not resting on the fabric, as this causes uneven feeding. Place the right hand approximately 4 inches in front of the needle so that your fingers can guide the edge. Gradually press on the foot control: use a slow speed to start with, increasing the speed as you gain confidence.

To start a seam, raise the take-up lever to its highest point by turning the handwheel toward you. With needle and bobbin threads lying diagonally to the right, slip the fabric under the presser foot with the bulk of the fabric to the left and the seam edge to the right. Lower the needle into the fabric, where the first stitch is to begin. Hold the thread ends and lower the presser foot. Stitch with a slow, even speed.

At the end of the seam, finish stitching (or turn the handwheel) with the take-up lever at its highest point. Raise the presser foot and remove the fabric by drawing it to the back and left. Snip the thread ends on the thread cutter.

As you stitch, guide firmly woven fabrics, just with the right hand. Unusual textures, fine fabrics, and stretch fabrics should be held both in front of and behind the needle. Apply gentle tension to the fabric as you guide it under the foot.

TURNING CORNERS

To turn sharp corners, stitch to the angle, finishing stitching with the needle in the fabric. Turn the handwheel to bring the needle to its upward stroke. Just before it leaves the fabric, lift the presser foot, and turn the fabric, pivoting it on the needle. Lower the presser foot and continue stitching. At very sharp points, particularly if there are several layers of fabric (and interfacing) take a couple of stitches diagonally across the point (see page 51).

To stitch curved seams, use a slow stitch. On sharp curves, it may be necessary to stop stitching occasionally, with the needle still in the fabric, and lift the presser foot and turn the fabric or remove any creases.

ZIG-ZAG STITCHING

Zig-zag stitching has both functional and decorative uses in dressmaking and home decorating.

Simple zig-zag stitch may be used for finishing raw edges and for stitching seams in stretch fabrics: with the stitch length closed up, zig-zag stitch becomes satin stitch, used for embroidery and appliqué, for example. Blind stitch hemming alternates straight stitches and zig-zag stitch, and is useful for quick and almost invisible hemming. It is also the basis for several decorative stitches. Other zig-zag stitches have been developed to suit different purposes – for example narrow zig-zag stitch has extra strength and stretch for seams in knitted fabrics, and elastic-stretch stitch is useful for finishing fabrics. Consult your sewing machine handbook for the stitches featured on your machine, and practice them on different types of fabric

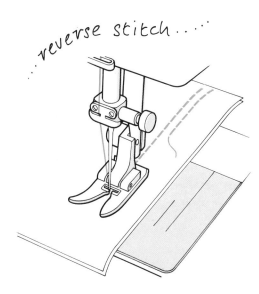

reverse stitch.....

to see how you can use them. For techniques using decorative zig-zag stitch, see page 58.

CHOOSING THE RIGHT FOOT

The foot you choose depends on the machine you are using and the type of fabric you are sewing. The standard foot has one toe slightly longer and broader than the other, to grip the bulkier part of the fabric more firmly. Most machines now include an all-purpose foot, usually made of clear plastic, which slips easily over most fabrics, and makes it easy to see your work.

The zipper foot, which is also used for cording, has only a single toe, which is adjusted to one side of the needle, enabling you to stitch close to the zipper or cording. The braiding foot has a slot through which you can thread fine braid or cord as you stitch, to strengthen a hairline seam, for example, or for decorative effect.

The rolled hem foot turns a small hem in the edge of fine fabric as you stitch, and the button foot is used to hold a button in place as you stitch it on. Other feet include eyelet plates, darning feet, feet for sewing loops or tailor's tacks, gathering feet, and so on. They vary according to the make and model of your machine.

Some machines have seam guide attachments to help you sew accurately in straight lines.

REINFORCING WITH REVERSE STITCHING
To strengthen seam ends, follow the normal procedure for stitching the seams, but lower the needle into the fabric about ½ inch from the end of the seam and reverse stitch to the end. Then stitch forward to the other end of the seam and finish with reverse stitching as before.

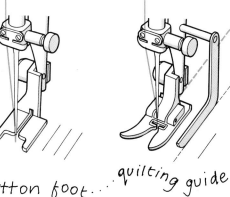

button foot.... *quilting guide* *gathering foot....*

Stitching and seams

Making a seam involves joining two or more pieces of fabric together, with one or more lines of stitching. You will use the sewing machine to make most of the seams you sew. In most cases, the pattern or instructions you are following indicate the seam allowance – which is normally ⅝ inch. Follow the throat plate markings on your sewing machine, or use a seam guide to help you keep the stitching straight and parallel to the raw edge of the fabric.

DIRECTIONAL STITCHING

It is important to stitch seams in the right direction to help the finished item hang well. In general, shoulder seams are stitched from the neckline to the armhole, bodice seams from underarm to waistline, and side seams downward. If in doubt, work out from the center of an item, and down seams that are meant to hang vertically. The main exception is when stitching velvet and corduroy, where you stitch with the pile up from hemline.

BASTING

Layers of fabric must be held in place before stitching. If you are inexperienced, or working with a difficult fabric, you should normally use hand basting (see page 36).

For machine basting, pin the seam at each end and at marks, and then fill in between, positioning the pins closer on curved seams. Always pin at right angles to the edge of the seam, with the point toward the raw edge. Use a long machine stitch – 6 to 8. Stitch on the seamline. After stitching, remove basting by clipping the top thread every four or five stitches, then pulling the under thread. Do not machine baste on fabrics where the needle puncture will show.

Pin basting may be used on straight seams in fabrics that are easy to handle. Place pins at right angles to the seamline, with the heads toward the edge. The pins should just nip into the fabric at the stitching line. Never position them on the underside of your work in contact with the feed of your machine. Machine stitch on the seamline, using a hinged presser foot.

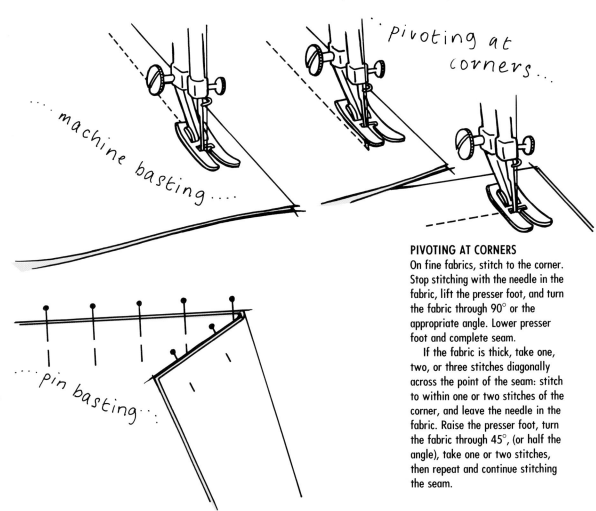

PIVOTING AT CORNERS

On fine fabrics, stitch to the corner. Stop stitching with the needle in the fabric, lift the presser foot, and turn the fabric through 90° or the appropriate angle. Lower presser foot and complete seam.

If the fabric is thick, take one, two, or three stitches diagonally across the point of the seam: stitch to within one or two stitches of the corner, and leave the needle in the fabric. Raise the presser foot, turn the fabric through 45°, (or half the angle), take one or two stitches, then repeat and continue stitching the seam.

RULES FOR STITCHING SEAMS

Follow these steps when forming a seam:

1 Pin the seam edges together at ends, at notches, and at the center. Then pin between these points.
2 Hand baste the seam. If your fabric is easy to handle and if you are reasonably skilled in stitching, you can pin it together instead of basting it. Machine basting is another alternative.
3 Stitch the seam with thread the exact color of the fabric. Set the stitch selector for the stitch length appropriate for your fabric (see page 44), then test the stitch on a scrap of the fabric. Stitch along one side of the basting thread, close to it but not through it. Reverse stitch at each end of the seam to secure the threads. Remove the basting thread.
4 Finish the seam edges.
5 Press as stitched, then press open unless the pattern instructs otherwise. Press enclosed seams during construction and when finished. See page 24 for more information on pressing.

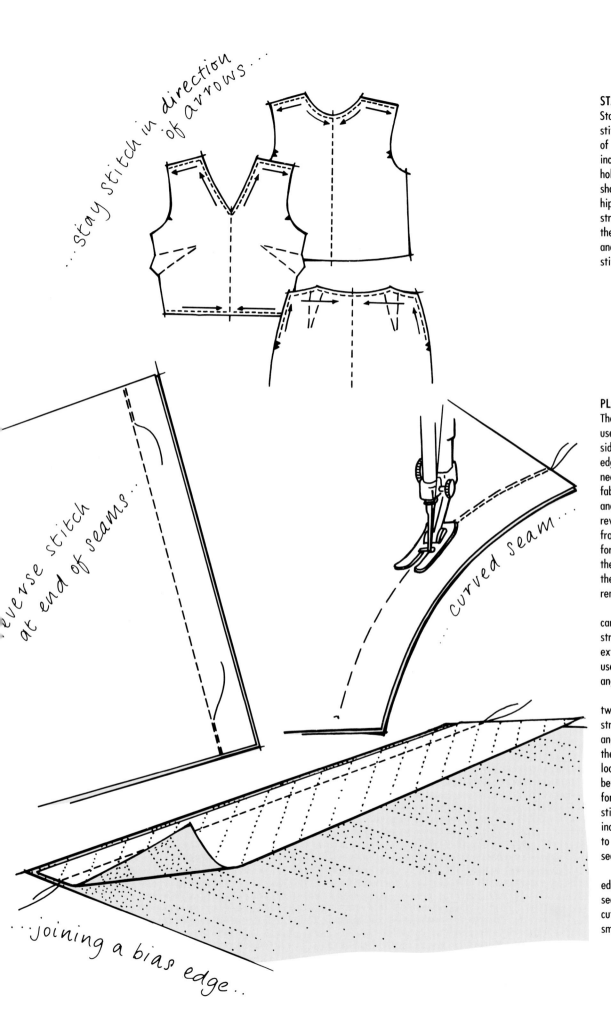

...stay stitch in direction of arrows...

...reverse stitch at end of seams...

curved seam...

...joining a bias edge...

STAYSTITCHING

Staystitching is a line of machine stitching through a single thickness of the seam allowance, worked ½ inch from the raw edge. It is used to hold the original shape of necklines, shoulder lines, waistline, and hiplines to prevent them from stretching when fitting and handling the garment. Use matching thread and the correct stitch length for stitching seams in the fabric.

PLAIN SEAMS

The plain seam is the one you will use most often. Stitch with right sides of fabric together and raw edges matching. Use an appropriate needle and stitch length for the fabric – normally a regular needle and 12 stitch length. Begin by reverse stitching, starting ½ inch from the starting point. Stitch forward to the end of the seam, then reverse stitch for ½ inch at the end. Raise the presser foot and remove the fabric. Trim the threads.

Curved seams require special care. Use a shorter stitch than for a straight seam – 15 – to ensure extra elasticity and strength. If you use a seam guide, position it at an angle to get a uniform edge.

Bias seams occur when you join two pieces of fabric on which the straight grain runs at a diagonal angle to the seamline. Hand baste the seam, leaving the thread ends loose. Hang the work overnight before stitching. Use a short stitch for a bias seam – for example, a 15 stitch length on normal fabrics – to increase the elasticity of the seam to suit the extra stretch of the bias seam.

To join a bias edge to a straight edge, pin and baste with the bias section on top. Stitch with the bias-cut fabric against the feed to ensure smooth, even joining.

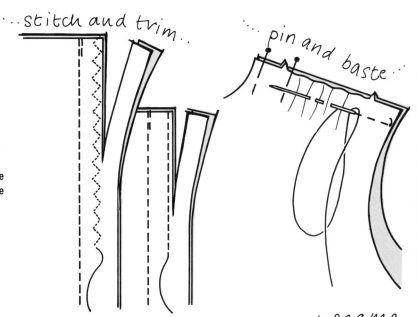

...stitch and trim...

pin and baste

DOUBLE-STITCHED SEAM

Use this seam in sheer fabrics and lace for curved as well as straight seams. Place the first row of stitching on the seamline. Press. Make a second row of stitching within the seam allowance, about ¼ inch from the first row, using a fine multi-stitch zig-zag. Straight stitching may also be used. Trim the seam allowance close to the outside row of stitching.

EASE IN A SEAM

A seam with slight ease often occurs at the shoulder or elbow, where a long seam edge joins a slightly shorter one. It gives shape to a garment without taking tucks.

Working from the long side, pin the edges together, matching them at the ends and at notches. The pattern should indicate where the easing should be fitted – usually between marked dots or notches. Pin at frequent intervals between marks, easing the long side to the short side and distributing the fullness evenly. Hand baste; stitch with shorter side against feed.

...trim...

...Lapped seams...

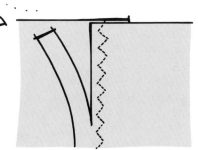

SEAMS THAT CROSS

These occur at the shoulder line, waistline, and underarm, and where darts join a seam or tuck.

Press the first seams open and finish the edges as required by the fabric. Pin the second seam, accurately matching the seams that cross by inserting a fine needle at the seamline, with only the point nipped into the fabric. Then pin on each side, on the seamline. The needle prevents one seam from slipping beyond the other during stitching, and will not mark delicate fabrics. Trim away the excess seam allowance at the point where the seams cross, and press the second seam as indicated on the pattern.

LAPPED SEAM

Use lapped seams when joining sections of interfacing and interlining to eliminate bulk. They may also be used for joining batting before quilting fabric, and sometimes for seams in fabrics such as felt or vinyl that do not fray.

Lap one edge over the other,

with the seamlines meeting in the center. Stitch through the center, using a multi-stitch zig-zag or straight stitching. If necessary, trim seam allowances after stitching.

...butt edges and stitch...

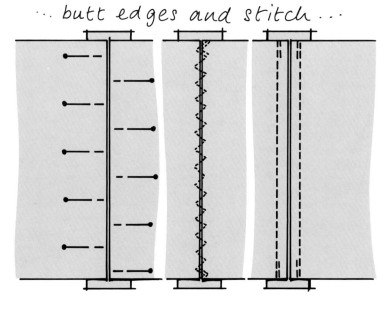

ABUTTED SEAM

Use an abutted seam for non-woven interfacings where a double thickness of fabric would create too much bulk. Trim away the seam allowance on both sections to be joined. Bring the two edges together and pin over an underlay of a lightweight fabric, 1 inch wide, and slightly longer than the seam. Stitch from the right side, using the multi-stitch zig-zag set to the widest stitch width and a 15 to 20 stitch length, aligning abutted line with center of the presser foot. Straight stitching may also be used.

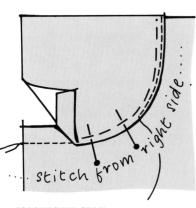

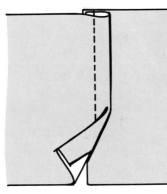

TOPSTITCHED SEAM

Topstitching is used as a styling point along the finished edge of a garment or along the seam within a garment. The technique described is used for curved topstitched seams.

Staystitch both edges to be joined, just inside the seamline. Fold under the seam allowance on the overlap and pin, tack, trim, and press. Lap the folded edge over the underlapping edge by the full width of the seam allowance, then pin and baste. Remove the first line of tacking. Stitch from the right side, close to the folded edge.

TUCKED SEAM

Use tucked seams as a design detail in blouses, dresses, skirts, and other garments.

Working from the right side, fold under the seam allowance on one side and pin; baste if necessary. Lay the folded edge on the seamline of the second section and pin, keeping the raw edges even on the underside. Baste the tuck, then stitch, following the even basted line. Trim off the seam edge on the undersection.

SELF-BOUND SEAM

Use this seam in sheer curtains, children's clothes and for fabrics that fray, when making items where you can include several layers of fabric in the seam.

Make a plain seam and press it open. Trim one edge to within ⅛ inch of the stitching. Turn under the other edge, and pin it to the seam at the line of stitching, enclosing the first edge. Stitch near the folded edge.

LINGERIE SEAM

This makes a flat, easy-to-finish seam. It is usually used where the seam is on the bias.

Stitch and press a straight seam. Pink edges of seam allowance, then press both sides in the same direction. From the right side, stitch with a fine zig-zag stitch, allowing the needle to pierce the seamline on one side and all three thicknesses of the fabric on the other side of the stitch.

FRENCH SEAM

This is used in fine fabrics, blouses, children's clothes, and lingerie to make a seam with enclosed raw edges. It is effectively a seam within a seam, and the finished width is usually ¼ inch or less. This technique is not suitable for curved seams.

Place *wrong* sides of fabric together and stitch about ¼ inch outside the seamline. Press as stitched. Trim seam allowances to within ⅛ inch of the stitching, and press the seam open. Turn the right sides of the fabric together, fold on the stitching line and press. Then stitch on the seamline.

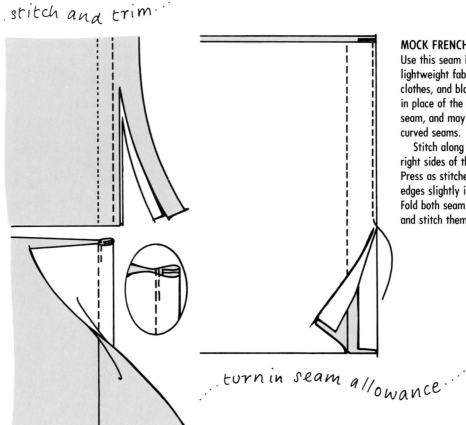

MOCK FRENCH SEAM

Use this seam in fine and lightweight fabrics, children's clothes, and blouses. It can be used in place of the conventional French seam, and may also be used on curved seams.

Stitch along the seamline with right sides of the fabric together. Press as stitched. Trim the seam edges slightly if they are too wide. Fold both seam edges to the inside and stitch them together.

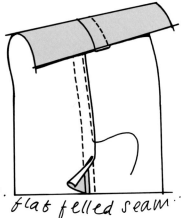

flat felled seam

FLAT FELLED SEAM

This gives a flat seam, with both edges enclosed in the seam. It is often used for men's and boys' clothes, and for sports clothes. It is also used for some details on tailored clothes.

With wrong sides of the fabric together, stitch a plain seam, taking the normal seam allowance. Press as stitched, then press open, then press both seam allowances to one side. Trim the under seam allowance to half its width. Turn the upper seam allowance over the trimmed edge, pin and baste if necessary, then topstitch. This gives a seam with one line of stitching showing on the right side. The seam may also be stitched the other way round, so that two lines of stitching show next to the seamline.

Opinions differ on which way you should press the seam allowances. On men's wear, the seam edges are normally pressed to the back side and sleeve seams, toward the sleeve on the top of shoulders, downward on yoke seams, and to the front on shoulder seams.

Zig-zag stitching gives strength and durability to flat felled seams. Stitch the seam as before, using a 15 stitch length and a medium-width zig-zag stitch.

...channel seam...

CHANNEL SEAM

This is a decorative seam, used for heavy- and medium-weight fabrics.

Pin and machine baste on the seamline, leaving one long thread at each end. Press as stitched, then press the seam open. Clip the machine basting on one side every four or five stitches. Cut an underlay of the same or contrasting fabric, 1 inch wider than the two seam allowances. Working from the wrong side, pin the underlay over the seam, so that the seam is centered on the underlay. Baste in place with two lines of stitching from the right side. Then from the right side, stitch along each side an equal distance from the seamline — about ¼ to ½ inch depending on the fabric and effect required. Use the presser foot to gauge the distance. Remove the long basting thread, and then use tweezers to remove any short ends that are visible.

WELT SEAM

This is similar to a flat felled seam, and is often used on suits and coats.

Stitch a plain seam on the wrong side of the fabric, then press as stitched. Press the seams open, and trim ³/₁₆ inch from one seam edge and press both seam edges to one side so that the wide edge covers the narrow edge. Baste flat. From the right side, stitch an even distance from the seamline.

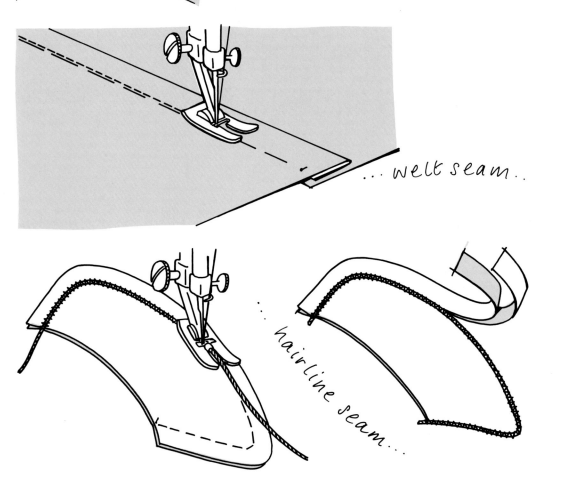

...welt seam...

hairline seam...

HAIRLINE SEAM

This is a perfect finish for enclosed seams on fine collars. Set the zig-zag to a short stitch length and narrow width. Baste the seam in place. Use a filler cord of pearl cotton or heavy buttonhole twist. Unwind sufficient filler cord to prevent strain or tension. Thread through the hole on the braiding foot. Stitch on the seamline, covering the filler cord. Press, then trim seam close to the stitching. Turn right side out and press.

A neat finish

There are several techniques that are used to eliminate bulk in curved, shaped, and enclosed seams. They all involve cutting away or grading some of the seam allowance to reduce the bulk in the seam. Stitch and press the seam, then clip, notch, and grade the seam allowances according to the methods described here before finishing the raw edges of the seam allowance. Always avoid cutting the stitching when trimming fabric. These techniques will ensure a smooth finish.

One area where grading is commonly used is on interfacings, and this is a point in the garment where understitching is frequently used. Understitching holds the facing and seam allowances together, and prevents a facing edge from rolling beyond the edge of the garment.

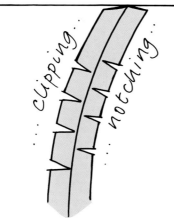

CLIPPING AND NOTCHING

These techniques are used on curved seams, so that when the seam is pressed open the seam allowances lie flat, without puckering or distorting the fabric.

On inside curves, clip into the seam allowance far enough to relieve the strain imposed by the seam edge. The depth of the slash and the spacing depend on the degree of the curve and the texture of the fabric. Sometimes, at sharp corners, only one clip is necessary.

On outside curves, cut small notches into the seam allowance, to remove the portion of fabric in the seam edge which would form a fold when the seam is pressed open. Avoid cutting out a wedge so large that a saw tooth effect is produced when the seam is pressed open.

Often an inside curve is joined to an outside curve, so one side must be clipped and the other notched.

GRADING

Grading is most often used in enclosed seams, where facings are joined around necklines for example, or inside collars or cuffs.

On straight seams, trim any interfacing close to the seamline. Trim the facing seam allowance to about 1/8 inch and the garment seam allowance to 1/4 inch. Press, then press the seam open. Turn right side out, ease the facing under at the seamline, and baste, using diagonal basting and silk thread. Press flat.

On inside curves, trim the interfacing, facing, and seam allowance of main garment as before, then clip into the seam allowance. Press.

On outside curves, trim the interfacing, facing, and seam allowance as before, then notch the seam allowance. Press, then press seam open over the curved edge of a seamboard or pressing mitt. Turn right side out, baste and press.

On square corners and points which have to be turned out, as on collars, patches, and pillows, take one or two stitches diagonally across the angle of the seam. The number of stitches depends on the thickness and texture of the fabric. Lightweight, crisp fabrics need only one, but woolens may need three.

Stitch to within one or two stitches of the corner, and leave the needle in the fabric. Raise the presser foot, turn the fabric 45°, take one or two stitches, then repeat and continue stitching seam.

Remove the fabric from the machine and grade the seam up to the corner. Clip away fabric diagonally across the point, then trim away seam allowance diagonally on either side of the point. Continue to trim seam allowance. Press as before.

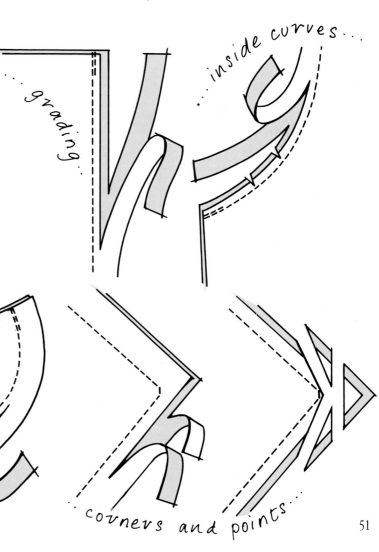

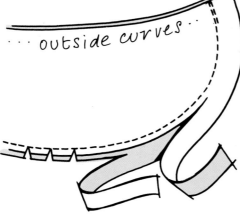

SEAM FINISHES

Seam allowances have to be finished or neatened to prevent fraying in use and during washing or dry cleaning. This also improves the appearance of the inside of the item and adds strength to the seam. Finish each seam as you stitch it, and before crossing another seam. Choose an appropriate finish, so that you do not add bulk that is visible and forms a ridge on the outside of the item when it is in use or being worn.

If you are in any doubt as to which seam finish would be best for the fabric you are using, join several seams and give them different finishes.

Press each sample well and check the right side.

For some fine fabrics, you may want a hand finish. Use a hand overcast stitch, see whip stitch, page 38.

Occasionally, you will be able to use the selvage of the fabric as the outer edge of the seam allowance: this quite often happens in flat household accessories, such as draperies and bedspreads. If you do decide to use the selvage as the seam finish, clip into it every 4 to 8 inches. The outer threads of the fabric are often pulled taut in the weaving process and distort the seam, preventing it from hanging well or lying flat.

ZIG-ZAG FINISH

The zig-zag is one of the most commonly used seam finishes. It does not distort any fabrics, and has enough "give" for knits and other stretch fabrics. Use it on plain seams – press them open before stitching. Set the zig-zag to a medium width and a 15 to 20 stitch length.

Stitch near the edge of the seam allowance but not over it. Press, then trim off the edge of the fabric close to the stitching.

The blindstitch zig-zag is a good finish for tweed, raw silk, double knits and heavy woolens. Stitch a plain seam and press, then press open. Use the blindstitch zig-zag, forming the stitches over the edge of the seam allowance.

When both seam allowances are turned in the same direction, press, trim them to about ¼ inch and finish together with an appropriate zig-zag stitch.

TURNED AND STITCHED SEAM

As its name implies, this seam finish involves turning under a narrow hem and stitching it in place. Use for light- and medium-weight fabrics, particularly on unlined jackets, as it gives a neat finish, with no raw edge showing.

Stitch a plain seam. Press flat, then press open. Pink or trim the edges, then fold each edge under ⅛ to ¼ inch, and stitch on the folded edge. Some machines have attachments for helping you to stitch evenly and very close to the edge.

PINKED SEAM

Use this only on fabrics that do not fray.

After stitching a plain seam, trim the edges with pinking shears. Remove only the very edge of the seam, using a medium stroke. Press.

For a pinked and stitched seam, which can be used on almost any fabric, stitch the seam, then make a line of stitching about ¼ inch from the edge of the fabric, using a 15 to 20 stitch length. Then pink and press as before. The stitching will prevent the seam from fraying and curling.

Facings and interfacings

TOPSTITCHING AND UNDERSTITCHING

These techniques add finishing touches to a seam and are frequently used around necklines and sleeve openings. In home furnishings understitching may be used in finishing shaped edges, such as scallops at the head of café curtains; topstitching is used as a decorative detail.

Topstitching may be used on openings, around the edge of an item, or to emphasize seams on fitted, tailored garments. It is also used on pockets and belts. Make more than one row of stitching for extra emphasis. When topstitching seams, position the stitching within the seam allowance. Finish the seam allowances before topstitching if the fabric frays easily. Stitch the seam, then press, grade, and understitch if necessary. Press again before topstitching. Test the stitch before the final topstitching – because this shows on the right side, you won't have a second chance.

Understitching is used to prevent a facing edge from rolling beyond the garment edge. It involves stitching the seam allowance to the facing. Understitch neckline and armhole openings, or other features, after attaching each section of facing. Press and grade the seam before stitching. Turn the facing to the underside, and ease it under slightly at the opening, then press again.

FINISHING WITH FACINGS

A facing is a strip of fabric, cut to the same shape as the edge to be finished. It is stitched to the right side of the fabric, then the seam allowances are trimmed or graded before the facing is turned to the wrong side. The edge may be understitched and/or topstitched.

In dressmaking, facings are used for collars, cuffs, necklines, front openings, and sleeve openings. Facings may also be used for curved hems, and for scalloped edges.

You can face an edge even if you do not have a pattern piece. Simply cut your own pattern by marking a facing strip on the edge to be faced and tracing it off onto a sheet of pattern paper. Normally, seams between sections of facing should match the main seams of the item you are stitching. An exception is when you have to join widths of fabric along the length of the facing – for example when facing a drapery heading: stagger the positions of the seams in the main fabric and facing to reduce bulk in the facing seam. Facing should be cut with the grain of the fabric running in the same direction as the section to be faced.

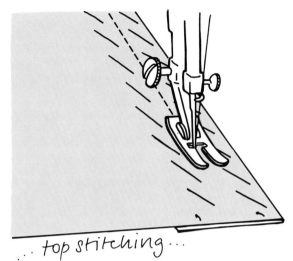

... top stitching ...

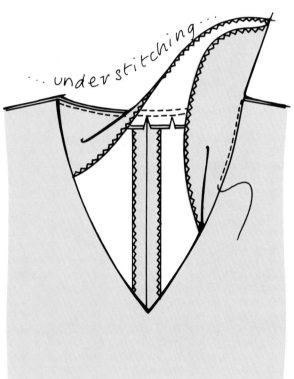

... understitching ...

INTERFACINGS

Interfacing is a third thickness of a carefully selected fabric; it is cut in the same shape as the edge to be finished and placed between the facing and main section. This adds body and helps to mold and hold the shape of curved sections.

The list of fabrics suitable for interfacing is long. It includes natural and synthetic, woven and non-woven, iron-on, heavy, and lightweight fabrics: make your selection according to the type of fabric you are using and the item you are making. If you

TOPSTITCHING

Use your usual thread, or use two spools; thread both through the upper tension control and needle. Or set the machine to a triple topstitch. Select a slightly longer stitch than for the rest of the item. Baste the layers to be topstitched to prevent slipping during stitching, using diagonal basting and silk thread. If the stitching is over ½ inch from the edge, make two rows. Use the foot, the throat plate or a seam gauge as a guide.

When you come to a corner, stitch to the point, stopping with the needle in the fabric. Lift the foot, pivot the fabric and then lower the foot and continue to stitch.

Leave thread ends of about 4 inches and finish by hand.

UNDERSTITCHING

Turn and press facing and both seam allowances away from the garment. Stitch from the right side of the facing, close to the seamline, through the facing and both seam allowances.

Finish the free edge of facings in the same way as you finish the seam allowances of the garment, taking into consideration the weight of the fabric, its elasticity, the amount the seams will show in use (in an unlined jacket, for example), the amount of wear on the seam and facing, and the weave and fiber – which affect how much the fabric will fray.

When buying interfacing, try this little test: lay the interfacing between two layers of your chosen fabric and roll between the fingers so that you can judge the final effect.

USING SEW-IN INTERFACING

With lightweight sew-in interfacing, cut the interfacing to the same size as the piece to be interfaced. Pin, baste and stitch seams, handling the two pieces as though they were a single piece.

With heavier sew-in interfacing, there are two methods.

First method: Mark seamlines where sections of interfacing are to be joined. Trim off seam allowance. On edges to be faced (around neck opening, along a scalloped edge, and round collar, for example) trim about ⅛ inch inside the seamline. Clip off corners. Join seams between sections of interfacing with an abutted seam, see page 48. Position interfacing on wrong side of piece to be interfaced. Baste in place, then herringbone stitch using sewing thread to match the garment. Catch one thread in the fabric, just outside the seamline, and stitch only through the interfacing on the opposite edge.

Second method: Mark and trim seamlines and join seams with abutted seams as before. Cut a strip of organza or similar lightweight fabric 1½ inches wide on the lengthwise grain, using the pattern to shape the edge. Join seams if necessary. Pin the organza strip over the interfacing, so that it overlaps by ¾ inch. Stitch in place using the multi-stitch zig-zag. Baste the interfacing in place so that the edge of the organza strip matches the edge of the fabric to be interfaced. When you stitch the seam, include only the organza, not the interfacing.

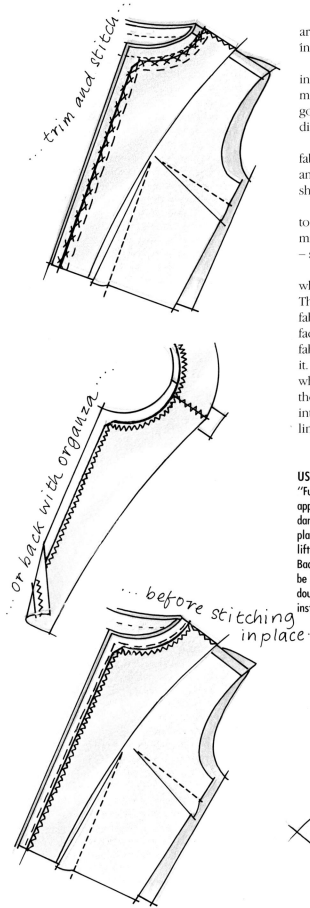

...trim and stitch...

...or back with organza...

...before stitching in place...

are using a good quality fabric, make sure the interfacing is of an equally high quality.

Patterns will give sound advice. Purpose-made interfacings are designed to be easy to handle and most are washable and dry-cleanable, so they are a good standby. Keep scraps, and have a range of different weights in your sewing cupboard.

Besides the fabrics listed, you can use the same fabric for interfacing as you use for the main fabric and facing. This is frequently done if the fabric is sheer, since any other interfacing would show.

Interfacing can be applied either to the facing or to the garment or main part of the item you are making. Cut it to the same size as the pattern piece – seams can be trimmed after stitching.

Iron-on, or fusible, interfacing has a shiny side, which has had heat sensitive adhesive applied to it. This holds the interfacing permanently against the fabric. Check washing instructions given for interfacing, as it may be more delicate than the main fabric. Always test iron-on interfacing before using it. Press under the same conditions that you will use when you start to sew. Wash the test piece to check the effect. When interfacing fine fabrics, trim the interfacing with pinking shears to prevent a hard line which might show through.

USING IRON-ON INTERFACING

"Fusible" interfacings are generally applied with a steam iron over a damp press cloth; the iron is held in place for several seconds, then lifted and moved to anothere area. Backings used in crafts may simply be ironed on with a dry iron. If in doubt, check the manufacturer's instructions.

...use a pressing cloth

CHOOSING INTERFACINGS

Name	Type	Description	Colours	Weight	Use	Care
Pellon sew-in, 905, 910, 930	Non-woven	Sew-in, no grain	White, also beige (905) and gray (910)	Light (905), medium (910) heavy (930)	Dressmaking, light to heavy fabrics	Wash or dry clean
Pellon fusible 906F, 911F, 931TD	Non-woven	Iron-on, no grain	White, also beige (906F) and gray (911FF)	Light (906F), medium (911FF), heavy (931TD)	Dressmaking, light to heavy fabrics	Wash or dry clean
Pellon Sof-Shape, 880F	Non-woven	Iron-on, no grain	White, gray	Light, soft	Dressmaking, for soft shaping, all fabric weights	Wash or dry clean
Pellon Stretch-Ease, 921F	Non-woven	Iron-on, crosswise stretch	White, charcoal	Light, soft	Knits and other stretch fabrics	Wash or dry clean
Pellon Stabilizer 30/35, 40, 50, 60	Non-woven	Sew-in, no grain	White, also black (40)	Light to extra-heavyweight	Home decorating, accessories	Wash or dry clean
Pellon Decor-Bond 809	Non-woven	Iron-on, no grain	White	Heavy, firm	Home decorating	Wash or dry clean
Pellon Shapewell, 70	Woven	Cotton	White	Light, stiff	Dressmaking	Wash or dry clean
Pellon Shapewell, 70F	Woven	Cotton iron-on	White	Light	Dressmaking	Wash or dry clean
Pellon KnitShape 85F	Knitted	Nylon, iron-on, crosswise stretch	White, natural, black	Light	Dressmaking, knitted fabrics	Wash or dry clean
Buckram	Woven	Various fibers	White, natural	Heavy, stiff	Crafts, drapery headings	Dry clean
Insulated lining	Composite, quilted	Cotton-polyester lining plus three insulating layers	Natural	Thick, soft	Home decorating, where insulation is required	Dry clean

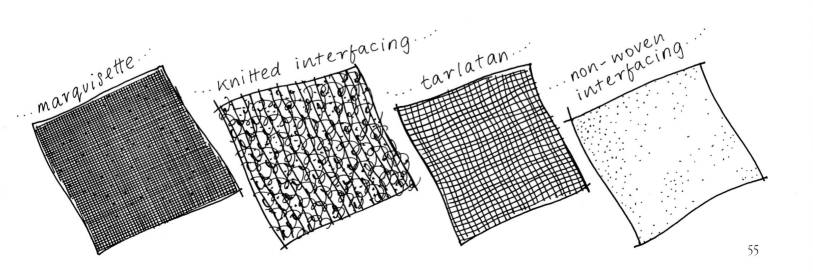

...marquisette... ...knitted interfacing... ...tarlatan... ...non-woven interfacing...

FACING A SLASHED OPENING

You can change the shape of a neckline by adding a simple, slashed opening, or use the same technique to finish an opening at a cuff. You may also want a slashed opening in some household or personal accessories, such as drawstring bags or dressing table items.

Mark the position of the slash. Do not cut. Stitch around the opening for the slash, using a short stitch. Begin at the edge of the fabric, about ¼ inch from the marked line.

Cut the facing the same shape as the edge to be faced and about 2 inches longer than the slashed opening. Finish seams and edges; position the facing on the right side of edge to be faced. Baste in place with markings and seams matching.

Stitch around opening, stitching to within ¼ inch of center front marking. Take one stitch diagonally, then stitch down one side of the slash opening, tapering to ¹⁄₁₆ inch at the point. Take one stitch across the point, then continue up the opposite side and around the edge in the same way.

Trim the facing seam allowance to ⅛ inch and the fabric seam allowance to ¼ inch. Snip into the seam allowance on any curves and trim at seams. Cut between rows of stitching, almost to point of slash, and cut off the corners at the top of the slash. Turn right side out and baste facing in place. Press then remove basting.

The opening cannot be understitched, but may be topstitched for a firmer, decorative finish.

To reinforce the point of the slash, fold a 1½-inch length of straight seam binding through the center and press. Pin it to the underside of the facing with the upper edge exactly at the point of the slash. Stitch near the top edge of the seam binding.

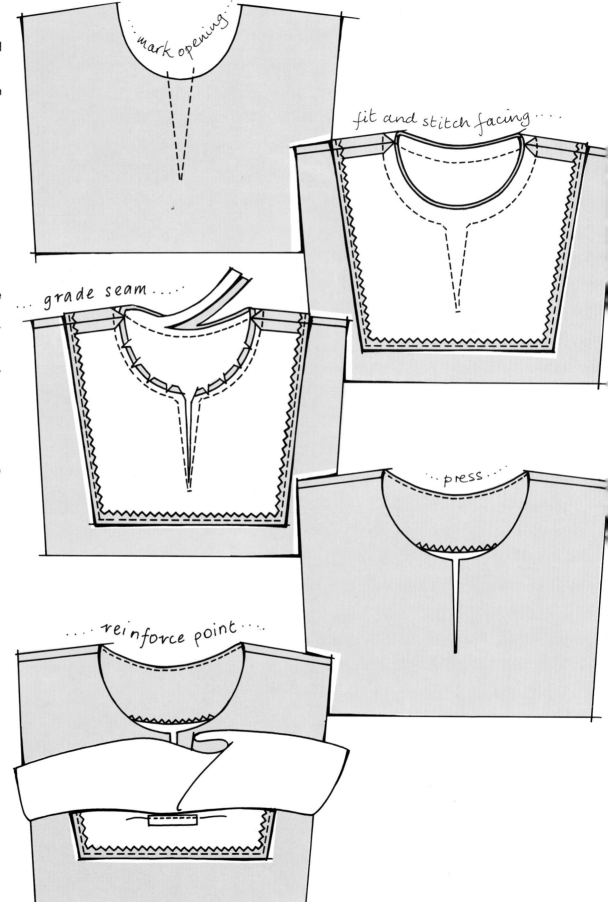

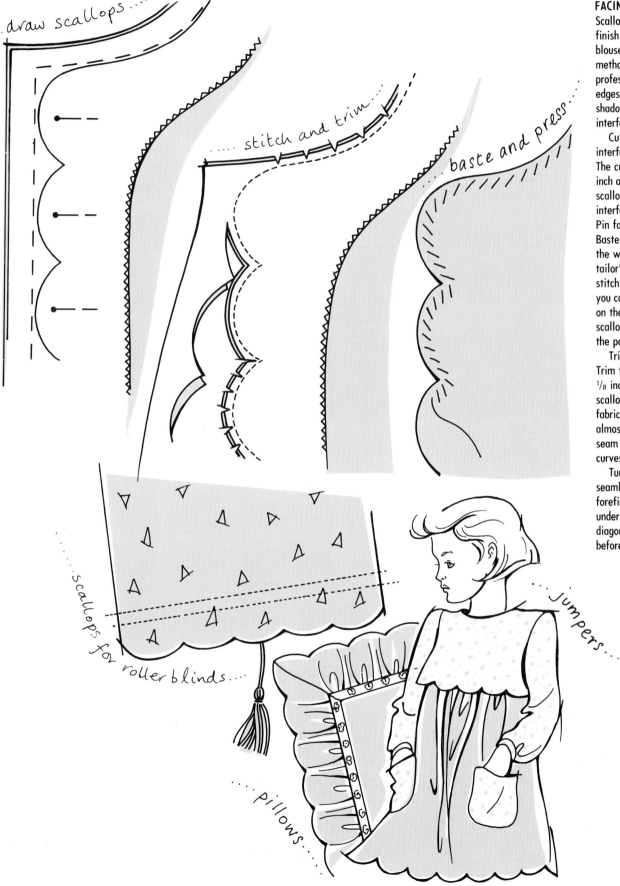

draw scallops....

stitch and trim....

....baste and press....

....scallops for roller blinds....

....pillows....

....jumpers....

FACING A SCALLOPED EDGE

Scalloped edges add a decorative finish to beds and table linens and blouses or tailored garments. This method of facing gives a professional touch. Avoid scalloped edges in sheers because of the shadow effect in the seams. Use interfacing where appropriate.

Cut fabric, facing, and interfacing without shaping edge. The cutting line should be about ⅝ inch outside the finished edge of the scallop at its deepest point. Attach interfacing to wrong side of fabric. Pin facing to right side of fabric. Baste in place. Draw the scallops on the wrong side of the facing, using tailor's chalk. Stitch, using a short stitch and a light pressure so that you can turn the fabric freely. Stitch on the traced outline of the scallops, taking one stitch across the point between each scallop.

Trim interfacing close to seam. Trim the fabric to between $1/16$ and $1/8$ inch according to size of scallops. Trim facing just inside fabric. Clip into angle of scallop, almost to stitching. Cut notches in seam allowance on outside of curves.

Turn facing to underside and roll seamline between thumb and forefinger to bring stitching just under the edge. Baste in place with diagonal stitches and silk thread before pressing.

Decorative stitches

The zig-zag facility has been refined in most machines to enable you to produce a wide range of decorative stitches. Always check your machine handbook before trying a new stitch, to see if there are any special adjustments to be made to the stitch length, tension, etc.

With some machines you may need to insert a special disk or template, which carries the instructions for making the stitch. The ease of setting a stitch varies from one machine to another: always check this point when you are buying a machine if you intend to do a lot of decorative stitching.

PLANNING DECORATIVE STITCHING

Plan your stitch patterns carefully, considering the fabric and the age of the person for whom the garment is intended, or the type of household article you are making. Pick up ideas from ready-made items, from magazines and from books. You can also pick up ideas from other printed images, such as fabric or wallpaper designs.

Plan stitching before assembling. Choose colors and threads carefully (normally sewing thread is used). If the stitching extends into the seam allowance, you will have to apply it before stitching the seam.

Make sure you have a backing fabric to use, particularly on fine or loosely woven fabrics. Normally, crisp lawn, organdy, or a proprietary, non-woven backing is used for this; and the backing is cut or torn away close to the stitching after the work is done.

SAMPLE STITCHES
This decorative sampler has been stitched by machine, using multi-colored threads for extra effect.

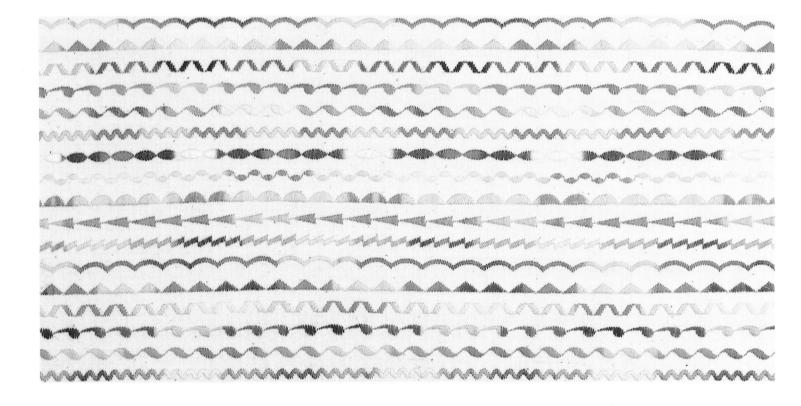

RULES FOR DECORATIVE STITCHING

1 Steam-press the fabric so that it is smooth.
2 Transfer the design to the fabric with chalk, lines of basting stitches or a tracing wheel.
3 Cut the backing on the same grain as the fabric (except with non-woven backing) cutting it at least 4 inches wider than the decorative stitching area.
4 Press the backing and place it on the wrong side of the fabric, where the stitching is to be. Pin, then baste in place.

5 Always test the stitch on a scrap of fabric, with your chosen backing, before starting to stitch. Find the beginning of the pattern unit if necessary.
6 When starting to stitch, align the stitching line with the center of the foot, rather than the needle, which may be off center.
7 After completing each line of stitching, press the work on the wrong side before doing any further stitching.

SATIN STITCH

Satin stitch consists of a series of closely spaced zig-zag stitches, which form a smooth, satin-like surface. Use a braiding foot, which will allow the extra bulk of stitching to move underneath it easily. Most of these feet also have a slot or eyelet, through which a filler cord can be threaded to raise the stitching for extra decorative effect.

Select a closed zig-zag stitch, and adjust the width of the stitch to suit your needs.

It is usually necessary to adjust the needle thread to a lighter tension, to give a balanced stitch. The fabric should not pucker.

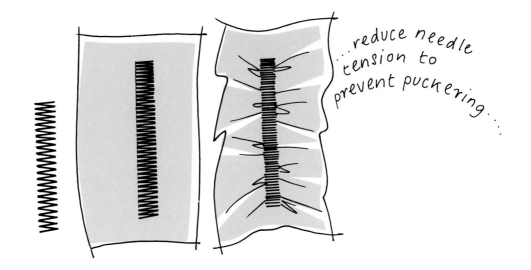

...reduce needle tension to prevent puckering....

TESTING THE PATTERN UNIT

It is often important to start decorative stitching at the beginning of a pattern unit, to give a neat finish to the embroidery. Stitch on a scrap of fabric before doing the actual stitching, stitching until you come to the end of a complete pattern unit. Remove the scrap of fabric from under the presser foot, and position the item to be embroidered under the needle, aligning the marking with the center of the presser foot. Lower the foot, and stitch. Repeat the process whenever you start a new line of stitching or a new motif.

...test on a scrap of fabric.....

...edge stitching....

EDGE-STITCHED FINISH

Edge-stitching is a delicate finish for babies' clothes, children's dresses, lingerie and fine linens. Use a closely spaced zig-zag stitch. Mark the seamline, with a scalloped shape if desired, then cut at least 1 inch away from the seamline. This increases the stability of the fabric. If edge-stitching is used on fine fabrics or a single thickness of fabric, baste a backing of crisp lawn to the wrong side of the fabric for added body. Set the stitch length for satin stitch. Place the work under the needle so that the outer edge of the stitching will fall barely inside the seamline. Guide the fabric with both hands as you sew. Remove basting and press. Trim the outer edge of the fabric and backing close to the stitching, using embroidery scissors. Then trim the backing close to the inside edge of the stitching. For extra body, insert filler cord as you stitch, using the braiding foot.

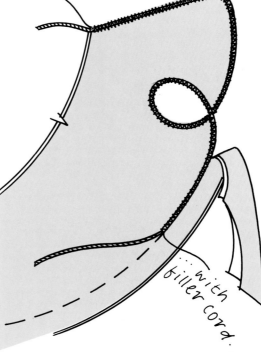

...with filler cord...

Mending

Some machines have special feet for darning, which act like an embroidery hoop, holding the worn area flat. These are suitable only for small holes.

Mending covers a wide range of garment repairs – re-stitching split seams, darning holes, mending tears, patching children's clothes, and so on. Many of these tasks are best done by machine to give a stronger repair. You can use zig-zag stitch, but in some situations you may need to use a straight stitch. Use straight stitch mending for large holes. For straight stitch mending you will need an embroidery hoop. Use a fine needle for both machine and hand mending. Match the thread to the fabric as closely as possible.

For large holes, patch rather than darn. Use matching fabric if possible. You may be able to cut a patch from a facing or pocket lining if you do not have a remnant. Trim the fabric away from around the hole to make a neat square or rectangular hole. With patterned fabrics, cut the patch to match the design of the pattern; it is easy to do this by laying the hole over the fabric and marking the outline of the hole. Then cut out the patch, cutting it 1 inch larger all around.

Rather than mending holes in garments by darning or patching, you may prefer to reinforce worn areas before holes appear. Common areas for this treatment are elbows and knees, particularly in children's clothes.

For some mending techniques, you will need to use an underlay of fabric, either to strengthen the area, or to hold torn edges of fabric together. Use a patch of the same for underlays, or a lighter fabric such as chiffon, nylon net or batiste. You can also use iron-on interfacing. Cut the underlay at least 1 inch larger all around than the area which is to be repaired.

DARNING

To darn a large hole, lower the feed or cover with the special plate. Remove the presser foot. Set the stitch to a short length. Trim any ragged edges from the hole. Place the worn section right side up in an embroidery hoop. Put the work under the needle and lower the presser bar to activate the tension. Hold the loose end of the needle thread, turn the handwheel and pull through the bobbin thread at the top left-hand corner of the area to be darned. Make a line of stitches down through the fabric on the left-hand side of the area to be darned. Then pull the hoop toward you so the thread goes back across the hole. Repeat, taking a few stitches in the fabric at each end of the area to be darned, with threads running

...move hoop back and forth...

back and forth across the hole. When you reach the bottom right-hand corner, turn the work and repeat, to cover the area with crosswise lines of stitching. Pull threads to the underside; tie and cut. Press.

Some machines have a special darning foot, so that you do not need to use an embroidery hoop.

To darn tears, which follow the grain of the fabric, using an embroidery hoop, start by cutting an underlay, of the same fabric if possible, for reinforcement. Press the tear and the underlay. Baste the underlay to the back of the fabric, stitching close to the tear. Place the fabric, right side up, in the hoop. Position the tear crosswise under the needle. Pull up the bobbin thread as for darning holes. Move the hoop backward and forward, making about six stitches across the tear, working down the length of the tear.

ZIG-ZAG STITCH MENDING

Baste underlay in place as for darning a tear, and set the machine to a multi-stitch zig-zag. Stitch along the line of the tear, reinforcing the stitches at the end and corner by using a shorter length stitch and stitching backward and forward.

To reinforce areas using zig-zag stitch, first cut an underlay and baste in place. Use a multi-stitch zig-zag set to short stitch length and medium width. Work from the right side, stitching up and down the worn area, making several rows of stitches parallel to the grain. Raise the presser foot and pivot the fabric on the needle at each end of the reinforcement. When working in confined areas, such as a trouser leg, turn the item inside out and roll up the leg to do the stitching.

...zig-zag to mend tears...

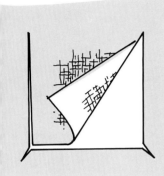

... trim ...

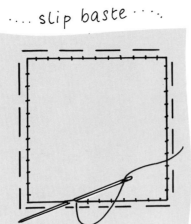

.... slip baste ....

... stitch ...

... finish seams ..

PATCHING
Baste the patch to the wrong side of the hole, and place, right side up, in an embroidery hoop. Stitch the fabric to the patch close to the edge of the hole. Then move the hoop backward and forward, making about six or eight small stitches over the edge of the patch. Turn at

corners and cross the stitches for added reinforcement. Press. Trim away edge of patch on underside close to stitching.

For a tailored patch, after trimming the hole, cut into the corners for about ¼ inch. Turn under and baste ¼ inch hems all around the hole. Pin the patch in

place under the hole, and slip baste the folded edges of the hole to the patch. Remove pins. On the wrong side of the fabric, turn seam allowances away from garment and stitch through the line of slip basting along the fold. Stitch around the patch, pivoting the fabric on the needle at the corners. Overlap

stitching when you get back to the starting point. Pull threads to wrong side and trim. Press. Stitch diagonally across the corners of the patch to reinforce. Herringbone stitch wide seam allowance of patch to garment, so that stitches do not show on the right side.

TOPSTITCHED PATCH
For a topstitched patch, trim hole and cut patch as before. Position patch and baste in place with even basting. Stitch in place from right side, near the folded edge. On the wrong side, turn under edges of patch and baste in place. Clip across corners to reduce bulk in turning. Stitch close to folded edge of patch. Pull threads to underside; tie and cut. Press.

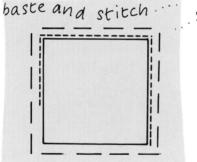

... baste and stitch ....

.. stitch from wrong side .....

REPAIRING SEAMS
When stitching at seams gives way, it is a fairly simple operation to make an invisible repair. Re-pin and baste the seam, following the exact line of the previous seam. If the fabric is loosely woven, and is gaping, press thoroughly before repairing. You may be able to strengthen the fabric by applying a little iron-on interfacing. But the problem should not occur if the garment fits correctly. Stitch along the seamline, continuing a little way beyond the end of the area of the repair.

If seams cross, it may be necessary to unpick one seam before repairing the crossing seam. Unpick hems before repairing side seams in skirts, etc.

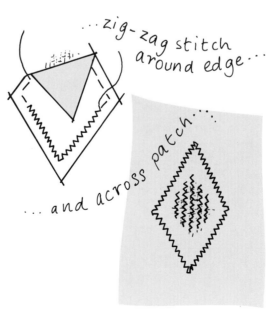

... zig-zag stitch around edge ....

... and across patch ...

REINFORCING WORN AREAS
Cut an underlay of lightweight fabric about 1 inch larger than the worn area. Position in on the wrong side of the worn area, and baste in place all around. Use a zig-zag or multi-stitch zig-zag stitch with a medium stitch width and short stitch length. Begin and end the work with backstitching. Stitch on the right side. (To do this on narrow trouser legs, turn the garment inside out and work from the inside.) At the end of each row of stitching, stop with the needle in the fabric and raise the presser foot. Turn the fabric, pivoting it on the needle. Lower the presser foot and continue stitching.

Kimono

ALTERNATIVES

Make the kimono in terry cloth, finishing the hem at mid-calf level, for a simple beach robe.

For a bathrobe, make the kimono full length, again in terry cloth, adding a contrasting front and neck band and sash – pink or blue trimmed with white, for example.

For an elegant evening wrap, use a luxurious satin, adding embroidered motifs around the shoulders.

Use seersucker, and make the kimono to above knee length for an easy-to-pack travel bathrobe.

SUITABLE FABRICS
Crisp cotton, medium-weight silk, satin, terry cloth.

TO FIT
Medium (size 10–14).

YOU WILL NEED
4¾ yds of 36 inch wide fabric
⅜ yd of 36 inch wide interfacing
Matching sewing thread

This elegant kimono, based on classic Japanese lines, is a useful addition to any wardrobe. The kimono is still worn by Japanese women on formal occasions, with a broad sash known as an *obi*. An informal version is worn by men when relaxing at home. The style shown here is made in crisp cotton, with a long, simple tied sash, as a lightweight housecoat, but you could adapt the cummerbund (see page 138) to make a more dramatic finish at the waist.

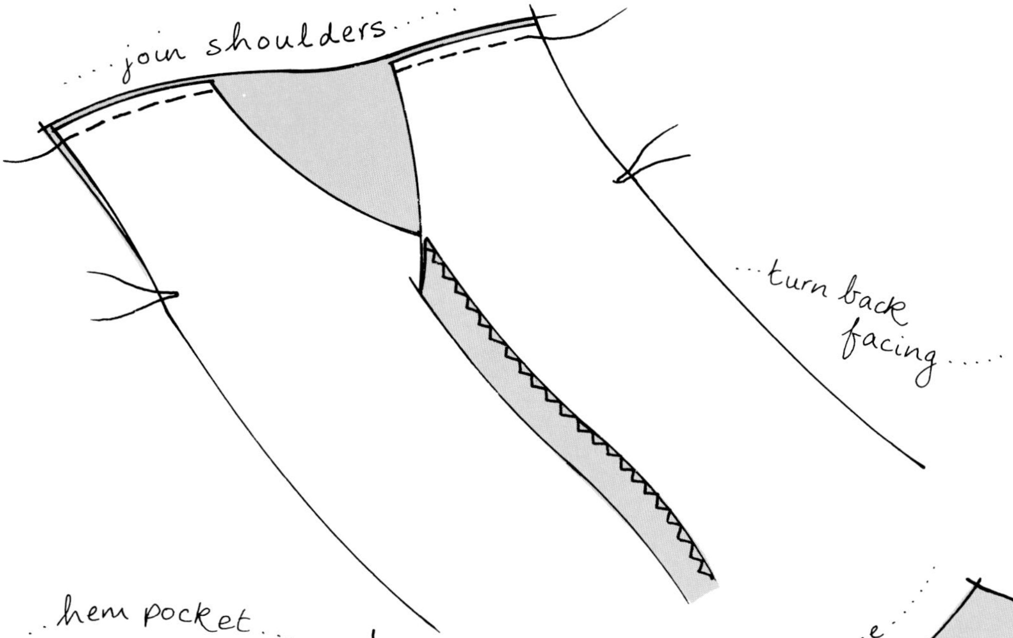

... join shoulders ...

turn back facing ...

... hem pocket ...

... stitch in place ...

join sleeve at shoulder ...

NOTE
Seam allowances are ⅝ inch unless otherwise indicated. Hems are indicated on the pattern. Cut out pattern pieces and fabric following the diagrams on page 65.

OPTIONAL
Plan positions for embroidery and work by hand or machine on back and pockets before assembling.

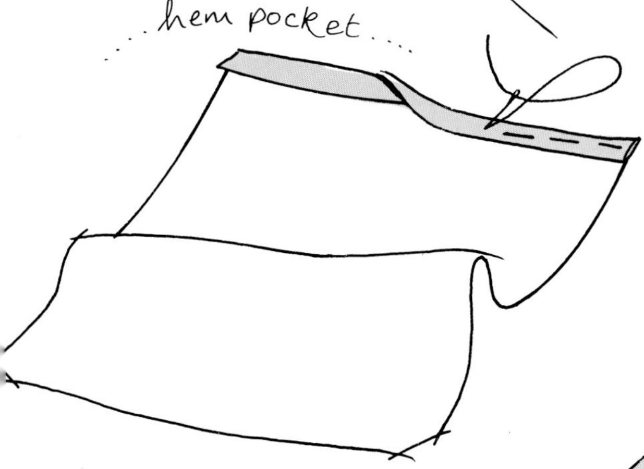

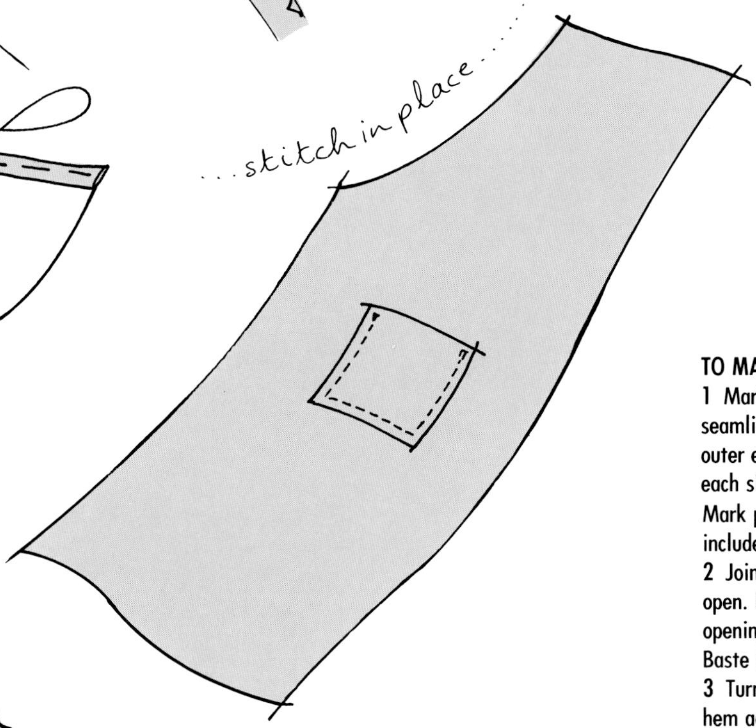

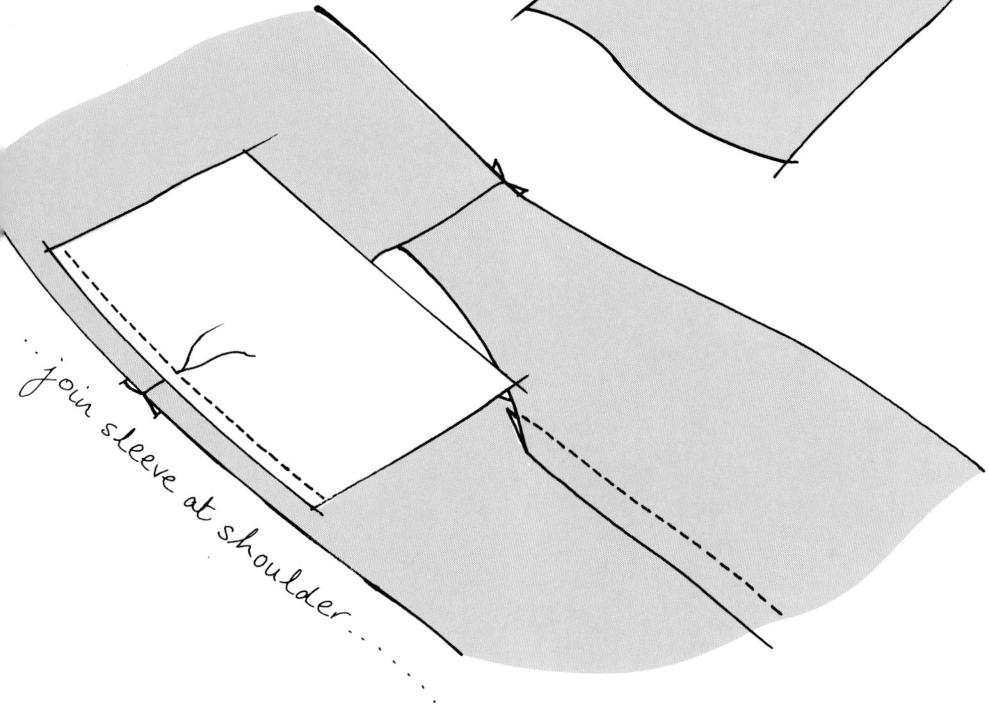

TO MAKE
1 Mark center top of sleeve at seamline. Measure 12 inches down outer edges of both front pieces and each side of back panel, and mark. Mark positions of pockets if included.
2 Join shoulder seams and press open. Finish edge of center front opening, and press under 4 inches. Baste in place.
3 Turn under a 1¼ inch double hem across top of each pocket, and slipstitch or topstitch in place. Clip away excess fabric from corners, and turn under a ⅝ inch hem all around. Baste to each front piece in marked positions. Topstitch in place around sides and lower edge of pocket, close to fold of fabric. Reverse stitch at each end and tie threads neatly.
4 Position sleeve over shoulder of garment, right sides matching and raw edges even, so that marked center points match shoulder seams. Pin and stitch in place. Finish seam allowances and press toward sleeve.

5 Stitch side seams. Clip into seam allowance on front and back of garment at underarm point. Continue stitching down sleeve seams to cuff.

6 Turn under ⅜ inch , and then 1 inch around sleeve cuff, and stitch in place by hand or machine (see page 100 for hem finishes).

7 Interface the front band, applying interfacing (iron-on or sew-in) to back of fabric, matching one edge to the center of the fabric.

8 Fold band in half, right sides facing, and stitch across ends. Trim seam allowances, clip across corners, and turn right side out. Press. Turn under ⅜ inch down long raw edges of front band.

9 Position band around neckline, right sides facing and raw edges matching (with faced part of band toward garment). Baste and stitch in place all around neckline, taking a ⅜ inch seam.

10 Turn band so that it stands out from the garment, and pin free folded edge to inside of garment. Slipstitch in place, just inside previous line of stitching. Slipstitch facing to garment down front edge if necessary.

11 Make belt by folding strip lengthwise, right sides together. Pin and stitch all around, leaving an opening in center of long side for turning through. Press. Turn right side out and press. Slipstitch opening.

12 Try on garment and turn up hem allowance – approximately 1½ inches. Check length, then finish to match sleeves, taking a deeper hem.

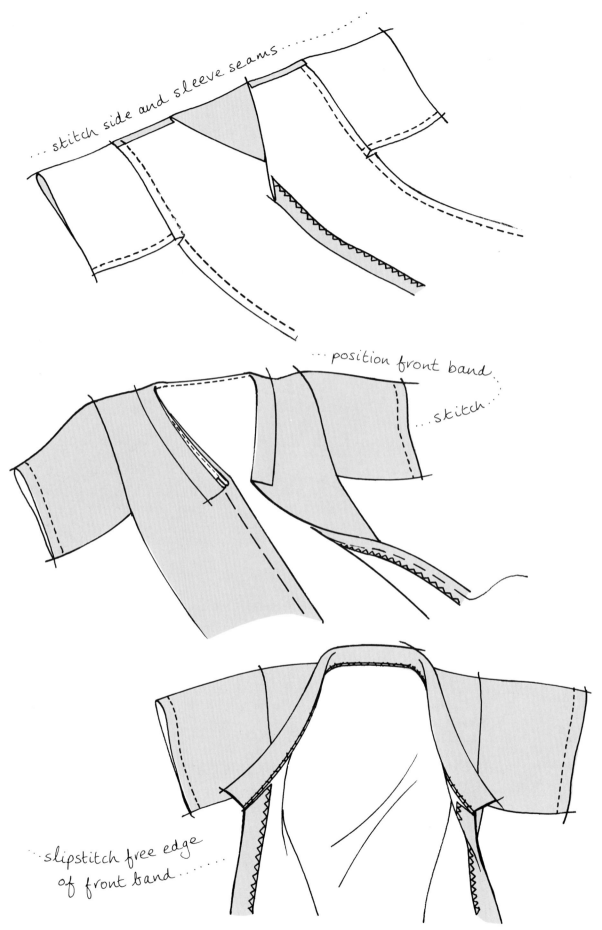

stitch side and sleeve seams

position front band

stitch

slipstitch free edge of front band

PATTERN DIAGRAM

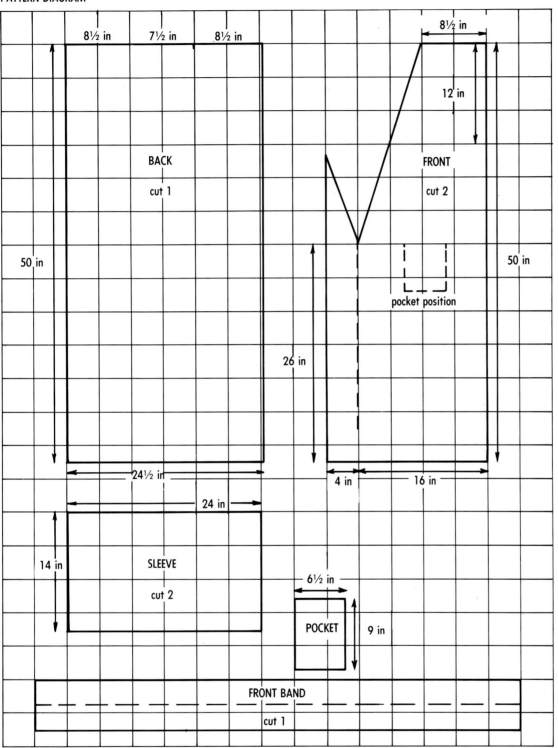

TO MAKE PATTERN
Following the diagram, in which each square represents 4 inches, draw full size pattern. Trace the pattern.

TO CUT OUT
Fold the fabric along its length, with selvages together. Cut out:
1 back
2 sleeves
2 fronts
2 pockets
1 front band
1 sash

FABRIC LAYOUT

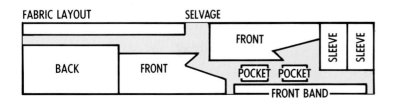

4 Trims and finishes

Once you have mastered the basic techniques of hand and machine sewing, there are many useful and decorative trims and finishes that you can apply to your work. For example, binding can be used to finish edges, and cording to emphasize seams. Appliqué, smocking, and quilting are ways of decorating the fabric. More functional elements include darts, tucks, and various kinds of fastening.

FABRIC FINISHES
Binding, cording, appliqué motifs, quilting, and smocking (opposite) all add an individual touch to your sewing projects.

If you are embarking on a home decorating project such as a slipcover with corded seams, or making a suit with bound seams, it is worthwhile preparing plenty of bias strips so that you do not have to stop and cut more. Join them together and roll them up ready for use. If you are making cording, make up as much as you think you will need before you start the project.

CUTTING AND JOINING BIAS STRIPS
Find the true bias of the fabric by cutting straight across the crosswise grain and folding the cut edge diagonally down to match the lengthwise grain. The diagonal fold is the true bias. Cut along the fold.

The width of the strips depends on what you are using them for. For cording, they should measure 1¼ inches plus three times the width of the cord. Use a ruler to measure the required width from the true bias edge of the fabric. Mark the line with tailor's chalk. Measure and mark as many strips as you will need, then cut on the markings.

For short lengths, avoid piecing the strips. Always join on the lengthwise grain. Overlap the diagonally cut ends of the strip, extending each point by the width of the seam. Pin and stitch, taking a ¼ inch seam. Take care to match any prominent weave, stripe or pattern of the fabric. Press the seams open and trim the corners.

Bias binding

Narrow strips of fabric, cut on the bias grain of the fabric, have many uses in dressmaking and home decorating. Folded bias binding can be used to give a neat finish to bulky fabrics at the hem or down seam allowances and for corded seams.

The fabric you use depends on the fabric you are sewing and the effect. For bound seams and hems you can use ready-made, folded bias binding, which is available in various widths and a limited range of colors. In a tailored, part-lined garment, you would do better to bind the seams in bias strips cut from the lining fabric.

Common widths for bias binding (or bias tape, as it is also called) are ½ and ⅞ inches. The sizes refer to the folded width, which may be single or double.

Binding can also be used to give a neat faced finish to hems, waistlines, and sleeve openings. With bias-cut binding, the strip can be shaped to suit the contours of the opening. Either use ready-made binding, in a plain color to match the main fabric, or cut your own binding in the main fabric.

TRIMMING WITH CORDING
For cording, it is more usual to use the same fabric for the bias strips as for the garment or furnishing itself. For emphasis, use contrasting fabric, but keep a similar, or lighter, weight of fabric. You could even use a fabric of a different texture – for example, satin cording on a velvet pillow. Bear in mind the wear on the cording: if you use a poor quality fabric it may wear out before the main fabric.

Filler cord is available in various sizes and qualities. A good size for cording seams in furnishings such as slipcovers and pillows in furnishing cotton is ³⁄₁₆ inch. If you are using cotton filler cord for an item that is to be washed, check that it is pre-shrunk, and shrink it if necessary.

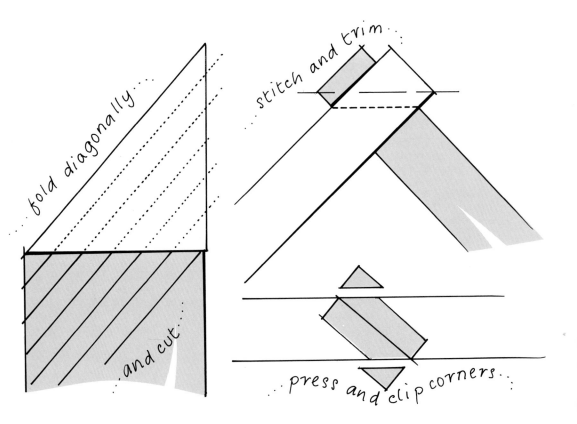

BOUND EDGE FINISH

To bind the edge of a straight piece of fabric, start by folding the binding. The width of the binding should be twice its finished width, plus seams. Turn in between ¼ and ⅝ inch down each raw edge, and fold the piping in half. Press. Open out the binding, then pin to the right side of the edge to be finished. Stitch along the foldline – this line of stitching will form the inner edge of the binding. Trim the edge of the fabric slightly. Turn the binding to the wrong side, and turn under the folded edge. Slipstitch in place. Alternatively, pin in place and stitch, either through both edges of binding, for a topstitched finish, or through the folded edge at the back, positioning the stitching so that it falls in the "ditch" where the binding is stitched to the fabric on the right side. The same method can be used for seams, using ½ inch wide ready-made binding.

For a less bulky seam finish, cut the binding narrower still – about ¾ inch wide. Fold under a ¼ inch seam allowance down one edge, then fold the binding in half. Open out the binding, and stitch the folded edge to the right side of the fabric down the seam. Trim the seam allowance slightly, then turn the binding to the wrong side of the seam. Stitch through the single layer of binding at the back of the seam – this side is protected from fraying with the seam pressed open.

When binding the edge of a rectangular panel, such as a pillow cover or a tablemat, you have to miter the corners. Prepare the binding. Stitch in place along one edge of the item, finishing the stitching the width of the finished binding from the corner. Fold the binding back on itself, making the fold at the edge of the fabric. Stitch or hand sew diagonally from the stitching line to the center of the binding at the fold to make a tuck. Continue down adjacent edge.

Turn the binding over the edge of the fabric, then hand sew a matching tuck on the back of the binding. Stitch the folded edge in place by hand or machine.

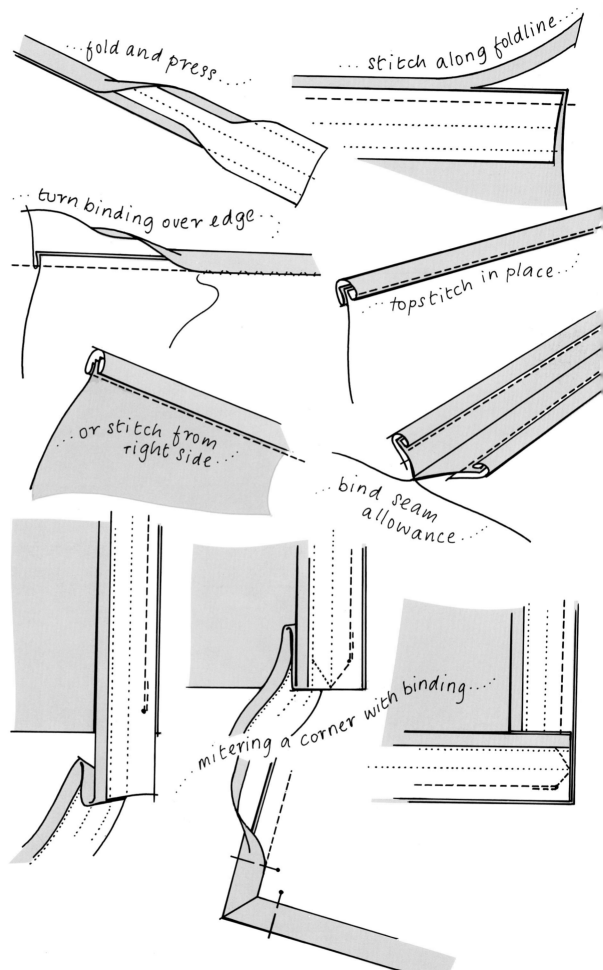

...fold and press...

...stitch along foldline...

...turn binding over edge...

...topstitch in place...

...or stitch from right side...

bind seam allowance...

...mitering a corner with binding...

USING CORDING

To cover filler cord, use a zipper foot. Position it to the left of the needle. Wrap the bias strip around the cord, right side out, so that raw edges match. Use a slightly longer stitch length than used for seaming the fabric. Stitch close to the cord. Press the stitching. Some machines have a foot with a built-in guide for covering cord.

To attach cording or corded piping to a straight edge, pin it to the right side of the fabric to be edged with edges matching. Position the first line of stitching over the seam. Adjust the zipper foot to the right of the needle. Stitch in place just outside the first

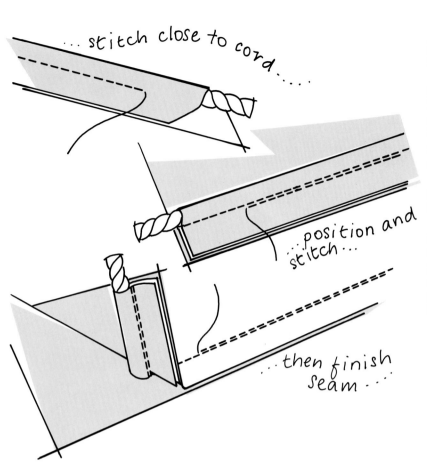

line of stitches. Press raw edges to inside.

To cord or pipe a seam, attach trim to one piece of fabric as before. Lay the other piece of fabric over corded edge and pin in place. With the corded side of the seam uppermost, stitch between the cord and the first line of stitching. Press.

Grade the seams, leaving the most exposed seam allowances the longest.

Trim the seam allowances as directed in the pattern: if the seam edge is enclosed, as on a collar or pillow cover, trim the seam allowance of the cording close to stitches, leaving seam allowance of the fabric slightly longer.

CORDING CURVES AND CORNERS

To fit cording round curves and corners, it is necessary to pin and baste it first, clipping into the seam allowance to ensure the cording will lie flat before stitching.

Pin cording in place so that raw edges match. The bias cut of the fabric should help to ease the fabric evenly around the curves. Clip into the seam allowance of the cording to ensure the cording lies close to the fabric, then baste in place. Stitch as for straight edges, using the zipper foot adjusted to the right of the cord.

For square corners, pin the cording along the first edge, then clip into the seam allowance of the cording in line with the corner. Turn the cord and continue pinning, ensuring that the cording lies as flat as possible.

After stitching the cording in place, layer and trim seam allowances in the usual way.

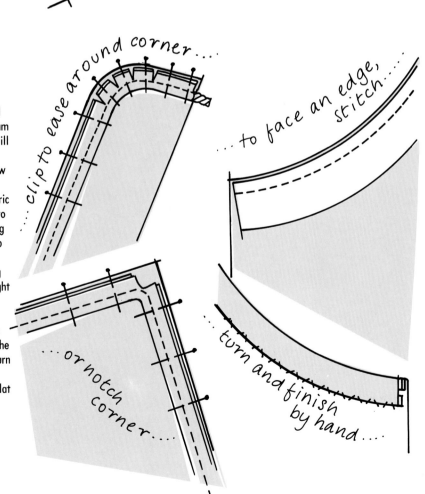

FACING AN EDGE WITH BINDING

Use ½ inch-wide ready-made bias binding, or cut your own, making it ¾ inch wide. Turn under and press a ⅛-inch wide seam allowance down each side edge. Do not fold the binding.

Allow a ¼ inch-wide seam allowance around opening (this will be trimmed to ⅛ inch).

Position the binding around the opening, with right sides together and raw edges matching. Pin and baste. Stitch with binding uppermost, following foldline of binding, taking ¼ inch seams. Press. Press binding to inside, folding main fabric on seamline. Slipstitch free fold of binding to inside of garment.

Allow ⅜ inch for turning under at each end of binding. Turn under ends and slipstitch them in place. For a neater finish on a circular opening, join ends of binding to make a ring to match opening before stitching in place.

Appliqué and quilting

Decorative techniques such as appliqué and quilting add a personal touch to your sewing. Often the instructions will be given with the pattern, but you may want to add a decorative panel or motif which you have designed yourself. Spend some time sketching and planning the design, to be sure that it creates the effect you are after.

APPLIQUE

Appliqué involves stitching (or applying) a patch to a garment so that it forms an outline design. You can use fabrics of similar textures, or add contrasting weaves, patterns, and textures, provided the motif can be laundered with the main fabric.

Use appliqué to decorate clothes and household furnishings. If you do not have a motif to follow, use a remnant of printed floral fabric, and stitch, following the outline of the motifs in the fabric.

Appliqué may be done by hand or machine. Machine appliqué gives a neat, durable finish, and is faster to do. For machine appliqué, trace the motif onto a patch of fabric, slightly larger than the finished motif. Use a narrow, short zig-zag stitch (see page 45).

MACHINE APPLIQUE

Do not cut out the outline. Pin the patch in place, then baste by hand, just outside the outline. Stitch along the outline with straight stitching.

Using a closely spaced zig-zag stitch, stitch over any lines that form part of the pattern inside the motif. Stitch over the straight stitch outline. Pull threads to underside

stitch . . . . .

. . . then trim . . . .

and tie. Press. Cut away the fabric close to the stitching, using embroidery scissors.

For an extra decorative effect, particularly on fine fabrics, use a braiding foot and add a filler cord as you stitch the close zig-zag stitch — this is known as corded appliqué. (See also Hairline seam, page 50.)

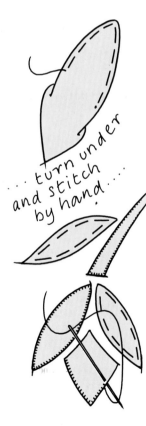

. . . turn under and stitch by hand . . .

HAND APPLIQUE

For stitching appliqué shapes in place by hand, cut out the motifs ¼ inch from the outer edge. Turn under seam allowance, clipping and notching where necessary. Baste in place and press. Baste the motif to the item, and either slipstitch or sew in place with blanket stitch.

. . . trim from beneath . . .

SHADOW APPLIQUE

Shadow hems are particularly effective in fine linen, organza, and similar fabrics. Turn up and baste the hem, mitering corners. Cut a piece of matching fabric, slightly larger than the motif. Pin in position on the wrong side of the fabric. Trace the design onto the right side of the fabric. Baste just outside traced outline.

Stitch around the design, using a fine filler cord. Remove basting, press, and trim away fabric on underside, close to stitching.

TRANSFERRING THE DESIGN

Choose the fabric to use for the appliqué, and cut a square or rectangle slightly larger than the motif. Then transfer the pattern to the fabric using one of the following methods. It may help to trace the outline of the motif on the main fabric, to make it easier to position the appliqué.

- Draw the printed pattern or your own design on a piece of stiff paper. Cut out around the outline, and draw around it on to the fabric with pencil or chalk. This method is particularly useful when you want to mark several matching motifs.

- With lightweight fabrics, draw the motif with a heavy line. Stick the motif to a window with tape so that the daylight shines through. Hold up the fabric and trace the design.
- With sheer and very light fabrics, use the same method, but lay the motif on the table — it will show through without light behind it.
- With heavy fabrics, place a piece of dressmaker's carbon paper on the fabric, coated side down. Position the motif on top, and trace the outline with a tracing wheel.

QUILTING

Quilting is the art of stitching two or more thicknesses of fabric together in a planned design. One layer of fabric should be a light padding, to create a puffed effect on the right side of the quilted panel. The stitching may be a grid of straight, usually diagonal, lines, or you can follow a pattern to create raised motifs.

Polyester batting is an ideal form of padding, and is available in several weights. It comes in a variety of widths; up to 120 inches. If you should need to join smaller pieces, use an abutted seam (see page 48). The batting should be backed with fine cotton, muslin, or voile, to prevent the fibers from catching in the feed dog, and to increase durability. Other fabrics to use for padding include outing flannel and lightweight interlining.

Many machines have a quilting foot, which makes the task of making even rows of stitches easier. It has a wide foot with a short toe, and a guide to help you space the rows of stitches. Use thread, needle, and stitch length to suit the fabric. Do not use a long stitch. Use a firm pressure. For hand quilting, use a short running stitch or prickstitch.

QUILTING

Sandwich the batting between the layers of fabric. For diagonal quilting baste together on both the lengthwise and crosswise grain to prevent the layers from slipping as you sew. Space the rows of basting 2 inches apart.

Draw a diagonal line to mark the first line of stitching in each direction. Using the appropriate foot, stitch the quilting, spacing each row of stitching by running the edge of the guide along the previous row. Roll bulky fabric so that you can slip it under the machine. Hold your left hand slightly in front of the foot, and your right hand slightly behind, so that they align on the lengthwise grain.

To quilt a pattern, mark the outline on the fabric as for appliqué. Baste the layers of fabric together, then baste round the outline before stitching.

In Italian, or corded, quilting, a design composed of parallel lines, is made to stand out in relief by the insertion of yarn through the channels. The fabric is backed with fine cotton, and the design is marked on the wrong side (or the right side if stitching by hand). Baste the fabrics together close to the outlines, then stitch along the lines. Thread yarn through the channels, bringing the needle up through the backing fabric, then back into it, at corners.

Trapunto quilting follows the same principle, but the design consists of small shapes, padded with bits of absorbent cotton. Cut small slits in the backing, insert the cotton with a needle, and then sew the slit edges together.

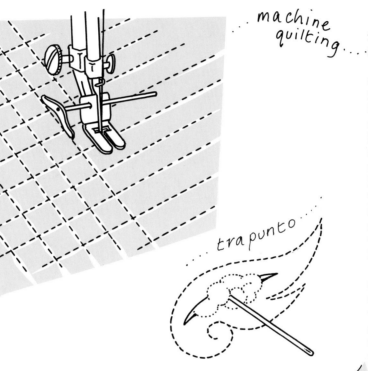

WORKING WITH QUILTED FABRICS

Because of the bulk of the batting, quilted fabrics need slightly different handling.

For a straight seam, stitch the seam as usual. Trim batting and backing close to line of stitching. Stitch seam as usual, but do not stitch through batting.

To make a seam in reversible quilted fabric, unpick quilting stitches for about half an inch down each side of seam. Trim batting from seam allowance. Stitch seam through just two layers of fabric. Press seam open, so that seam allowance folds over wadding. Turn under seam allowance down

remaining layers of fabric and slipstitch together. For a machine finish, fold under one seam allowance, then fold under a narrower seam allowance on the opposite side of the seam. Lap the narrower seam allowance over the normal seam allowance, and stitch in place through all layers of fabric.

Smocking

Smocking is a decorative way to control fullness in a garment. It is particularly appropriate for children's clothes, lingerie, and soft cotton and silk garments. Smocked bands are normally positioned at the yoke of a dress or blouse, or at the hipline of a gathered skirt. Traditionally developed as a hand technique, smocking can also be done by machine.

Patterns for smocked garments should indicate how much to draw up the gathering stitch. Work smocking before assembling the garment. If the smocking extends across seams, join the fabric with a flat seam and press and trim before smocking.

SMOCKING BY HAND

For hand smocking, the fabric has to be evenly gathered, and then embroidered to control fullness and allow a little "give" in the smocking. It is easiest to use a smocking transfer to mark the fabric: this is a piece of paper with evenly spaced dots marked on it. You simply trim the paper to suit the area to be smocked and position it on the fabric, then press according to the manufacturer's instructions to transfer the markings to the fabric. Use a long milliner's or straw needle, with two or three strands of embroidery floss.

GATHERING FOR HAND SMOCKING

Mark the wrong side of the fabric, using a suitable smocking transfer. Knot the end of the thread and run lines of gathering stitches along each line of dot, taking small stitches under each dot.

Draw up the gathering threads to the required fullness, and fasten ends securely.

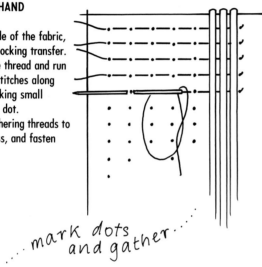

...mark dots and gather...

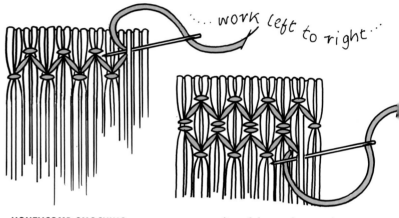

...work left to right...

HONEYCOMB SMOCKING

For honeycomb stitch, two rows of dots are joined with each line of stitching. Work from left to right, with the needle pointing to the left. Knot the end of the thread, and take the first stitch from right to left through the end pleat at the second row of gathering stitches from the top of the panel. Take a stitch over the first two pleats, stitching back through the second pleat. Move the needle up and to the right, to the next line of dots, and repeat the process, stitching through the next two pleats. Then move back down to the first row of dots, and so on.

To produce a honeycomb effect, repeat the stitch, starting from the same point and working down to the next row, then back up to meet the previous row of stitching, forming a diamond or honeycomb pattern. Rows of stitching may be made all the way down the panel of smocking, or in pairs.

ROPE AND CABLE STITCH

Both these stitches are small backstitches taken at each dot, so fasten the thread behind the first dot at the top left-hand corner of the work.

For rope stitch, take a backstitch under each dot, angling the needle so that you bring it out slightly beneath the previous stitch. Alternatively, bring the needle out above the previous stitch, so that the rope "twists" the opposite way.

For cable stitch, work in a similar way, alternating the angle of the needle so that the finished stitch looks like two staggered rows of running stitch.

Control your tension carefully to ensure even stitches and gathers. If you are not working to a pattern, make a sampler to test the effect of combining the various stitches.

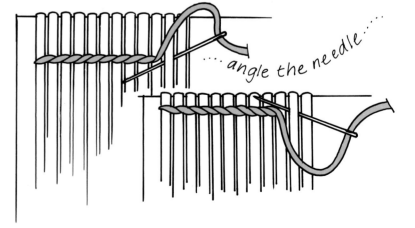

...angle the needle...

MACHINE SMOCKING

Machine smocking can speed up the work, and is particularly suitable for children's dresses, where it is important to work quickly, to make sure that the finished garment fits well.

As with hand smocking, make up the smocking before constructing the garment, so that you can ensure that the gathers are controlled to suit the situation. Mark the area to be gathered carefully, and check how much fullness must be drawn in before stitching.

There are several methods of achieving a smocked effect with the sewing machine. Some have more elasticity than others.

The main difference between the two methods shown here is that the first involves gathering the fabric, then stitching it to embroider a pattern and control the gathers; while the second method involves stitching a pattern on the fabric first, then gathering it by using elastic thread in the bobbin.

Elasticized smocking can be used as a finish in its own right for waistbands on gathered skirts or for softly gathered cuffs on full sleeves. Do a test sample, using the fabric and threads you plan to use for the finished garment, but omitting the embroidery. This enables you to check that the elastic in the bobbin will draw the fabric up sufficiently to fit the waist or wrist.

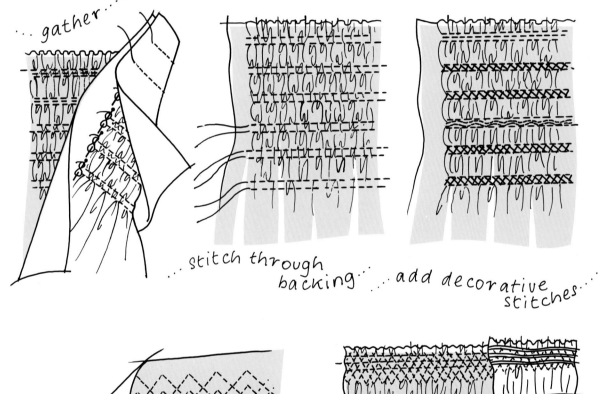

... gather.....

... stitch through backing... ...add decorative stitches...

... stitch trellis pattern...... ...use elastic thread in bobbin...

MACHINE SMOCKING

Position pairs of rows of machine gathering stitch down the area to be smocked, with about ⅛ inch between the rows, and each pair about ½ inch apart. Draw up the fabric to the required width.

Cut an underlay of lawn, organdy, or non-woven interfacing, and baste to the wrong side of the gathered area.

Select a decorative zig-zag stitch and stitch between the pairs of gathering stitches. Different patterns may be alternated down the panel.

ELASTICIZED SMOCKING

Use a slightly heavier thread than usual to stitch a pattern over the area to be smocked. Make a trellis pattern, all over the area or in bands of varying density.

To gather the area, wind the bobbin with elastic thread, using the bobbin winder on the machine. The elastic thread should stretch slightly as it winds onto the bobbin. Use a strong thread for the needle. Stitch from the right side, across the trellis pattern you have already made.

Crib quilt

Bring a touch of fun to bedtime, with this crib quilt with its bold appliqué motif. When possible, use remnants of fabric from your sewing basket for appliqué – but make sure that they are of a similar weight, and can be laundered in the same way as the main fabric. Of course, you can adapt the instructions and use a different motif to match other furnishings in the room.

The design here, with the clown's head on a matching pillowcase, is for older children; never give a child under one a pillow to sleep on.

QUILT

FINISHED SIZE
47 × 39½ inches.

YOU WILL NEED
Graph paper
2¾ yds of 48 inch wide wide pale yellow medium weight cotton
1⅜ yds of 36 inch wide muslin
1⅜ yds of 36 inch wide high loft batting
Piece of plaid fabric 24 × 20 inches
Piece of light blue fabric 30 × 20 inches
Scraps of printed and solid-colored fabrics for appliqué
Transfer fusing web
Black embroidery thread
16 inches of 48 inch wide blue satin
Matching sewing threads

PILLOWCASE

FINISHED SIZE
22½ × 14 inches.

YOU WILL NEED
Graph paper
1½ yds of pale yellow fabric, as for quilt
Appliqué fabrics, as for quilt
Transfer fusing web
Matching sewing threads

position appliqué

add suspenders

stitch laces

quilt background

bind edges

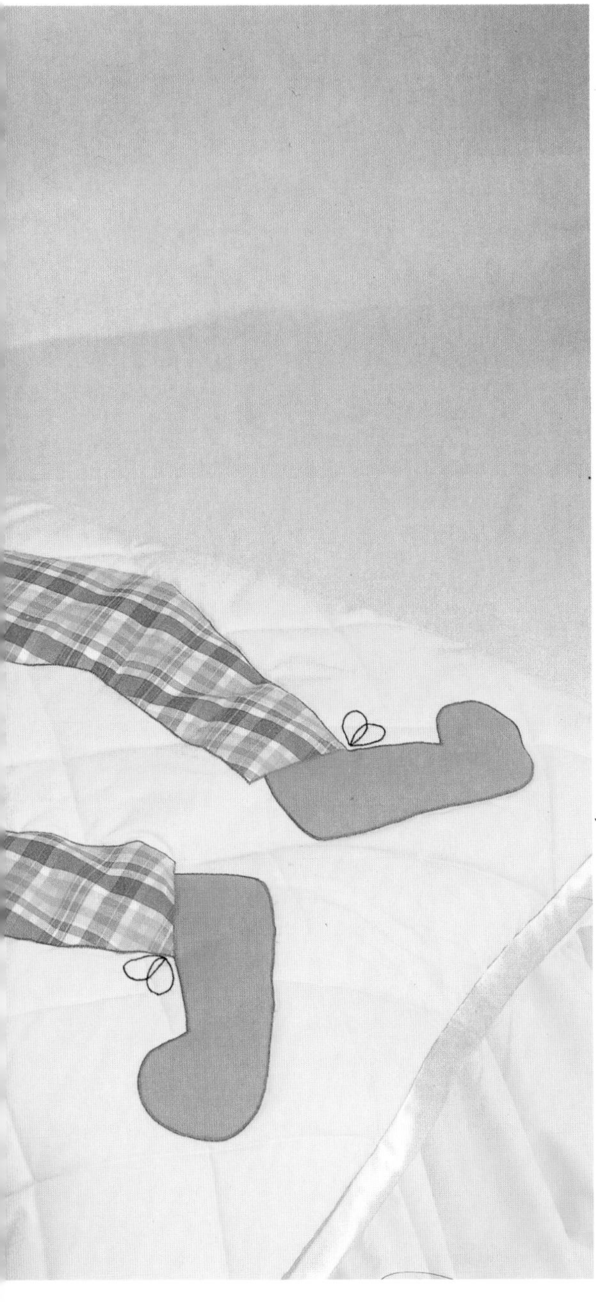

QUILT

TO CUT OUT
From main fabric cut out two pieces, each 49 × 41½ inches. Mark center of front.

TO MAKE
1 Enlarge the clown body appliqué shapes on pattern paper, following diagram overleaf. Each square on the diagram equals 2 inches. See page 33 for details of enlarging patterns. Cut out paper pattern.

2 Iron transfer fusing web to the wrong side of appliqué fabrics. Mark each shape in reverse on the web side of the fabrics, marking a blue top, plaid trousers, printed bow tie, white hands, and dark pink shoes. Mark buttons. Cut out.

3 Center the pieces on the front quilt piece, sliding the trouser tops under top, hands under sleeve ends, and top of shoes under trouser ends. Pin, when the result looks good, then piece-by-piece peel off backing and iron in place. Using matching threads, zig-zag stitch around each piece in turn. Add buttons in the same way.

4 Cut two strips from plaid fabric, each 18 × 1½ inches. Turn under raw edges and pin on each side of top, for suspenders; stitch in place.

5 Work boot laces in stem stitch using black embroidery thread.

6 Mark diagonal quilting lines on front, 5 inches apart. Center batting then muslin behind appliqué front; baste all around clown, around edge, and across quilt at intervals. Quilt.

7 Place back on front with wrong sides together. Pin and baste. Trim quilt to 47 × 39¼ inches, then stitch together around the edge.

8 From blue satin fabric cut out 3½-inch-wide binding strips, two 50 inches long and two 42 inches long. Stitch in place to edges of quilt front, taking ⅝ inch hem on strip and stitching 1¼ inches from quilt edge. Turn under raw edges; slipstitch.

PILLOWCASE

TO CUT OUT

From main fabric cut out one piece 52¾ × 15¼ inches for pillowcase.

TO MAKE

1 At one end, turn under a double 1¼-inch deep hem; pin and stitch hem in place.

2 At opposite short end, turn under a double ⅜-inch deep hem; pin and stitch hem in place.

3 Turn in narrow hemmed edge 4½ inches for flap. Fold pillowcase in half widthwise with deep hem level with folded edge; press. Mark center front of pillowcase, and unfold the fabric.

4 Enlarge clown face appliqué shapes from diagram below. Each square on diagram equals 2 inches. Cut out pattern shapes.

5 Apply transfer fusing web to wrong side of dark pink, pink, white, and printed fabrics. Mark patterns in reverse on fusing web side of fabrics. Mark dark pink hair, pink fabric, white eyes, and printed fabric nose. Cut out each piece.

6 Center the pieces on the pillowcase, tucking the edge of the face underneath the hair. Peel off the backing and iron in place. Using matching sewing threads, zig-zag stitch each piece in position.

7 Using a tight zig-zag stitch, work a cross for each eye, using black thread.

8 Turn in flap to wrong side and press edge. Fold pillowcase in half widthwise with wrong sides together, so hemmed edge is level with fold of flap. Pin and stitch side edges, taking ¼ inch seam allowance.

9 Turn pillowcase so right sides are together; press side edges. Stitch sides again, taking ⅜ inch allowance, to complete French seams. Turn right side out.

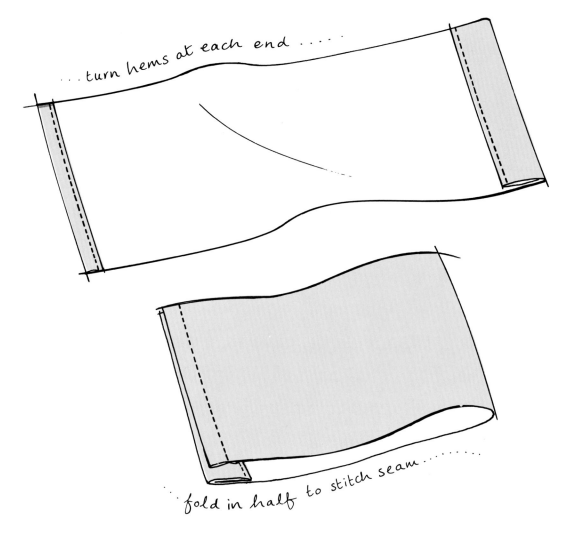

...turn hems at each end......

...fold in half to stitch seam......

Scale: 1 square represents 2 inches

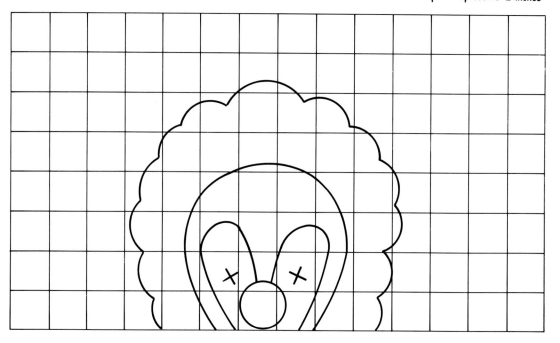

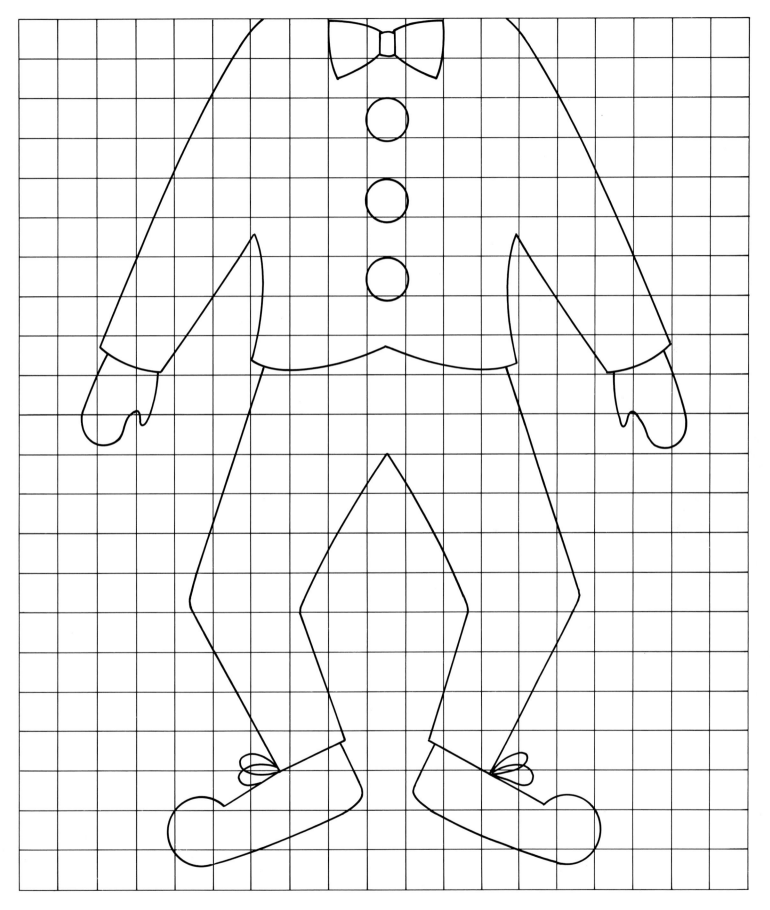

Shaping techniques

For slight shaping, without taking any tucks in the fabric, you can add ease to a seam: this involves cutting one edge to be joined very slightly longer than the opposite edge. The fullness is eased into the seam as you stitch. See page 48.

In order to fit flat pieces of fabric to curved, three-dimensional shapes, darts and tucks have to be made. You can also take in the fullness of fabric by gathering it. The method you use for shaping or controlling fullness will depend on the pattern and the effect you want. As a rule of thumb, use darts on firm fabrics, tucks in fine, smooth fabrics, and gathers in soft and sheer fabrics.

Other methods of shaping fabric to give fullness are pleats – for instance, in a skirt or in a ruffle in furnishing fabric, and godets – extra panels in a flared skirt which give flare to the hemline.

DARTS

Darts provide fullness at the bust, hip, shoulder, and at the elbow in tight-fitting sleeves. In home furnishings they may be used to shape corners in slipcovers. They point toward the fullest part of the garment or furnishing.

In dressmaking, it may be necessary to change the position of darts to match your figure. Darts up from the waistline may be moved closer to the center or farther apart to bring them under the point of the bust. To accommodate a low bustline, waist darts must be made shorter and underarm darts moved down. This should be done when fitting the pattern, before cutting out.

Darts are normally made on the wrong side of the garment, but are sometimes stitched on the right side as a styling detail. In this case, use the continuous thread method, which leaves no knot at the point of the dart. They are stitched from the point. This method should also be used for sheer fabrics.

For information on pressing darts, see page 26.

TUCKS

Tucks are another way to provide fullness, and are usually positioned on the front of a garment at the shoulders, on the front and back running up from

DARTS

Fold the dart, matching markings. Pin at raw edge and point, and at intervals between. Place the pins at right angles to the stitching line of the dart. Baste from the seam edge to the point. Remove tailor's tacks. Stitch from the raw edge, reinforcing with reverse stitching, tapering gradually to the point. The last three or four stitches should be parallel to the fold of the dart, just a thread's width from the fold. Continue stitching to form a short chain beyond the point.

Cut the threads about 2 inches from the point of the dart. Tie the thread chain in a single knot, using a pin to set the knot close to fabric.

In heavy fabric, such as tweed and flannel, darts are frequently slashed and pressed open. Finish edges by overcasting or pinking.

For contour darts, which shape dresses, coats, and jackets at the waistline or under the bust, fold the dart, matching markings. Pin at each end, then at the widest point and evenly between. Stitch the dart in two stages, stitching from just inside the stitching line at the waist to the point. Slash the dart to within ¼ inch of the stitching at the waist.

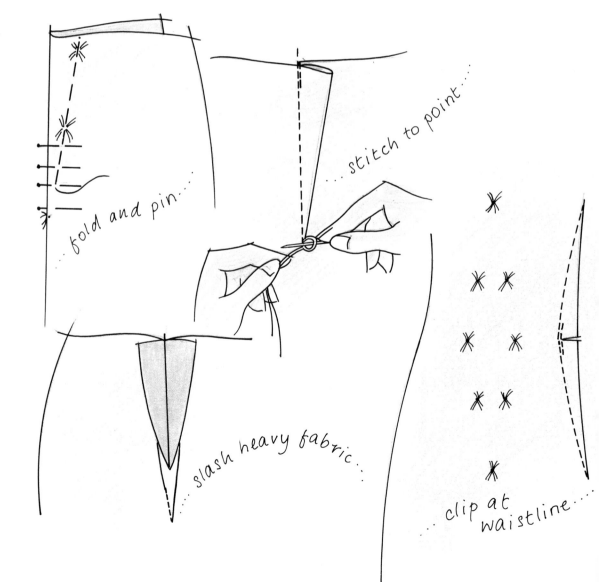

... fold and pin ...

... stitch to point ...

... slash heavy fabric ...

... clip at waistline ....

the waistline, and on the front of a skirt. Tucks running up and down the front of a bodice should be in line with the fullest part of the bust, and tucks on bodice and skirt sections should meet at the waistline when sections are joined.

As with darts, they are normally stitched on the wrong side of the fabric, but may also be stitched on the right side as a styling point. Use the continuous thread method when tucks are on the right side, or on sheer fabrics.

GATHERS

In dressmaking, gathers are used to control fullness at waist, yoke shaping, over the cap of puff sleeves and at cuffs. In home decorating, gathers are frequently used for decorative effect in ruffles.

Normally, two rows of stitching are made to gather the fabric. Some patterns indicate extra rows of stitching, which will hold the gathers in place to give a crisp effect on the garment: these extra rows show when the gathered edge is set into the waistband or yoke.

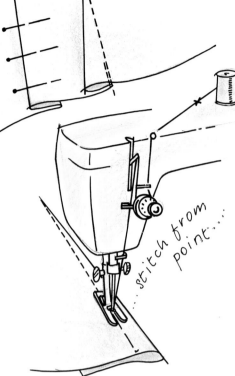

stitch from point...

stitch downwards....

CONTINUOUS THREAD DARTS

Thread the bobbin thread through the needle in the opposite direction to usual, and tie it to the upper thread in a single knot. Rewind the upper spool so the knot passes onto the spool so there is enough thread to stitch the full length of the dart. Position the tip of the needle in the point of the dart just a thread's width from the fold. Pull the slack out of the thread by turning the spool. Lower the presser foot and stitch, carefully shaping the dart. At the raw edges, reverse stitch to strengthen. With some machines you can wind the upper thread onto the bobbin, without removing it from the machine.

For continuous thread contour darts, start from each point in turn, overlapping the stitching for about ¾ inch at the waistline. Slash and press as usual.

TUCKS

Fold the tuck, match the markings and keep the raw edges even at the top. Pin and baste. Start stitching at the seam edge and reinforce with reverse stitching. Continue stitching to the end of the tuck, then reverse stitch to finish.

When tucks are on the right side of the fabric, so that the fold and stitching lines show, avoid unsightly reverse stitching by using the continuous thread method.

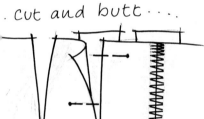

cut and butt....

DARTS IN INTERFACING

To eliminate bulk, cut the dart on the stitching line. Bring the two cut edges together and pin over an underlay of a lightweight fabric.

Cut the underlay about 1 inch wider and slightly longer than the dart. Stitch from the right side, using a multi-stitch zig-zag set to the widest stitch width and 15 to 20 stitch length. Align the abutted line with center of the presser foot.

GATHERS

Position the first row of gathering stitches just inside the seamline, with a second row about ⅛ inch outside the first, in the seam allowance. Use a long stitch – 8 to 10 in medium-weight fabrics and 12 to 15 in soft and fine fabrics. Loosen the upper tension so that you can draw the bobbin thread.

At one end, draw the threads through to the underside. Tie each pair of threads by forming a single knot in the strands and set the knots tightly against the fabric. Fold the fabric across the end of the gathering stitches so that the ends of the threads extend outward. Stitch a pin tuck in place, stitching

close to the fold. Cut off the ends of the gathering stitches ½ inch from the tuck.

At the other end of the stitching, anchor the threads on the right side of the fabric by winding in a figure eight around a pin set across the end of the gathering stitches. On the wrong side of the fabric, take the remaining threads from each row of stitches and twist them together. At the same time ease the fabric back on the stitches to form uniform gathers. When gathering is tight enough, pull all the threads to the wrong side of the fabric, tie each pair together, and make a pin tuck as before.

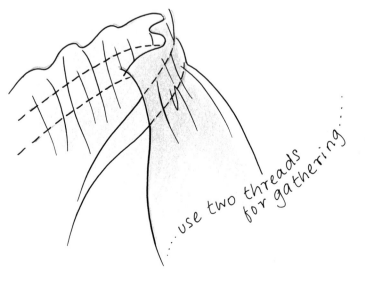

...use two threads for gathering...

PLEATS AND GODETS

These are two methods of giving fullness to the hemline of a skirt. Pleats are also used as a design detail, on shirts and jumpers, for example, and for decorative effect in home furnishings – on skirts, round the lower edge of slipcovers, for drapery headings, and for ruffles around pillows.

There are several different styles of pleat, and the pattern should give detailed instructions. On skirts,

they may be used to give fullness all around the waistline, or they may be positioned in the lower part of the skirt, particularly at the back in straight skirts. They may also be positioned at the front of a skirt – as a single pleat, in pairs, or grouped.

Godets are carefully cut panels which add fullness to a hemline. They may be set into a panel cut out of the main part of the skirt or set into a seamline. Set them in before joining side seams.

KNIFE PLEATS

Knife, or wrap pleats usually fold in one direction, from right to left, although they may fold outward from the center if they are on each side of the front of a skirt. This method does not need any stitching on the right side of the pleat.

If the pattern does not extend the pleat allowance the entire length of the skirt, do so by marking the fabric with chalk before cutting. Mark the position of the pleat and seamline above the pleat with tailor's tacks. Pin and baste the seamline and the extension for the pleat, then stitch close to the basting. Remove basting and press the seam allowance above the pleat to one side.

Baste the foldline for the pleat and remove tailor's tacks. On the wrong side, cut out the seam allowance from the top layer of fabric above the pleat, leaving a ⅝ inch seam allowance. This will eliminate bulk, but the second layer of fabric holds the pleat in position. Clip into the seam allowance and press the seam open above the

pleat. Press the pleat to one side, but avoid pressing the hem area, as the folds are reversed once the hem has been made.

For extra strength, the pleat may be topstitched in place at an angle from the seam to edge of the pleat.

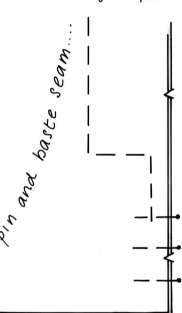

...pin and baste seam...

trim seam allowance...

...press pleat to one side...

TOPSTITCHED PLEATS

This method is often used for panels of pleats, or skirts that are pleated all around. The topstitching runs from the waistline to the hipline. Mark, fold, and press the pleats, then pin and baste in position. Pin-mark the length to be stitched on the right side of each pleat. On the underside, fold back the preceding pleat, to avoid stitching through extra layers of fabric. On the right side, stitch the pleat in place from the marking up to the waistline. Stitch each pleat, then pull threads to underside and tie.

...fold, baste and topstitch pleats...

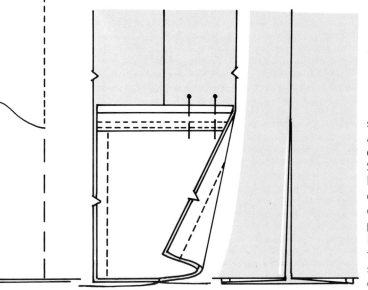

... baste pleat .... stitch underlay...

...finish hems...

INVERTED PLEAT

An inverted pleat with an underlay is made in the seam of a skirt. The underlay is joined to the main fabric down the inner folds of the pleat. If the pattern does not extend the pleat allowance the entire length of the skirt, do so by marking the fabric with chalk before cutting out. Mark the position of the pleat and seamline above the pleat with tailor's tacks. Pin and baste the seam the entire length of the skirt and pleat. Stitch from the waistline to the top of the pleat, reinforcing the stitch by reverse stitching. Remove basting along stitching line, but not down pleat. Press. Press wide seam open down the length of the seam and pleat. Press lightly in the hem area.

Position an underlay over the pleat section, right side down, so that the top of the underlay extends for ⅝ inch above the top of the pleat. Pin and baste the underlay to each side of the pleat, stitch side

seams, and press. Cut a strip of straight seam binding the width of the pleat. Fold it lengthwise through the center and press. Pin the stay across the top of the pleat with the lower edge of the tape at the top of

the pleat. Pin, then stitch in place, stitching one half at a time, through tape, underlay, and pleat/wide seam allowance.

The Dior pleat is similar to an inverted pleat, but there is no

stitching down the side of the pleat. Allow a 2 inch-wide seam allowance down the back seam. Stitch the seam in the usual way, leaving about a 6 inch opening above the hemline. Press the seam open and stitch the hem. Cut a piece of fabric 4 inches wide by 7 inches, plus hem allowance. Finish the sides of the panel with zig-zag stitching or binding, then finish top edge. Pin and baste to the seam allowances, 1 inch above the opening. Hem it in place, checking that the stitching does not go through to the right side of the skirt. Turn up the hem, making it ¼ inch shorter than skirt so there is no danger of it showing.

GODETS

For a godet set into a cut-out, the cut-out has a sharp inside curve, while the godet has a more gentle outside curve. Staystitch ⅝ inch from the seam edge of the cut-out. Press and slash the seam allowance around the curve almost to the stitching. Pin the godet in place, pinning from the center to the lower edge. Baste by hand with small stitches and check the right side to see that the godet hangs well. Leave to hang overnight before stitching. Stitch slowly, with the godet next to the feed, in a continuous line from one hem to the other.

For a godet in a seam, stitch the seam above the opening and reinforce each end with reverse stitching. Finish seam edges. Snip into the seam allowances at the top of the opening, almost to the stitching. Press, then press the seam open.

Position godet in the opening, right sides together, matching the marking at the point with the end of the seam above the opening. Pin at the point. Pin and baste one side

from the point to the lower edge. Keep seam edges even. Stitch on the garment side, from lower edge to point. Pin, baste and stitch the opposite side in the same way. At the point of the godet, pull all threads to the underside and tie together in a single knot. Remove basting and press. Finish seam edges.

To reinforce the seam at the point, cut a piece of seam binding about 1¼ inches long. Fold it lengthwise through the center and press. Pin across godet and garment seam allowances, aligning the lower edge of the stay with the top of the point. Stitch to seam allowances. Cut off point of godet ¼ inch from stitching.

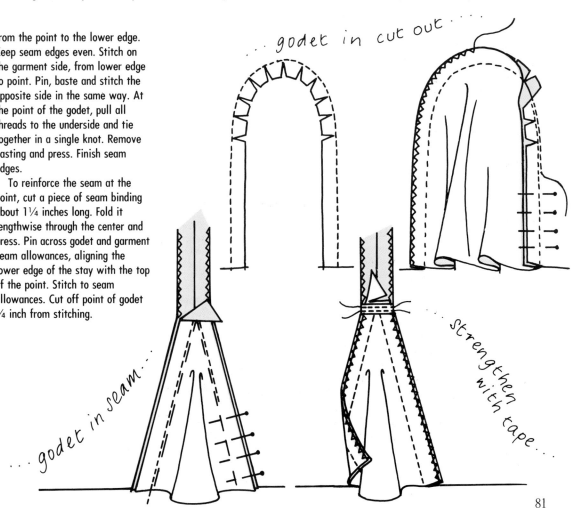

... godet in cut out.....

...godet in seam...

strengthen with tape...

Ruffles and trims

In both dressmaking and sewing for the home, decorative ruffles, gathered or pleated, and lace trims have their place. Fashion trends may come and go, but gathered and eyelet lace trims continue to be used on children's clothes, while pleated trims give a crisp finish to many home furnishings.

GATHERED RUFFLES

The fullness of a ruffle may be given in the pattern you are following. If you are adding a trim without a pattern, cut the strip for the ruffle at least twice the length of the piece of fabric it is to be attached to. Ruffles may be cut across the fabric or on the bias. In the case of fine fabrics, particularly on sheer curtains, for example, they are cut along the length to reduce seams to a minimum.

There are several ways to finish the long, free edge of the ruffle. A popular choice for furnishing trims is to cut it from a double width of fabric, folding it in half lengthwise to make a strip with a folded outer edge, and the right side of the fabric showing on both sides of the ruffle. You can add extra color by binding the outer edge of the ruffle with bias binding, or simply turn over a double hem down the outer edge of the ruffle, using the rolled hem foot if preferred.

PLEATED RUFFLES

Pleated ruffles are used in many of the same ways as gathered ruffles – to trim the hems on children's clothes and to edge pillows in home furnishings, for example. Finish the long raw edge of the ruffle as for gathered ruffles making it double thickness,

or turning under a narrow hem. A bound finish is less suitable for a pleated ruffle.

The strip may be pleated into knife pleats or box pleats. The diagrams indicate how to mark the fabric and fold it before pressing and setting it in place.

LACE AND BRAID TRIMS

Lace is available in many different styles and finishes. Traditionally, it was woven of silk or cotton, but fine lace is now normally machine made from nylon fiber, or embroidered onto a net backing. Crochet effect cotton lace is also available for heavier cotton. Eyelet lace is an embroidered cotton trim. Lace and eyelet lace trims may be finished along one edge, with the raw edge set into a seam or tuck. The long raw edge may be gathered, or set flat against the edge of a panel of fabric.

Lace may also be finished along both edges, to use for appliqué or insertion. This type of trim may also have eyelets, through which you can thread ribbon for an extra decorative touch.

There are many other different types of braid, fringes, and edgings, for finishing home furnishings, garments, and accessories. It is worthwhile browsing through the notions and furnishing trimmings racks, and buying some short lengths of trim to use in experimenting with different ways of adding trims. Always use a fine needle and short stitch. Light braids may be topstitched in place, but heavier braids, particularly furnishing trims, should be slipstitched to a finished edge or along a seamline.

STEPS IN ADDING A RUFFLE

- Cut the ruffle to the appropriate measurements: for a double thickness ruffle, the width of the strip should be twice the finished depth of the ruffle plus twice the seam allowance. For a bound edge, the strip should be the finished depth of the ruffle plus seam allowance. A turned double hem may measure anything from 1/8 inch to 3/8 inch wide, so allow twice the depth of the hem plus the seam allowance. The length of the strip can measure anything from twice to three times the length of the gathered or pleated ruffle, depending on the weight of the fabric, the depth of the ruffle and the effect required.
- Finish the fabric by folding the strip in half, binding or turning a double hem, using the rolled hem foot for a fine finish.
- Gather the fabric by hand, or machine stitch or pleat it as described on page 84. Stitch the gathering or pleats firmly in place by machine (or by hand for very fine fabrics) so that fullness is distributed evenly. Press, then pin to the edge to be trimmed: position it with right sides facing and

raw edges matching. Baste, then stitch in place on the seamline, and finish seam allowances by one of the methods described on page 84. Many machines have special accessories to gather and stitch ruffles in place in one go. It is advisable to run a second line of stitching to hold the pleats in place.
- Where the ruffle is applied to the corner of a panel of fabric (around the corner of a collar, a pillow or a tablecloth, for example) pin the ruffle in place without stitching the gathers in place: pin along a straight edge, then draw extra gathers together to ease the fullness around the corner. Finish pinning the ruffle in place, then baste and stitch before pressing and finishing raw edges.
- If the trim is to be set into a seam, pin to one side only. Stitch in place just inside the seamline. Then finish the seam, sandwiching the ruffle or pleat in place as you stitch the seam. Trim away seam allowance of gathered fabric and zig-zag stitch raw edges together, or press open and finish raw edges separately.

GATHERING BY HAND OR MACHINE

To gather fabric by hand, run two lines of gathering stitches through the edge of the strip of fabric to be attached to the panel of fabric or set into the seam. Position the rows of stitching inside the seam allowance and ⅛ inch apart. Draw up the fullness to the finished measurement of the ruffle and tie the threads in place around a pin.

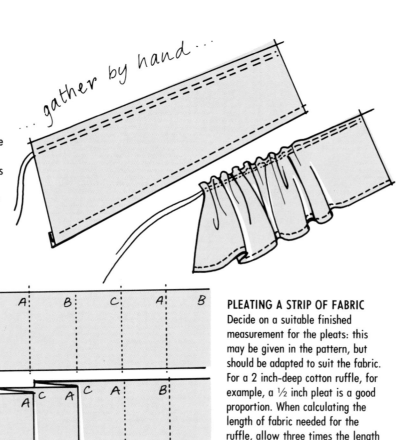

...gather by hand...

To gather by machine, either use the method described on page 79, drawing up the bobbin thread to control fullness, or use the gathering foot. Experiment with the gathering foot and the fabric you are using to test what fullness to allow when cutting the strip for the ruffle. Most machines enable you to gather and stitch the ruffle in place in one movement.

PLEATING A STRIP OF FABRIC

Decide on a suitable finished measurement for the pleats: this may be given in the pattern, but should be adapted to suit the fabric. For a 2 inch-deep cotton ruffle, for example, a ½ inch pleat is a good proportion. When calculating the length of fabric needed for the ruffle, allow three times the length of the fabric it is to be attached to, plus seam or hem allowance at each end. Fold the fabric or finish the edge of the strip and press. Mark off distances the width of the pleats down the length of the raw edge of the strip, marking the points A, B, C, A, B, C, etc. down the length of the strip. Fold and pin point A to point C down the length of the strip. Baste, press, and stitch just inside the seamline.

FINISHING THE RAW EDGES

To finish straight edged lace by hand, baste the lace over the seam allowance where the fabric meets the lace, with the wrong side of the lace facing the right side of the fabric. On the underside, roll the edge of the fabric and overcast through rolled hem and lace. On the right side, the lace covers the hem.

To finish gathered lace by hand, baste the gathered edge to the seamline of the fabric, right sides together. Trim the fabric seam allowance to ¼ inch. Roll the fabric edge over the stitching line and overcast through the rolled hem and lace. When finished, press lace away from rolled hem. If you want the rolled hem on the right side in the finished work, baste the gathered lace on the seamline of the fabric, wrong sides together.

To finish a ruffle applied to an edge, trim the seam allowance of the ruffle close to the seamline. Fold the straight edge under ⅛ inch, and then fold it over the trimmed seam allowance of the gathered edge. Pin, baste, and stitch in place. Some machine accessories turn and stitch this self-bound hem in one movement.

To finish seam allowances in a seam, trim the seam allowance of the ruffle, then, in a faced or enclosed seam, zig-zag stitch raw edges together. In a garment, press ruffle downward, press seam allowances upward, and finish together.

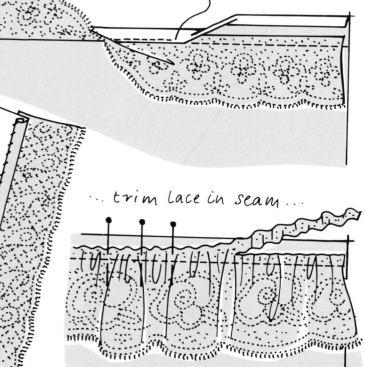

...self bound lace trim...

...baste to right side...

...roll and overcast...

...trim lace in seam...

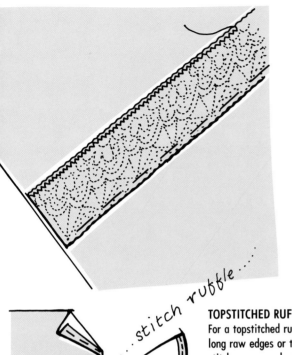

... stitch lace ...

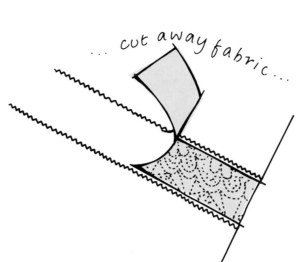

... cut away fabric ...

INSERTING LACE

Bands of lace can be set into lingerie; this method is used to set lace in on the bias in woven fabrics, to prevent the fabric from stretching and make sure that the work is straight. Mark seamlines for the lace without cutting the panels where it will be inserted. Pin, baste, and stitch the lace to the fabric from the right side, then cut away the fabric 1/8 inch from the stitching. Press seam allowance away from lace. For fabrics that fray easily, or as an alternative finish, cut the fabric to allow for the lace insertion, leaving a 1/2 inch seam. Turn under seam, and topstitch lace in place.

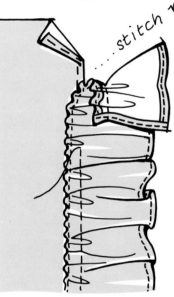

... stitch ruffle ...

TOPSTITCHED RUFFLE

For a topstitched ruffle, bind both long raw edges or turn under and stitch a narrow double or rolled hem. Allow a seam allowance or heading to suit the design of the item. Turn under a double hem on the edge of the panel where the ruffle is to be attached. Finish the ends of the ruffle and gather it along the seamline, drawing up threads so the ruffle fits the panel. Pin and baste in place, distributing fullness evenly. Topstitch along first line of stitching.

draw thread to gather ...

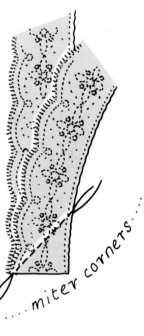

... miter corners ...

APPLYING LACE TO CURVES AND CORNERS

Mark the seamline where the lace is to be stitched on the right side of the fabric. Pin the lace in place around the curve, then draw the thread on the top edge of the lace and shape it to fit the curve. Alternatively, run fine gathering stitches along the inner edge of the lace, and draw up fullness. Pin and baste lace along seamline, then sew in place by hand, using a whipping stitch, or by machine, using a straight or narrow zig-zag stitch.

For corners on applied, straight lace, fold the lace diagonally to match the corner, and stitch by

machine along foldline or whipstitch by hand. Trim away excess lace from underside and stitch to garment or item being made.

When fitting edging lace around a corner, you can either miter the corner in the same way or gather the lace by drawing a thread or running gathering stitches along the inner edge of the lace trim around the corner. Pin and fit lace at corners carefully before stitching.

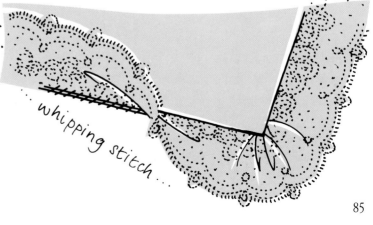

... whipping stitch ...

Simple dress

ALTERNATIVES
Omit sleeves and cut away fabric around armholes; face the neck and armholes to make a simple top.

Drop the waistline, and omit the elastic. Shorten the pleated skirt. Tie with a bold sash at the waist. Add a front, slashed opening.

SUITABLE FABRICS
Cotton, cotton mixtures, silk, linen, and synthetics.

TO FIT
Size 12.

YOU WILL NEED
2½ yds of 58-inch wide fabric
Matching thread
¼ yd of 30 inch wide lightweight interfacing
⅞ yd of narrow elastic

Versatile and easy to wear, this dress has a wide neckline and dropped shoulder line. The bodice is gathered up with elastic and fitted to a more formal skirt with topstitched pleats. For smaller or larger sizes, it is a good idea to make the dress first in unbleached muslin, and check the fit before cutting it out in your chosen fabric. Crisp weaves will hold the pleats better than soft fabrics.

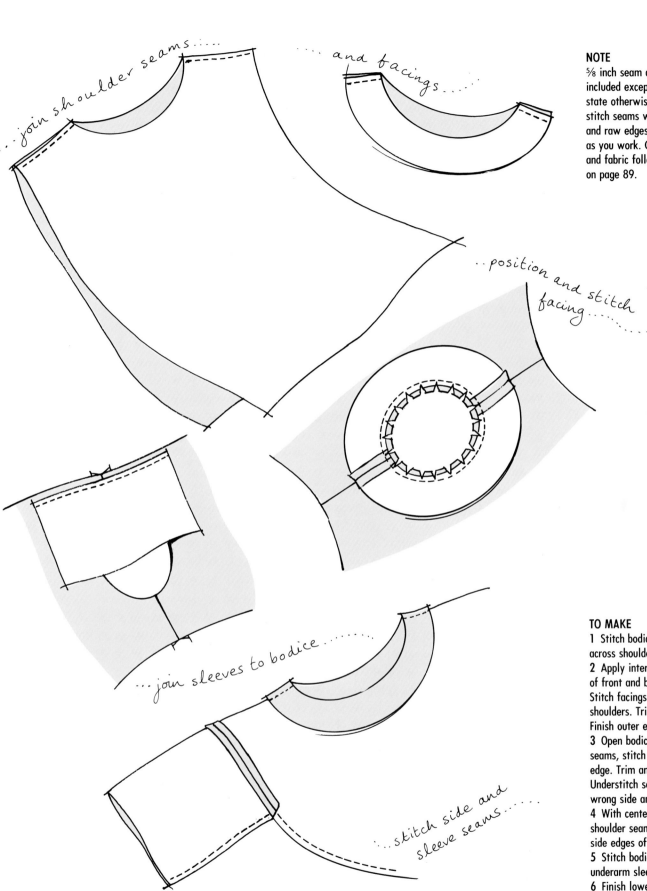

...join shoulder seams......

... and facings ......

..position and stitch facing.........

... join sleeves to bodice ....

...stitch side and sleeve seams ......

NOTE
⅝ inch seam allowances are included except where instructions state otherwise. Pin, baste and stitch seams with right sides facing and raw edges even. Finish seams as you work. Cut out pattern pieces and fabric following the diagrams on page 89.

TO MAKE
1 Stitch bodice front to bodice back across shoulder seams.
2 Apply interfacing to wrong side of front and back neck facings. Stitch facings together across shoulders. Trim and press seam. Finish outer edge of facing.
3 Open bodice out flat. Matching seams, stitch facing around neck edge. Trim and clip seam. Understitch seam. Turn facing to wrong side and press.
4 With center of sleeve level with shoulder seam, stitch sleeves to side edges of bodice.
5 Stitch bodice side seams and underarm sleeve seams.
6 Finish lower edge of sleeves. Press ¾ inch hems to wrong side and stitch.

7 On wrong side, fold skirt front so pleat lines indicated by arrows match. Form four pleats and stitch along pleat lines from waist to dots.

8 Press folds of pleats toward center. Press in pleats down length of skirt. Topstitch pleats on right side about ¼ inch away from stitching.

9 Stitch skirt front to skirt back along side seams.

10 Matching side seams, stitch skirt to bodice taking ¾ inch seam allowance. Stitch seam allowances together with a second row ⅜ inch from first, leaving opening for elastic. Finish edges together. Alternatively, use the method on page 126.

11 Trim elastic to fit, allowing ¾ inch for joining. Thread through waist seam. Overlap ends and stitch together.

12 Finish lower edge of skirt. Press up a 1½ inch hem and stitch it in place.

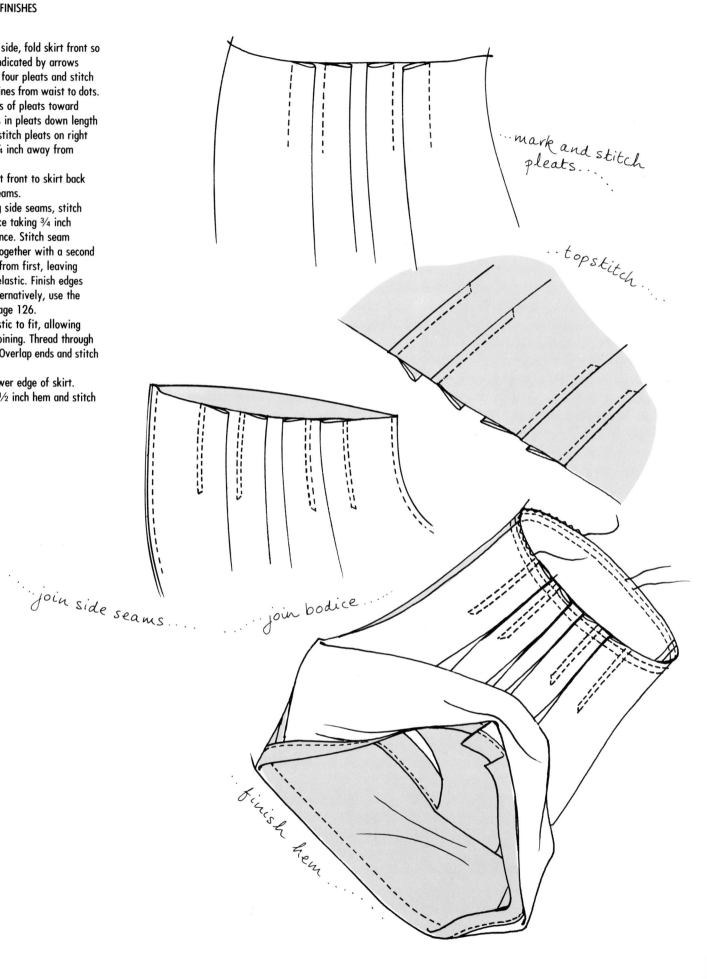

...mark and stitch pleats.........

...topstitch.........

.......join side seams......... ....join bodice.........

finish hem ....

PATTERN DESIGN

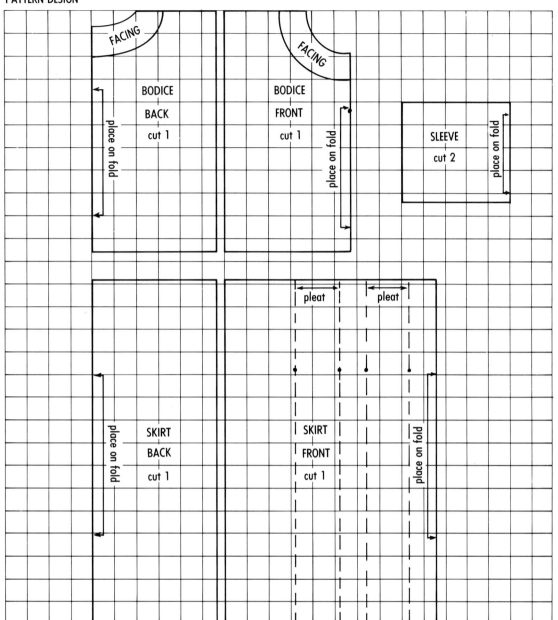

TO MAKE PATTERN

Following diagram, in which each square represents 2 inches, draw the full-size pattern. Trace the 2¼ inch deep shaded area around front and back necklines to make neck facings. Mark fold edge on facings.

FABRIC LAYOUT

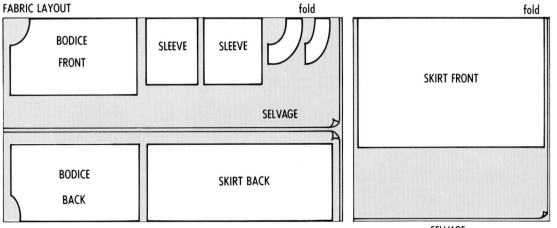

TO CUT OUT

Fold fabric as shown with selvages meeting near center so there is a fold at both edges. Cut out through the double thickness:

1 bodice front
1 bodice back
2 sleeves
1 skirt back
1 front neck facing
1 back neck facing

Refold remaining fabric in half lengthwise and cut out:

1 skirt front

Fastenings

A knowledge and understanding of the different types of fastening enables you to give a distinctive finish to the items you make, and to adapt patterns if you do not like the suggested fastening. Many patterns do not give detailed instructions for finishing fastenings, so the following hints should prove useful.

Fastenings may be decorative or discreet: toggles on a duffle coat, for example, or closely spaced covered buttons and fine loops of tubing set the tone of the garment, whereas zippers and hooks and eyes or thread loops can make a skirt placket almost invisible.

MAKING BUTTONHOLES

The method of making a buttonhole depends on the style of the garment and your sewing skills. Hand- and machine-made buttonholes take a bit of practice, as do bound buttonholes, which are normally used for heavier fabrics. Tubing loops, made of a strip of fabric, are fairly simple, provided that you measure and pin the fabric carefully. Thread loops are one of the simplest ways of fastening a button, but are suitable only in certain situations.

As a general guide, corded and bound buttonholes are usually preferred in women's dresses, suits, and coats; machine-worked buttonholes are used in sportswear, children's clothes, and men's wear; and hand-worked buttonholes are found in babies' clothes and blouses of soft, fine silk, linen, or cotton.

The length of the buttonhole depends on the size of the button, so select buttons before marking and making buttonholes. Mark with basting stitches, according to the type of buttonhole. Where the buttons are not positioned down the center front of an item, mark the button position, rather than the center line.

Buttonholes should be interfaced or stayed to strengthen the finish and give extra body to the surrounding fabric. Machine-stitched and hand-worked buttonholes are made after the garment is finished, so they will have to be stitched through whatever interfacing is sewn into the item. For bound and other fabric-finished buttonholes, use a lightweight interfacing. If the garment demands a heavier interfacing, use a patch of lightweight batiste or organza as a stay to strengthen the buttonhole. Never make bound buttonholes through hair canvas or heavy facing.

However experienced you are at sewing and making buttonholes, always make a practice one in a scrap of the fabric you are using. This gives you a chance to see how easy it is to handle the fabric, and enables you to check the size of the buttonhole with the button.

CHOOSING BUTTONS

Choose buttons to suit the style of the garment: small pearl buttons for blouses; buttons shaped like animals or flowers for children's clothes; bold wooden buttons for a tweed coat; brass buttons for fitted jackets and blazers – the choice is almost unlimited. The size of the button should be appropriate to the fabric – smaller buttons for finer fabrics.

Flat buttons with two or more holes can be sewn without a shank, but on bulky fabrics stitch them with a thread shank, which will accommodate the layers of fabric around the buttonhole. Some buttons have a built-in shank. Most modern machines can be used to sew on flat buttons, so check your sewing machine handbook. For where there is a thread or built-in shank, you will have to sew by hand. Use cotton-wrapped polyester thread on lightweight fabrics and button thread on heavier fabrics and larger buttons.

More elaborate fastenings include frogging, which is made from braid twisted into a decorative shape and is available ready-made, and toggles; use leather for loops and toggle fastenings for a classic duffle coat style, or use strips of fabric or tape for a hint of Chinese practicality.

MARKING BUTTONHOLES

- Buttonholes in women's and girls' clothes are placed on the right side; in men's and boys' wear on the left side.
- Down center front and center back openings on a garment, position horizontal buttonholes so that they extend ⅛ inch beyond the center line basting; vertical buttonholes are placed so that the center line basting falls down the center of the buttonhole.
- If buttons and buttonholes are not placed on the center front of the garment, mark the button positions. Again, horizontal buttonholes should extend ⅛ inch beyond the button position, and vertical buttonholes are centered on the button position.
- When considering the size of button to use, make sure that the space from the center-line basting/button position to the finished edge is at least three-quarters of the diameter of the button. This will ensure that the button does not extend beyond the edge when the opening is buttoned.
- Space the buttons evenly down the opening, unless they are unevenly spaced as a styling detail. If you have to adjust the length of the opening, adjust the spacing accordingly.
- Check the positions of the buttons for fit by trying on the garment or fitting the cover if making a slipcover. Pin at the marked buttoning positions. If the buttons are not positioned for a good fit, the opening will bag, wrinkle, and distort. It is essential to position a button at the neckline, at the fullest part of the bust, at the waistline, and at the hips. On a shirt waist dress, position the lowest button about 4 inches from the hem edge.

...mark...

...and stitch...

MACHINE-WORKED BUTTONHOLES

The length of the finished buttonhole should be the length of the opening plus ⅛ inch at each end for bar tacks. Mark the cutting line and ends of the buttonhole with chalk or hand basting. Set the sewing machine for a plain zig-zag stitch, in satin stitch.

Stitch down one side of the buttonhole, across the end, back up the other side, and across the other end, following the instructions in your sewing machine handbook.

For corded buttonholes, use gimp or buttonhole twist, and stitch over the filler cord as you make the buttonhole. Thread the filler cord through the braiding foot.

Some machines have a special buttonhole attachment, which saves having to mark the ends of the buttonhole on the fabric. The buttonhole size is set on a special plate attached to the foot, and the foot is centered over the buttonhole opening as you stitch.

HAND-WORKED BUTTONHOLES

Mark the length and line of the buttonhole with chalk or hand basting along the grain of the fabric. Pin the layers of fabric together. Machine stitch around the buttonhole for reinforcement, using a 20 stitch length and stitching ¹/₁₆ to ⅛ inch from the marking. Press. Cut the buttonhole between the two lines using sharp, pointed scissors.

For horizontal buttonholes, work buttonhole stitch along one edge of the opening, starting from the inside edge. See page 38 for details of working buttonhole stitch.

At the outside edge, fan the stitches, making about five or seven stitches, slightly longer than the side stitches. Work down the opposite edge to the inside, turning the buttonhole around so you always hold the needle at the same angle.

Make a bar tack across the inside end by taking two straight stitches through the fabric, and working blanket stitches across the bar right through the fabric.

For vertical buttonholes, make a bar tack at each end.

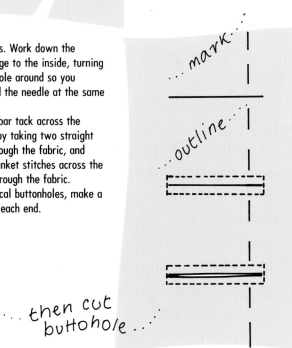

...mark...

...outline...

...then cut buttohole...

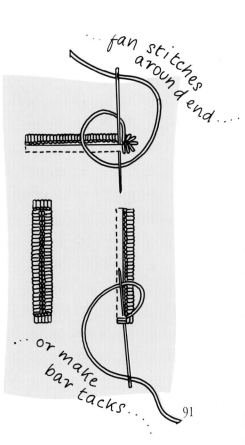

fan stitches around end...

...or make bar tacks...

BOUND BUTTONHOLES – PATCH METHOD

Mark the buttonholes with lines of machine basting. On the back of the lightweight interfacing, mark a stitching line on each side of the buttonhole position, 1/8 inch from the line of basting or up to 1/4 inch for bulky fabrics.

For each buttonhole, cut a patch of fabric on the crosswise grain or on the bias, about 2 inches wide and 1 inch longer than the finished buttonhole. Crease lightly through the center of the patch.

Position a patch, centered over each buttonhole marking, right sides together. Pin and baste. On the wrong side, stitch around the buttonhole, following the markings. Begin at the center of one side and stitch to the end. Pivot the needle on the fabric, to turn each corner, taking four or five stitches across each end of the buttonhole. Press.

Remove basting threads across each end of the buttonhole. Cut along the line of basting marking the buttonhole, cutting to within 1/4 inch of each end, then snip diagonally to each corner.

Draw the patch through the opening to the underside. Carefully pull out the triangular ends to square the corners. Press the triangular ends and seam allowances away from the opening.

Fold each side of the patch to form pleats that meet at the center of the buttonhole and cover the opening. Carry the folds to the edge of the patch. From the right side, baste along the center of each fold, then overcast the folds together. Remove all basting. Press.

Place the garment, right side up, on the machine, fold back the garment edge, and stitch the pleats to the seam allowances: first stitch across the triangular ends on the original stitching line, beginning and ending the stitching at the raw edge of the patch. Then stitch along the seams on each side, just a hair's breadth from the original stitching line. The side stitching crosses the end stitching – no stitching shows on the right side. Press and trim the patch to within 1/4 inch of the stitching.

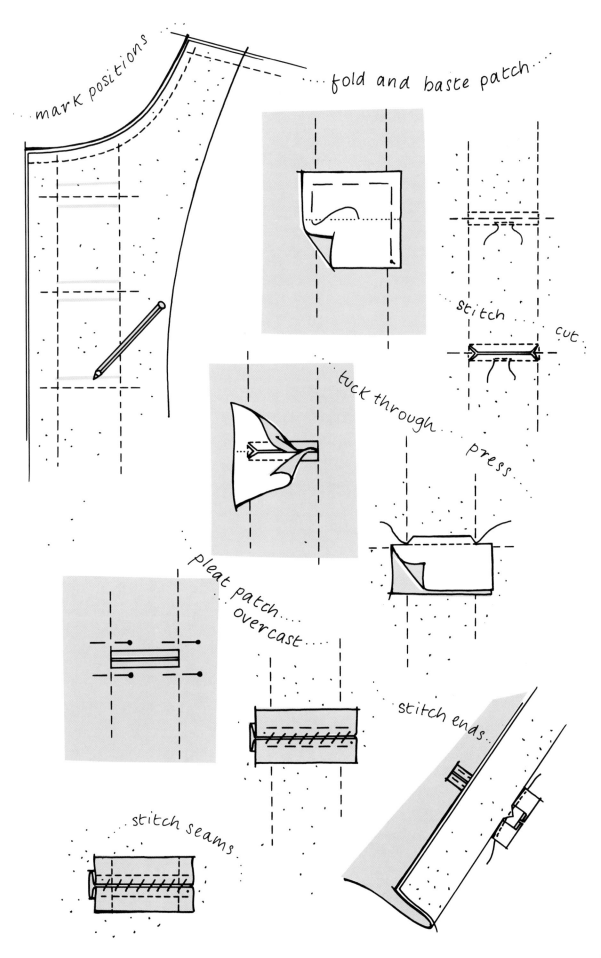

mark positions

fold and baste patch

stitch

cut

tuck through

press

pleat patch

overcast

stitch ends

stitch seams

FINISHING BOUND BUTTONHOLES

The back of bound buttonholes is normally finished with the facing of the garment. Attach the facing in the normal way, then baste it in place all around the buttonhole. The method you use depends on the weight and weave of the fabric.

If the fabric does not fray easily, and the facing will not show when the garment is being worn, start by marking the corners of the buttonhole on the facing, by sticking four pins through from the right side. Slit the facing along the line of the buttonhole to within ¼ inch of the corners, then carefully snip diagonally to the corners. Use the point of the needle to turn under the edges of the opening, and slipstitch the facing in place. The facing side has the same rectangular shape as the front of the buttonhole.

For tweeds and fabrics that fray easily, mark just the ends of the buttonhole on the facing. Cut the facing between the pins. Turn under the edges with the point of the needle and slipstitch in place, forming an oval shape.

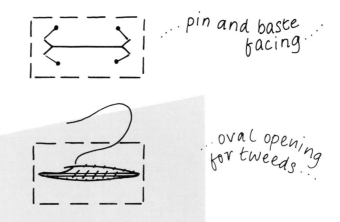

pin and baste facing

oval opening for tweeds

BOUND BUTTONHOLES – ONE PIECE METHOD

Mark the ends and center of each buttonhole with basting. For each buttonhole, cut a strip of fabric on the crosswise grain, 1 inch wide, and 1 inch longer than the finished buttonhole. Fold the cut edges to the center down the length of the strip, wrong sides together, and baste along each fold, to make a strip ½ inch wide. Press.

On the right side of the garment, place a buttonhole strip, centered, over each buttonhole marking with a pin at each end. Baste through the center of each fold, to hold the strip in place. Stitch the strips in place down each side of the buttonhole, using a short stitch, positioning the line of stitches half way between the folded edge and the center of the strip. Begin and end the stitching exactly on the basted lines marking the length of the buttonhole. Remove basting. Tie threads on back. Press. Cut through center of buttonhole strip.

Working from the back of the fabric, cut between the two lines of stitching, through the fabric and the interfacing, to within ¼ inch of the ends of the buttonhole, then snip diagonally to each corner. Draw the cut strip of fabric through the opening to the underside, so that the folded edges meet at the center of the opening. Pull the triangular ends away from the opening to make it square. Press. Overcast the folded edges.

Place right side up on the machine. Fold back the garment edge and stitch the triangular ends to the strip at each end of the buttonhole. Remove basting. Trim ends of strip to within ¼ inch of the stitching and press. Apply heavy interfacing, and finish the facing as for the patch method.

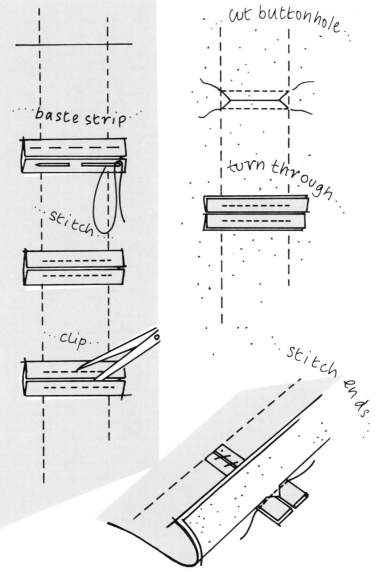

baste strip

stitch

clip

cut buttonhole

turn through

stitch ends

BOUND BUTTONHOLES – TWO PIECE METHOD

This method, for bulky fabrics, is a variation on the one-piece method.

Place a stay of lightweight fabric on the underside, and baste guidelines to mark the buttonhole positions. Mark the stitching lines about 3/16 inch from the buttonhole position in pencil on the wrong side of the stay. Cut a piece of organza measuring 1 inch wide and 1 inch longer than the finished buttonhole. Center the patch over the buttonhole marking on the right side of the fabric. Pin; baste if necessary. Turn the garment to the wrong side and stitch around the buttonhole, following the markings.

Cut through the center of the buttonhole to within ¼ inch of each end, then snip diagonally to each corner. Turn the organza patch through to the underside. Carefully pull out the triangular ends to square the corners, and press them away from the opening. Turn the seam allowances and organza patch

away from the opening along the sides, fold on the stitching line, and press flat against the fabric.

For cording the buttonhole, cut two strips of fabric on the straight crosswise grain, cutting them 1½ inches wide and 1 inch longer than the finished buttonhole. Place them right sides together and baste through the center. Press, then press the basted seam open.

With the garment right side up, place the basted strips over the wrong side of the opening, so that the basted seam is in the center and the ends extend ½ inch beyond the opening. Pin them in place at each end.

Place the garment, right side up, in the machine and turn back the edge. Stitch the seam allowances and organza patch to the strip, using a 20 stitch length, and place the stitching barely outside the previous stitching, so that the organza patch will not be visible on the top side of the garment. Stitch the triangular ends first, then the long edges of

the buttonhole. Pin with fine needles.

Trim the ends of the strip to within ¼ inch of the stitching and grade the seam allowances of the strip along the side. Before pressing, slip brown paper between the garment and seam allowance.

Interface and finish facing as for patch method. Remove the basting.

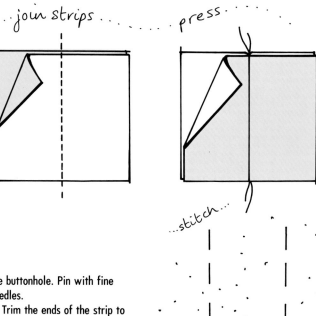

join strips ... *press*

...stitch...

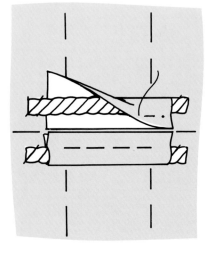

position corded strips ... *stitch* ... *cut* ... *turn through*

CORDED BUTTONHOLES

Apply stay of light interfacing. Mark the ends and stitching lines of the buttonhole as for the patch method, basting all markings so that they show on both sides. Prepare a length of cording from a 1 inch-wide bias-cut strip, using an appropriate size filler cord. Stitch

with the zipper foot.

For each buttonhole, cut two strips, 1 inch longer than the buttonhole. Place two strips over each buttonhole marking, on the right side, aligning the corded edges with the outer markings, with the raw edges toward the center. Baste in position. Stitch on each side of

the buttonhole, between the cord and the previous line of stitching. Use a short stitch, with the zipper foot to the left of the needle. Begin and end the stitching exactly on the guidelines marking the buttonhole length. Remove hand basting. Pull the threads through to the underside and tie. Remove all horizontal

basting. Cut buttonhole from the underside of the garment. Draw the strips through to the underside so the corded edges meet at the center of the opening. Pull out the triangular ends, then overcast the corded edges together.

Stitch ends and finish facing as before.

94

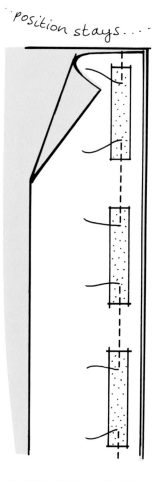

Position stays....

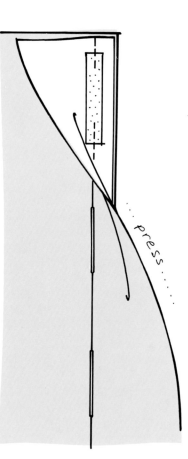

....press....

BUTTONHOLES IN A SEAM

Mark the position of the buttonhole in the seam with tailor's tacks. With right sides together, pin and baste a ⅝ inch seam. Cut two stays for each buttonhole, 1 inch longer than the buttonhole and 1¼ inches wide. Use batiste, organza, or similar lightweight fabric. Position the stays on each side of the seam over the buttonhole marking and pin.

Stitch the seam to the buttonhole marking, lift the presser foot, pull out thread from bobbin and spool to give enough to tie ends, then continue stitching the seam from the other end of the buttonhole. Cut threads, pull through, and tie. Remove tailor's tacks and basting where seam has been stitched. Press seam, then press open. Trim the stay on each side to within ⅜ inch of the opening. Treat interfacing and finish facing as described for the patch method.

MAKING TUBULAR CORDING

Use bias-cut strips, 1 inch wide, plus three times the width of the filler cord. The size of cord you choose depends on the weight of the fabric, and the effect desired. See page 66 for bias strips. Cut one end of the strip to a point.

Use a cord twice the length of the bias strip. Match the point of the strip to the middle of the length of cord. Machine stitch the center of the cord to the wrong side of the pointed end. Stitch for about ⅜ inch, starting from the point.

Turn the stitched section to the right side of the bias strip, then fold the bias in half around the cord. You now have a covered cord, with half of cord extending beyond bias strip.

With the zipper foot to the right of the needle, use a short stitch to stitch the bias strip in place. Avoid catching the pointed end in the stitching. Stitch close to the cord, stretching the bias slightly as you stitch. Press, then trim the seam allowances to ⅛ inch.

Pull the tube back over the extended cord, by pulling the encased cord.

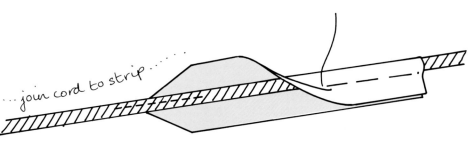

....join cord to strip.....

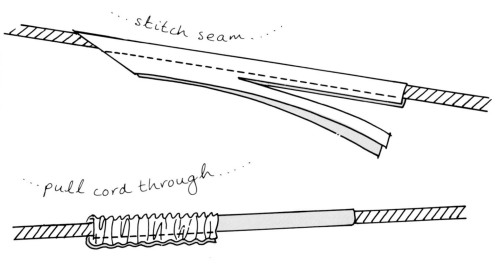

....stitch seam.....

....pull cord through.....

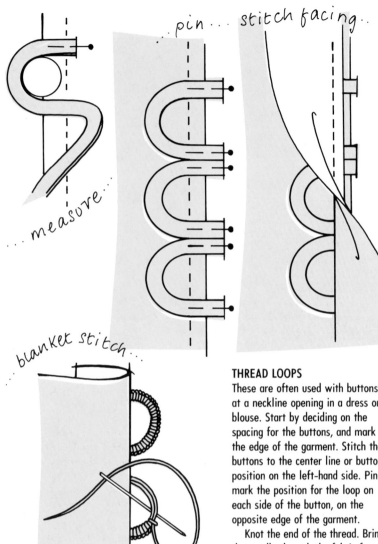

pin... stitch facing...

...measure...

...blanket stitch...

BUTTON LOOPS

Button loops made from lengths of tubing are normally set into the seamline where a facing joins the main fabric. The length of tubing for each loop and the spacing of the loop depends on the size of the button. To get the precise measurements, make a paper pattern.

Mark the seamline $5/8$ inch from the edge of the paper, and mark a second line in the seam allowance, $1/4$ inch from it. This indicates the position of the loop ends. Place the exact center of the button on the seamline. Pin the end of the tubing to match the mark on the paper. Bring the tubing around the top edge of the button, with the seam to the inside of the loop. Pin the other end of the tubing in place, and

mark the tubing at the $1/4$ inch line. This gives the length for each loop. Mark the points where the tubing crosses the seamline on the paper, then measure between the marks.

Mark the fabric down the seamline to indicate loop spacing. Mark the tubing down its length to indicate the loop length. Clip into the fabric and cord at each marked point, but not through seam.

Mark seamline and position of loop ends on right side of fabric, and pin the tubing loops in place. Pin the loops in place with fine needles, then baste them together close to the seamline. Stitch loops in place just within seam allowance, then apply facing and interfacing in the normal way. Stitch on seamline, press and fold facing back. Baste and press.

THREAD LOOPS

These are often used with buttons at a neckline opening in a dress or blouse. Start by deciding on the spacing for the buttons, and mark the edge of the garment. Stitch the buttons to the center line or button position on the left-hand side. Pin-mark the position for the loop on each side of the button, on the opposite edge of the garment.

Knot the end of the thread. Bring the needle through the fabric from

the underside near the edge of the opening. Take a stitch in the edge at the bottom, leaving a loop large enough to slip easily over the button. Take two or three long stitches, back and forth, then work blanket stitch over the strand of thread. Fasten the threads securely on the underside.

BUTTONS

Choose a thread that matches the button. Knot the end. Place the button over the marking, on the center line if the opening is down the front of the garment. Bring the needle through the fabric from the underside and up through one eye of the button. Place a pin across the button between the holes, then bring the needle back through the second eye and through the fabric. Take about six stitches, then fasten the thread with two or three backstitches close to the threads on the underside. With four-hole buttons, you can sew on the button crossing the threads from one hole to the diagonally opposite hole or in parallel lines.

To make a shank, use a

matchstick or bodkin in place of the pin. After stitching the button, remove the bodkin and pull the button away from the fabric. Wind the needle thread evenly around the threads between the fabric and button to form a thread shank.

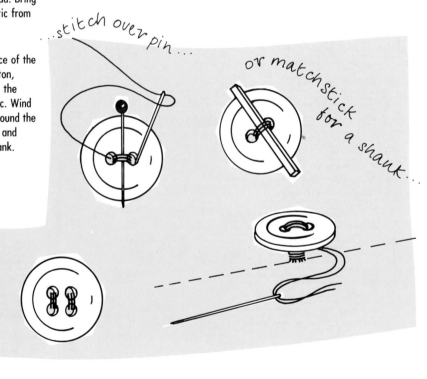

...stitch over pin...

or matchstick for a shank...

REINFORCED BUTTONS

On some garments, it is a good idea to strengthen the button and neaten the back of the button at the same time by sewing a small button on the underside at the same time as you sew on the top button.

Position the top button and make the first stitch as before, working over a bodkin between the eyes of the button. As you bring the needle back through the fabric, take it through the eye of the bottom button. Make about six stitches, through both buttons, then finish the thread shank and fasten the thread as before.

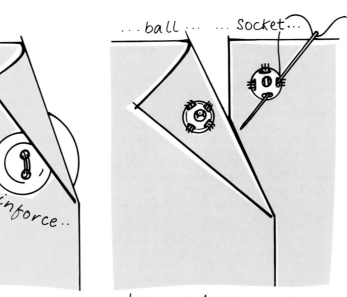

...ball... ...socket...

...reinforce..

.... where edges meet ....

SNAP AND HOOK FASTENINGS

These fastenings are more discreet than buttons, and are usually sewn on by hand.

Snap fasteners may be made of either metal or plastic. Choose a suitable weight and size for the item you are making. Snaps are normally stitched to both sides of an overlapping opening, about ⅛ inch from the finished edge. Stitch the ball part of the snap to the underside of the overlap, and the socket to the right side of the underlapping edge.

Hooks and eyes are often used at the waistband of a skirt, and at the end of an open-ended zipper. They are available in a wide range of sizes, for different weights of fabric. A straight eye is generally used where there is an overlap, and a round eye where the edges meet.

Snap fasteners are also available attached to ready-made strips, for machine stitching to garments. These are often used in baby clothes, for crotch openings in trousers, for example; in duvet covers and in slipcovers. They may be stitched into a lapped seam or into the seam allowance of straight seams, as in duvet covers, so that no stitching shows on the right side. Choose the weight and color of the strip to suit the item you are sewing.

Touch-and-close nylon tape is another way of fastening edges; this is often used in sewing for the home. The two halves of the strip are stitched to opposite sides of the opening, in the same way as in applying a strip of snaps. However, the touch-and-close fastening produces a stiffer finish, and is not suitable for all the same situations. Some types of touch-and-close fastening can be glued to solid surfaces, such as wood, which gives them several special applications. Consult the back of the package for fixing instructions.

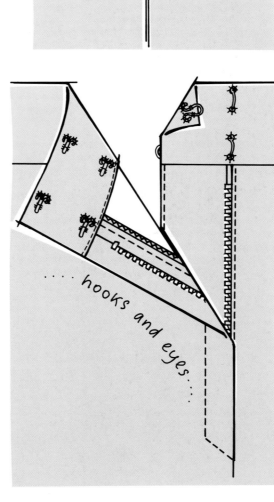

...hooks and eyes...

SNAPS

Sew the ball side in place first. Take about six stitches through each hole in the snap, finishing with a couple of backstitches in the fabric. Mark the position for the socket part by rubbing chalk on the ball and pressing in position.

With some snaps, you can position the socket by passing a fine needle through the hole in the center of the ball and through the socket, into the underlap of fabric.

HOOKS AND EYES

Where edges meet at an opening, sew the eye in place first, extending the end of the loop very slightly over the edge of the fabric. To mark the position of the hook, fasten the hook and eye, and bring the edges of the fabric together. Sew the hook in place.

Where there is an overlap, stitch the hook in place on the overlap first. Then wrap the opening and pin-mark the underwrap directly opposite the end of the hook. Place a straight eye over the marking and sew in place.

To make a thread eye, sew the hook in place and mark the position of the eye as before. Use thread to match the fabric. Knot the end of the thread and bring the needle through from the underside at one marked end of the eye. Take a stitch at the opposite end. Work back and forth two or three times, then blanket stitch over the strands of thread, making firm stitches. Fasten securely on the underside.

INSERTING ZIPPERS

Zippers are available in a wide range of weights, lengths and colors, to suit most needs. There are also special purpose zippers, such as open-ended and double slider zippers, often used in sports and children's wear. The pattern should specify the type and size of zipper required. There are several ways of inserting a zipper, depending on whether the zipper is positioned to one side of the opening, in a lapped seam or opening, or centered in the opening. The lapped method is more often used at side seams in garments and the centered, channel seam is used for center front or back openings, and openings in a panel of fabric (such as cushion covers). The opening for a zipper should be ⅜ inch longer than the zipper, plus seam allowance at the open end of the zipper as necessary. The pattern should give detailed measurements.

Zippers should be inserted at the same time as the rest of the seam is stitched, when possible. Any seams that run across the zipper (at the waistline of a dress, for example) will have to be stitched before the zipper can be set in. In a skirt, set in the zipper before attaching the waistband. In a faced opening, set in the zipper then turn under the ends of the facing and finish by hand, stitching the turned-under facing to the zipper tape. More details, and variations in method, may be given in the pattern.

The instructions here are for setting in the zipper by machine. If you prefer, hand finish the work by using prick stitch (see page 37) instead of topstitching by machine. On open-ended zippers, strengthen the stitching with machine stitches across the top of the zipper tape within the seam allowance.

ZIP IN A LAPPED OPENING

Check that the end of the permanent stitching is reinforced with reverse stitching, and that the two edges to be joined are exactly the same length. Mark the foldline on each side of the opening. Pin and baste the zipper opening and press. Working from the wrong side, fold under the back seam allowance ⅛ inch from the basted seamline. Place the folded seam allowance over the right side of the zipper, positioning it with the slider ¾ inch below the top of the opening, with the end stop ⅛ inch above the lower end of the opening. Pin and baste to zipper tape.

With the zipper foot positioned to the left of the needle and the pull tab extended, stitch from lower end to top, near the edge of the fold. Remove basting.

Turn work right side up. Pin through main fabric, front seam allowance and zipper tape, at right angles to the seam. Baste in place, ½ inch from the basted seam, using uneven basting. Adjust the zipper foot to the right of the needle and, starting from the end of the permanent stitching in the seam below the zipper opening, stitch across the lower end and up the length of the zipper. If cording is set into the seam, it may be continued down the zipper opening. Pin and baste it to the back seam allowance, so it is sandwiched between fabric and zipper.

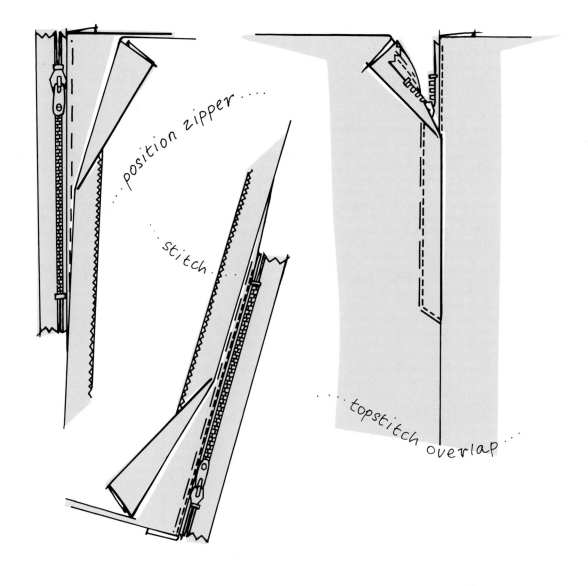

position zipper . . . .

stitch . . . .

. . . . topstitch overlap . . . .

HAND-FINISHED ZIPPER
For a professional finish, particularly on fine fabrics, finish the zipper by hand as follows: Stitch the zipper in place as before, omitting topstitched finish. Use a fine needle and matching thread, and start from the lower end of the zipper. Fasten the thread with two backstitches on the underside of the zipper tape. Bring the needle through from the underside at the seamline, and use a prick stitch to finish the zipper, taking only one or two threads of the fabric in each stitch. Stitch across the end of the zipper, up the side, and across the top of the zipper if the top is enclosed.

...finish with prick stitch...

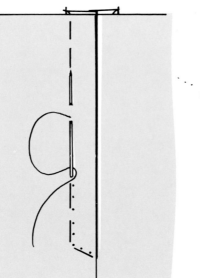

PROBLEMS WITH THE PULL TAB
The pull tab sometimes creates bulk, which makes stitching difficult. Pull up the pull tab when stitching the zipper so that the tab lies over the upper end of the zipper, reducing bulk.

If the slider is too bulky, start stitching with the zipper closed. When you are half way down the line of stitching, stop stitching with the needle in the fabric, lift the foot, and ease the slider down the zipper, past the needle. Stitch to the top with the zipper open.

BLINDSTITCHED INSERTION
As an alternative to topstitching or hand finishing, you can do the final stage of stitching using the blindstitch zig-zig setting. Stitch the zipper to the back seam allowance as before and baste the zipper to the seam allowance down the front edge. Set the stitch to a 15 stitch length and narrow width and position the foot to the right of the needle. With the garment inside out, open out the seam allowance and place the work under the needle with the zipper tape over the feed of the machine. Position the fold of the fabric against the foot, and make a line of stitching through the seam allowance and zipper tape, catching the fold of the fabric with the zig-zag stitch. Finish ends by pulling to underside and tying. Sew the front seam allowance to the zipper tape at the end of the zipper. Remove basting and press.

...stitch on fold...

...open flat...

CENTERED ZIPPER
Working from the wrong side, hand or machine baste along the length of the opening. Press the seam, then press it open. Position the zipper on the wrong side of the opening, and pin in place, positioning the pins across the zipper, avoiding the teeth. Baste by hand, ¼ inch from seam, down each side of opening.

Using the zipper foot, adjusted to the left of the needle, stitch down the right-hand side of the zipper, across the lower edge, and back up the other side.

If the end of the zipper is closed, the seam continuing beyond the zipper, follow the same method, stitching across both ends of the zipper.

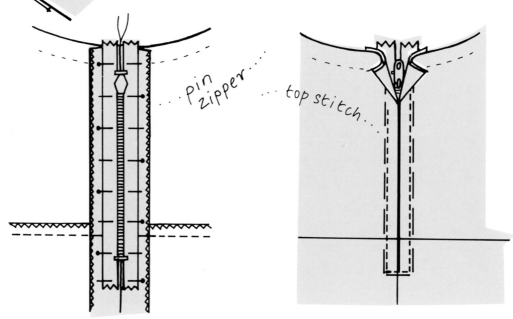

...pin zipper... ...top stitch...

Finishing hems

The usual aim when hemming is to make the hem as invisible as possible from the right side. On some items, and on narrow hems, the edge may be turned and topstitched by machine. Whichever finish you choose, mark and baste the hem in place, positioning the basting close to the finished edge. Press carefully, without marking the top fabric with an impression of the hemline. After marking and basting, trim the hem allowance so that it is an even depth, as given in the pattern. Trim seam allowances from the hemline to half their width.

Choose the method of hemming according to the weave and weight of the fabric, and the type of garment or home furnishing. There are special techniques for ensuring a smooth finish on curved and flared hems.

Narrow hems can be finished by hand or machine. Hand-rolled hems are used for fine fabrics, where an invisible finish is needed. For a plain finish, some machines have an attachment that turns and stitches the hem in one movement. Decorative stitches can often be used.

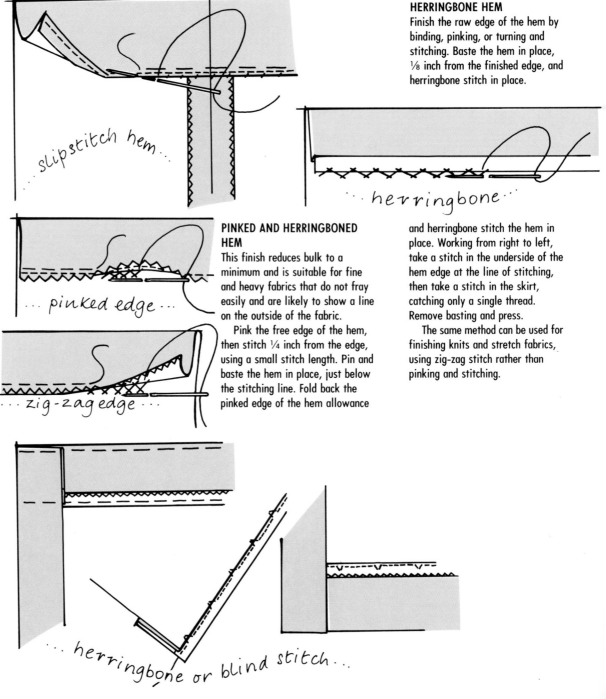

EDGE-STITCHED HEM
Fold under the free edge of the hem about ¼ inch, and stitch near the edge of the fold. Press. Pin the hem to the skirt and baste. Finish with slipstitch. Remove basting and press.

... slipstitch hem ...

PINKED AND HERRINGBONED HEM
This finish reduces bulk to a minimum and is suitable for fine and heavy fabrics that do not fray easily and are likely to show a line on the outside of the fabric.

Pink the free edge of the hem, then stitch ¼ inch from the edge, using a small stitch length. Pin and baste the hem in place, just below the stitching line. Fold back the pinked edge of the hem allowance

... pinked edge ...

... zig-zag edge ...

HERRINGBONE HEM
Finish the raw edge of the hem by binding, pinking, or turning and stitching. Baste the hem in place, ⅛ inch from the finished edge, and herringbone stitch in place.

... herringbone ...

and herringbone stitch the hem in place. Working from right to left, take a stitch in the underside of the hem edge at the line of stitching, then take a stitch in the skirt, catching only a single thread. Remove basting and press.

The same method can be used for finishing knits and stretch fabrics, using zig-zag stitch rather than pinking and stitching.

BOUND HEM
Bind the free edge of the hem, using the binder attachment or one of the methods on page 68. Press. Pin the hem in place and baste just below the binding. Herringbone between the hem and skirt. Remove basting and press.

... herringbone or blind stitch ...

BLINDSTITCHED HEM

This machine-stitched hem is almost invisible on the right side of the fabric. The raw edge of the hem may be taped, bound, pinked, zig-zag stitched or left unfinished. Baste the hem to the skirt about ¼ inch from the free edge. Set the machine to blindstitch zig-zag, with a medium stitch width and a 12 to 20 stitch length. Turn back the bulk of the fabric from the line of basting so that you can place the free edge of the hem under the foot. Stitch, making straight stitches in the hem edge and allowing the zig-zag stitch to catch only one or two threads of the soft fold. It may be helpful to use the seam guide attachment, so that it rests next to the soft fold. Remove basting and press.

HAND-ROLLED HEM

Mark the line of the hem. Machine stitch ⅛ inch outside the marking for the hem, using a short stitch. Trim the hem allowance ⅛ inch outside stitching. Press stitching. Fold the edge to the wrong side. Fold raw edge to wrong side, so stitching just rolls over the edge of the fold. Using a fine needle, and working from right to left, or toward you, take a stitch through the fold. Then, ⅛ inch from the fold, take a stitch in the fabric, catching only a single thread. Continue, spacing the stitches about ⅛ inch apart. After making about six stitches, pull the thread to draw the fold down and form a neatly rolled hem.

FLARED AND CURVED HEMS

The fullness in the hem allowance has to be reduced in a flared hem. Lower the tension on the upper thread, and make a line of stitching ¼ inch from the free edge of the hem from one seam to the next. Pin the hem in place and draw the bobbin thread, easing the fullness evenly until the hem lies smoothly on the fabric. Press to shrink out fullness. Baste in place ⅛ inch from the hem edge and finish with a blind hemming stitch (see page 38). Remove basting and press.

In a circular hem the hem must be narrow. Hang the finished item overnight to drop before marking the hem. Mark the hemline and trim the allowance to ⅜ inch. Pin bias binding to the free edge of hem allowance, right sides facing, ¼ inch from the raw edge. Stitch in place. Turn binding to underside, and fold along hemline. Baste hem in place, close to folded edge of binding. Press. Stitch hem by hand, using a blind hemming stitch or slipstitch. Remove basting and press.

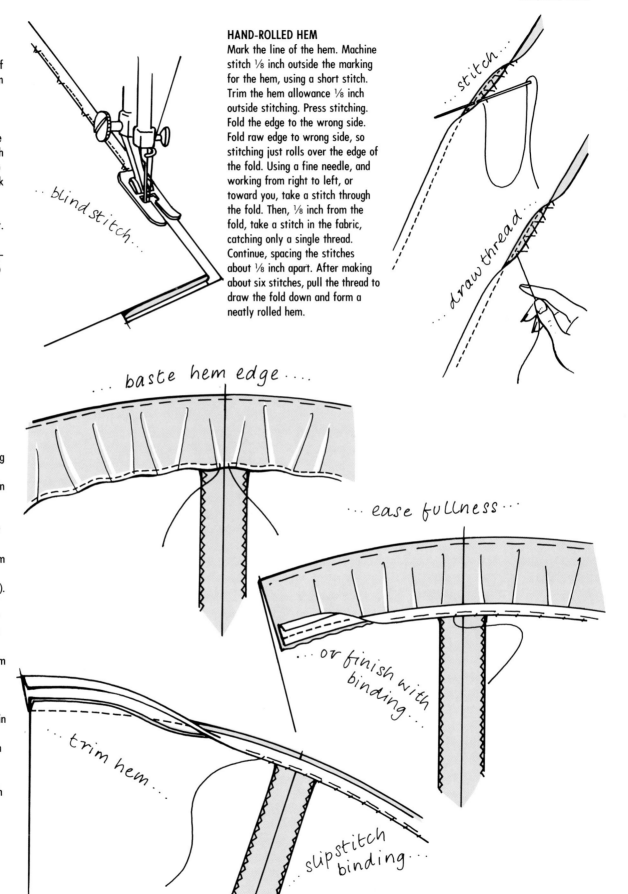

Camisole and skirt

ALTERNATIVES

Add ruffles of eyelet lace around upper and lower edge of camisole, and around hem of skirt. Make wider shoulder straps and trim with eyelet lace.

Use richly colored silk or satin for an evening outfit. Add panels of insertion lace in place of, or between, the pin tucks.

This simple outfit is particularly effective in white cotton lawn, but could also be made from silky fabrics for evening wear or a floral print for a vacation two-piece. Fullness at the bust and waist is drawn in with ribbons threaded into casings, and the front opening is formed with loops of tubing for an edge-to-edge finish. Pin tucks around the hem and down the front add a classically simple finish.

SUITABLE FABRICS
Soft lightweight woven fabric such as lawn, chambray, or other fine cotton.

TO FIT
Size 12.

YOU WILL NEED:
Paper for pattern
3 yds of 36 inch-wide fabric
Matching thread
4½ yds narrow ribbon
13 small buttons
2½ yds seam tape

stitch pin tucks.....

....join side seams.....

...position loops.....

...fit casing tapes.......

NOTE
⅝ inch seam allowance is included except where instructions state otherwise. Pin, baste and stitch seams with right sides facing and raw edges even. Finish seams as you work. Cut out pattern pieces and fabric following the diagrams on page 105.

TO MAKE
Camisole
1 On camisole fronts press and stitch first tuck 3¾ inches in from center front edge. Make five more tucks, placing them ¾ inch apart.
2 Stitch fronts to back along side edges.
3 Fold tubing strip in half and stitch 3⁄16 inch from fold. Trim seam and turn right side out.
4 Form tubing into 13 equal-sized loops (or use the method on page 96) to fit buttons down center edge of right front. Pin and baste.
5 Place camisole facings level with center front edges with right sides facing. Stitch top, center, and lower edge. Trim seam, turn facing to wrong side, and press.
6 Press and stitch a double hem along top and bottom edges.
7 Tucking raw ends under, pin two pieces of seam binding around inside of camisole. Position top tape so top edge is ⅝ inch down from top of camisole and waist tape with top edge 11 inches down from top. Stitch along both edges to form casings for ribbons.
8 Cut ribbon into three equal lengths and thread one through each of the camisole casings. Reserve third ribbon for skirt.

9 Fold straps in half lengthwise and stitch along length. Trim seam, turn right side out, and press.

10 Stitch on straps following lines of casing stitching. Stitch front ends level with third tucks and back ends 3½ inches to either side of center back.

11 Sew buttons to left front edge to match button loops.

Skirt

1 Stitch skirt pieces together along side seams, leaving a 4¼ inch opening at top of one seam.

2 Press and stitch first tuck 3¼ inches up from lower edge. Make five more tucks, each ¾ inches above previous one.

3 Finish lower edge. Press up and stitch hem so top of hem is level with first tuck.

4 Press ⅝ inch to wrong side along edges of opening. Stitch along opening edges ⅜ inch in.

5 Press ¼ inch then ⅝ inch to wrong side around waist edge. Stitch near both edges to make a casing. Thread remaining ribbon through casing.

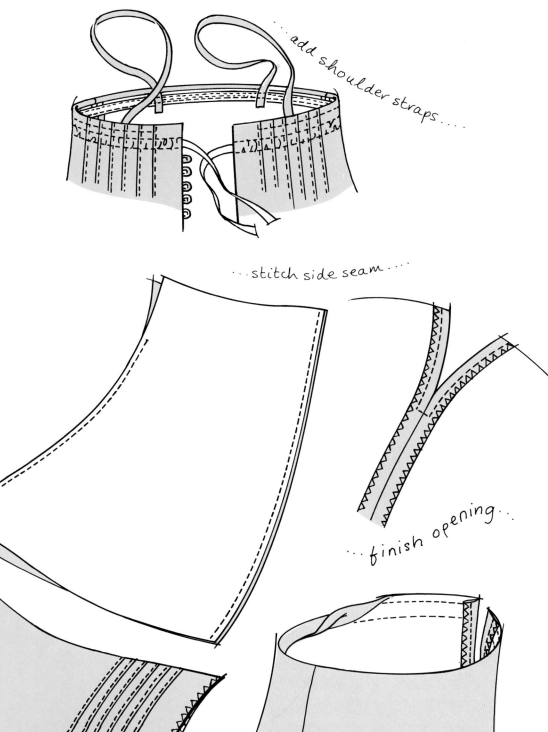

...add shoulder straps....

...stitch side seam....

...finish opening...

...make casing.....

...stitch tucks.....

PATTERN DIAGRAM

TUBING STRIP cut 1

CAMISOLE STRAP

cut 2

CAMISOLE FRONT

cut 2

CAMISOLE FRONT FACING

cut 2

CAMISOLE BACK

cut 1

place on fold

SKIRT FRONT AND BACK

cut 2

place on fold

TO MAKE PATTERN
Following the diagram, in which each square represents 2 inches, draw the full size pattern.

FABRIC LAYOUT

fold

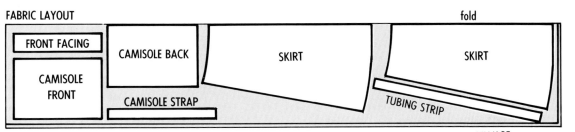

FRONT FACING

CAMISOLE FRONT

CAMISOLE BACK

CAMISOLE STRAP

SKIRT

TUBING STRIP

SKIRT

SELVAGE

TO CUT OUT
Fold fabric in half lengthwise. Through double thickness of fabric cut out:
2 camisole fronts
2 camisole front facings
1 camisole back on fold
2 camisole straps
1 camisole tubing strip
2 skirts

105

5 Dressmaking

For most garments, certainly when you are starting to learn dressmaking, you will need a paper pattern. These are made in a range of sizes and styles to suit different figure types: choose the type of garment according to your needs, your sewing abilities, and your figure shape. For more information on pattern types, see page 28.

USING PAPER PATTERNS

Dressmaking pattern envelopes contain a set of tissue paper pattern pieces and a detailed instruction sheet explaining how to arrange the pattern pieces on the fabric and how to make up the garment. The back of the envelope and the pattern book in the store give charts of the amount and type of fabric required, and any notions, such as zippers and decorative trims, that you may need.

When you begin work on the garment, inspect the pattern pieces and take out the pieces you need for the garment – many patterns include a range of garments. Press the pattern pieces, and prepare the fabric, if necessary (see page 30).

PATTERN MARKINGS

Most manufacturers use a standard system of marking the patterns. A solid line marks the cutting line, with a line of dashes inside it to mark the seamline. Center front and back are also marked with dashes where appropriate. Black dots, in various sizes, are used to mark features such as darts, the position of the shoulder seam on the sleeve cap, pocket positions, and so on. Black squares may also be used. Around the seamline, notches mark points that need to be matched. These may be single or double, to avoid confusion when assembling. For example, around armholes and sleeve caps, single notches are used on the front seamline and double on the back, so that by matching the notches you can be sure the sleeve is set in the right way around. All these marks have to be transferred to the fabric at the cutting-out stage.

The grainline is also marked on the pattern, by a straight line with arrowheads at each end. This is used as a guide when positioning the pattern pieces on the fabric, and does not normally have to be marked on the fabric.

See page 32 for information on different methods of transferring marks from the pattern to the fabric.

POSITIONING PATTERN PIECES

The pattern gives instructions for folding the fabric and arranging the pattern pieces to make best use of the fabric. With some fabrics, such as patterns with large floral motifs, checks or stripes, you have to take extra care in cutting out, to make sure that the pattern will match at the seams and run the right way down the garment. There are also special points to consider when cutting out pile fabrics (see page 158).

WORKING WITH PLAIDS AND CHECKS

Choose a pattern that the manufacturer suggests is suitable for plaids. Avoid patterns with a lot of darts or shaping: too many seams will break the continuity of the plaid. Convert darts at the waistline to tucks or gathers if necessary.

Allow extra for pattern matching when using a plaid or checked fabric – ¼ to ½ yard, depending on the size of the repeat and the number of pattern pieces.

The design must match at side seams, center seams or openings, shoulder seams, waistline, armholes, and sleeves. Slip baste all seams (see page 36) to enable you to match checks accurately.

Plaids may be even or uneven. Even plaids repeat their design on both the lengthwise and the crosswise stripes. Uneven plaids may be uneven in either or both directions.

STRIPED FABRICS

Stripes, like plaids, may be even or uneven. They are cut in the same way as plaids. Position the pattern on the fabric so that notches to be joined fall on the same stripe. Extra care must be taken when cutting stripes on the bias.

RULES FOR CUTTING OUT

- Use bent-handled dressmaker's shears with 6- or 7-inch blades. Do not use pinking shears; they are for seam finishing only.
- Keep the fabric flat on the table and cut along the marked chalk line, cutting line, or edge of the pattern. Pin pattern through all layers of fabric.
- Use long, smooth strokes, but do not close the shears to the point. If you do, you will get an irregular edge. Leave pattern pieces pinned to the fabric until all markings have been made.
- Cut out the entire item at once – whether it is a dress or a pair of curtains. Then you will be sure that you have enough fabric to complete the project. Cut out any facings, interfacings, and trimmings at the same time.
- Pin layers of fabrics to prevent their slipping as you cut: you can pin the pattern pieces in place at the same time.

PRINTED PATTERNS
Check that you know what all the markings on the pattern mean before you start cutting out a garment.

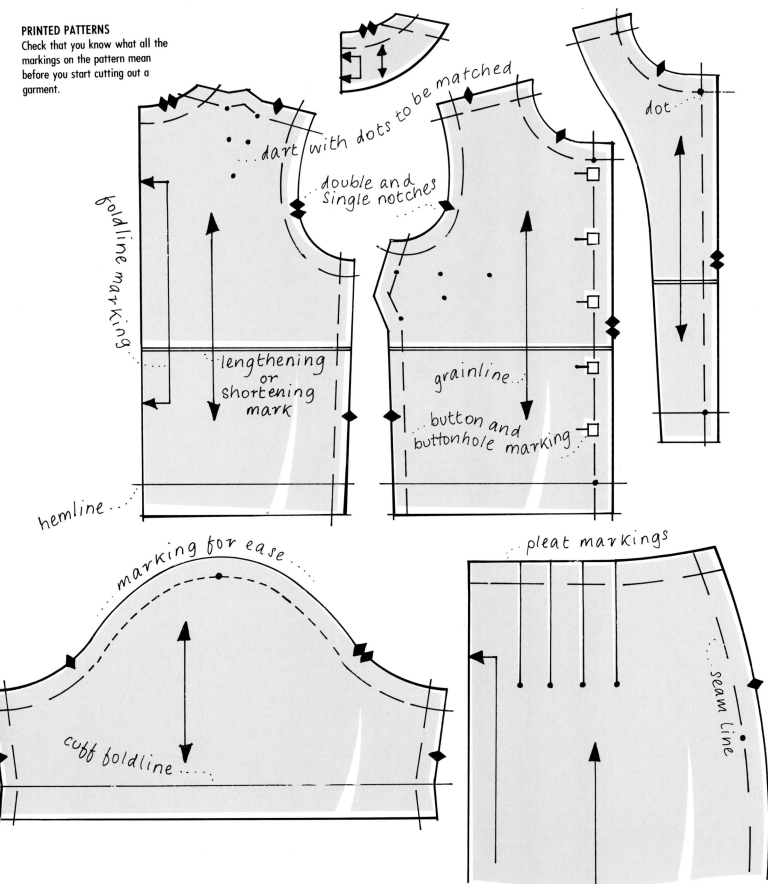

dart with dots to be matched

double and single notches

dot

foldline marking

lengthening or shortening mark

grainline

button and buttonhole marking

hemline

marking for ease

cuff foldline

pleat markings

seam line

BOLD MOTIFS

Try to center any bold motifs on the pattern pieces, and match the pattern at the seamlines where possible. Be particularly careful how you position motifs at the bust: avoid positioning them at the fullest part of the bust.

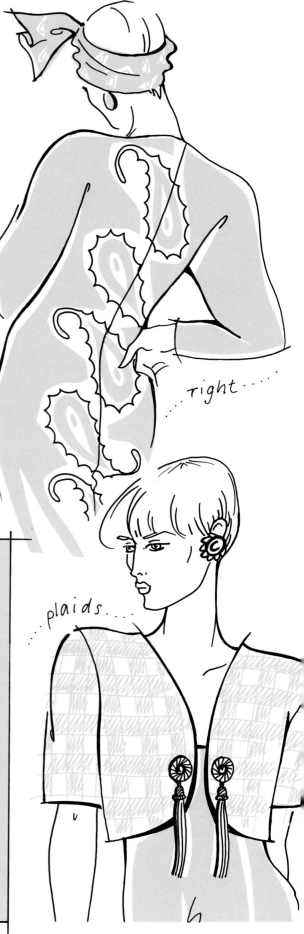

CUTTING OUT EVEN PLAIDS

For even plaids, fold the fabric right sides together, so that the center (or a bold stripe) of the plaid falls on the foldline (center front and/or back of the garment). Check that the upper and lower layers of the folded fabric match exactly, and pin them together along the stripe lines to prevent slipping during cutting. Lay the pattern pieces on the folded fabric, making sure that notches that will be joined are placed on the same color stripe. Be careful to match the pattern at the seamline, rather than the cutting line. If possible, position back and front pieces side by side to ensure a good match. Match crosswise stripes at sleeve cap and armhole as accurately as you can.

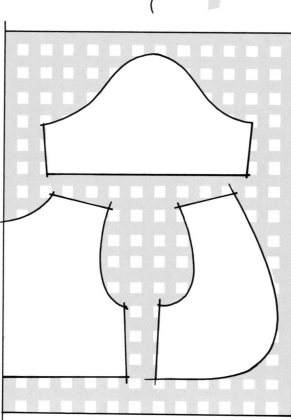

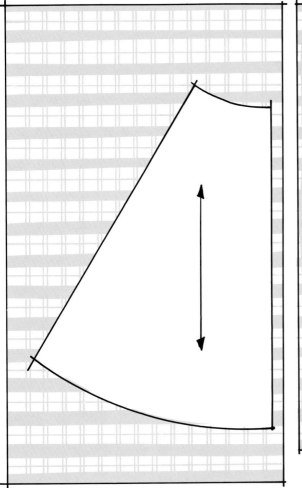

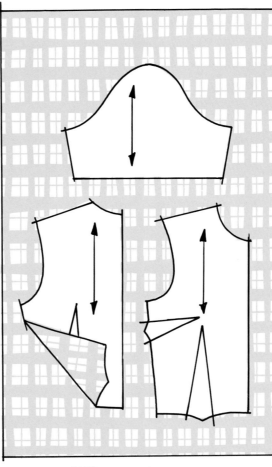

....uneven plaids.....

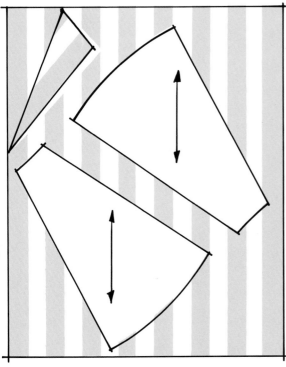

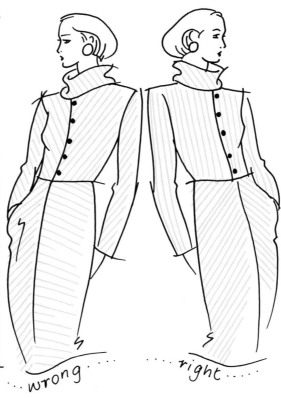

....wrong....   ....right....

CUTTING OUT UNEVEN PLAIDS

If only the crosswise stripes are uneven, fold the fabric lengthwise, right sides together, as for even plaids. Lay all the pattern pieces in one direction, so that pattern matches at the seamline.

If only the lengthwise stripes are uneven, you can match the pattern only if the fabric has no nap. Choose a pattern with a center seam or opening at both back and front. Fold the fabric in half across the width, right sides together, and match the stripes in the upper and lower layers. Lay the pattern pieces in one direction, making sure to position center back and front on the same part of the pattern, so that stripes match at the waistline.

If the plaid is uneven in both directions, and the fabric is woven so that both sides of the fabric are the same, cut out the pattern pieces through one layer of fabric, so that notches match at the seamline. Then lay the pattern pieces out a second time on the reverse side of the fabric, with the pattern pieces still pinned to the first half, matching identical lengthwise and crosswise stripes. Assemble the garment with one half of the pattern "inside out".

CUTTING OUT STRIPES ON THE BIAS

Choose a pattern with a center seam or opening in the front and the back. Fold the full width of the fabric on the crosswise grain, right sides together. Lay the pattern with a grainline parallel to the selvage, so that notches to be joined are on the same stripe, matching the pattern at the seamline. If the stripes are uneven, lay all the pattern pieces in the same direction – you may need extra fabric.

109

The perfect fit

Before cutting out the fabric for a garment, you have to make sure the finished garment will fit. Few people are an exact pattern size, so unless you are making a loosely fitted garment, a certain amount of alteration is inevitable. Large alterations and changes to the proportion of the pattern have to be done before the fabric is cut out. Smaller alterations can be made as the garment is stitched and fitted. Measure yourself and keep a chart of your measurements, or use a dressmaker's dummy adjusted to your size, to ensure a good fit.

With paper patterns, you are given a sheet of instructions for constructing the garment, to follow step by step. This makes it unnecessary to give detailed instructions for making garments, but in this chapter you will find some general principles for making features like collars, waistbands, and belts, to give details of different styles and enable you to adapt patterns and add extra features.

TAKING YOUR MEASUREMENTS

You not only need basic body measurements, such as bust, waist, hips and shoulder to waist measurements. These are needed for determining pattern size, but for finer adjustments there are extra measurements to be taken. The diagrams indicate where measurements should be taken: of course, the actual measurements you need will depend on the garment you are making. When measuring, follow the seamlines of the garment where possible.

Wear the same underwear and shoes as you intend to wear with the garment when it is finished. To make measuring easier, tie cords around yourself. Mark the neckline, at the base of the neck, over the pit of the throat and the prominent vertebra at the back of the neck; mark your waistline, and your hipline at its fullest points. Also mark your bustline with pins.

MEASURING UP

1 **Chest**
Position tape just above bustline and straight across back

2 **Bust**
Measure at fullest point, with tape slightly higher at back

3 **Waistline**
a) Measure natural waistline
b) Measure across front from side seam to side seam

4 **Hipline**
a) 3 inches below marked waistline
b) 7 inches below waistline – this is normally the fullest point
c) 9 inches below waist

5 **Shoulder length**
Measure from neckline to shoulder seamline at top of shoulder joint. Measure both left and right shoulder

6 **Sleeve length**
a) Shoulder to elbow
b) Elbow to wrist
c) Inside sleeve

7 **Sleeve width**
a) Upper arm
b) Elbow
c) Wrist

8 **Underarm to waistline**
From 1 inch below armpit (left side)
From 1 inch below armpit (right side)

9 **Shoulder to waistline**
Measure from junction of shoulder and neckline

10 **Center front**
Measure from neckline to waistline

11 **Shoulder to bustline**

12 **Center front to bustline**

13 **Back length**
a) Neckline to waistline
b) Highest point of shoulder to waistline (left)
c) Highest point of shoulder to waistline (right)

14 **Shoulder to shoulder**
Measure across back

15 **Back width**
Measure 4 inches below neckline, with arms forward and raised slightly

16 **Full length (from waistline to floor)**
a) Center front
b) Center back
c) Left side
d) Right side

17 **Skirt length**
Include appropriate hem allowance

18 **Crotch measurement**
a) Length
b) Depth (depth of waist above chair when seated)

ALLOWANCE FOR EASE

If patterns fitted precisely, and fabrics had no give, you would not be able to move once you put the garment on. So most patterns have an allowance built in for ease. When checking pattern measurements, include the following allowance for ease:

Bustline:	3 inches
Waistline:	1 inch
Hipline:	2 inches
Sleeve width	
at upper arm:	2 to 3 inches
Shoulder to	
waistline:	½ to 1 inch
Back length:	½ to 1 inch
Back width:	½ to 1 inch

Of course, some patterns have extra ease to suit the style of the garment.

CHECKING THE FIT

After taking all your measurements, check the measurements of the pattern. Start by pressing the tissue paper pattern pieces with a cool iron to remove creases. Measure the pattern from seamline to seamline in the same places as you took your own measurement. Check there is enough ease.

As an extra check, and to help you decide whether the style will suit you, you can pin the pattern pieces together and try on the tissue pattern. Trim the pattern along the fabric cutting line, and pin darts, tucks, and ease allowance in place. Pin shoulder seams, side seams, and any seams within the bodice, placing pattern with wrong sides together and positioning pins along the seamline. Pin pieces together at waistline, if appropriate. Slip the pattern over the right half of the body, slipping shoulder pads in place if they are part of the garment. Check that the shoulder seam is on top of the shoulder, and side seams hang straight from armpit to lower edge. Ensure that the fullest parts of the bust and hips are in the right place and the waistline is at the right height.

PATTERN FITTING

The simplest type of pattern adjustment is lengthening and shortening at points other than hem or seams: positions for making such adjustments are marked on the pattern, so that they avoid any important features such as darts or pockets and so on.

More tricky adjustments – for example to accommodate a full bust, a low bust, a large upper arm – are essential for a professional finish.

Both types of adjustment involve cutting or folding the pattern: if you want to keep the original pattern intact, trace new pattern pieces.

LENGTHENING AND SHORTENING

You will find lengthening and shortening marks across the pattern at various points: usually between the bustline and the waistline, below the hipline, and on the sleeve above and below the elbow. Be sure to adjust front and back pattern pieces by the same amount.

To lengthen, slash across the pattern at the marked lengthening line. Place a strip of tissue under the pattern. Spread the pattern the necessary amount and pin it to the tissue. Keep the grainline straight. If the grainline does not extend as far as the adjusting line, extend it the full length of the pattern before slashing. Adjust facing pieces the same amount.

To shorten, fold the pattern on the printed line and pin in a tuck of an even width across the pattern pieces. Adjust the facing by the same amount.

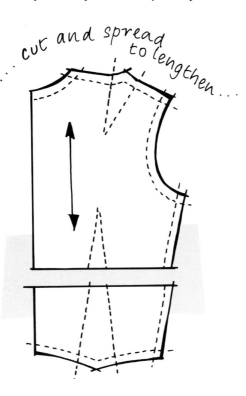

cut and spread to lengthen...

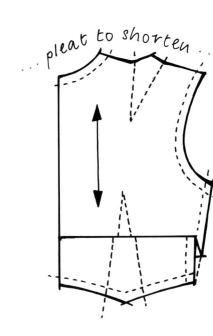

...pleat to shorten...

RULES FOR PATTERN ADJUSTMENTS

1 When you need to lengthen or widen a pattern, use tissue paper for the adjustment. Cut it 1 inch wider than the adjustment, so the pattern overlaps the tissue ½ inch on each side of the adjustment.

2 Make a clean, straight cut across the pattern at the point where the adjustment is to be made, following the printed lines or your own marked line.

3 Pin the pattern to the tissue, placing the pins parallel to the adjustment. If the pattern is one you may use more than once, machine baste the pieces together, or use tape to hold pieces firmly.

4 When making a pattern piece narrower with tucks or darts, remember that the tuck or dart should be only half the amount to be removed at each point.

5 Always measure the pattern again after making adjustments, and measure both halves of a seam where you have made adjustments that affect the length of a seamline.

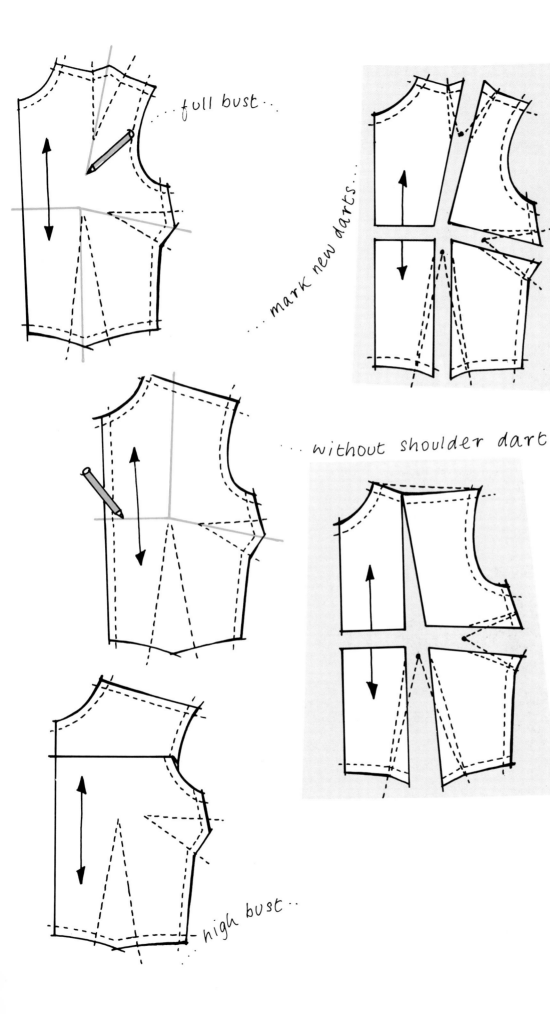

full bust...

...mark new darts...

...without shoulder dart...

...high bust...

FITTING THE BUST

When a pattern fits everywhere except at the bust, buy the pattern by the hip measurements and adjust the bustline.

If the pattern has shoulder darts, draw a line from the center of the waistline dart, through the fullest part of the bust, and another from the center of the shoulder seamline to the same point. Then draw a horizontal line across the fullest part of the bust. Place a large piece of tissue under the pattern and slash along these lines. Spread the four pieces apart, keeping the cut edges parallel and making sure that the grainline remains straight. Mark a new dart at the shoulder, and adjust existing darts to take up the extra fabric. If you do not want a dart from the shoulder, angle the two outer panels so that the shoulder seamline remains the same length, still keeping the horizontal adjustment an even width across the pattern.

For a flat bust adjust the necessary amount by folding a tuck across the chest, decreasing in width at the armhole. Pin in place. Make a corresponding dart in the front of the sleeve so that the armhole and sleeve will fit correctly. Remember, the width of the dart and tuck are only half the amount to be removed.

For a low bust, you have to lower the dart at the underarm. Slash across the pattern the length of the dart, approximately 1 inch below the armhole; then slash down toward the waistline. Place the tissue underneath and pin it to the pattern along the upper edge of the slash. Slide the dart section down, taking a tuck at the lower end of the vertical slash, until the point of the dart is in line with the fullest part of the bust. Pin the top edge of the slash to the tissue and pin down each side of vertical slash.

FITTING THE SHOULDERS

For round shoulders, slash across the pattern from the center to the armhole at the fullest part of the back. Place the tissue underneath, and raise the pattern at the neck to add the necessary amount across the shoulders. Pin the pattern to the tissue. Add a dart at the neckline to regain the original neck size. Add the amount needed at center back to keep center back line straight.

For square shoulders, slash across the pattern front and back, from the armhole toward the center just below the shoulder line. Place a piece of tissue underneath, and raise the shoulder line the necessary amount. Pin the pattern to the tissue. Raise the armhole at the underarm by the same amount to retain size. Straighten the dart at the shoulder as illustrated by the dotted lines.

For sloping shoulders, slash across the pattern front and back, from the armhole toward the center, just below the shoulder line. Lap and pin the slashed edges the necessary amount at the armhole, tapering to a point. Lower the armhole by the same amount at underarm to retain the shape and size of the armhole, as illustrated by the dotted lines. Straighten the shoulder dart.

For broad shoulders, slash the pattern front and back, from the center shoulder down as far as the armhole notches. Then slash across almost to the armhole edge. Place tissue underneath and spread the outer edge of the shoulder the necessary width. Pin the pattern to the tissue. Straighten the shoulder line, as illustrated by the dotted lines.

For narrow shoulders, slash the pattern front and back from the center shoulder line diagonally to the notches in the armhole. Lap and pin the slashed edges the necessary amount at the shoulder. Adjust the shoulder seam as illustrated.

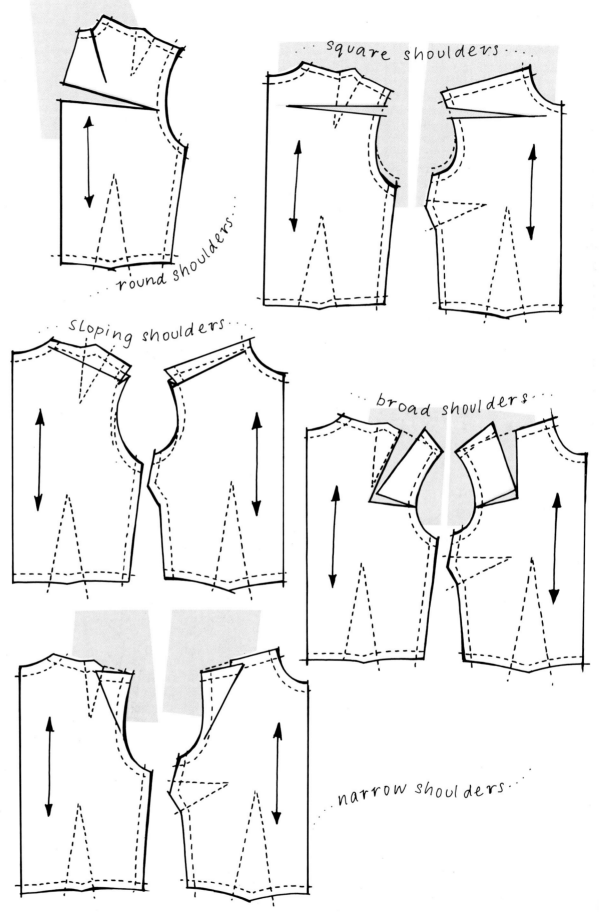

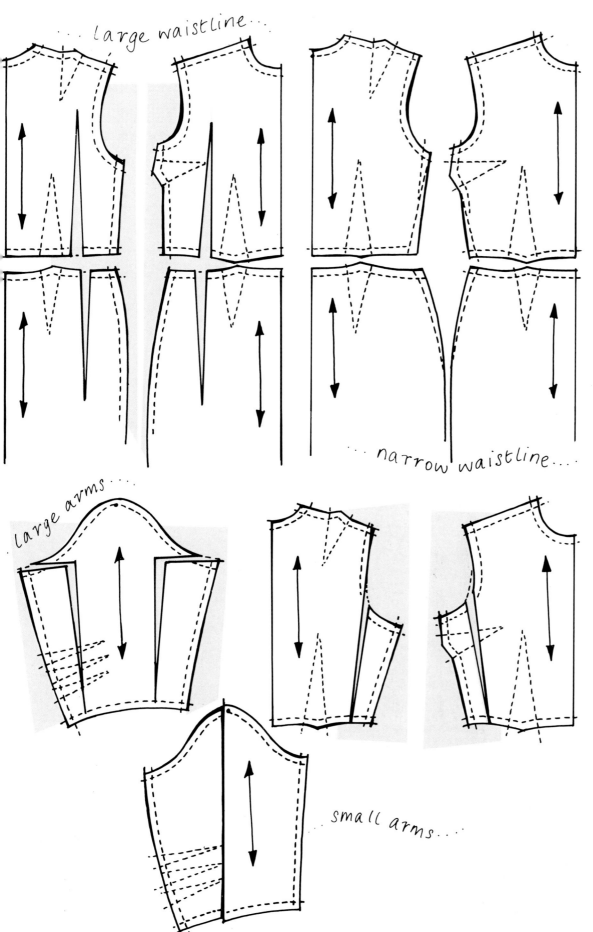

large waistline

narrow waistline

large arms

small arms

FITTING AT THE WAIST

For a large waistline, you have to adjust pattern pieces both above and below the waist. To adjust the bodice, slash the pattern front and back from the waistline toward the shoulder. Place the tissue underneath. Spread both front and back bodices to add the necessary width. Divide the required amount into quarters and add one quarter to each section. Pin the pattern to the tissue. Adjust the pattern pieces below the waist in the same way.

For a small waistline, take in equal amounts on the bodice and the skirt by increasing the size of each waistline dart or tuck and adjusting the seams.

FITTING THE SLEEVES

For a large arm, on each side of the sleeve draw a horizontal line about 3 inches long, beginning at the underarm. Then draw vertical lines to the lower edge on each side. Slash the pattern on these lines and place the tissue underneath. Spread the pattern, tapering to the cuff on a long sleeve. To adjust the armhole seam, slash from the armhole almost to the waistline on the front and back bodice. Place tissue underneath, spread the pattern and adjust the armhole sleeves as illustrated, checking they match the length of the sleeve cap.

For a small arm, fold a lengthwise tuck through the center of the sleeve. Raise the armhole at the underarm the same amount so that the sleeve and armhole will fit correctly.

FITTING AROUND THE HIPS

For full hips, slash the front and back skirt, near the side seams, from the lower edge to the waistline. Keep the grainline straight. Place the tissue underneath and pin it to the inside edge of the slash. Spread the outer edge of the pattern to add the necessary width at the hipline. Add one quarter of the amount needed to both the front and the back of the skirt. Pin the other slashed edge of the pattern to the tissue from the waistline to the hipline. Fold a dart in the pattern below the hip, tapering to the side seam as illustrated, to remove excess fullness at the lower edge. Add the necessary length to the lower outside edge to compensate for the dart. Make exactly the same adjustments to back and front.

For narrow hips, form a lengthwise tuck in the skirt front and back to take up one quarter the amount in each section. Taper the tuck to a point at the waistline, but keep it the same width from hipline to lower edge. Make the adjustment near the side seam to avoid crossing darts and grainline.

For a large seat, first extend the grainline the full length of the pattern. Slash down through the waistline dart to the hemline, and across the hips from center back to side seam at the fullest part. Slip tissue paper underneath and spread the pattern to add one half of the extra fullness needed across the hips. Pin the upper sections in place. Fold a dart below the hipline at the inside edge of the outer, lower section, as shown. Pin lower sections of pattern in place, and adjust hipline and hemline as shown. Finally, re-draw the dart at the waistline.

For a hollow back, slash across the skirt from the center back to the seam edge approximately 2 inches below the waistline. Lap and pin the slashed edges at the center back, to take in fullness, tapering to the seamline. Re-draw the center back line and dart.

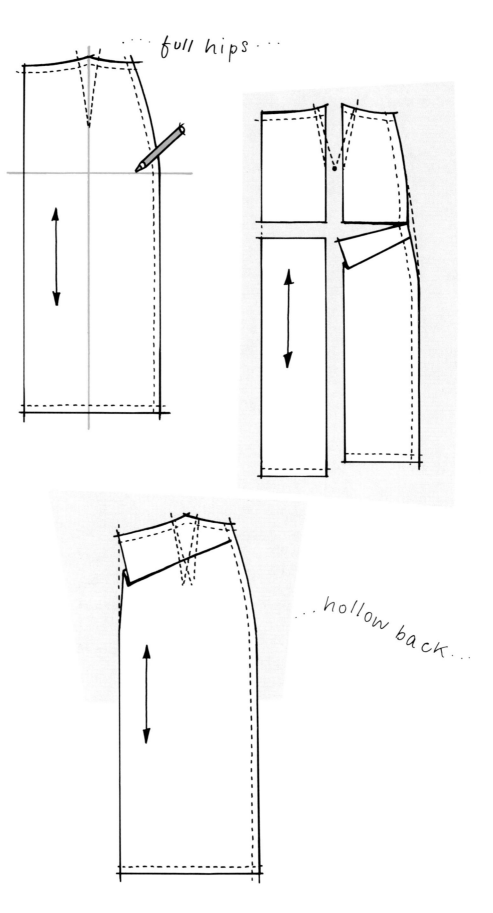

full hips

...hollow back...

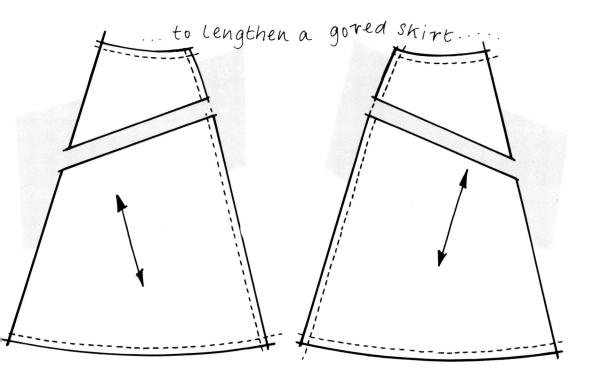

... to lengthen a gored skirt .....

GORED OR FLARED SKIRTS

To lengthen or shorten skirts that are cut on the bias, or to adjust the waistline, adjustments have to be made across or along the lengthwise grain of the fabric. Extend the grainline the full length of the pattern.

To lengthen, draw a line across the pattern at right angles to the grainline, below any pattern markings on the hips, and spread the pattern the required amount, keeping the grainline straight. Pin tissue paper in place. To shorten, fold along the marked line.

To enlarge the waistline, draw a line parallel to the grainline, from the waistline to the lower edge. Spread the pattern and pin tissue paper in place. To reduce the waistline, take a tuck along the same line.

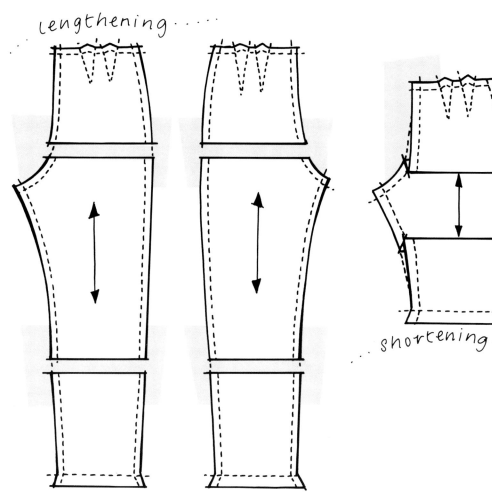

lengthening .....

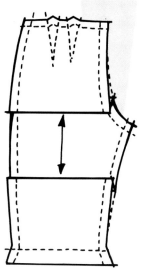

... shortening ...

FITTING PANTS AND SHORTS

To add extra depth to the crotch seam, slash across the pattern above the crotch and spread the pattern, pinning tissue in place. Reduce by taking a tuck at the same point.

To lengthen or shorten pants or shorts, slash across the legs below the crotch and spread the pattern, or take a tuck.

FITTING AS YOU SEW

Besides adapting the pattern to suit your figure, it is usually necessary, on closely fitted garments, to make minor adjustments as you sew. Test the fit at every stage of construction, after basting each seam, unless you are sure the fit is correct. If you are using a delicate fabric, or one that will show pin holes, make a muslin shell first, and adjust the fit on that before cutting out (see page 167).

BALANCE LINES

Balance lines are imaginary lines across the pattern, which correspond with certain body measurements. When fitting, these should be kept level all around the garment, to ensure that it hangs well, with straight seams. If you are inexperienced, it is worthwhile basting these lines on the pattern pieces so that you can see they are running horizontally or vertically.

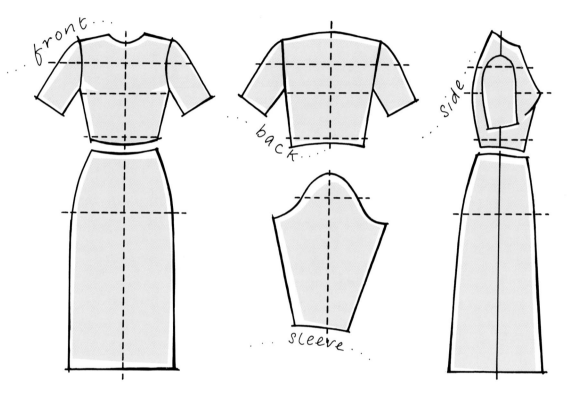

POSITION OF BALANCE LINES

BODICE FRONT

Chest	About 4 inches below the base of the neck, on the crosswise grain.
Bust	Across the fullest part of the bust, on the crosswise grain.
Waist	About 1½ inches above the waistline, on the crosswise grain.
Center front	Center of body, from base of neck to waistline, on the lengthwise grain.

BODICE BACK

SHOULDER	About 4 inches below the prominent vertebra, on the crosswise grain, to correspond to chest on front.
Underarm	About 1½ inches below the armhole, across the shoulder blades, to correspond to the bustline on the crosswise grain.
Waist	About 1½ inches above the waistline, to correspond to the front waist line, on the crosswise grain.

Center back	Center of body, from prominent vertebra at neck to waistline, on the lengthwise grain.

SLEEVES

Center	From shoulder line marking to center of wrist, on the lengthwise grain.
Sleeve cap	About 3 inches below the shoulder line, across the sleeve cap at a right angle to the lengthwise grain. This line is on the crosswise grain and corresponds to the chest and shoulder grainline of the bodice.

SKIRT

Center	Down front and back following center of body from waistline to hemline, on the lengthwise grain.
Hips	Across the fullest part of the hips, usually about 7 inches below the waistline, parallel to the floor on the crosswise grain.

PIN FITTING

Wear the same underwear you intend to wear under the finished garment, and the same shoes. (You may find you stand slightly differently in high heeled shoes than in flat shoes.) If the garment has shoulder pads, keep them handy so that you can insert them at each stage of fitting.

Cut out the pattern and transfer all pattern markings. Staystitch shoulder seams and any other seams if necessary. Baste any darts and tucks and gather up any fullness by machine. Baste any sectional seams, such as curved bustline seams, and center front and back seams, so that you have four pieces: front and back bodice and front and back skirt. Pin the bodice pieces together at the shoulder, down the underarm seams and at the sides of the skirt. Position pins so they run along the seamline.

Try on the garment, right side out, in front of a full length mirror. Pin any buttoned opening in place at the button and buttonhole markings. Pin seams together at zipper openings; pin the bodice to the skirt at the waistline. Adjust the shoulder line and check that the center lines run down the center of your body. Bear in mind that the neckline has an extended seam allowance, which makes it seem smaller than it will be when the neckline is finished. Ease allowances are included in the pattern – make sure they are sufficient to allow comfortable movement.

Check the following points:

Shoulder adjustments Sloping shoulders will cause the balance line to drop at the armholes and form wrinkles. To correct, re-pin the shoulder seams, making them slightly deeper as you approach the shoulder points. This means lowering the armhole so that the sleeve will fit as it should. Baste the position of the new seamline. Lay the pattern on the fabric with the shoulder seamline of the pattern on the basted line of the fabric, and re-cut the armhole. Shoulders are often different heights, so it may be necessary to cut each side of the bodice and each sleeve separately, from differently adjusted pattern pieces.

Square shoulders cause the balance line to swing up at the armholes and wrinkles to form diagonally toward the bustline and below the back neckline. Re-pin the shoulder seams, making them deeper at the neckline and tapering the seam allowance at the shoulder points.

Bustline adjustments Check the length and angle of the darts. If there is fullness below the bustline and the balance line seems to drop below the fullest part of the bust, raise the underarm darts to bring the points in line with the fullest part of the bust. If there is fullness above the bustline and the balance line is above the fullest part of the bust, lower the underarm darts.

A small flat bust will cause the balance line to sag at the center front. Decrease the underarm darts to correct the balance line position, then try on again, to check the length of the front bodice. If it is too long, take a tuck across the pattern, and re-cut the lower edge of the pattern.

Skirt adjustments If one hip is higher or larger than the other, adjust fit on one side only. A hollow back will make the balance line sag at the center back. Raise the waistline by marking an adjusted seamline up to ⅝ inch below the original one, tapering the allowance to the side seamlines.

If the skirt lifts in the front, and the side seams jut forward, raise the back and sides of the skirt at the waistline to bring the balance line to a horizontal position.

Move the darts if necessary, to match the fullest part of the hips. Check that the hemline is level, and the right length.

BASTED FITTING

Join the first seams of the garment, following any adjustments made at the pin fitting stage: the darts, any seams within the bodice or skirt sections, and the shoulder seams. Baste the sleeve seams, and check the fit of the sleeves, then baste the side seams and fit the sleeve into the armhole. Baste in place. Then baste bodice to skirt at waistline and try on the garment. Check the fit, both sitting and standing, and with arms forward, to make sure that there is enough ease. Pin-mark any further adjustments needed, and baste the new adjustments and fit again before stitching.

Check the fit as often as you feel necessary, first pinning, then basting seams and features. Check the positions of buttons and openings, pockets, and other features, before basting and stitching in place. You may need to ease some seams slightly after making adjustments, or make further adjustments to the opposite part of the seam to make sure of a smooth fit.

Patterns for children

Children's patterns are available in a variety of styles. Avoid making children's clothes extra large, for the child to "grow into". Both fit and fashion are lost along the way, and the garment may be worn out and discarded before the child grows to fit it. However, do try to build in allowances for growth, such as deep hems, adjustable waistlines, and growth tucks.

TAKING MEASUREMENTS

As for adult clothes, measure the child accurately and record the measurements. It may be easier to measure a garment that fits a child, if the child is

small and won't keep still. The level of the hemline for a girl usually varies with age. Crawling babies need a very short skirt, so that they do not kneel on it. Generally, skirts get longer as a girl grows older, but this may vary with fashion trends and pattern styles.

FITTING PATTERNS FOR CHILDREN

Children's patterns should be fitted and adapted as for adults' garments. Obviously, this may be impossible for small children. Apart from the normal adjustments, you may also need to adjust the pattern to fit a chubby child.

JACKET, TROUSERS AND SHORTS

1 Chest
2 Waist
3 Hip
4 Height – Neckline to floor
5 Back length of shirt – Neck to waistline
6 Shoulder to shoulder
7 Finished length of pants
8 Finished length of shorts
9 Finished length of jacket
  a) Front
  b) Back
10 Neck circumference
11 Sleeve length

Allowances: 5 to 7 inches for ease across chest; tuck-in allowance plus 1½ to 2 inches ease down back length; ½ to 1 inch for ease across shoulders. Check pattern for hem allowance.

DRESS MEASUREMENTS

1 **Chest**
2 **Breast**
3 **Waist**
4 **Hip – 3 inches below waist**
5 **Neck circumference**
6 **Shoulder length – Right**
        Left
7 **Shoulder to shoulder**
8 **Waist length**
   a) Front
   b) Back
9 **Sleeve length**
   a) Shoulder to elbow
   b) Elbow to wrist
   c) Inside from underarm seam to wrist
10 **Skirt lengths**
   a) Front
   b) Back

Allowances: include 1½ to 2½ inches ease around chest; ½ to 1 inch ease across shoulders and in waist length; 3 to 5 inch hem allowance should be added to skirt length.

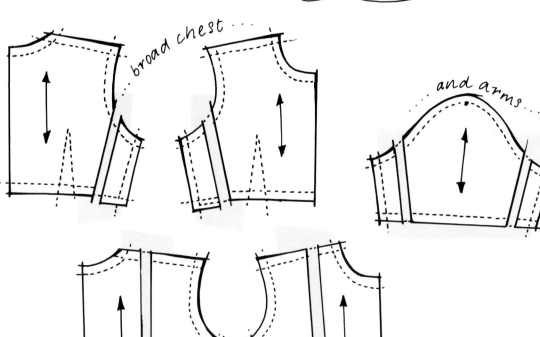

CHUBBY CHILDREN

To add width across the chest, around the waist, and in the sleeves, slash the front and back bodice and sleeve from lower edge to armhole, as illustrated. Place tissue paper under the pattern and spread it to add a quarter of the width required around the waist at each point. Redraw the seamlines if necessary.

To add width across the shoulders and around the waist, without increasing the sleeve size, slash the front and back bodice from the center of the dart (if any), to the shoulder line. Spread the pattern as before, adding a quarter of the width required at each point. Redraw darts and seamlines.

Make any adjustments to the skirt or pants section (if any) to match those made to the bodice.

121

Attaching collars

The collar is attached to the garment after the shoulder seams are stitched and finished, and any facing and interfacing has been attached to the front opening. It is easier to finish the collar if the side seams are left open at this stage. Of course, patterns give instructions for a specific collar, but there are some general principles that apply, and you may want to adapt your pattern and make a different style of collar.

COLLAR STYLES

The simplest finish for a collar is to cover and face the seam with a bias strip. It is suitable for light cotton garments and children's clothes. As with all styles, the collar is faced and interfaced, then stitched and pressed. Trim and grade seams, and clip off fabric at corners or notch curves before turning right side out and pressing again.

For a smoother finish, and for styles with an open neck, the opening has to be faced. The facing may be continued around the back of the neck, or extend up the front and lapels, if any, only as far as the shoulder seam.

Some collars, particularly on men's garments, have a neckband between the collar and the garment. With this finish, the front of the opening may be faced, or there may be no facing, apart from down the button and buttonhole bands.

COLLAR WITH BIAS FACING

With the garment and collar right side out, pin the collar to the neckline edge, matching markings, shoulder, and center lines and baste by hand. Roll the collar so it sits as it will be worn, allowing a little ease in the top collar so that it fits smoothly over the roll. If there is a front facing, fold it back over the right side of the collar and pin.

Cut a bias strip of fabric 1¼ inches wide and long enough to extend around the neckline. Pin it over the collar at the neckline, taking ¼ inch seam allowance and extending the ends of the strip ⅜ inch over the front facing. Stitch in place around the neckline from one front edge to the other, reinforcing by reverse stitching at each end.

Grade and clip into seam allowances, and cut off corners of seams at the shoulder line. Press. Turn the front facings and bias strip to the underside. Fold under ¼ inch along free edge of bias strip and pin to garment across the back of the neckline. Hem in place by hand. Finish front facings according to fabric.

assemble collar

...fit around neck...

...add binding..... trim....

...finish by hand....

COLLAR AND LAPELS WITH BACK FACING

Join front and back facings at shoulder and stitch to the garment, right sides together, along the front seams, leaving neckline edges free. Press, trim seams and press open, and finish free edge. Clip into neckline seam allowance almost to staystitching. Pin and baste the undercollar and the interfacing to the neckline of the garment, matching markings, shoulder, and center lines. Stitch in a continuous seam, from within 1/8 inch of one collar edge to the same distance from the other collar edge.

Pin and baste the neckline facing to the top collar, matching

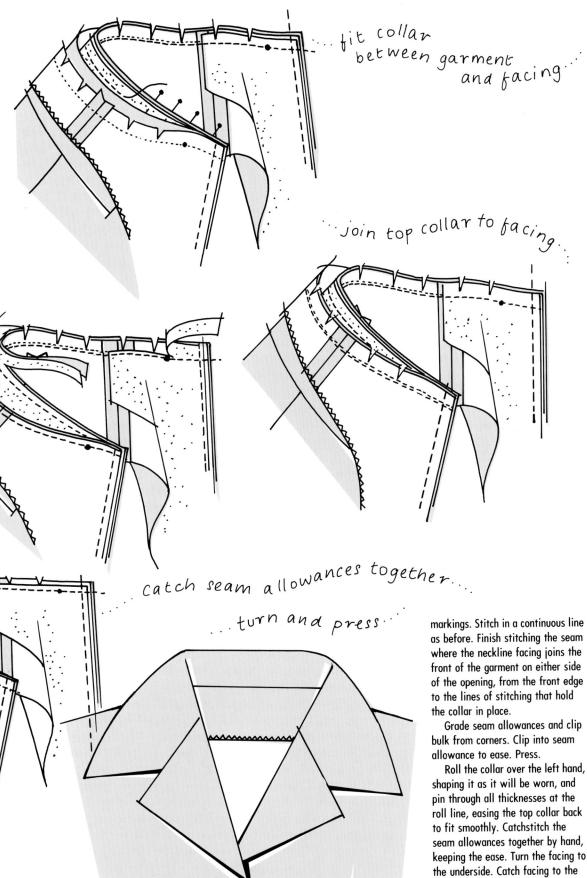

fit collar between garment and facing

...join top collar to facing...

trim seams...

...catch seam allowances together...

...turn and press...

markings. Stitch in a continuous line as before. Finish stitching the seam where the neckline facing joins the front of the garment on either side of the opening, from the front edge to the lines of stitching that hold the collar in place.

Grade seam allowances and clip bulk from corners. Clip into seam allowance to ease. Press.

Roll the collar over the left hand, shaping it as it will be worn, and pin through all thicknesses at the roll line, easing the top collar back to fit smoothly. Catchstitch the seam allowances together by hand, keeping the ease. Turn the facing to the underside. Catch facing to the shoulder seam allowance.

123

COLLAR AND LAPELS WITHOUT FACING

If there is no facing around the back of the neckline, the front part of the top collar is stitched to the neckline facing, but the back of the collar has to be eased and stitched to the undercollar and garment neckline, then turned under for a neat finish.

After joining shoulder seams and staystitching around neckline, clip into the neckline seam allowances almost to stitching.

Assemble the collar as before, then pin undercollar and interfacing to the neckline across the back, from shoulder seam to shoulder seam, leaving the top collar free. Match the markings and center lines.

Then pin the undercollar, top collar, and interfacing to the neckline from shoulder to center front on each side, matching markings.

Turn the front facing over the collar, right sides together, and pin, matching markings. Baste from the front edge to the shoulder seam. Clip into top collar at shoulder seam, in line with end of facing, for the depth of the seam allowance. Baste undercollar and interfacing to neckline across the back. Continue basting to the opposite edge, clipping into seam allowance of collar at shoulder as before.

Stitch all around neckline, from one faced front edge to the other, leaving top collar free across the back.

Trim the interfacing seam allowance close to the stitching. Trim the garment and collar seam allowances to 1/4 inch. Clip into seam allowance on neckline curve at even intervals and clip across corners of facing. Trim excess fabric where seams cross. Press, and turn facing to underside. Turn under seam allowance of collar around back neckline.

Roll and shape collar over left hand, and pin and slipstitch folded edge of top collar in place. Catch front facings to seam allowance at shoulder.

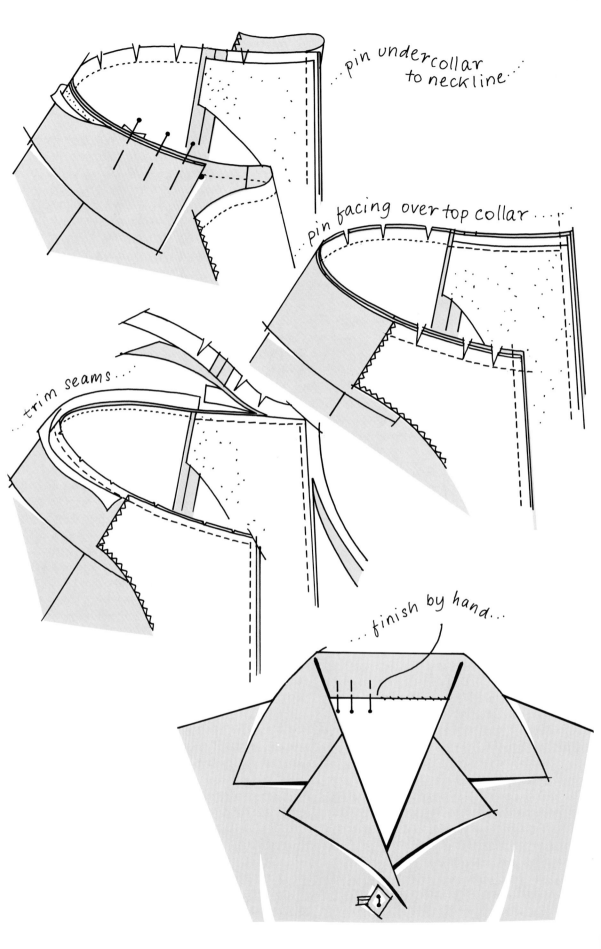

...pin undercollar to neckline...

...pin facing over top collar...

...trim seams...

...finish by hand...

Finishing waistlines

There is a wide range of finishes for waistlines – depending on the style of garment. Where the bodice is joined to a straight or slightly flared skirt, the waistline should be strengthened with straight seam binding. This is not usually necessary for a gathered skirt. In a straight dress, the waistline may be drawn in by elastic, or a casing with a drawstring. Drawstrings may also be used at the waistline of a gathered cotton skirt, loose shorts, or pajama bottoms. Most skirts and pants are finished with a plain waistband – shown in these diagrams with a pointed end for clarity, but equally often waistbands have square ends. Waistbands normally measure 1 to 1¼ inches wide. There may be a wrap on the overlapping part of the band, on the underlapping side, or on both edges.

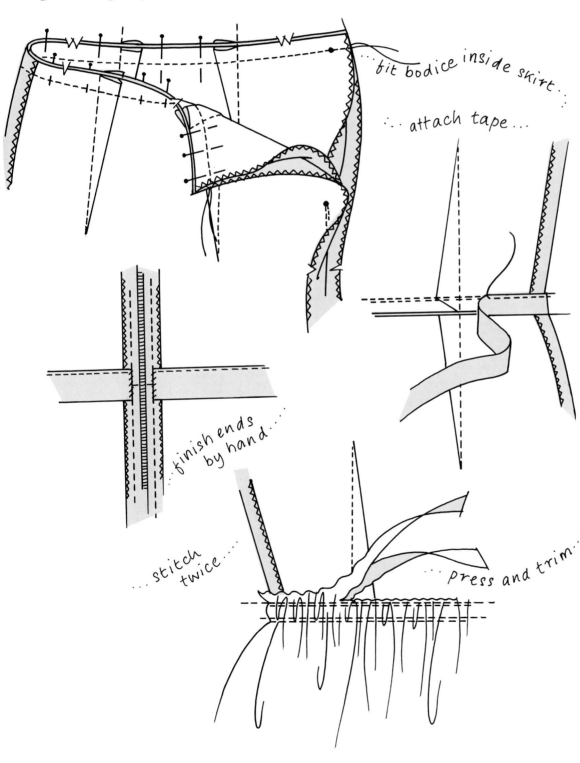

fit bodice inside skirt...

...attach tape...

...finish ends by hand...

...stitch twice...

press and trim...

JOINING BODICE TO A STRAIGHT OR FLARED SKIRT

Turn skirt to wrong side and bodice to right side. Place bodice inside the skirt, right sides together, and pin at the waistline, matching center lines, seams, darts and notches. Baste.

Stitch around the waistline from one edge of the placket opening to the other. Reinforce with reverse stitching at each end. Press.

Turn the seam allowances away from the garment. On the bodice side, stitch pre-shrunk straight seam binding to the seam allowance, barely below the first line of stitching. Begin and end the stitching about 1¼ inches away from each side of the opening. Press. Cut off corners where seams cross at darts. Press. Turn the seam allowance down toward the skirt. After the zipper is inserted, turn under the ends of the seam binding and catch them to the zipper tape.

JOINING BODICE TO A GATHERED SKIRT

Turn skirt to wrong side and bodice to right side. Pin the bodice and skirt together at the waistline, matching center lines, side seams and markings. Adjust the gathers to fit the waistline, and pin and baste. Stitch the seam with the bodice next to the feed. Place a second row of stitching in the seam allowance, ¼ inch from the first. Pink the edges. If the fabric is loosely woven, overcast the edges either by hand or by machine. Turn seam allowance upward.

ELASTICIZED WAISTLINE

This method provides controlled, even gathers at a waistline. Mark the waistline with chalk or a line of basting. Fit the elastic comfortably at the waistline, allowing 1 inch for finishing at the opening, or for joining.

Divide the garment waistline and elastic into quarters, allowing about ½ inch at each end of the elastic for finishing. Pin the elastic to the inside of the garment waistline at

WAISTBAND WITH FACING AND DOUBLE WRAP

Cut the fabric for the waistband on the lengthwise grain, twice the finished width of the band, plus seam allowances, and the length of the waistline measurement plus 2 inches for seam allowance and wrap on the overlap, and 2½ inches for seam allowance and wrap on the underlap of the opening.

Fold waistband lengthwise through the center, wrong sides together, and crease. Cut the interfacing twice the width of the finished waistband less ¼ inch and the same length as the fabric for the waistband. Fold it lengthwise through the center and press. Cut overlapping end to a point, trimming seam allowance, as shown, if required. Stitch interfacing to wrong side of waistband lining section just below the crease and along the opposite edge, so that the point aligns with the seamline.

Mark the overlap allowances on the wrong side of the waistband and check that the distance between the marks matches the waist measurement. Open the zipper. Place the waistband over the waistline of the skirt, right sides together, with the part of the waistband without interfacing matching the top of the skirt. Extend the pointed end 2 inches beyond the front edge of the placket and pin. Pin the opposite end so that it extends 2½ inches beyond the back seam of the placket opening and pin. (This underlap should match the zipper underlay.) Pin waistband to right side of

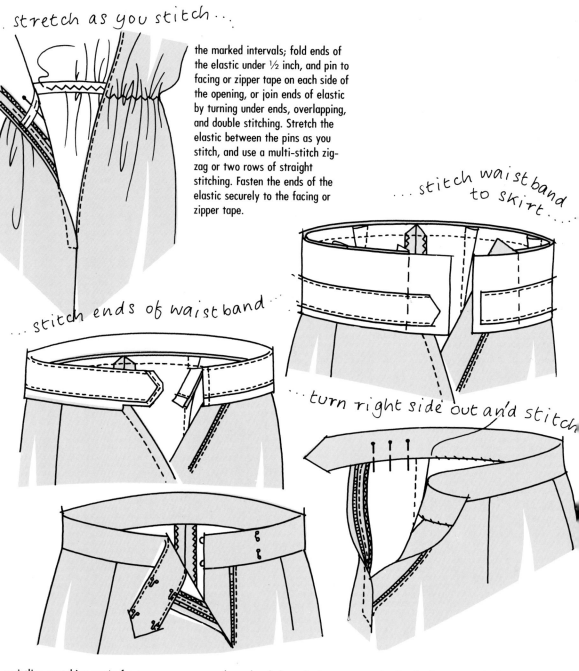

the marked intervals; fold ends of the elastic under ½ inch, and pin to facing or zipper tape on each side of the opening, or join ends of elastic by turning under ends, overlapping, and double stitching. Stretch the elastic between the pins as you stitch, and use a multi-stitch zig-zag or two rows of straight stitching. Fasten the ends of the elastic securely to the facing or zipper tape.

waistline, matching center front, side seams and center back points, and any other markings. Distribute ease evenly. Pin and baste all around. Stitch on seamline, reinforcing with reverse stitching. Cut off the corners of the seam allowance where seams cross and at darts. On firmly woven fabrics trim the waistline seam allowance to ¼ inch.

Remove basting and press. Turn the waistband away from the skirt and press the seam allowance toward the waistband. Fold the pointed end of the waistband in half, right sides together, and pin across the end and along the lower edge as far as the placket opening. Stitch just outside the interfacing, taking one stitch across the point. Reinforce ends of seam with reverse stitching. Repeat at the other end, making a straight line of stitching across the end. Trim seam allowances and press. Turn waistband to right side and press the ends. Fold waistband in half and pin along the fold. Turn under the seam allowance on the free edge of the waistband and pin to the seam at the waistline, enclosing the seam allowances. Finish by hand using a hemming stitch and press. Topstitch

(optional), then sew on hooks and eyes as illustrated, stitching through the underside of the waistband and interfacing.

For a machine-stitched finish, take a slightly narrower seam allowance in the free edge of the waistband, then baste in place over previous line of stitching. Stitch from the right side of the garment, following the line of the seam between the waistband and the garment, so that the stitches barely show.

WAISTBAND WITH GROSGRAIN BELTING AND NO WRAP

Cut the waistband on the lengthwise grain twice the finished width plus seam allowances, and the length of the waistline plus 1 inch for the depth of the point and seam allowance on the overlap and 2½ inches for the underlap and seam. Open the zipper. Place the waistband (without interfacing) over the waistline of the skirt, right sides together, matching marked lines to placket opening. Pin waistband in place, matching all markings and distributing ease evenly and baste. Cut a length of 1 inch wide grosgrain belting, cutting it to the same length as the waistband; cut one end to a point. Lap the belting over the waistband side of the seam allowances, keeping the edge even with the seamline. Pin, baste, and stitch on the edge of the interfacing with the skirt next to the feed. Remove basting. Press.

Turn waistband away from the skirt and press the seam allowances and interfacing toward the waistband. Trim seam allowances under the interfacing to ¼ inch and cut off the corners where seams

USING PRE-CUT INTERFACING

Waistband interfacing is available in pre-cut strips. Choose a width to suit the width of the waistband. The interfacing has three slotted lines: the center one runs along the top of the waistband and the outer ones along the seamline where the waistband is joined to the garment. Cut the waistband fabric to the width of the interfacing and to the length specified in the pattern.

Position interfacing on wrong side of waistband and press with a warm, dry iron for about 15 seconds, or as specified by the manufacturer. Zig-zag stitch interfacing to fabric along the raw edge of the fabric that will form the inside of the waistband. Position waistband on garment, allowing appropriate overlaps at each end, and stitch along outer slotted line, through waistband and garment. Press, then press seam allowances

cross and at darts. Pink and stitch free edge of the waistband.

Fold ends of waistband, right sides together, and pin across the end. Stitch barely outside the interfacing at pointed end, and straight across straight end. Trim seam allowances and interfacing at straight end. Turn to right side. Press.

Turn free edge of waistband over the interfacing and pin to the seam at the stitching line, enclosing seam allowances. Sew in place by hand, and attach hooks and eyes.

toward waistband. Finish ends of overlap. Turn waistband right side out; press along center foldline. With inside of waistband positioned under the previous seamline, sew in place from right side, following previous seamline, through garment and inside of waistband.

stitch stiffening to seam...

press upwards...

turn right side out...

iron on interfacing...

stitch through slotted line...

fold waistband...

stitch along seamline...

Fitting sleeves

Sleeves are an important style element of a garment – and show up poor dressmaking work if they are not correctly fitted. Sleeves may be constructed in a variety of ways – loose or tight, tapering to the wrist, or drawn into a cuff – and with a wide choice of finishes at the sleeve cap.

SLEEVE CONSTRUCTION

Dropped shoulder seams are easier to fit, since the contours do not have to be fitted to the body, but set-in sleeves are the most usual type. For a more tailored look, the sleeve cap may extend over the shoulder, to form an epaulette. Puffed sleeves are often found on children's clothes, blouses, and shirt dresses. Raglan sleeves normally have extra seams or darts down the outside of the sleeve, while magyar or dolman sleeves are cut in one piece, and need extra strength under the arm. On a sleeveless garment, the sleeve edge is normally finished with a fitted facing.

ASSEMBLING A FITTED SLEEVE
Three-quarter and full-length sleeves have fullness at the elbow, which is controlled with darts or gathers. Stitch darts and press them downward over a pressing mitt. If gathers are marked, control the fullness with a row of stitching between the marks, just outside the seamline. Fold the sleeve, right sides together, and pin on the seamline, matching markings. Draw the thread to ease the fullness and distribute it evenly at the elbow. Baste, then stitch underarm seams and finish seam edges. Press the seam, then press open.

For a two-piece sleeve, there is slight ease in the upper sleeve section at the elbow. Pin seam at ¼ inch intervals to ease the fullness. After basting and stitching the seam, press to shrink fullness.

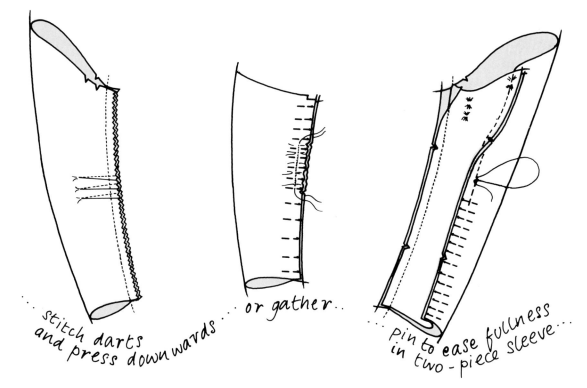

stitch darts and press downwards... *...or gather...* *...pin to ease fullness in two-piece sleeve...*

HINTS FOR CONSTRUCTING AND SETTING IN SLEEVES

1 Transfer markings accurately from the pattern to the sleeve and the armhole.
2 Never omit pinning and basting.
3 Always press during construction.
4 Check the fit of the sleeve carefully: do not fit the fashion out of the sleeve if it extends beyond the natural shoulder line. Check that shoulder lines match on fitted sleeves.
5 Check that there is room for shoulder pads if they are included in the garment.
6 Always check that you have set the right sleeve into the right armhole: pattern markings should indicate this clearly, with double notches at the back of the garment and single notches at the front.
7 With some patterns, it is easier to set the sleeve in before stitching the underarm seam. For the techniques shown here, the sleeve is assembled and fitted before the armhole seam is stitched. Check also whether the cuff should be finished before or after the sleeve is set in.

...pin sleeve in place...

...distribute ease...

...stitch seam...

SET-IN SLEEVE

Turn sleeve inside out, and make one or two lines of stitching around the cap of the sleeve between notches to control ease. Place stitching in seam allowance, close to seamline. Use the same stitch length, but loosen the upper tension so you can draw the bobbin thread. Leave the threads long. Turn sleeve to right side. With wrong side of the garment out, slip the sleeve into the armhole, right sides together. Pin,

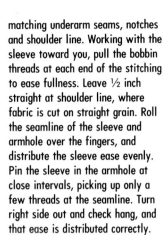

matching underarm seams, notches and shoulder line. Working with the sleeve toward you, pull the bobbin threads at each end of the stitching to ease fullness. Leave ½ inch straight at shoulder line, where fabric is cut on straight grain. Roll the seamline of the sleeve and armhole over the fingers, and distribute the sleeve ease evenly. Pin the sleeve in the armhole at close intervals, picking up only a few threads at the seamline. Turn right side out and check hang, and that ease is distributed correctly.

With the sleeve toward you, baste, using a short stitch. If necessary, shrink fullness in woolen fabric before basting. Try on garment before stitching in the sleeve, and adjust if necessary. Stitch from the sleeve side, just outside the stitching used to control the ease. Stitch from underarm seam and continue around the sleeve cap, overlapping stitches about 1 inch at underarm seam. Remove basting. Trim seam allowance, cut off corners where seams cross, and press. Turn the seam allowance into the sleeve.

...stay stitch...

...pin into opening...

...pin epaulette...

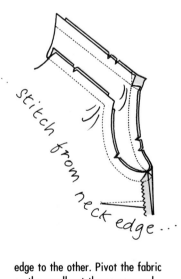

stitch from neck edge...

EPAULETTE SLEEVE

At the cap of the sleeve, where the epaulette begins, staystitch the point at which the angle of the seamline changes, where the seam allowance will be slashed. Use a short stitch. Press. Stitch the underarm seams of the sleeve and bodice. Finish seams and press open.

Turn sleeve to right side. With wrong side of bodice out, place the sleeve in the armhole, right sides together. Pin, matching underarm seams, shoulder markings, and notches. Then with the sleeve toward you, pin at close intervals. Baste in one continuous line from one shoulder to the other. At the shoulder line of the sleeve, slash

almost to the stay-stitched point. Pin the epaulette to the shoulder line of the bodice on each side, matching markings. Check that the corners do not pucker. Baste with a short stitch. Turn right side out and check fit.

Stitch the seam from the epaulette and sleeve side, in a continuous line from one neckline

edge to the other. Pivot the fabric on the needle at the corners and take one stitch across the point. Pivot again and continue stitching. Remove basting, and cut off corners where seams cross. Finish edges. Press seam as stitched, then press seam allowances toward shoulder on epaulette section and toward sleeve in armhole section.

PUFF SLEEVES

Stitch underarm seam. Turn sleeve wrong side out; from the inside, stitch two lines of gathering around the sleeve cap, between the markings. Place the first line of stitching just outside the seamline in the seam allowance and the second line in the seam allowance, about 3/16 inch from the first. At the lower edge of the sleeve, run a line of gathering between the markings. Gather and finish the lower edge.

Turn sleeve right side out. With the wrong side of the garment toward you, slip the sleeve into the armhole, right sides together. Pin, matching seams, notches and markings. With the sleeve toward you, gather the sleeve between the notches to fit the armhole. Distribute the fullness evenly and pin. Baste, using a short stitch. Stitch from the sleeve side, just beyond the first line of gathering stitches, overlapping the stitching about 1 inch at the underarm. Stitch again on the second line of gathering stitches. Trim the seam allowance close to the second line of stitching. Press. Finish the seam edges with binding, or blindstitch zig-zag. Turn seam allowances

toward the sleeve.

For a self-finished sleeve in sheer fabrics, position the lines of gathering stitch very close to the seamline. Stitch the seam with a single line of stitching. Then trim seam allowance on the sleeve side to 1/4 inch, and turn under the cut edge 1/8 inch on the bodice side. Fold this seam allowance over the sleeve seam allowance to the stitching line, enclosing the cut edge. Pin. Slipstitch the sleeve seam in place barely above the stitching.

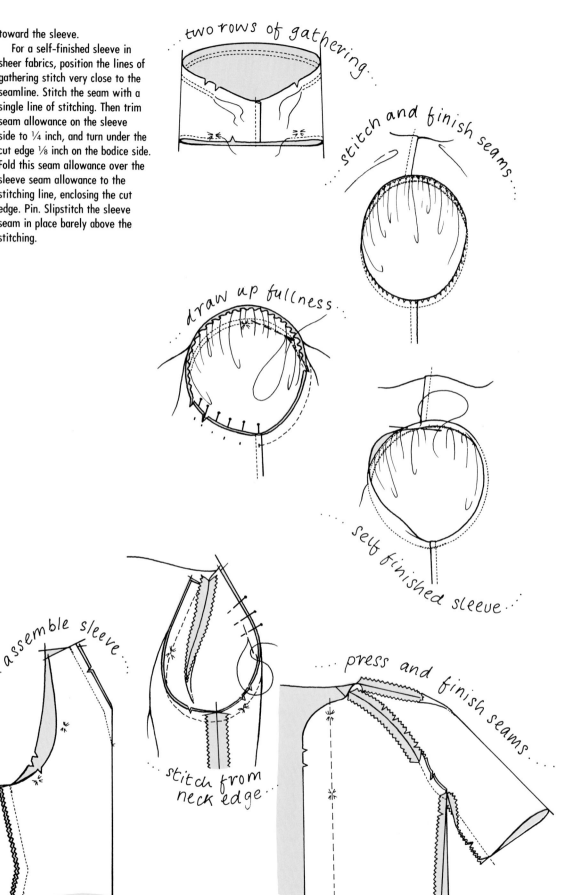

RAGLAN SLEEVE

Pin, baste and stitch the shoulder seam or dart. Stitch underarm seams of sleeve and bodice. Finish the seam edges and press the seam open. Turn the sleeve right side out. Pin to the front and back bodice, right sides together, matching markings and underarm seams. Baste. Stitch in one continuous line from one neckline edge to the other. Remove basting. Slash the seam allowance on the inside curve and notch on the outside curve. Cut off corners where seams cross. Finish seam edges to suit the fabric and garment. Press seam open from neckline to curve of underarm. Press seam allowances toward the sleeve at the underarm.

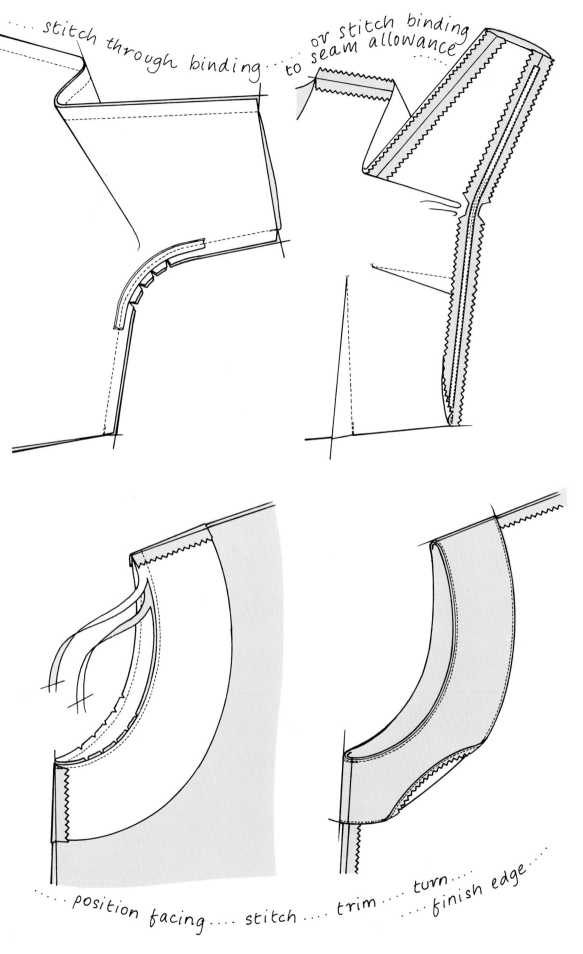

stitch through binding.... or stitch binding to seam allowance

....position facing.... stitch.....trim..... turn.... ....finish edge....

MAGYAR SLEEVE WITHOUT GUSSET

Pin and baste the seam. Fold a 6 inch strip of straight seam binding in half lengthwise, and pin it over the seamline at the curve. Stitch the seam through the binding. Slash seam allowances at the curve to relieve the strain. Press the seam, then press open.

Alternatively, pin, baste and stitch the seam, using a shorter stitch on the curved section. Slash the seam allowances almost to the stitching line on the curve to relieve the strain. Press the seam, then press it open.

Place straight seam binding over the open seam from the hem fold in the sleeve to the lower edge of the bodice. Turn the seam allowance away from the garment and stitch binding to each side of seam allowance. Stitch again down the center of the seam binding, close to the seamline. The binding is stitched only to the single seam allowance and will not show from the right side. Press seam open.

FACED ARMHOLE

Cut the facings the same shape as the edges to be faced. Join seams at the shoulder and the underarm on both garment and facing. Turn garment to right side. Pin the facing around the armhole, right sides together, matching notches and seams at the shoulder and underarm. Baste. Stitch around the armhole on the seamline, overlapping a few stitches at the starting point. Press.

Trim the facing seam allowance to ⅛ inch measure and the garment seam allowance to ¼ inch. Slash the seam allowance on the inside curves, and cut off corners where seams cross. Turn the facing to the inside and ease it under slightly at the seamline. Baste, then press. Understitch the seam to prevent the facing from rolling out of place. Press.

Finish the free edge of the facing then turn the facing into the armhole and press. Catch the facing to the seam allowances at the shoulder seam and underarm seam.

131

SLEEVE HEMS AND CUFFS

The lower edge of a sleeve may simply be turned or bound and hemmed in place, like the hem on any item. However, there are several other choices, and your pattern should give details of a suitable finish. If the sleeve is tight fitting, it will have to have some sort of opening: this may be finished with snaps, or with a zipper, for example. With buttoned cuffs, the opening may not coincide with a sleeve seam, and in this case a bound opening (or placket) should be made. (A similar finish may be used in home decorating projects.)

Cuffs may be cut in one piece with the garment, and stitched to form a turn up, or added as a separate section, particularly on tapered sleeves. Buttoned cuffs, set onto the end of a sleeve with or without gathering, are a favorite finish for shirt-style garments.

WRIST OPENING

Turn sleeve to wrong side. Pin, then stitch straight seam binding to the front edge of the wrist opening, ⅛ inch from the seamline, extending it to a point ½ inch above the opening. Slash diagonally into this seam allowance from the top of binding to opening. Press.

At the back edge of the opening, fold the binding to the underside and pin the free edge to the sleeve. Finish by hand, using a hemming stitch. At the top of the opening, stitch the front and back seam edges together the depth of the seam allowance. At the front edge of the opening, fold the binding to the underside and pin the free edge to the sleeve. Finish by hand, using a hemming stitch.

At the lower edge of the sleeve, pin, then stitch binding ¼ inch from the edge, extending the ends to a point ¼ inch beyond the edges of the opening. Press. Cut diagonally across corners of the sleeve seam allowance close to the stitching. Fold the binding to the underside, miter the corners, and baste the free edge to the sleeve. Press. Finish by hand. Sew on small snaps.

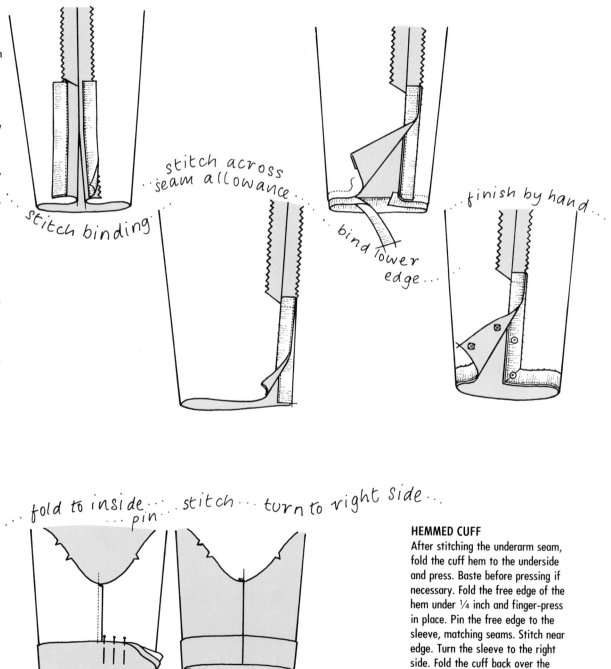

HEMMED CUFF

After stitching the underarm seam, fold the cuff hem to the underside and press. Baste before pressing if necessary. Fold the free edge of the hem under ¼ inch and finger-press in place. Pin the free edge to the sleeve, matching seams. Stitch near edge. Turn the sleeve to the right side. Fold the cuff back over the sleeve, about ½ inch below the stitching.

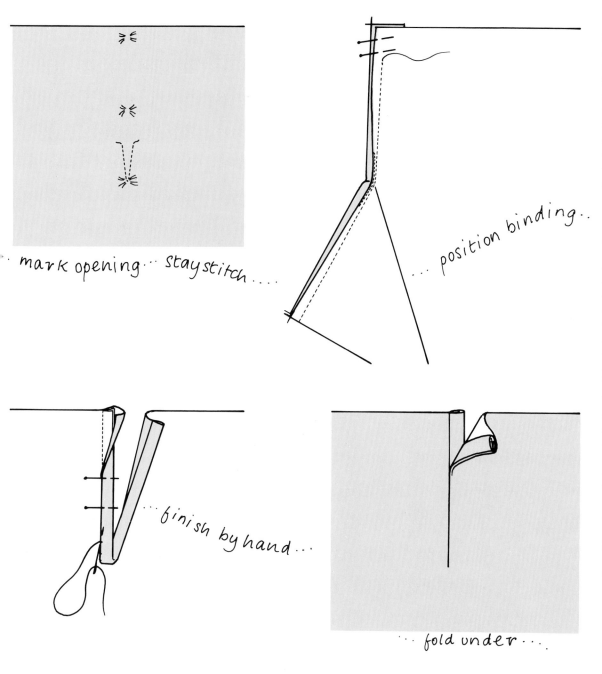

mark opening··· staystitch···

··· position binding··

··· finish by hand···

··· fold under···

··· fit zipper···

··· finish with binding···

CONTINUOUS BOUND PLACKET

Mark the position for the slashed opening with a line of tailor's tacks. Staystitch around the point of the slash, taking a single stitch across the point. Cut the opening to within a couple of threads of the staystitching. Cut a strip of fabric on the lengthwise grain, 1¼ inch wide and twice the length of the slash.

At the open end of the placket, pin the strip to the fabric, right sides together, keeping the cut edges even. Angle the fabric so that at the point the raw edge of the fabric is 3/16 inch from the edge of the strip. Pin in place. Baste. From the garment side, stitch ¼ inch from the edge of the strip, beginning at one end. When you reach the point, stop stitching with the needle in the fabric, raise the presser foot and fold the garment back, forming a "V" at the point. Then lower the foot and finish stitching. Press, then turn the strip away from the garment and press the seam allowance over the strip. Fold under ¼ inch on the free edge of the strip, and crease. Then fold the strip over the seam edge to the stitching line on the underside, enclosing the seam allowances. Pin in place and finish by machine, or by hand. Press.

Fold the strip under on the side that will overlap. Press

ZIPPER OPENING

Choose a fine neckline zipper, about 4 to 6 inches long. Insert the zipper by the channel seam method. Then open the zipper and finish the lower edge of the sleeve with straight seam binding, as for the opening with snaps.

TURN-BACK CUFF

This cuff is made from a top cuff and under cuff piece, which are interfaced and assembled before they are attached to the end of the sleeve. It is a particularly suitable finish where the sleeve is tapered.

Stitch the ends of the cuff together on the under cuff piece and the upper cuff. Press, then press seam open. Cut interfacing and join ends with a lapped seam (or an abutted seam for heavier interfacing). Baste interfacing to wrong side of under cuff, matching seams. Baste to cuff along seamlines. Turn under cuff right side out, then slip upper cuff over under cuff, right sides together. Pin along top edge. Baste then stitch. Grade seams. Press, turn right side out, and ease under cuff to underside. Baste and press.

Turn sleeve and cuff to right side. Slip the cuff over the sleeve. Pin, then baste the under cuff and interfacing to the lower edge of the sleeve, matching markings and seams. (Fold the upper cuff back out of the way.) Stitch from the sleeve side, overlapping a few stitches at the starting point. Trim the interfacing seam allowance close to the stitching; trim the under cuff seam allowance to 1/8 inch and the sleeve seam allowance to 1/4 inch.

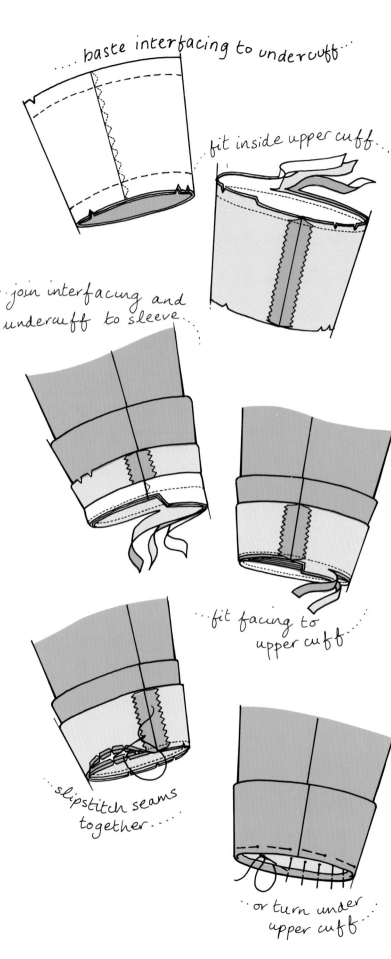

baste interfacing to under cuff

fit inside upper cuff

join interfacing and under cuff to sleeve

...fit facing to upper cuff

...slipstitch seams together...

...or turn under upper cuff...

Cut off the corners where seams cross and clip into any curved seam allowance. Press, then press seam open. Cut a sleeve facing about 3 inches deep, using the sleeve pattern as a guide. (The facing must not be deeper than the cuff.) Stitch the ends together, then press the seam and press it open. Pin and baste the facing to the free edge of the upper cuff, matching markings and seams. Stitch, overlapping a few stitches at the starting point. Trim seam allowance to 1/4 inch and cut off corners and clip into seam allowance. Press, then press the seam open. Pin cuff sections together just above stitching lines, and slipstitch open seams of the two cuffs together, allowing sufficient ease in the upper cuff for it to fit smoothly over the fold of the interfacing and under cuff. This prevents the under cuff from slipping out of place at the top. Finish the free edge of the facing, then turn the facing into the sleeve and pin the free edge to the sleeve. Finish by hand.

Where a facing is not used, turn under a seam allowance on the upper cuff, then turn the edge over the seam, allowing ease for the upper cuff to fit smoothly. Hem in place by hand.

FRENCH CUFF

This cuff, also known as a button link cuff, is cut from two pieces of fabric, twice the depth of the finished cuff. Position cuff pieces with right sides together. Position interfacing on wrong side of cuff, and baste in place. Cut off corners of interfacing to reduce bulk. Stitch round three sides, leaving open the edge that will join the sleeve. Take a stitch across the corners as you pivot the fabric. Remove basting, press, and grade seam allowances.

Press. Turn cuff to right side. Pull out corners to square them. Ease the under cuff slightly to the underside at the seamline and baste. Press.

Mark the position for the opening in the sleeve, and finish it with a continuous bound placket before stitching underarm seams. (See page 133). Turn the sleeve to wrong side and make two lines of gathering stitches around the lower edge, just inside the seamline. Loosen the upper tension slightly. Leave thread ends long enough to draw up.

Turn the sleeve to the right side. On the right side, wind the thread ends around a pin, forming a figure eight at each end of the stitching. Place the cuff over the sleeve, with the upper cuff and right side of the sleeve together. Pin the upper cuff

and interfacing to the sleeve, matching markings and extending the placket binding beyond each end of the cuff. Working with the wrong side of the sleeve toward you, draw both threads at the same time and gather the sleeve to fit the cuff. Distribute the fullness evenly, then pin the sleeve to the cuff at close intervals. Pull the gathering threads to the underside and tie. Fold the placket binding back over the gathers, and pin. Baste the cuff to the sleeve. Stitch from the sleeve side, just beyond the first line of gathering stitches. Trim the interfacing close to the stitching and the cuff seam allowance to ⅛ inch and the sleeve to ¼ inch. Press the seam, then turn the cuff away from the sleeve and press seam allowance toward cuff. Fold the cuff smoothly through the center. Slip the fingers of the left hand between the fold to be certain there is enough ease in the upper cuff for it to fit smoothly over the fold of the interfacing and under cuff. Pin through all thicknesses, about ½ inch above the fold. Fold the free edge of the cuff under for ¼ inch, and pin it to the sleeve at the stitching line, enclosing the gathered seam allowance inside the cuff. Slipstitch in place. Check positions for buttonholes, and insert cuff links.

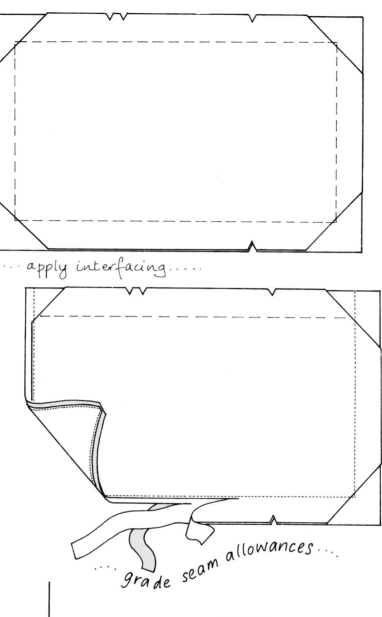

.... apply interfacing ....

.... grade seam allowances ....

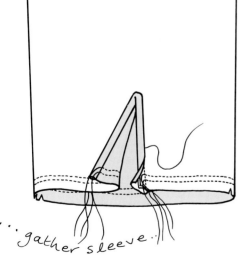

... gather sleeve ...

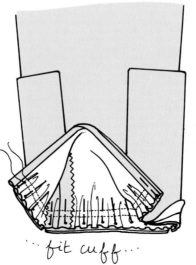

... fit cuff ...

... fold cuff and slipstitch ....

135

Belts and belt carriers

Belts can be the focal point of an outfit, providing a contrast in colour and texture, or they can be an integral part of the design, made of matching fabric. Often you can alter the appearance of an outfit, simply by changing the belt.

STYLES FOR BELTS

The simplest belt is a narrow tie belt, cut on the lengthwise grain of the fabric, with a finished width of 1 to 1½ inches and long enough to tie or knot at the waist. A wider, sash belt, cut on the bias with pointed ends, makes a bolder statement, or a braided belt, made from three lengths of tubing and knotted at the end, adds a delicate touch.

The classic, buckled belt, used for coats, dresses, skirts, and pants, has a pointed end and is stiffened with "belting" or non-woven interfacing, whereas fitted dresses often demand a softer style, with buttoned ends. Another alternative is a shaped belt, curved to fit just below the waist.

A cummerbund, stiffened at each side, can be adapted to suit many outfits.

When choosing a belt style, first check to see what types of ready-made belt suit you; if you are short-waisted, you may not want to wear a deep, tight-fitting belt, which will further shorten the distance from your bustline to your waist. Similarly, low, loose-fitting belts do not suit large hips.

Check belt positions carefully at the fitting stage, to make sure that they sit well on the garment.

BUCKLES

You will find a wide range of buckles in notions departments, including styles to cover yourself. Buckles are available with or without prongs, in a wide range of finishes, and as metal forms for covering.

Buckles without prongs can simply be stitched to the end of the belt. With prongs, you have to make an eyelet or buttonhole in the belt to slip the prong through.

Choose the buckle before making the belt; you can make a belt to any width, but there may be a limited choice of widths of buckle available to you.

NARROW TIE BELT
Cut the belt to the finished length plus seam allowance, and four times the finished width.

Fold the fabric in half lengthwise, through the center, right sides together, and pin. Baste through the center. Stitch ¹⁄₁₆ inch from the basting, toward the cut edge. The seam allowance is very slightly narrower than the finished

belt, to allow the seam allowance to fit smoothly inside the finished belt. Press, fold back one seam allowance, and press seam open. Clip off corners of seam allowance at ends. Trim off one seam allowance close to stitching if fabric is bulky. Turn right side out, fold on stitching line, baste and press. Turn in raw edges at ends and slipstitch together.

... baste .... stitch.....

... turn right side out ....

BELT WITH STIFFENING
Cut belting to waist measurement plus 4 inches. Cut fabric on the lengthwise grain, 1 inch longer than belting and twice the width plus seam allowances. Fasten a safety pin on the right side of the fabric about 1½ inches from the shaped end. (This is used later to turn belt right side out.)

Wrap the fabric around the belting, wrong side out, and use the zipper foot to stitch in place, close to the belting. Press seam.

Move fabric around the belting,

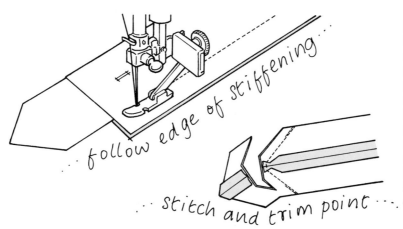

... follow edge of stiffening ...

... stitch and trim point ...

bringing the seam to the center. Press seam open, then trim the seam allowances to ¼ inch. Stitch the point barely outside the edge of the belting and reverse stitch at each end. Trim seam edges to ¼ inch and withdraw the belting. Use the safety pin to turn fabric right side out, then insert the belting again, keeping seam down center back and easing belting to point of belt. Topstitch if desired, then sew on buckle.

TOPSTITCHED, INTERFACED BELT

Interfacing is easier to handle than belting, and is a suitable stiffening for soft belts, on raincoats, and on tied coat belts. Topstitching helps to hold the shape of the belt.

Use medium- or heavy-weight, iron-on interfacing. Cut to twice the width and the same length as the finished belt. Cut fabric for belt to the same measurements, adding a seam allowance all around. Position interfacing on wrong side of fabric and press in place, leaving a seam allowance all around. Fold

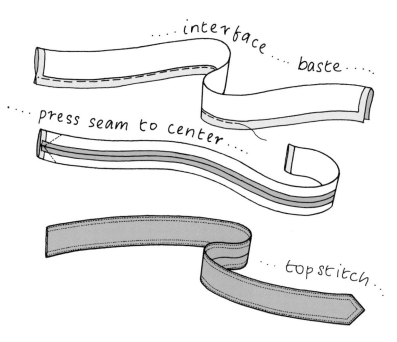

fabric in half, right sides facing, and join long raw edges of belt. Press, then center seam down back of belt and press again. Stitch seam at pointed end of belt. Turn belt right side out. Press, baste, and topstitch all around edge of belt: position stitching close to folded edge, and then ¼ inch inside the first line. Stitch end of belt to buckle. For a tie belt, turn in and slipstitch raw edges at end of belt before topstitching. Extra rows of topstitching may be added if desired.

LINED SOFT BELT

Cut fabric on lengthwise grain, 4 inches longer than waist measurement and twice width of finished belt plus seam allowance. Fold lengthwise, wrong sides together, and crease. Cut interlining of lawn, lining, or non-woven interfacing, the length of the fabric and twice the finished width of the belt. Crease lengthwise through center, and shape one end to a point. Clip off the end of the point to eliminate bulk when turned through. Place folded edge of interlining along crease on wrong

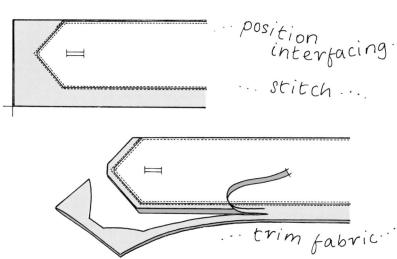

side of belt, with point of interlining ¼ inch from the end. Stitch in place along each side and around the point. Press. Fasten a safety pin through the lining and fabric near the shaped end. This will be used later to turn the belt right side out. Fold the belt, right sides together, and pin the seam edges together. Stitch just outside the edge of the interlining around the shaped end and down the side. Trim, press, and turn right side out, using the safety pin. Fold on stitching line and press. Topstitch if desired. Attach buckle or buttons.

SHAPED BELT

Cut belt and lining from the same fabric, allowing ⅝ inch seams. Use two layers of heavy interfacing, cut to the size of the finished belt. Make lines of zig-zag stitch across interfacing to hold layers together.

Staystitch around edge of top section of belt, in the seam allowance ¼ inch from seamline. Staystitch lining just outside seamline. Lay out top belt fabric on a flat surface and position interfacing on top. Pin through center, and wrap fabric over interfacing, working from center to outer edge. Clip into seam if necessary. Herringbone stitch seam allowance to interfacing. Press.

Trim seam allowance of lining to ⅜ inch on all edges except the straight end where the buckle will be fixed. Clip and notch seam allowances, then turn under and press; place lining over the belt, wrong sides together, and pin. Slipstitch by hand to finish. Add buckle.

FITTING THE BUCKLE

To fit the buckle to the end of the belt, first overcast the raw edges by hand or machine.

Allow about 2 inches for turning under at the end. If there is a prong, make an eyelet for it, 2 inches from the end, by piercing the fabric with a stiletto or stitch ripper, or other sharp point, then working buttonhole stitch all around, to finish the hole neatly. Slip the buckle onto the belt, and slip the prong through the hole.

Sew the end of the belt to the back with two rows of stitching, reverse stitching at each side for extra strength.

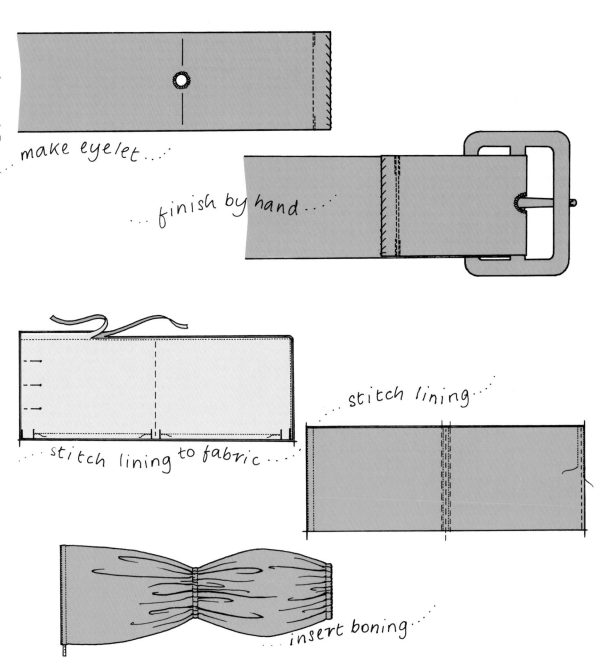

make eyelet...

...finish by hand...

...stitch lining

...stitch lining to fabric...

...insert boning...

CUMMBERBUND WITH BONING

For a cummerbund, the fabric is cut on the bias, and the belt is lined. Use matching fabric, or a softer silk or satin for lining heavy fabrics.

Cut the fabric and lining to the same size, making it the length of the waist measurement plus 2 inches for overlap and seams and about 9 inches wide.

Mark the position for the boning at the side opposite the fastening by folding the cummerbund in half across its width, adjusting the fold

so that the front section is 1 inch longer than the back (because the front waist measurement is always longer than the back waist). Baste along the foldline to mark it. Position lining on top fabric, right sides together and raw edges matching. Pin on the seamline. Stitch along top edge of cummerbund and down one end. Along lower edge, leave ¾ inch for the opening in the casing, then stitch to within ⅜ inch of side boning mark, leaving a ¾ inch

opening, and stitch to end, leaving seam allowance and opening of casing unstitched.

Grade the seam allowances, leaving both seam allowances ¼ inch wide at openings. Press. Turn cummerbund right side out. Fold on stitching line, baste and press. At the open end, turn seam edges to inside for ½ inch and pin. Baste and press. Stitch from right side, close to the edge. Stitch again ⅜ inch from the first row of stitching to form the casing for the

boning. Baste and stitch the other two casings. Tie all threads.

Cut three pieces of boning 3½ inches long, and slip into casing; work them up to top edge. Make two rows of stitching across top of casing, through boning, to hold top in place. Gather fabric onto boning, turn in seam allowances and stitch across lower end of casing in same way. Slipstitch folded edges at end of casing. Pull all threads to underside and tie. Stitch four hooks and eyes in place.

BELTS TO SUIT YOUR SHAPE

Sometimes the position of the waistline or waist-band dictates the position of a belt. But clever use of belts can flatter your figure and improve the look of a garment.

For example, if you have large hips, avoid low belts, which will only emphasize a pear-shaped figure. If you have a short waist (your waist is high in relation to your bust and hips), you may be able to fit a belt below your natural waistline to give better proportions. Your existing wardrobe should give you some guidance as to what suits you.

You can also use belts to alter the look of a loose fitting dress, or to add extra style to a straight coat or jacket.

BELT CARRIERS

Choose between simple thread carriers, for an inconspicuous finish, or fabric belt carriers made to match or contrast with the garment. Where possible, fit the ends of carriers into a seamline, for extra strength. Fabric carriers may be topstitched in place for a more conspicuous finish.

crossover belt carriers

cummerbund

simple sash

buckle belt

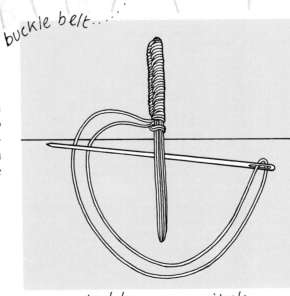

work blanket stitch

BLANKET-STITCH CARRIERS

Pin-mark positions of belt carriers at side seams, above and below the beltline. Use a double strand of thread and knot the ends together. On the underside of garment, take two backstitches to tie the thread at the top marking. Bring the needle through to the right side, then take a stitch at the opposite marking, leaving enough slack in the thread to fit over the belt. Work back and forth two or three times to make a group of strands of the same tension. Blanket stitch over the strands of thread, drawing up the stitches firmly. Fasten the thread on the underside with a couple of backstitches.

CHAIN-STITCH CARRIERS

Mark ends of carrier, and use a double thread. Knot and take a couple of backstitches to secure at one of the marked points, on the wrong side of the garment. Bring the needle through to the right side, then take a small stitch and draw the thread partway through, leaving a 2 inch loop. Hold the loop open with the needle. Reach through the loop with the thumb and one finger of the left hand and grasp the needle thread, pulling it through to form a new loop. Draw the released loop down to the fabric. Make the chain the length required, then pass the needle through the last loop to lock the chain. Stitch through the fabric and fasten the thread with two backstitches on the underside.

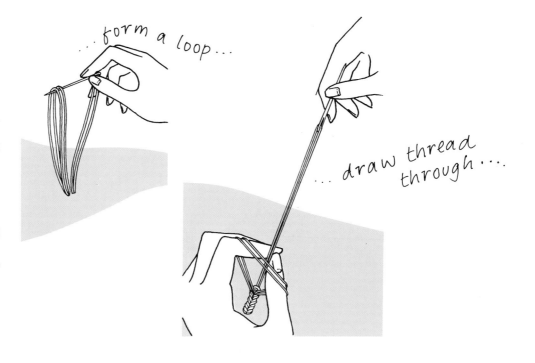

... form a loop ...

... draw thread through ....

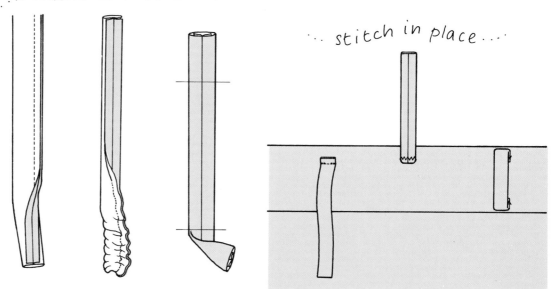

... make carriers ....

... stitch in place ....

FABRIC CARRIERS

Plan the position and size of the carriers if they are not given with the pattern.

Cut a strip of fabric on the lengthwise grain, twice the finished width plus an extra ½ inch for seam allowances, and long enough to make the number of carriers required. Fold strip lengthwise and stitch ¼ inch from the edge. Trim seam allowances to ⅛ inch. Ease the seam to center of strip and press open with fingers. Stitch across one end.

Turn strip right side out, pushing fabric through with an orange stick. Turn the stitched end to the inside and trim off. Ease seam to center and press. Cut each carrier long enough to fit over the belt with ease, plus 1 inch for seam allowances. Fold under ½ inch at each end and press.

Mark the position for the finished end of the carrier on the garment. Place the carrier right side up, with the cut end ⅛ inch inside the marking. Stitch ⅛ inch from the edge. Reverse stitch at each end. Do not stitch beyond ends of carrier. Trim the end close to the stitching and press.

Fold carrier back on the stitching line and press. Stitch ⅛ inch from the fold, using a closely spaced zig-zag stitch. Finish the opposite end in the same way.

Pockets

The choice of pocket depends on the style of the garment and the current fashion: changing the style of a pocket, or adding pockets to patterns that did not have any, is an easy way to adapt a pattern to suit your needs.

The simplest style is a rectangular patch pocket, topstitched in place on the garment: for extra style, you can add buttoned flaps, or shape the pocket, adding a pleat for a more military look. Other styles include pockets with bound edges, made in the same way as a buttonhole; and stand pockets, with just a narrow band of fabric showing on the right side, across the top of the pocket; welt pockets are similar to stand pockets, but the strip of fabric

edging the top of the pocket is cut separately from the rest of the pocket, rather than being cut in a single piece, so it is more suitable for heavy fabrics and tailored garments. Pockets may also be stitched into the side seam of a garment: if the pattern you are using does not include a pocket, it is quite easy to take the pocket pieces from another pattern and adapt the shape to suit the garment you are making.

The instructions given here are for pockets cut on the straight grain, with the opening following the grain of the fabric: the opening may also be angled, but it is advisable to develop your skills on straight pockets first. Always make a practice pocket in the same fabric before working on the garment.

UNLINED PATCH POCKET

Cut the pocket piece the width and depth desired, plus seam allowances and a hem at the top. Curve the lower corners if required.

Fold under ¼ inch across the top edge of the pocket. Stitch near the fold; press. Fold the top hem to the right side. Pin and stitch across the ends of the hem, on the seamline. Press. Stitch around the curve of the pocket, within the seam allowance, using a loose upper tension and leaving long ends. Trim seam allowance to within ¼ inch of the stitching, and clip across corners at the top of the hem.

Turn hem right side out, pull out corners, turn under seam allowance around pocket piece, and press. Draw up bobbin thread, easing the fabric to give a smooth curve. Notch seam allowance to remove bulk so that the seam will lie flat. Press.

Pin the hem in place at the top and slipstitch.

Pin and baste the pocket over the markings on the right side of the garment. Stitch close to the edge, or slipstitch in place. Pull threads to the underside and tie. Remove basting and press.

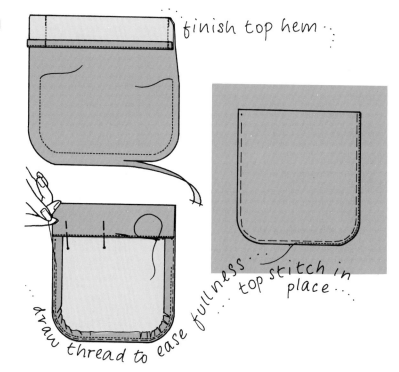

finish top hem

draw thread to ease fullness

top stitch in place

MARKING POCKET POSITIONS

1 Plan the position of pockets before cutting out the garment: mark the position of the pocket on the pattern, avoiding darts and curved seamlines (patch pockets may be positioned over straight seamlines, in loose fitting jackets, for example)

2 Mark the position of the pocket with tailor's tacks before removing the pattern from the fabric.

3 Mark patch pocket positions with lines of machine basting down the sides and across the lower edge of the pocket. Mark position for flap, if required.

4 For bound, stand, and welted pockets, place an underlay of batiste or non-woven interfacing under the stitching line to reinforce the opening and retain the shape of the pocket.

  Cut the underlay about 1½ inches longer than the pocket opening and 3 inches deep. Center it over the markings on the wrong side of the garment, and pin in place.

5 From the right side, machine or hand baste across the ends of the pocket to mark the width. Then machine baste through the center, extending the stitching about ¾ inch beyond the ends. Use a contrasting thread so that it will be easy to see when you come to remove it.

6 On the wrong side, draw pencil lines on each side of, and ¼ inch from, the center basting to mark the stitching line. This distance may vary, depending on the style of the garment and size of pocket.

PATCH POCKET WITH FLAP

Cut the pocket and lining the depth and width of the finished pocket plus seam allowance. Pin lining to the pocket, right sides together, and stitch around the pocket, leaving 2½ inches to turn through. Trim seam allowances, clip corners, press, and turn right side out. Ease lining under slightly at stitching line, baste and press again. Slipstitch open edges together. Pin and hand baste the pocket over the markings on the right side of the garment. Baste a second line, ⅜ inch from the edge to mark the stitching line. Use a seam gauge to keep the line even. Topstitch in place around three sides. Tie ends.

For the flap, cut flap and facing the width of the pocket and depth required, plus seam allowance. Cut interfacing if desired. Assemble flap, stitching around three sides. Trim seams, clip across corners (or cut notches if corners are curved), and turn right side out. Ease lining under slightly at stitching line and baste. Press. Pin the free edges together and baste about ⅝ inch from edge. Topstitch around flap (optional). Pin and baste flap to garment, above pocket, so the seamline is ½ inch above the pocket. Stitch. Pull threads to the underside and tie. Press seam. Turn under the cut edge and slipstitch in place. Press.

POCKET IN A SEAM

Cut two pocket pieces, allowing ⅝ inch seam allowance all around. Mark pocket opening on seam line of garment. Staystitch front section of garment just within seam allowance between marked points. Pin and baste front pocket section to front of garment, taking just under ⅝ inch seam allowance. Trim seam allowance down seam of pocket piece and finish raw edges. Repeat for back, but do not trim seam.

Pin, baste and stitch side seams, beginning and ending stitching at pocket opening. Press seam open and press pocket toward front of garment. Stitch around pocket, then finish raw edges together.

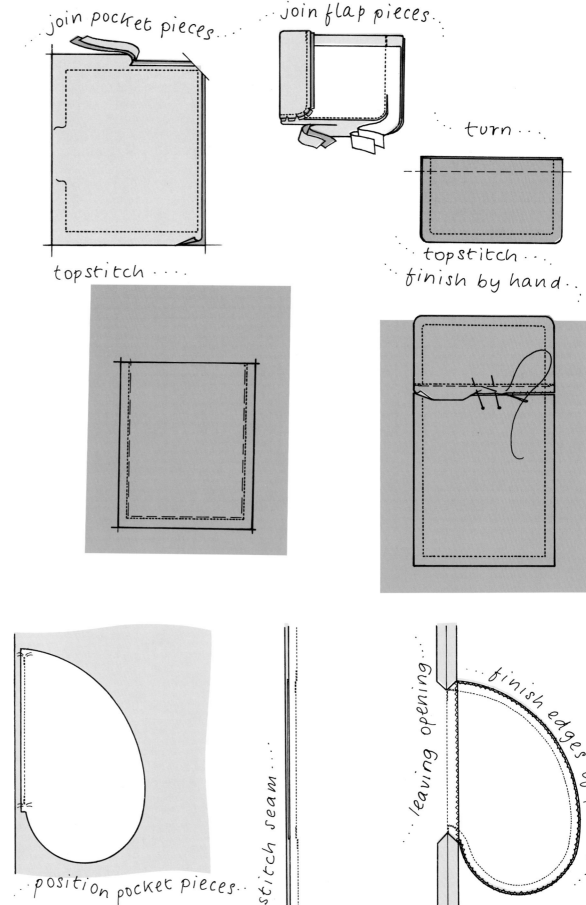

join pocket pieces...

join flap pieces...

turn...

topstitch...

topstitch....

finish by hand...

position pocket pieces...

stitch seam....

leaving opening...

finish edges of pocket

BOUND POCKET

Cut one pocket section to measure the depth of the pocket plus 2 inches, and 1 inch wider than the opening. Cut another section the depth of the pocket plus seam allowance and 1 inch wider than the opening.

On the right side of the garment, place the long section of the pocket, right side down, extending the edge for 1½ inches below the marking. Pin. Baste if necessary. On the wrong side, stitch around the pocket opening, following the guidelines. Use a short stitch, and begin stitching at the center of one side. Pivot the fabric on the needle at the corners, and take the same number of stitches across each end. Overlap the stitching at the starting point. Remove the basted guidelines at the ends and press. Cut between the two lines of stitching, through all thicknesses, to within ½ inch of the ends, then cut diagonally to each corner. Do not cut through the stitching. Draw the pocket through the opening to the underside. Pull out the triangular ends to square the corners. Press the triangular ends and seam allowances along the sides away from the opening. Fold the pocket section to form a pleat on each side which meets at the center and covers the opening. Check both the right and wrong side of the garment to be sure the pleats are even in width. Baste along folds, then overcast the folded edges together. Baste to the raw edge of the pocket section and press.

Place garment right side up, fold back edge, and stitch the seam allowance to the pleats: first stitch across the triangular ends, on the original stitching line, then stitch across the seam at the top, just a hair's breadth from the original stitching line. The side stitching crosses the end stitching and squares the corners. Place the second pocket section under the bottom seam, right side up; then stitch the seam allowance to the pleat and the lower pocket section in one operation. Turn down the lower pocket section, and remove all basting except the overcasting

holding the pleats together. Press.

Turn down the upper section of the pocket and pin it to the lower section. Place the garment, right side up, on the machine. Fold back the edge of the garment and stitch the two pocket sections together. Stitch across the triangle at one end, around the pocket bag, and across the triangle at the opposite end. Stitch the triangular ends on the original line of stitching. Tie thread ends. Trim seam allowances evenly and finish edges. Remove all basting and press.

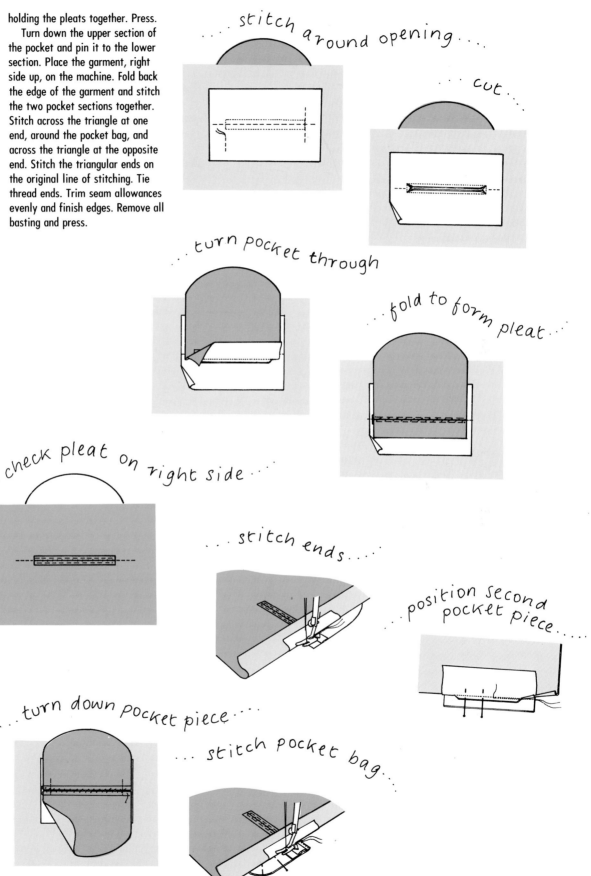

STAND POCKET

Cut a piece of fabric on the lengthwise grain, twice the pocket depth plus twice the depth of the stand, plus seam allowances, and 1 inch wider than the opening. Crease the pocket section 1 inch above the center.

Place the pocket section on the right side of the garment, right sides together. Align the crease with the marking on the garment so the long end extends below the marking. Pin and baste.

On the wrong side, stitch around the pocket opening, using a short stitch and overlapping stitches at starting point. Remove basted guidelines and press.

Cut between the two lines of stitching, through all thicknesses, to within ½ inch of the ends, then cut diagonally to each of the four corners. Do not cut through the stitching. Draw the pocket through the opening to the wrong side. Pull out the triangles at the ends to square the corners. Press the triangular ends and seam allowances along the side away from the opening. Fold the lower section of the pocket to form a pleat to cover the opening. Check both the right and wrong sides to be sure that the pleat is even and covers the opening. Hand baste on the folded edge, carrying the basting to each end of the pocket. Press the folded edge. Overcast the fold to the top edge of the opening (pin the upper section of the pocket to keep it out of the way). With garment right side up, fold back edge, and stitch seam allowances to the lower pocket section to hold the pleat in place. Turn down the upper section of the pocket and pin it to the lower section. Press the top seam open. Place garment, right side up, on machine; fold back the edge and stitch the two pocket sections together. Stitch across the triangle at one end, around the pocket bag, and across the triangle at the other end. Tie thread ends. Trim seam allowances evenly and finish the edges. Remove all bastings and press. Trim underlay to within ½ inch of stitching.

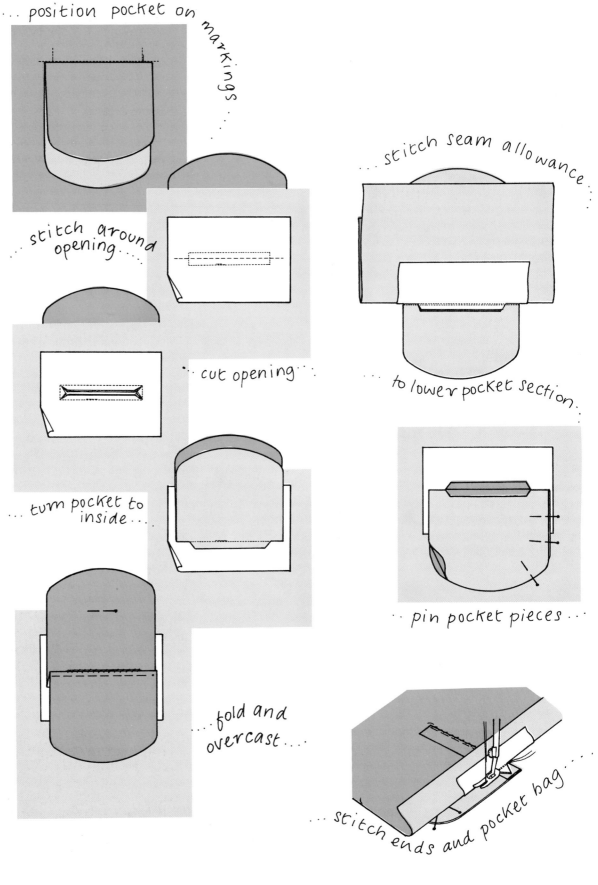

... position pocket on markings ...

... stitch around opening ...

... cut opening ...

... turn pocket to inside ...

... fold and overcast ...

... stitch seam allowance ...

... to lower pocket section ...

... pin pocket pieces ...

... stitch ends and pocket bag ...

WELT POCKET

Cut a welt twice the depth of the finished welt and the width of the pocket opening, plus seam allowance all around. Interface the welt, then fold in half, right sides together, and stitch across ends. Trim seam allowances and press. Turn right side out and press. Machine stitch ¼ inch from the lower edge to hold layers of fabric together.

Cut one pocket section the depth of the pocket plus 2 inches and 1 inch wider than the opening. Cut another section the depth of the pocket plus seam allowance, and 1 inch wider than opening. With garment right side up, position welt below pocket marking, right side down, with raw edge on center line and ends matching guidelines. Pin and baste in place. On right side of garment, place upper pocket section (the long one) over marking, right sides together, extending the edge for 1 inch below the center marking. Pin. On the wrong side of the garment, stitch around the pocket opening, following the guidelines. Use a short stitch, and begin stitching at the center of the upper side; pivot at the corners and take the same number of stitches across each end. Overlap stitches at starting point. Check that stitching does not extend beyond the welt. Remove basting and press.

From underside, cut between lines of stitching, through all thicknesses, to within ½ inch of ends, and clip diagonally to the corners. Turn pocket through the opening to the underside. Pull out triangular ends to square corners, and turn welt up on the right side to cover the opening. Press the triangular ends and seam allowances along the sides away from the opening. Turn extended lower edge of pocket away from opening and press. Pin upper section of pocket out of the way.

Place garment right side up and fold back the lower edge. Place lower pocket section under the opening, right side up, keeping cut edges even along the lower edge of the opening. Turn back seam allowances and stitch the pocket

sections together close to previous stitching line, beginning and ending the stitching at the outer edges of the fabric. Press. Turn down the lower pocket section and press. Turn down upper pocket section and pin the two sections together. Trim both sections to the same length. Fold back the edge of garment and position it right side up. Stitch the pocket sections together, stitching across triangle, around bag, and across triangle at opposite end. Stitch triangular ends on the original line of stitching. Tie the threads. Remove all basting and press.

Finish seams as required. Trim underlay to within ½ inch of stitching. On right side, slipstitch the ends of the welt to the garment.

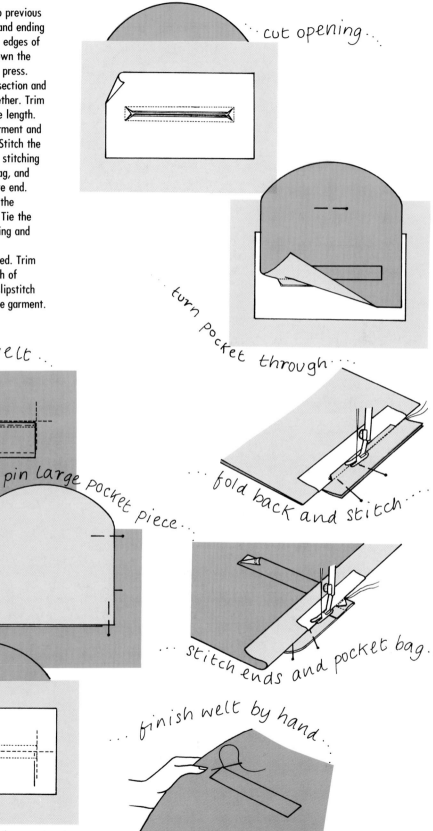

cut opening

turn pocket through

position welt

fold back and stitch

pin large pocket piece

stitch ends and pocket bag

stitch around pocket opening

finish welt by hand

Looking at patterns

Once you have some experience at dressmaking, you can start to develop your own designs, adapting simple dressmaking patterns which you know fit you well. On this and the following pages are some ideas for making simple alterations or additions to patterns. Bear in mind your figure proportions when altering a pattern: emphasize good points; but avoid drawing attention to bad points.

...take a simple dress...

FITTED DRESS

This simple dress with a plain, round neckline, gently fitted to the waist, can form the basis for any number of adaptations. For evening wear, use soft crepe and bands of satin at the cuffs and dropped waistline, with a flowing pleated skirt. Other variations can be made up in fabrics to suit the occasion: a simple shirtwaist dress, to knee or mid-calf length, or a softly fitted dress with a slightly gathered skirt can be equally appropriate for formal or everyday wear.

CLASSIC COAT

A single-breasted coat takes on a stylish look with the addition of a velvet collar and pocket flaps; the crow's feet at the point of the darts add extra detail. For a light jacket, reduce the length of the coat and either widen the lapels for a double-breasted finish or add patch pockets and flaps to create a safari-style jacket.

...or a classic coat......

T-SHIRT TOP

A basic T-shirt top pattern can be given a variety of stylish finishes: add a topstitched facing in matching or contrasting fabric, on the right side of the garment around the neck and cuffs; or make a deep, slashed opening down the center front (see page 56). For a softer finish, add fullness to the sleeves and a Peter Pan collar for a pretty neck finish.

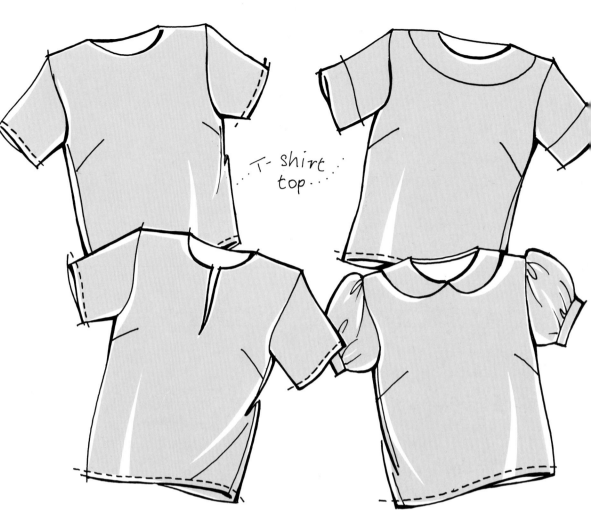

T-shirt top

PENCIL SKIRT

A slim-fitting skirt can be seamed and pleated for an alternative daytime look. On the right and far right, the skirt takes on a casual look, particularly effective in denim, chambray, or drill: patch pockets, topstitched in place on either side of the back opening, or a gathered skirt fitted to a yoke, both emphasize a slim-hipped figure.

pencil skirt

blazer-style jacket

straight cut pants

BLAZER-STYLE JACKET

A topstitched finish gives extra interest to this simple, collarless, blazer-style jacket. The jacket takes on a classic designer look with a square-cut front opening, gilt buttons, and a braid trim. Emphasize a slim midriff with a short, cropped, double-breasted version of the jacket, made in a silky fabric for evening wear.

STRAIGHT-CUT PANTS

A good fit is particularly important with a simple pants pattern like the one on the far left. Follow all the instructions for fitting the pattern and the garment before assembling. Give the pants a more tailored look with welt pockets and cuffs, or for evening wear, use silk or crepe, adding extra fullness down the length of the garment. For summer adapt the pattern for Bermuda shorts, with cuffs and patch pockets.

149

6 *Special sewing techniques*

The fabrics you use and the type of garment you are making mean that you have to use some special techniques for professional results. For example, stretch fabrics need a particular type of stitch; with fine fabrics you have to prevent the layers from slipping around as you stitch them; and with pile fabrics there is extra bulk to cope with. Tailored garments and children's clothes also demand careful stitching.

Knits

Knitted fabrics, with varying degrees of stretch, are suitable for a wide range of garments. Choose patterns with simple, uncluttered lines, which are designated as suitable for knits. Some patterns, in which the amount of stretch in the fabric is important to the fit of the garment, give a stretch gauge on the pattern; this indicates how much a certain sized piece of fabric should stretch.

LOOKING AT KNITS
Patterned, ribbed, bouclé, and plain knits all require careful handling to retain their stretchy quality.

PREPARING THE FABRIC AND CUTTING OUT
Many knitted fabrics should be washed before they are cut, to remove finish and pre-shrink the fabric. Fold in half lengthwise, square the ends on a table top, and baste the edges together before shrinking.

Always use a "with nap" pattern and fabric allowance. Arrange pattern pieces so they run in the same direction, following a straight rib of the fabric rather than the lengthwise grain. If there is a heavy center crease down the fabric, it is almost impossible to press out. Try to avoid positioning pattern pieces over it; add extra seams to center front and center back of a garment if necessary. Use fine pins, positioning them within seam allowances. Do not allow fabric to hang over the edge of the cutting table, as it may stretch. Use sharp, heavy-bladed scissors. Cut notches outward.

Use hand basting and tailor's tacks to mark features like button positions and darts. Tracing wheel and dressmaker's carbon paper are not effective on most knits.

NEEDLE AND THREAD
Use a ball-point needle for knitted fabrics. These are designed with a slightly rounded point, to slip between the fibers without piercing them (which would cause snags). Coated needles are available to run smoothly through knitted fibers. Choose an appropriate size for the weight of the fabric (see page 16).

With loosely knitted fabrics, use a flat-fronted, no-snag foot, if you have one, or wrap a ¼ inch wide strip of tape around the front of a standard foot, to prevent the "toes" from catching in the fabric. Adjust the pressure of the presser foot if necessary, so that it does not mark the fabric or cause the top layer to drag. Most knits require medium pressure.

Use a strong thread, preferably with some degree of elasticity. For most knitted fabrics, cotton-wrapped polyester is preferable to cotton, since it is stronger. Avoid using harsh synthetic threads on soft cotton or wool jersey knits.

PRESSING HINTS
Regulate the temperature of the iron according to the fiber content. Never use the iron directly on the fabric. Protect with a damp pressing cloth of thin cotton. Use a softly padded ironing board. Trim as much bulk as possible from seams, darts, and hems before pressing.

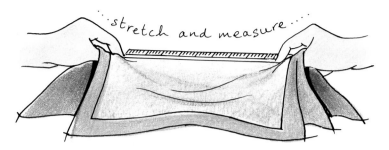
stretch and measure

narrow zig-zag

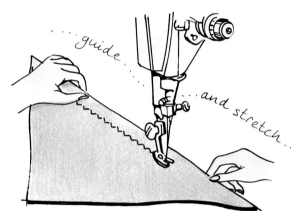
guide
and stretch

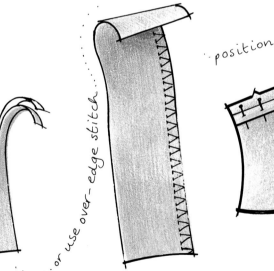
stitch .... then trim

or use over-edge stitch

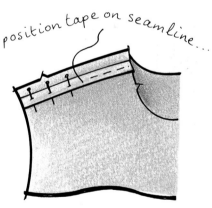
position tape on seamline

USING A STRETCH GAUGE

Knitted fabrics have varying degrees of stretch – and they stretch different amounts along the length and across the width of the fabric.

To check the stretch of a fabric before buying, make the following test. Fold the fabric along its length and grasp it firmly in one hand. Measure and mark a set distance – 4 inches – and grasp the fold with the other hand at the measured point. Stretch the fabric as far as it will go without straining, and measure the stretched marked length between your hands. Repeat across the fabric if necessary.

STITCHING KNITTED FABRIC

For most seams, a narrow zig-zag stitch is best, as it gives a slight degree of stretch to the seam. Experiment with various stitch widths and lengths to see which suits the fabric, giving a similar degree of stretch. Normally, a stitch width of 1 to 2 and length of 15 to 20 is appropriate. Guide the fabric with both hands, stretching it slightly as you stitch.

FINISHING SEAMS IN KNITTED FABRIC

Many knitted fabrics do not require finishing: if you do wish to finish the edges, use one of the following methods.

For a mock over-edged, double-stitched seam, use a straight stretch or narrow zig-zag stitch to stitch on the seamline, then stitch again, just outside the seamline, using blind-stitch, over-edge stretch stitch, multi-stitch zig-zag, multi-stretch zig-zag or plain zig-zag if your machine does not have the other facilities. Trim seam allowances close to stitching and press.

Alternatively, stitch the seam as before, then trim seam allowance and finish the edges together with an over-edge stitch.

For a quick finish, trim the seam allowances to ¼ inch or less and stitch and finish the seam in one operation, using overedge or over-edge stretch stitch.

TAPING SEAMS

Neckline, shoulder, and waistline seams usually need to be stayed by stitching straight seam binding or bias binding into the seam to control the amount of stretch. After basting the seamline, place the center of the stay tape on the seamline and stitch in place. Press seam as stitched, then press open.

INTERFACING

Collars, cuffs, and front openings are normally faced and interfaced in the same way as those in woven fabrics. Suitable interfacings include stretch, non-woven interfacing, sew-in or iron-on, and soft woven interfacing. Heavier interfacings may be used on heavier fabrics, particularly in tailored garments. To reduce the amount of stretch in some sections of the garment, such as collars and yokes, and to reduce bulk, a lining of taffeta, lining fabric, or other crisp fabric may be used.

BOUND, PIPED, AND CORDED EDGES

These finishes are frequently used on garments made from stretch fabrics, and eliminate the need for a facing. Use fabric strips cut lengthwise, crosswise, or on the bias, according to the amount of stretch and ease required and the amount of stretch in the fabric. Staystitch any curved edges, on garment necklines, for example, before finishing. Choose the method according to the finish required. The edge may also be topstitched: this is often done around the back of a neckline, to control the amount of stretch. Choose a straight stitch, narrow zig-zag stitch, or stretch stitch for the seams, according to the fabric you are using. On single knits, a straight stitch is normally used, to control the stretch and reduce the amount of distortion at necklines and armholes. Stretch the fabric as you stitch to maintain a bit of give.

BOUND EDGE

For a ¼ inch wide bound edge, cut a fabric strip 1¼ inches wide and finish one edge with overedge stitch. Trim the garment on seamline. Place bias strip over the garment with edges level and right sides facing. Stitch ¼ inch from edges. Press seam allowances open. Turn strip over one seam allowance and baste through center of binding. Stitch from wrong side, through seam allowance and finished edge of strip, 1/16 inch outside first stitching line. Remove basting and steam-press binding in place.

PIPED EDGE

Cut a strip 1½ inches wide and finish one edge as for "bound edge". Fold back the other edge ½ inch and press. Place the prepared strip right side down and position garment edge over it, right side down, so that raw edge of garment matches raw, folded edge of strip. Stitch ¼ inch from edges, through three layers of fabric. Fold strip to underside and steam press. Topstitch finished edge if required.

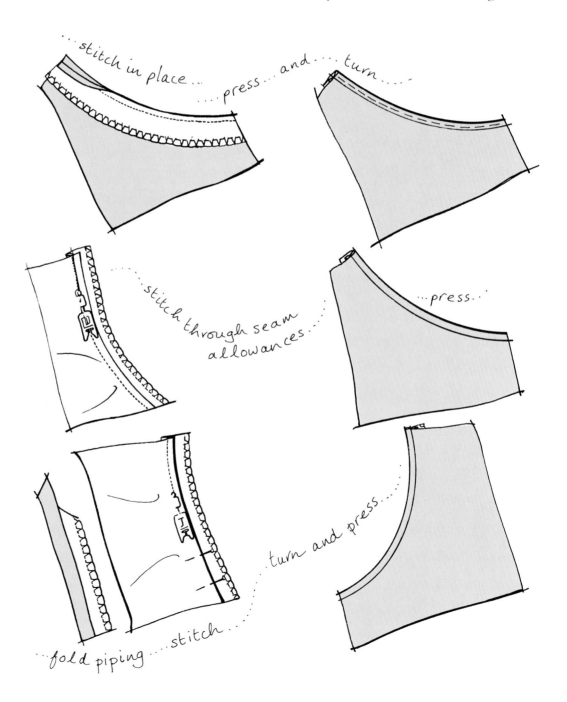

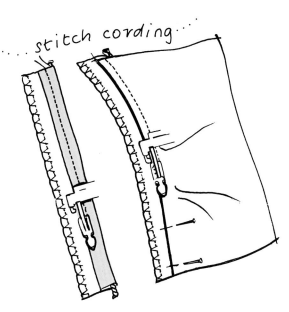

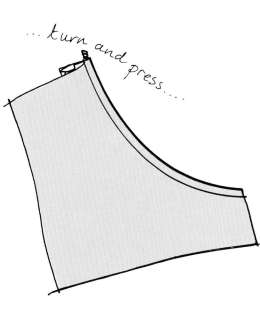

CORDED EDGE

For a corded edge, cut a fabric strip 1½ to 2 inches wide, according to the diameter of the piping cord. Fold the strip over cord, so that ¼ inch of strip extends beyond stitching line on one side and ¾ inch on the other. Baste in place. Finish wider edge of strip. Position edge of garment over corded strip as for bound edge, and stitch, using the zipper foot. Fold cording to edge of garment and press to finish as before.

READY-MADE COLLARS AND CUFFS

Bands of ribbing can be used to finish collars, waists, ankles, and cuffs on knitted garments. They may be sold as a circular band, which you can adjust to suit your needs if necessary, or you can make your own to length from strips of ribbed fabric, folding them in half lengthwise to make the band double thickness. The length is determined by the body measurement it is to fit or pass over and the amount of tension that you want on the band in wear. The seam allowances for both band and garment are ¼ inch. If you are cutting a band, make sure that the direction of greater stretch runs along the length of the band.

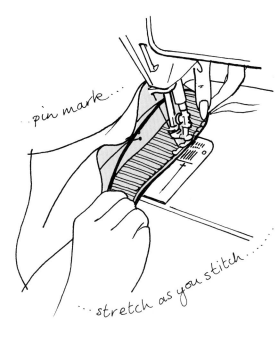

ATTACHING STRETCH BANDS

Join the ends of the band with a double-stitched seam and fold in half, right side out, if necessary. Pin seam allowances together. To make sure that the ease is evenly distributed, divide the ribbed band and the opening it is to be joined to into four equal parts and pin mark. With garment inside out, pin band to right side of garment with seam edges level, matching pin markings. Stitch with the band up, using an overedge stretch stitch to seam and finish at the same time. Stretch the fabric as you stitch, holding the seam in front of and behind the foot, but allowing the feed to carry the fabric under the foot. Stretch so that the edge of the garment matches the edge of the band. Steam-press the seam.

BLOCKING BANDS TO SHAPE

If the bands are fitted to a curved edge, on pocket flaps, deep necklines, and down front openings, for example, they have to be steam-pressed or blocked into shape.

- Trace the outline of the finished edge on a large piece of unbleached muslin. Pin this to a well-padded ironing board to use as a shaping guide.
- Cut the strip for the shaped band twice the finished width plus two ½ inch seam allowances. Cut, either lengthwise or crosswise: test a short strip to see which will hold the shape best.
- Baste the edges of the strip together, leaving one end of the basting thread long and unknotted. Press lightly to form a crease.

- Pin-mark the band at center and place center of band at center of marked shaping guide. Baste band to guide across center.
- Use the surface of the band that is upward as the underside in the garment, in case some shine develops during pressing.
- Using a damp cloth over the band, and working from the center basting, apply steam, stretch the outer edge of the band, and pin it along the cut edges, keeping the folded edge level with the marked line. Work on a short length at a time, easing the folded edge and stretching the cut edge. When the entire length is pinned, steam-press again to set the shape.

Tracksuit

ALTERNATIVES

Use a contrasting color for the stretch bands at neckline, wrists, waist, and ankles.

Add bands of contrasting color, or piece together blocks of fabric to make the tracksuit, joining the "patchwork" of pieces first.

SUITABLE FABRICS
Knitted fabrics only: sweatshirt knit, stretch terry cloth, cotton and synthetic jersey.

TO FIT
Size 12.

YOU WILL NEED
2¾ yds of 59-inch wide fabric
Thread
3⅝ yds of ready made ribbing for   cuffs and waistband
⅞ yd of 1-inch wide elastic

If you've never owned a tracksuit before, you'll wonder how you ever managed without one, once you've made this go-anywhere outfit. Whatever your favorite leisure activity – serious sport, pottering around in the garden, working at your sewing machine, or just relaxing with a good book – you'll find that this comfortable, practical garment is the ideal thing to wear. Stretch ribbing draws the cuffs and ankles in to fit and shapes the neckline. Make it in classic sweatshirt knit, or in a loosely woven cotton for a cooler version.

join front, back and sleeves......

......and ribbing

...pin mark cuff.......

...stretch as you stitch........

NOTE
A ⅝ inch seam allowance is included except where instructions state otherwise. Pin, baste, and stitch seams with right side facing and raw edges even. Finish seams as you work. Cut out pattern pieces and fabric following the diagrams on page 157. For patchwork version, piece blocks of fabric together as on page 156.

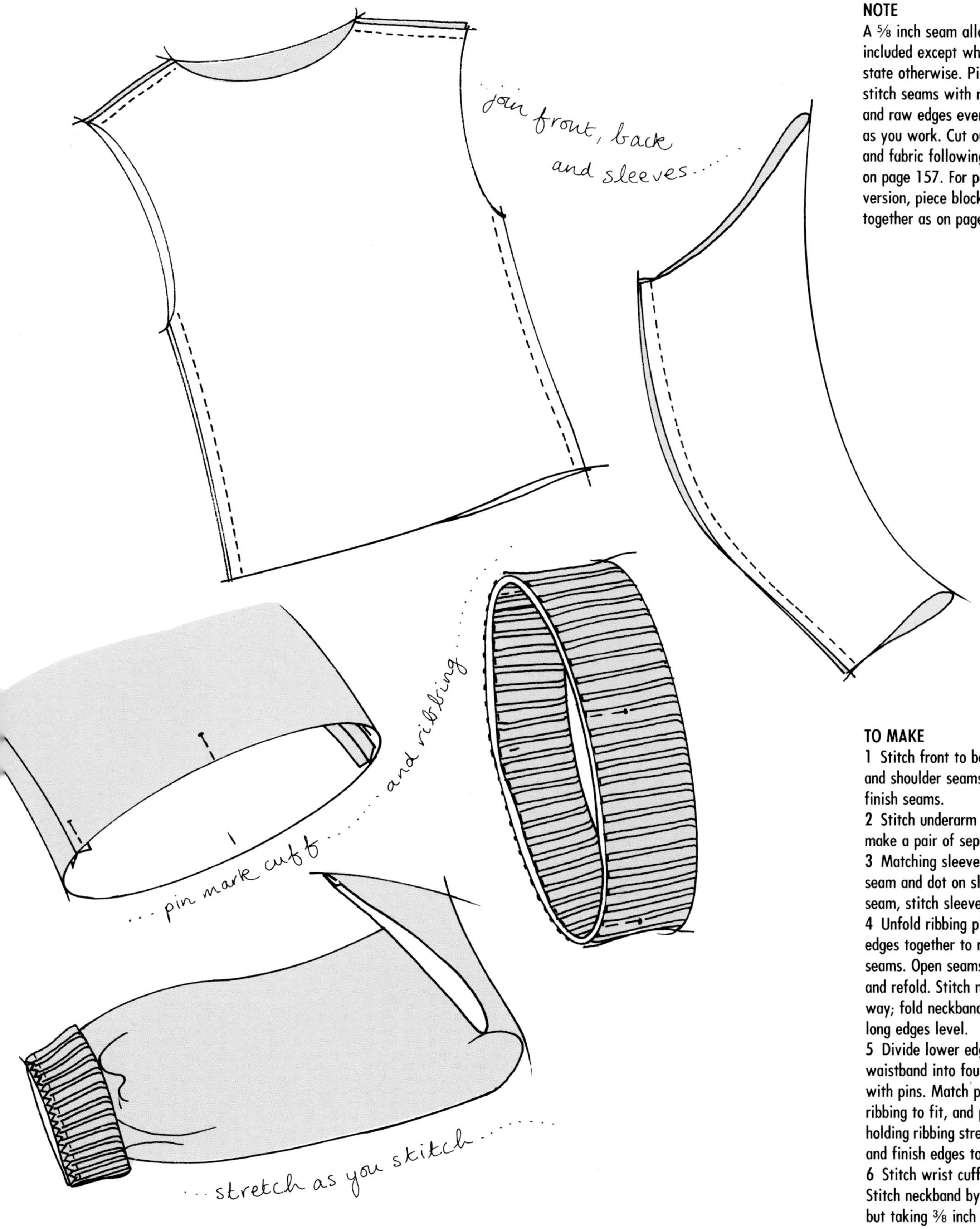

TO MAKE
1 Stitch front to back along side and shoulder seams. Press and finish seams.
2 Stitch underarm sleeve seams to make a pair of separate sleeves.
3 Matching sleeve seam to side seam and dot on sleeve to shoulder seam, stitch sleeves into armholes.
4 Unfold ribbing pieces, and stitch edges together to make rings. Trim seams. Open seams with fingers and refold. Stitch neckband in same way; fold neckband in half with long edges level.
5 Divide lower edge of top and hip waistband into four equal sections with pins. Match pins, stretch ribbing to fit, and pin. Stitch while holding ribbing stretched to fit. Trim and finish edges together.
6 Stitch wrist cuffs in same way. Stitch neckband by same method but taking ⅜ inch seam allowance only.

7 Stitch pants front to pants back along inside and outside leg seams to make two separate legs.

8 Turn one leg right side out and thread inside other leg so crotch edges are level. Stitch crotch seam from front waist to back waist.

9 Finish waist edge. Fold 1½ inches over to wrong side. Stitch around near top edge and again 1¼ inches down, leaving an opening to insert elastic.

10 Trim elastic to fit, allowing ¾ inch for joining. Thread elastic through casing. Overlap and join ends. Close opening. Stitch on leg cuffs in same way as wrist cuffs.

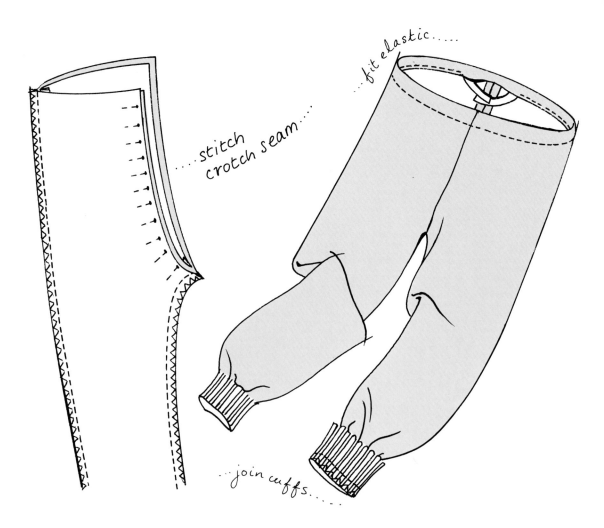

JOINING BLOCKS OF FABRIC

For the "patchwork" version choose three or more colors for the fabric blocks. For each section of the garment, assemble a rectangle of blocks — suggested combinations and overall dimensions are shown on the right. Each square represents 2 inches. Join the blocks using one of the same seams suggested on page 151 — include appropriate seam allowances when cutting out blocks of fabric. Cut out each pattern piece from the patchwork panels and make up the garment as before.

RIGHT SLEEVE

LEFT SLEEVE

FRONT

BACK

LEFT LEG (FRONT AND BACK)

RIGHT LEG (FRONT AND BACK)

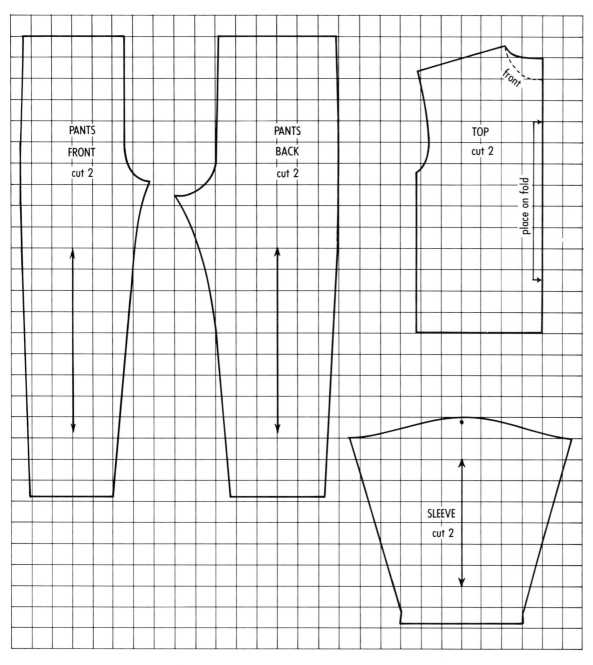

TO MAKE PATTERN

Following diagram, in which each square represents 2 inches, draw up a full-size pattern. The front and back are the same except for the neckline: follow the high neckline for the back pattern and the lower dashed line for the front neckline.

PANTS FRONT cut 2

PANTS BACK cut 2

TOP cut 2

place on fold

front

SLEEVE cut 2

TO CUT OUT

Cut out:
1 front (on fold)
1 back (on fold)
2 sleeves
1 pair of pants fronts
1 pair of pants backs

From ribbing cut:
2 wrist cuffs 6¾ inches long
2 ankle cuffs 7¼ inches long
1 hip waistband 30 inches long
1 neckband 13½ inches long and
half the width of other ribbing

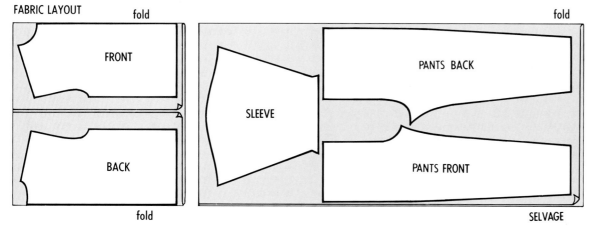

FABRIC LAYOUT

fold

fold

FRONT

BACK

SLEEVE

PANTS BACK

PANTS FRONT

fold

SELVAGE

Pile, leather and suede

From ball gowns to teddy bears – there is a wide range of types of pile fabric, and different items that can be made from pile fabrics. Pile fabrics are those with surface fibers which stand up from the fabric, on either a woven backing (velvet, velveteen, and corduroy) or on a stretch backing (imitation fur fabric). The pile may also be of a looped construction (terry cloth and stretch terry cloth).

PREPARING TO SEW WOVEN PILE

First determine which way the pile runs: see page 20. With a woven backing the pile should normally run up the garment. Long pile, like that of imitation fur, should run down the item you are making. The most important point is to make sure that it runs the same way throughout.

Woven pile Choose patterns with a minimum of seams and stitched darts, to show off the fabric. Fit the garment carefully before starting to cut out and sew. Cut out with the pile side upward, cutting pieces separately (reverse the pattern, if necessary). Use long, fine needles to pin pattern pieces in place and transfer markings with tailor's tacks. Use a lightweight interfacing, or hair canvas for coats and suits. Line or underline the garment, or sections like yokes and jacket fronts, using silk crêpe or a

suitable synthetic lining.

STITCHING AND HANDLING WOVEN PILE FABRICS

Basting Baste with fine thread. Fit the garment and make all necessary adjustments before stitching.

Needle and thread Use cotton-wrapped polyester, mercerized cotton, or polyester thread suitable for the weight and fiber content of the fabric. Use a size 14 needle, or finer with soft velvets.

Stitch length and pressure A 12 stitch length is usually suitable. Reduce the pressure on the presser foot if necessary.

Stitching Stitch with the pile. Since the pile normally runs up, this means that seams are stitched from the lower edge to the top. Use plain seams whenever possible.

Seam finishes Raw edges may be finished by pinking, binding with nylon net, overcasting by hand, or over-edging using the blindstitch zig-zag.

Darts Slash through the center of darts to reduce bulk.

Underlining and lining Most garments should be lined to help them keep their shape. Line garments or sections of garments, rather than using facings, to keep bulk down. Underlining is necessary in tailored coats and suits.

Zipper openings Hand sew the zipper for a professional finish.

Hems Never turn and stitch the edge of a hem: use synthetic seam binding or nylon net to finish hem edges, and hand finish them, positioning stitches between the hem and the garment.

WORKING WITH STRETCH PILE FABRICS

Lay out the fabric to "relax" before cutting out, particularly with stretch terry cloth. Lay out the pattern on the wrong side of the fabric. Cut out long pile fabrics with sturdy shears, cutting through the backing only, with short snips, or use a single blade – a razor blade or craft knife. Use a strong synthetic thread, and a size 14 ball-point needle. Check the tension and stitch length before starting to stitch.

If using a zig-zag stitch, to maintain the stretch on pile fabrics, trim seam allowances to ⅛ or ¼ inch. Items may be basted using an overcasting stitch, then stitched with a small zig-zag stitch. Seams can be stitched and finished in one go. Use straight seam binding to tape any seams that should not stretch (see page 151).

PILE IT ON
Rich colors for rich weaves – cotton and synthetic velvets, corduroy, and fake furs all have a definite pile direction or nap.

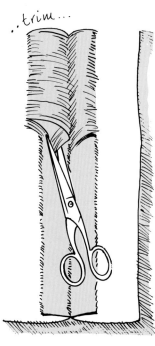

..trim...

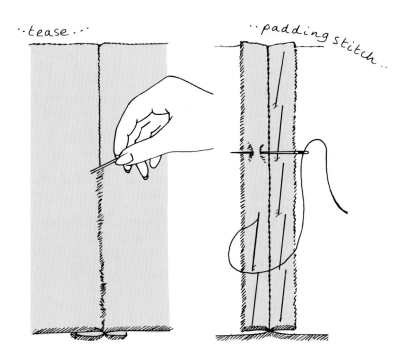

..tease..   *..padding stitch..*

TEASING AND TRIMMING PILE

After stitching a seam in a pile fabric, steam-press (or finger-press for stretch pile) and turn to the right side. Check that no pile is caught in the stitching: if it is, tease it out with the eye end of a darning needle.

On long pile fabrics, reduce bulk by trimming the pile from the seam allowance, either before or after stitching the seam.

If the seam allowances tend to roll on long pile, stretch fabrics, hold them flat with padding stitch.

NOTES ON SEWING STRETCH TERRY CLOTH

Stretch terry cloth is particularly popular for closely fitting garments with plenty of give, such as baby suits.

- Aim to maintain stretch in seams, and keep bulk to a minimum.
- Choose patterns specifically for stretch knit fabrics. Make any alterations before cutting out. Bear in mind that fitting does not have to be precise, due to the stretch in the fabric.
- Hold seams taut as you stitch.
- Use a general purpose presser foot: wrap the toes with a strip of tape to prevent them from catching in the loops of the pile if necessary.
- It is normally better to trim after stitching, as the fabric tends to distort if you stitch too close to the edge.
- Either stitch and finish in one operation, with the overedge stretch stitch, or first stitch the seam with a straight stretch stitch, then use a multi-stretch stitch to finish, before trimming the seam allowance close to the stitching.
- Machine-stitched buttonholes can be used, but snap fastenings (available in strips) are more convenient on babies' suits.

LEATHER AND SUEDE FABRICS

Of course you *can* buy the real thing, but most dressmakers prefer to use imitation leather and suede. It is convenient to buy and easier to handle. Most have a knitted backing, which gives a more supple, easier to handle finish than a woven backing. There are several different materials used for the surface, which give different textures, but most are handled in the same way. Check the notes on using knitted fabrics when using stretchy leather fabrics.

PREPARING TO SEW

Avoid patterns with gathers, sharp pleats, or tucks: simply shaped seams are often the best way of shaping leather garments. Do not pin through the fabric: hold the pattern in place with weights or tape if necessary. Mark the fabric with chalk or marking pencil.

Use a good pair of scissors, but not your best, to cut out the fabric. Avoid basting on right side.

STITCHING AND HANDLING LEATHER AND SUEDE FABRICS

Basting Avoid basting, especially on lapped seams. Instead, use tape to join pieces together.

Needle and thread Use size 14 leather sewing needle, and polyester thread. Increase needle thread tension if necessary.

Stitch length and pressure Use a 10 stitch length for straight stitching.

Stitching Topstitched seams are best, since they control and hold the seam allowances in place. Stitch carefully, since any unpicking will show.

Seam finishes Seam allowances do not normally need finishing, but a thin line of fabric glue can be used to hold them down.

Facings and interfacing Choose a stiff interfacing if necessary, to structure the garment.

Underlining and lining Underlining and lining are not essential, but they add to the comfort.

Hems Turn and topstitch hem in place, or use fabric glue.

Using silk and lace

Silk is available in any weight from sheer chiffon to heavy tweed. It is used for dressmaking, tailoring, decorating projects. Whatever the project, silk must be treated with a light and gentle hand.

PREPARING TO SEW SILK FABRICS

Choose patterns and fabric according to the weight of the silk – heavy silks for tailored dresses, suits, and coats, soft silks for blouses and sheers, and soft, knitted silk (or synthetic imitations) for lingerie. Be particularly careful when choosing patterns for sheer silks: choose a pattern with no facings, or adapt a pattern, since any facing will show through the garment. Similarly, styling seams and darts may cause problems.

Cut out on a non-slip surface, such as cork or felt if possible, or pin an old sheet tightly over the table or cutting board.

Use fine pins or, better still, needles, when pinning the pattern to the fabric. Place them close together within the seam or dart allowance. Use sharp scissors of medium length. Careful cutting will give accurate seam width and maintain the garment proportions. Use tailor's tacks to mark the fabric.

For a professional look, you should either underline or line silk fabric (see page 164). Select any interfacing with care: with sheer silks, use the fabric itself for both facing and interfacing collars and cuffs.

STITCHING AND HANDLING SILK

Basting Hand baste the seams and darts: most silks show the needle marks from machine basting. Use very fine thread (a strand of embroidery floss, if necessary) and a size 8 or 9 needle.

Needle and thread For machine stitching use silk thread if possible, or a mercerized cotton or all-purpose synthetic thread (particularly for imitation silks). Use a size 11 needle for lightweight silks, up to a size 14 on heavy or rough silks. It is normally necessary to reduce the thread tension to prevent puckering.

Stitch length and pressure Use a 15 to 20 stitch length for fine silks and a 12 stitch length for heavier silks. If necessary, reduce the pressure on the presser foot.

Stitching Medium and heavy silks need only to be guided from the front in the normal way. Crêpe weaves and chiffon require gentle support; when stitching, hold the seam behind the presser foot as well as in front. Do not pull the fabric through the foot – simply keep it taut. Use the straight stitch throat plate and presser foot for best results: a non-stick foot is useful. (Knitted silks may be stitched with zig-zag or stretch stitch.)

Darts If the silk is underlined (see page 164) make darts in silk and lining separately, unless the fabric is sheer, in which case they should be treated as a single layer of fabric. Unstitched gathers and tucks are better than darts in sheer fabrics.

Seams and seam finishes The aim is to reduce bulk: some closely woven silks require no seam finish, and some may be pinked. But many silks have a tendency to fray, so if you are not using a self-finished seam use the blindstitch zig-zag or multi-stitch zig-zag.

Sheer silks need narrow French seams. The hairline seam is useful in collars and cuffs, or satin binding may be used to edge openings.

Zipper openings Zippers should normally be stitched by hand at the final stage of insertion, using a fine prick stitch.

Buttonholes Avoid buttonholes on fine silks; otherwise any method may be used, so long as a firm underlay of interfacing or woven lawn or muslin is used.

Hems Seam binding may be used, or a pinked and stitched, hand-finished hem. Rough open weaves may be finished with blindstitch zig-zag or multi-stitch zig-zag. Hand sew the hem, using silk thread if possible, positioning stitches between the hem and the garment rather than over the edge of the hem.

Hand-rolled hems are a popular finish for silk fabrics – see page 101. Lingerie edging may be used for stretch silks.

PREPARING TO SEW LACE FABRICS

Lace fabrics may be made from a number of fibers: cotton, rayon, wool, linen, silk, nylon, and so on. It is used for a wide range of different types of garment, according to current fashions.

Choose simple patterns, with a minimum of

seams and darts which break up the continuity of the lace design. Avoid neckline and sleeve facings, unless you plan to mount the lace with an opaque fabric. If you do use facings, cut them in matching plain net to eliminate bulk and prevent patterns from showing through. Avoid shoulder pads with sheer lace.

When cutting out, be careful to match the designs of the lace. Use sharp pins (or needles) and pin within seam allowances. Use sharp, lightweight shears. Use tailor's tacks to transfer marks.

Most lace garments should be underlined to support the delicate weaves and patterns. Skirts, and items made of more opaque lace, such as eyelet lace, may be lined with a smooth, firm fabric. Taffeta, satin, *peau de soie*, polished cotton, or even wool crêpe may be used, but to maintain a sheer feel to the fabric use silk organza, fine net, or chiffon and use a plain underslip with the garment.

STITCHING AND HANDLING LACE

Basting Use a size 8 or 9 hand sewing needle and baste all seams. If there is a design, slip baste from the right side.

Thread and needle Select silk thread, if possible, for the machine stitching on silk, wool, or synthetic lace, mercerized cotton or all-purpose thread for cotton, wool, or synthetic fibers. Use a fine needle if you can do so without the thread breaking.

Stitch length and pressure In stitching the fine openwork of lace, use a 15 stitch length and light pressure.

Stitching Guide fine lace through the machine with both hands, keeping it taut without pulling or stretching.

Darts Use darts only if underlining is opaque.

Seam and seam finishes With an opaque lining seam allowances will not show, so you can use plain seams and pink the edges. Otherwise, make fine, narrow French or double-stitched seams.

Seam grading Grade curved seams in the usual way (see page 51) to eliminate bulk.

Finishing edges A fine, double-fold silky bias binding is a better finish than a shaped facing for neckline, sleeves, and front or back opening.

Zipper openings Use a fine zipper, and insert it by hand, finishing with a fine prickstitch.

Fastenings Do not use buttonholes; thread loops and small buttons are more appropriate fastenings.

Hems If the lace has a border or scalloped edge, use that as the finished hem of the dress. (This requires careful fitting before cutting out, as there is no room for adjustment in length later.) Otherwise make a hand-rolled hem, or finish the edge with a multi-stitch zig-zag, or pink and stitch, then hand

finish the hem with herringbone stitch between the hem and the garment (see page 100).

Pressing Use the steam setting on the iron and a wool-faced pressing pad (or a good thick towel) on the board. Lay the lace, right side down, on the pad. Cover with a thin pressing cloth before pressing, adding extra moisture if necessary. This prevents flattening any raised design in the fabric.

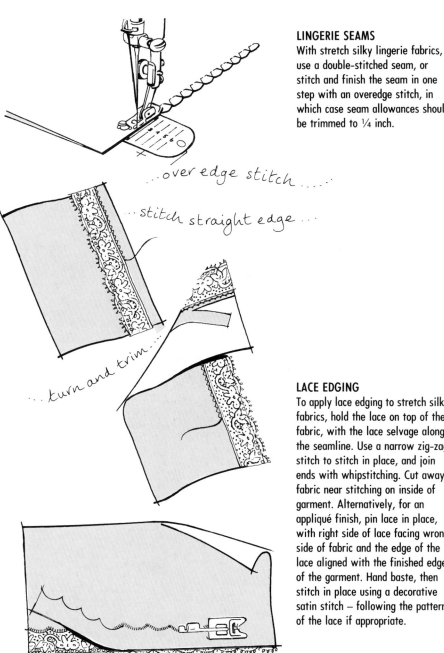

over edge stitch

stitch straight edge

turn and trim

trim close to stitching

LINGERIE SEAMS

With stretch silky lingerie fabrics, use a double-stitched seam, or stitch and finish the seam in one step with an overedge stitch, in which case seam allowances should be trimmed to ¼ inch.

LACE EDGING

To apply lace edging to stretch silky fabrics, hold the lace on top of the fabric, with the lace selvage along the seamline. Use a narrow zig-zag stitch to stitch in place, and join ends with whipstitching. Cut away fabric near stitching on inside of garment. Alternatively, for an appliqué finish, pin lace in place, with right side of lace facing wrong side of fabric and the edge of the lace aligned with the finished edge of the garment. Hand baste, then stitch in place using a decorative satin stitch – following the pattern of the lace if appropriate.

Teddy and slip

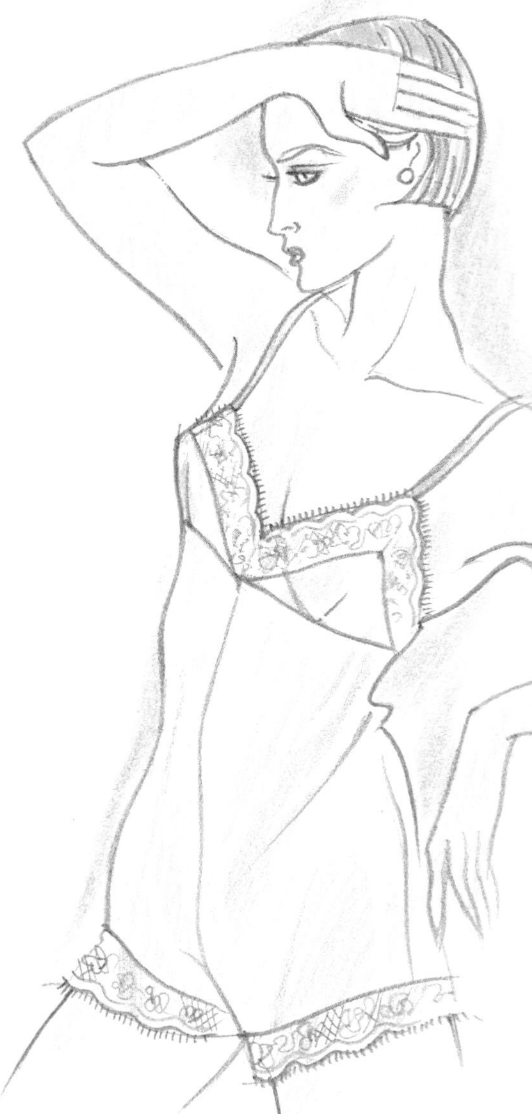

SUITABLE FABRIC
Silk or synthetic satin or crêpe de chine.

TO FIT
Size 12.

YOU WILL NEED
Teddy
1⅝ yds of 36-inch wide fabric
Matching thread
3⅜ yds lace trimming
2 buttons, ⅜ inch in diameter
Slip
2⅝ yds of 36-inch wide fabric
Matching thread
3⅜ yds lace trimming.

NOTE
A ⅝ inch seam allowance is included except where instructions state otherwise. Pin, baste, and stitch seams with right sides facing and raw edges even. Trim and finish seams as you work. Cut out following diagrams opposite.

TO MAKE
Teddy

1 Stitch darts on bra pieces. Trim dart ¼ inch from stitching and finish edges together. Press.
2 Matching notches, stitch bra pieces together along center seam.
3 Stitch fronts together along center front seam, and backs along center back seam.
4 Stitch lower edge of bra pieces to top edge of front.
5 Stitch front to back along side edges.
6 Stitch lace around top edge by one of following methods. Fold ¼ inch to right side, lap lace over fabric and straight stitch both edges of lace, mitering at corners. Or overlap lace and stitch outer edge with a small close zig-zag stitch and inner edge with straight stitch.

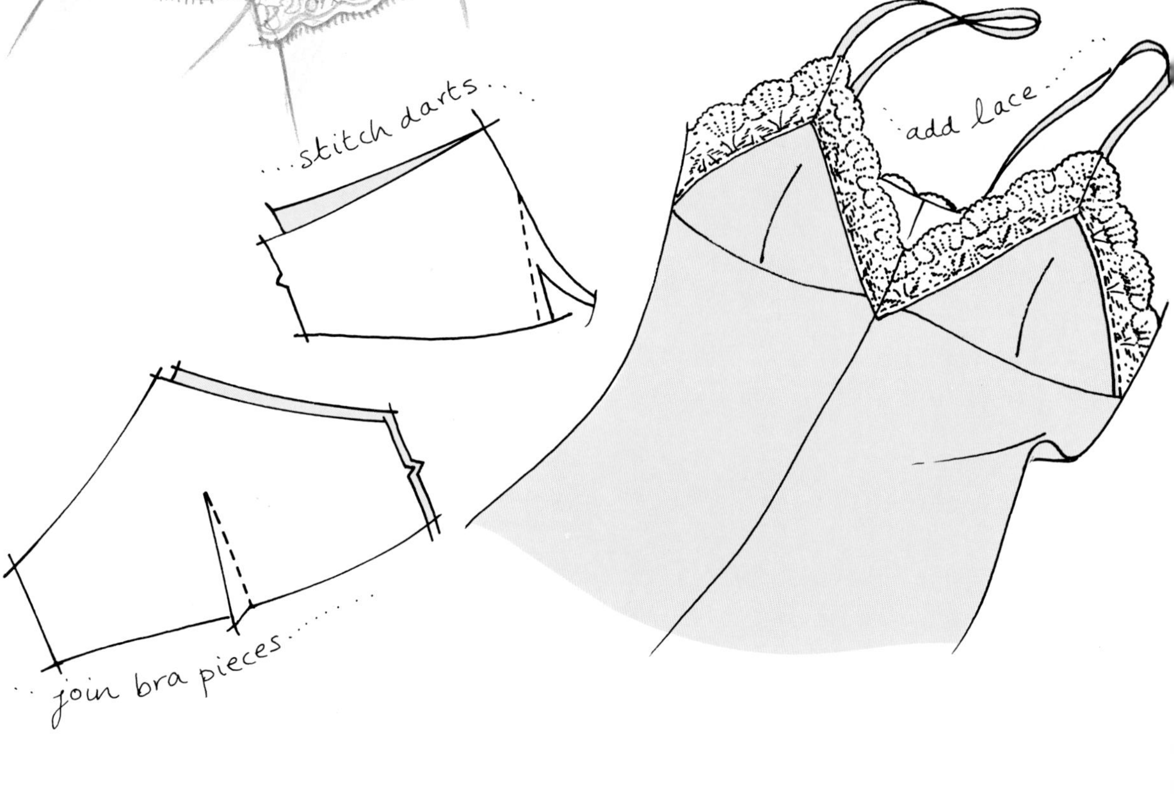

Silky lingerie may seem an indulgent luxury, but it is also practical, helping garments to fit smoothly, without lumps and wrinkles. The same bodice shape can be used for a teddy with an opening crotch or for a full length slip: plan the length to suit the outfit you intend to wear it with.

...stitch darts...

...join bra pieces...

...add lace...

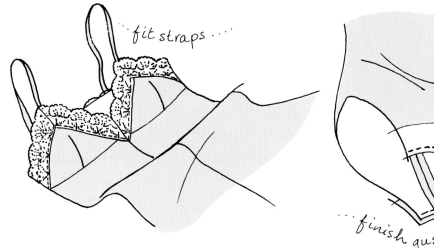

fit straps

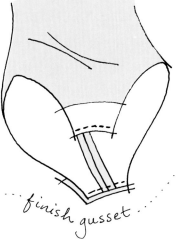

finish gusset

7 Fold straps in half lengthwise and stitch along length. Trim seams and turn right side out.

8 Stitch straps 4 inches either side of center back seam; adjust length if necessary and stitch to bra points on front.

9 Stitch gusset facings to lower edge of front and back down sides and across ends of gusset. Trim seams. Turn facings to wrong side. Tuck under raw edge and stitch.

10 Make two ½ inch-long buttonholes parallel to front gusset edge and ¼ inch in. Stitch buttons to match on back gusset so edges overlap by about ½ inch when fastened.

11 Stitch lace around legs by overlapping edge of lace over raw edge and zig-zag stitching. Alternatively if fabric frays fold back ¼ inch onto right side before stitching lace.

Slip

Make as for teddy to step 8. Stitch lace around lower edge of slip following method for teddy legs in step 11.

PATTERN DIAGRAM

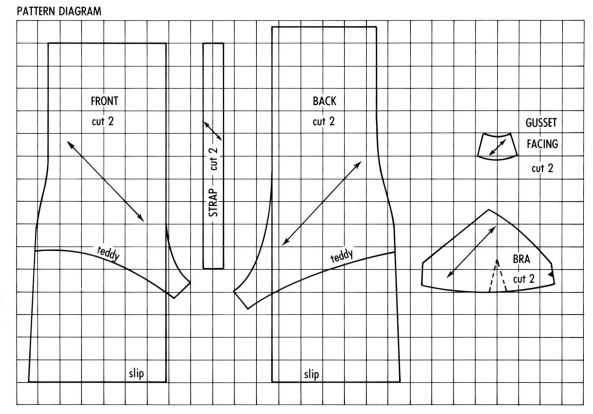

FRONT
cut 2

STRAP — cut 2

BACK
cut 2

GUSSET
FACING
cut 2

teddy

teddy

BRA
cut 2

slip

slip

TO MAKE PATTERN

Following the diagram, in which each square represents 2 inches, draw the full size pattern. The upper part of teddy and slip are the same; follow appropriate line for lower part of teddy or slip.

TO CUT OUT

Unfold fabric to full width, and refold widthwise so that there are selvages at top and bottom. For teddy, cut out through double thickness:

2 fronts
2 backs
2 bras
2 straps
2 gusset facings

For slip omit gusset facings.

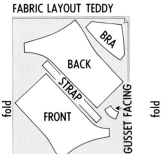

FABRIC LAYOUT TEDDY

BRA

BACK

STRAP

FRONT

fold

GUSSET FACING

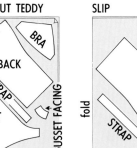

SLIP   SELVAGE

BRA

BACK

FRONT

STRAP

fold

Underlining and lining

Adding underlining or lining to any garment helps to achieve a professional, tailor-made look. Simply defined, both are a second layer of fabric which supports the fabric and adds resistance to strain. The difference is that underlining is included in the seams of the garment, providing an extra layer of fabric for some finishes: for example hand stitches used to hold down facings are made in the lining fabric, rather than in the garment itself.

A loose lining is constructed separately and joined to a skirt at the waistline seam or to a dress at the neckline, armhole, and waistline seam. Around openings, the lining may be stitched to the edge of the facing, or it may replace the facing (edge-to-edge lining).

CHOOSING FABRICS

The most popular fabrics for underlining and lining are silk organza and china silk, for soft, silky garments. The same fabrics may be used for heavier silks, wools, and rayons, but obviously heavier fabrics are also suitable – Bemberg taffeta and silk crêpe are all used for lining. When lining very sheer fabrics, use self fabric for underlining and lining. Synthetic, non-woven interfacings may also be used for underlining. Synthetic lining fabrics are economical, and available in a wide range of colors – but if the main fabric was expensive it is worthwhile spending extra on the lining.

UNDERLINING

The whole garment may be underlined, or part of it – just the bodice, or part of the skirt, for example. In skirts, the underlining may extend to the fold of the hem, to the top of the hem, or to about 12 inches below the hipline.

Cut out underlining in the same pattern pieces and on the same grain as the garment. Transfer all markings. Stitch darts and shaping seams within the main part of the bodice and skirt sections separately, then place the corresponding pieces together, wrong side of fabric facing right side of underlining. Both pieces must be smooth and wrinkle-free. Pin together along center line, side seams, and waistline, then make several lines of diagonal basting to hold the layers of fabric together. Hand baste along seamlines. Machine stitch underlining to garment at waistlines, ½ inch from raw edge. Treat fabric and underlining as one piece of fabric.

To hem underlined garments, if the underlining extends to the top of the hem, pink the lower edge of the hem, then turn under and stitch near the folded edge, using a multi-stitch zig-zag.

If the underlining extends into the fold of the hem, fold the hem over the underlining and sew by hand, taking the stitches through only the underlining and hem. Then finish the hem of the garment according to the type of fabric (see page 100).

When underlining sheer fabrics, use a smooth, firm, opaque fabric of a similar fiber content. Either underline the complete garment, or underline the bodice section and loose line the skirt if it is full.

To create the illusion of a sheer yoke and sleeves on the upper part of a bodice, underline the upper part of the bodice with net or chiffon and the lower part with a firm, opaque fabric.

UNDERLINING A DRESS

Hold the underlining in place with rows of diagonal basting, with stitches ⅜ to ½ inch long and about 2 inches apart. Do not draw the thread tightly. Do not remove this basting until the hem is finished. (If the two fabrics are different lengths the skirt will not hang evenly.) Hand baste on seamlines. Stitch underlining to garment within seam allowance at waistline.

..... underline with diagonal basting....

SKIRT WITH A PLEAT

When underlining a straight skirt with a kick pleat, finish the underlining at the top of the hem. Stitch seam above pleat to top of pleat, then trim off excess fabric. Pink the seam edges and lower edge of the underlining back and front. Fold the pinked edges under and stitch around the lower edge and both sides of the slit, using a multi-stitch zig-zag for added strength. Then baste and stitch underlining to skirt as for the dress, above.

.... finish underlining at top of hem .....

LINING DRESSES AND SKIRTS

Lining has the advantage of covering seams, reducing the need for time-consuming seam finishes. The lining is made in the same way as the garment, omitting features like collars, cuffs and pockets. The lining normally replaces facings (except with tailored garments; see page 166). The lining is fitted to the garment with right sides facing, and the garment is joined to the lining around openings before pressing, turning right side out, and pressing again so that it extends slightly beyond the lining. In order to facilitate construction and make a neat finish at openings, the shoulder seams may be left open, and slipstitched by hand when the garment has been turned right side out. At waistbands, collars, and cuffs, finish after lining.

LINING A SKIRT

Cut the lining in the same pattern pieces and on the same grain as the skirt. Transfer all markings as usual. Stitch and press the darts and all seams in the skirt and sew in the zipper. Stitch and press the darts and all seams in the lining. Make the opening for zipper the same length in the lining as in the skirt fabric. Place the lining inside the skirt, wrong sides together, and pin together at the waistline, matching seams, darts, and markings. Turn the skirt wrong side out with lining outside. At the end of the placket opening in the lining, slash diagonally on each side ¼ inch beyond the seamline. Fold under the edges and pin them to the zipper tape. Slipstitch in place. Stitch the skirt and lining together at the waistline, ½ inch from the seam edge. Add the waistband in the usual way. Hem the skirt and lining separately, so that lining is 1 inch shorter than the skirt.

If the skirt has a slit in it, the lining can be used to hold an underlay in place behind the slit. Cut the lining and notch and mark each section. Assemble front and back panels of skirt, leaving the seams open the depth of the slits plus hem. Reinforce with backstitching. Machine baste the seams together down the slits.

Assemble the lining so that the seams will face the seams in the skirt. Stitch darts and the full length of the seams that correspond to the slits in the skirt. Cut a facing of skirt fabric 5 inches longer than the slit plus hem and seam allowances, and 8 inches wide so that it will extend 4 inches on each side of the slit. (The skirt illustrated has two slits in the back and is faced with a single panel.) Fold under seam allowance at top and sides of facing. Place facing, right side up, on wrong side of skirt lining, keeping lower edges even. Baste in place, then stitch near folded edges. Pin lining panels together down side seams, leaving lower ends of seams open to correspond with length of slits, and leaving opening to correspond to zipper as before. Finish the seam edges. Press, then press seams open. Turn lining wrong side out, and skirt right side out. Place lining inside skirt, with faced side to wrong side of skirt. Pin around waistline, matching markings, and finish as before. Hem the skirt, facing, and lining separately.

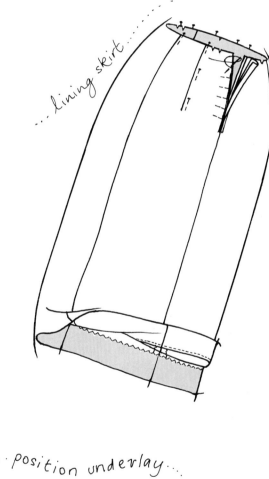

...lining skirt...

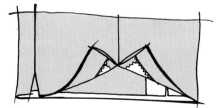

...position underlay...

...so it hangs beneath slit...

Tailoring techniques

Tailoring is an advanced stage of dressmaking. You should attempt tailoring in luxury fabrics only if you have a thorough knowledge of sewing techniques, good workmanship, and plenty of experience. It is also important that you understand the principles of fitting garments and the use of underlining and interfacing, which are important in molding and shaping garments.

PATTERNS AND FABRICS

Choose a pattern that is right for the fabric you wish to use and classic enough to be fashionable for several years. Choose the same size coat and suit patterns as you use for dress patterns, since ease is included in the garment.

There is a wide choice of fabrics for tailored garments – firmly woven wool, tweed, flannel, wool broadcloth, double knits, raw silk, heavy cotton, linen, heavy silk, velvet, corduroy, and all the variations on these in synthetic fibers. The important point is to choose one which is heavy enough so that the interfacing, and the stitching securing it, will not show through.

Prepare the fabric and adjust the pattern to fit before starting to work. Press out all creases, but check pressing techniques first. Be careful not to give the fabric any shine.

LINING AND INTERLINING

Choose a lightweight fabric for lining suits – silk crêpe, china silk, or a synthetic alternative – that matches the color of the main fabric. Or make a feature of the lining, choosing a pattern or contrasting color. For coats use heavier linings. For added warmth, coats are usually interlined with lambswool or a fabric specifically for this purpose. The interlining should be cut to match the foldline of the lining hem. It is basted to the lining, in the same way as underlining on a garment, and the interlining and lining treated as one.

INTERFACING AND UNDERLINING

Interfacing fabrics are available in many weights and textures. Choose them according to the weight of the garment fabric, the effect desired, and personal preference (see page 55). For most coats and suits, hair canvas is suitable: it gives extra body to the garment, so it will hold its shape better. Nonwoven interfacing is also suitable. With loosely woven fabrics, use china silk or batiste for underlining.

LININGS WITH STYLE
Add a dramatic flourish to jackets and coats with solid-color, printed, and pattern-woven linings in real silk or synthetic fibers.

MUSLIN SHELL

With any garments, and particularly with tailored garments, it is a good idea to construct the garment in muslin before cutting out the fabric. This will ensure a perfect fit. Use good quality unbleached muslin. Make any major pattern adjustments, then cut out the garment. Transfer pattern markings, and mark center front and back. Mark balance lines across the muslin.

Stitch and press the darts and shaping seams within the bodice or skirt. Then stitch shoulder and side seams. Apply facings and undercollar. Grade all seams and press them open. Seam the sleeves and baste them into the armholes. Fold, baste, and press the hems. Try on the muslin shell with the clothes you intend to wear with the finished garment. Slip shoulder pads in place if necessary. Lap openings and pin in place at button markings. Check the fit, as for a pin fitting (see page 119). Make and stitch any adjustments to the muslin shell and check the fit again before adjusting the pattern and cutting out the main fabric.

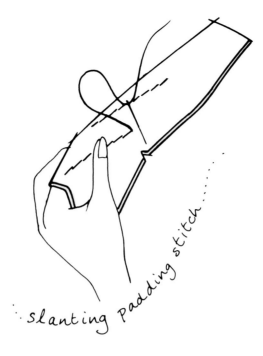

slanting padding stitch

PADDING STITCH

This stitch is used in tailoring to hold two layers of fabric together to prevent them from slipping. For example, when making a jacket or coat, use padding stitch to hold the interfacing in place along the roll line of lapels and collars.

First baste the interfacing in place. Work toward you, with the wrong side of the fabric facing, using thread to match the fabric. Hold the work between the thumb and forefinger of the left hand, taking a short stitch from right to left through the interfacing and fabric, catching only a single thread of the fabric. Space the stitches about 3/8 inch apart.

The long slanting stitches on the wrong side are visible, but the short crosswise ones on the right side are not.

MAKING A SUIT JACKET

The steps in making a simple tailored suit jacket, with collar and lapels, illustrates many of the techniques of tailoring. Don't forget to fit the jacket at each stage.

1 Pin, baste, and stitch seams of jacket within front and back bodice sections, then press them open.

2 Make buttonholes at this stage: bound buttonholes are normally used – see pages 92–93.

3 Stitch darts, and with heavy fabric and wide darts slash through the center of the dart and press open. (See pages 78–79.)

4 Pin and baste interlining in place about 1 inch from the raw edges.

5 Fit front interfacing, trimming interfacing at seamline and lapping it over a strip of organza or non-woven interfacing, zig-zag stitched in place. Pin interfacing over wrong side of each front jacket section. Fit to jacket, keeping the roll, using padding stitch (see above).

6 Join front and back at shoulder line, making seam through garment fabric only. Clip corners of dart in seam allowance, press, then press seam open. Lap interfacing over underlining at shoulder and herringbone stitch in place, holding shoulder over your hand to allow ease. Or turn seam allowances over interfacing and underlining and herringbone stitch edges in place.

7 Join interfaced undercollar to jacket, leaving seam allowances free at each end. Trim and grade seam allowances.

8 Finish buttonholes in interfacing, cutting away interfacing around buttonholes.

9 Join facing at shoulders and press seams open. Join top collar to facing, leaving seam allowances free at ends of collar.

10 Position top collar and facing over jacket, and join around edges, but do not baste through the seam allowances of crossing seams where collars join. Stitch in place, taking care not to catch seam allowance into seam where collar meets facing. Tie ends neatly. Trim seams and clip off fabric at corners. From the top of the lapel to the top button, trim the garment seam allowance to 1/8 inch and the facing seam allowance to 1/4 inch. Reverse the grading below the top button. Press, then press seams open. Turn facing to underside, ease out corners and baste, using diagonal basting. Ease the garment under slightly at the seamline. Press, then press lapels and collar over a tailor's ham or pressing mitt.

Check how the collar sits, easing top collar and facing over the roll. Pin along roll line. Where collars join neckline, catch the open seams together, without drawing stitching taut.

11 Join side seams. Make and set in sleeves. To maintain the roll of the sleeve cap, cut sheet batting on the true bias, 1 1/4 inches wide. Fold it through the center, then pin it to the sleeve side of the seam allowance over the cap between the notches, keeping the fold even with the stitching line. Stitch in place by hand. Fit shoulder pads, catching them to seam allowance of sleeve cap.

12 Finish edges of facing, then finish jacket hem and sleeve hems.

13 If the jacket is lined, cut the lining narrower down front edge and around neckline where there are facings. The edge of the lining is stitched to the edge of the facing, with the jacket inside out. It is important to allow ease down the center back of the lining, and a little ease in the length, so that it forms a slight fold over the hem of the jacket.

UNDERLINING

A back underlining of linen, batiste or cotton broadcloth is normally fitted to jackets, covering the shoulders. Use the jacket pattern as a guide for cutting. If the jacket is cut with a center back seam, place this seam on a foldline when cutting out underlining. It should measure about 10 inches deep at the center back and be shaped to fit around the armholes. Slash through the center of shoulder darts. Lap one cut edge over the other, so seamlines meet, and stitch using a multi-stitch zig-zag. Press. Position underlining over wrong side of back of jacket, matching center lines and seam edges.

INTERFACING THE UNDERCOLLAR

Cut the undercollar in interfacing, making it ¾ inch smaller all around than the main undercollar piece. To edge the undercollar, cut another collar of fine non-woven interfacing. Lay the heavy collar over the lightweight one. Zig-zag stitch in place, then trim away the lightweight interfacing inside stitching. Pin interfacing over wrong side of undercollar. Baste along the roll line. Using thread to match the main fabric, stay interfacing to undercollar with padding stitch, first working around neckline, then filling in with rows of padding stitch to seamline.

STAYING THE FRONT INTERFACING

Make lines of padding stitch to hold the interfacing to the back of the lapel. Place a ruler along the marked roll line of the lapels, and mark interfacing with chalk. Pin along marked line, then stay interfacing to lapels with padding stitches, catching only one thread of the fabric under the interfacing. Start at the neckline edge, following the roll line. Roll the lapel as you work, and hold it firmly with the thumb to shape it as it will be worn. Baste interfacing in place along seamline. Make a few rows of diagonal basting across free section of interfacing to hold it.

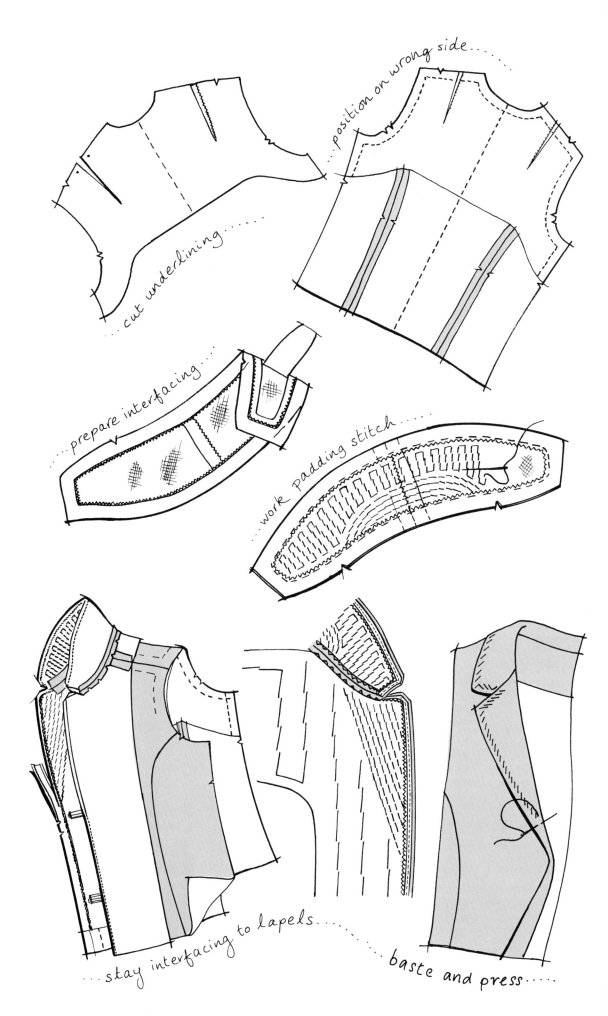

...cut underlining...

...position on wrong side...

...prepare interfacing...

...work padding stitch...

...stay interfacing to lapels...

...baste and press...

SHAPING SHOULDERS

To help to maintain the roll of the sleeve cap in tailored garments, use a piece of lambswool or sheet batting (a loosely woven, thick fabric, specially sold for this purpose in dressmaking departments).

Cut a strip on the bias, 1¼ inches wide. Fold it through the center, then pin it to the sleeve side of the seam allowance over the cap, between the notches (or from about two-thirds of the way up the armhole on each side). Check that the folded edge of the strip aligns with the stitching line. Stitch the shaping to the seam allowance of the sleeve by hand.

Shoulder pads are available ready-made, or you can make them up from soft synthetic batting fabric, and cover them with lining, to create the shape you require.

The pads should be roughly triangular in shape, and you can add extra bulk to the outer edge for emphasis. Make each pad from a diamond-shaped piece of batting, covered in lining fabric cut slightly larger all round.

Fold batting in half, then wrap lining fabric over it, and finish edges with zig-zag stitch. Since the pads are fitted between the jacket (or coat) and lining, the finish will not show.

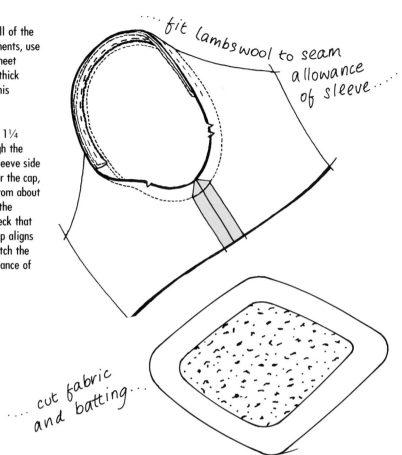

fit lambswool to seam allowance of sleeve

cut fabric and batting

fold and stitch

INTERFACED JACKET HEM

This technique gives extra body and weight to the hem. Use pre-shrunk linen or non-woven interfacing. If you use linen, cut it on the bias to make sure it does not distort the hem. Cut the strip 1 inch wider than the finished hem, and the length of the lower edge of the garment, plus 1 inch for seam allowances.

Mark the hemline of the garment with a row of basting and turn the hemline away from the garment.

Place interfacing along hem of jacket, aligning the lower edge of the interfacing with the crease of the hem, extending the ends ½ inch over the front interfacing. Pin and then herringbone stitch the interfacing to the jacket along each edge, catching only one thread of the main fabric (or stitching through interfacing only at side edges). Press.

Turn up the hem over the interfacing and pin the free edge in place, matching seams. Baste.

Herringbone the hem to the interfacing as far as the facing seam. Make a stitch in the hem, then a stitch in the interfacing over the hem edge.

At the front edges, turn the facing to the inside of the garment and pin it to the hem. Slipstitch in place, then herringbone over the cut edge the depth of the hem.

For a sleeve hem, cut interfacing on the straight grain, using the sleeve pattern as a guide. Join the ends of the interfacing with a lapped seam, then herringbone stitch in place and turn up hem as before.

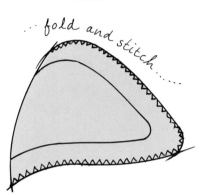

herringbone stitch

turn up hem over interfacing

Duster coat

This loose fitting, lightweight coat is a useful extra layer for a spring day. Make it in a crisp fabric or, for a better drape, use a softer fabric such as wool crêpe or knit.

ALTERNATIVES

Make the coat in silky fabric, with contrasting satin lapels, and wear it over slacks and a simple top for evening wear.

Shorten the pattern, and make a jacket in tweedy fabric, with a tie belt and patch pockets. Fit a lining from facing to facing for a more structured effect.

SUITABLE FABRICS
Cotton, linen, linen looks, wool crêpe, double knit.

TO FIT
Size 12.

YOU WILL NEED
5 yds of 44/45-inch wide fabric
Matching thread
1¾ yds of 30-inch wide interfacing

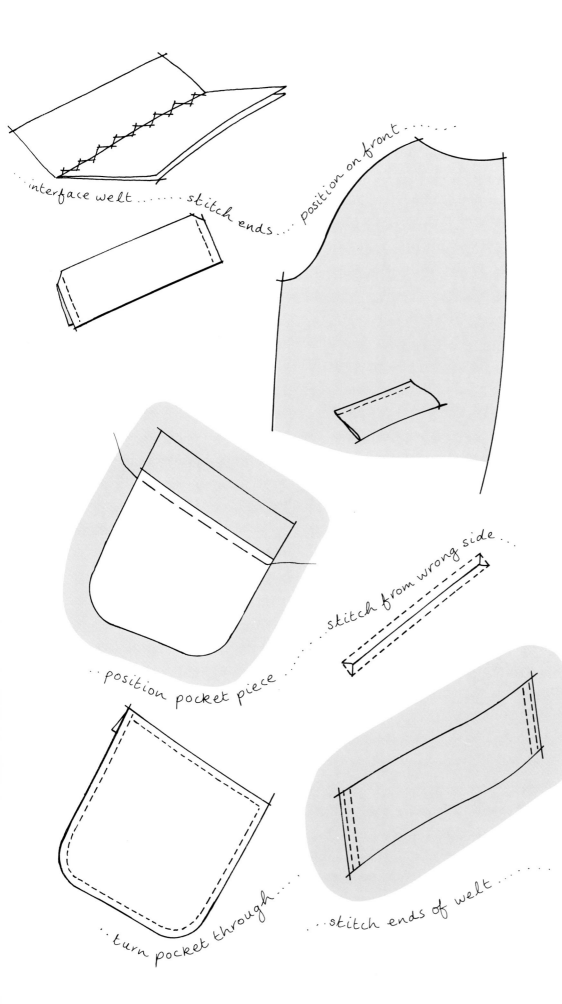

interface welt .... stitch ends .... position on front ......

position pocket piece .... stitch from wrong side .....

...turn pocket through ....stitch ends of welt ....

NOTE
A ⅝ inch seam allowance is
included except where instructions
state otherwise. Pin, baste, and
stitch seams with right sides facing
and raw edges even. Finish seams
as you work. Cut out pattern pieces
and fabric following the diagrams
on page 173.

TO MAKE

1 Apply interfacing to half pocket
welts up to dashed line. Fold welts
in half along dashed line and stitch
ends. Trim, turn right side out, and
press.

2 Mark pocket position on fronts on
both sides of fabric. On right side,
place welt top edge downward so
raw edges overlap pocket position
by ¼ inch. Baste.

3 With pocket pointing upward, lap
slanting edge of large pocket piece
over raw edge of welt for ¾ inch.
Baste.

4 Working from wrong side, stitch
around the rectangular pocket
position through all thicknesses.

5 Cut along center of pocket
position and into corner. Turn
pocket piece through opening to
wrong side and turn welt upward.
Press.

6 Stitch slanting edge of small
pocket piece to lower edge of
opening on wrong side.

7 Stitch pocket pieces together
around side and lower edges.

8 Stitch ends of welts to front with
a double row of topstitching at
each end.

9 Stitch backs together along center seam.

10 Stitch one sleeve front to one sleeve back along top arm seams. Make a pair.

11 Matching notches, stitch sleeves to front and back along raglan armhole seams.

12 Stitch undercollars together along straight center seam, trim, and press open. Stitch curved edge of undercollar to neck edge.

13 Apply interfacing to wrong side of front facing/collar. Stitch together across top straight edge for center back seam. Trim and press open. Finish long inner edge of facing/collar.

14 Stitch facing/collar to front and undercollar edges of coat. Trim seam and turn facing to wrong side. Press seam to edge.

15 Snip to dot at inner corner of collar neck edge. Tuck under raw edge along back neck and hand stitch to undercollar seam. Also hand stitch straight edges to shoulder seams.

16 Stitch fronts to back and sleeve underarm seams in one continuous line.

17 Open out facing at lower edge. Finish lower edge of coat. Press and stitch a 2½-inch hem on to wrong side. Refold facing, press and stitch to hem.

18 Finish edges of sleeves. Press and stitch 1½-inch hems on to wrong side.

19 Make belt, stitching and trimming the ends at an angle. Make sleeve bands, leaving ends raw. Also make a strip for loops, and cut into four equal loops.

20 Stitch loops to top arm seams just above hem. Thread sleeve bands through and join ends with an open seam at underarm.

21 Try on to establish belt position. Stitch on belt loops at side seams (see page 140), and thread belt through.

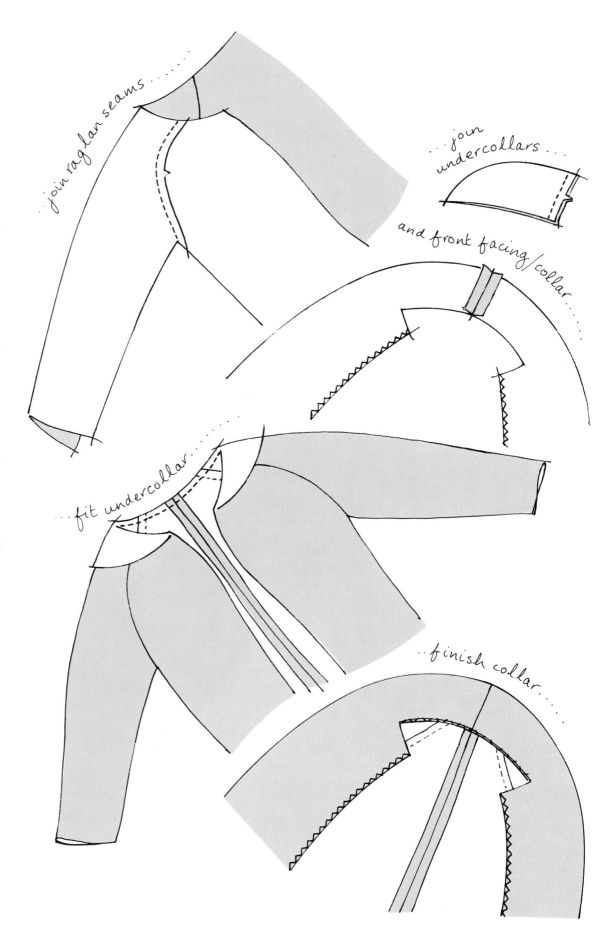

join raglan seams

...join undercollars...

...and front facing/collar...

fit undercollar

...finish collar...

PATTERN DIAGRAM

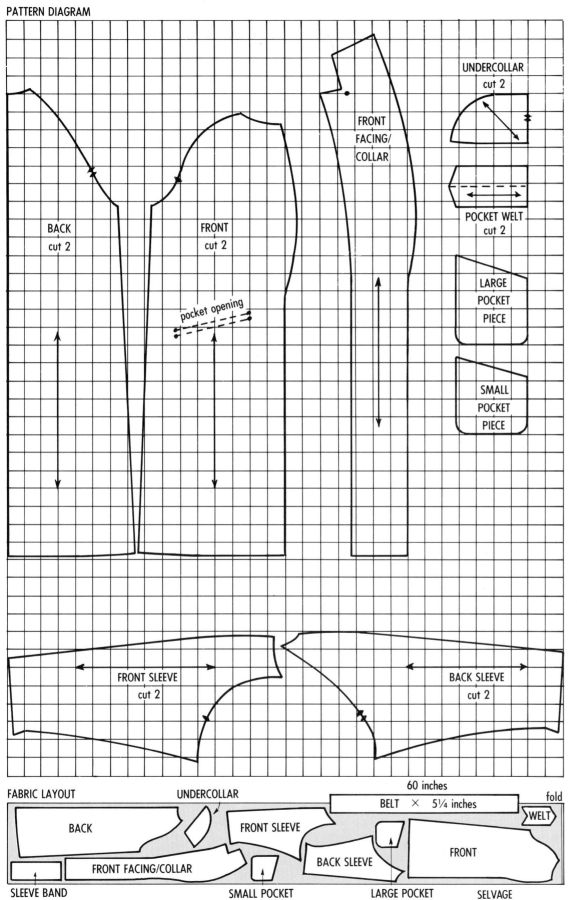

TO MAKE PATTERN
Following diagram, in which each square represents 2 inches, draw the full-size pattern.

TO CUT OUT
Fold fabric in half lengthwise. Cut out through double thickness:
2 backs
2 fronts
2 front facings/collars
2 undercollars
2 front sleeves
2 back sleeves
2 small pocket pieces
2 large pocket pieces
2 pocket welts
2 sleeve bands 16¼ inches × 5¼ inches
Cut out through single thickness:
1 belt 60 inches × 5¼ inches

173

Children's clothes

Because of their scale and relatively loose fit (at least for the under-fives), children's clothes are quick and economical to make. For details of pattern sizing, measuring and adjusting the fit of children's clothes, see page 120. Of course, if you enjoy hand sewing, delicate items, like christening gowns and party dresses, are an ideal way to put your hobby to good use – and create a family heirloom. These styles require slightly different treatment from the techniques for everyday clothes given here.

FABRICS FOR CHILDREN

Whatever the type of garment you are making, choose washable, hard-wearing fabrics. Very small babies are often dressed in suits of knitted fabric or stretch terry cloth fabric, which conform to the baby's body, and do not get tangled as he or she turns over. For toddler's suits, you will need tougher fabrics: canvas and corduroy are ideal. Choose soft fabrics – brushed cotton and wool-cotton blends for winter shirts and dresses, and crisper, crease-resistant fabrics for summer.

If you want the garments to dry quickly after washing, choose fabrics of synthetic fiber.

STYLES AND DESIGN POINTS

Children grow fast, so it is worthwhile including design points that allow for this. With very small babies, the natural give of stretch fabrics will allow for growth. On items such as overalls and jumpers, include some adjustable features, particularly in the straps: two buttons on the straps make them instantly adjustable, or you can use special adjustable suspenders for children's shoulder straps. It is a good idea to fit elastic around wrists and ankles, to draw the fullness of the garment out of the way, even if it is slightly on the large side. Alternatively, fit buttoned cuffs at wrists and ankles. Trousers and overalls can be adjusted at the hem without too much trouble by including cuffs as a design feature. These may be lined with soft cotton fabric, so that the cuffs contrast with the rest of the garment.

Yoked dresses and tops have been a traditional choice for girls' dresses, because below the yoke a minimum of fitting and fastening is required.

Knees and elbows are always faster to wear out than the rest of the garment, so reinforce them before you start with decorative patches, or be prepared to patch or darn them (see pages 60–61).

SEAM FINISHES

Make strong seams that will withstand washing and rough wear. For fine fabrics, in girls' dresses and blouses, for example, use French seams. For cottons and canvas, use a flat felled seam, particularly for play clothes. Velveteen and corduroy look neater if the seams are pressed open and finished by hand with overcasting, but this does not give such a tough finish.

HEM FINISHES

Always allow between 3 and 4 inches for hems in full, gathered skirts, and about 2 inches in closer fitting skirts. Finish hem with edge-stitching, and stitch by hand, or use a blindstich machine hem finish.

Children tend to grow upward rather than outwards from 18 months to three years, so the life of trousers can be extended if you make rolled hems. Line the lower 4 inches or so with contrasting fabric, to give a cheerful and practical trim around the cuffs.

FINISHING TOUCHES

Watch for accessories and personal touches to add to children's clothes. Bold appliqué initials on the bib of a jumper or overalls, or lacy trims for party dresses; purpose-made motifs to stitch to clothes, and cheerful buttons – in the shape of ladybugs or teddy bears, for example. D-rings and suspender fastenings or clips that look like brooches are also practical as well as decorative touches.

You can create a patchwork effect, and use up remnants of fabric, by making different sections of a garment in different fabrics: for example, make the yoke of a dress in a plain color, with the skirt and sleeves in a floral print; or use different primary colors for different sections of a pair of overalls to create a harlequin effect.

For small babies, remember to make clothes easy to remove, and easy to open at changing time. Use purpose-made snap fastener tape around inner leg seams and across shoulders or down the front of garments.

GROW TUCKS

Tucks are frequently put into children's clothes to allow for growth. The tuck must be on the straight grain of the fabric, and may be placed in the hem, on the skirt just above the hemline, in the bodice near the waistline, or vertically, over the shoulder. Of course, the tuck is likely to show when it is unpicked, so be prepared to add a decorative trim along the line of the tuck.

Overalls

These practical overalls have an elasticized waist, roll-up hems, and adjustable straps, so that they can grow with their proud owners. The plain cotton version has a topstitched detail around the bib and suspenders – the corduroy version is more appropriate for winter months. Contrasting pockets and facings for the bib, waistband, and straps add fun and color. Snap fasteners at the waist make them easy to slip on and off, and clips in the shape of hands and feet add a distinctive touch. For young children, make them with an opening at the crotch to make diaper changing easy.

SUITABLE FABRICS

Corduroy, cotton drill, denim, solid-color or striped furnishing cotton, plus printed fabric for pockets and facings.

TO FIT

Toddlers, 18–36 months.

YOU WILL NEED

1⅝ yds of 36-inch wide fabric in main colour
¾ yd of 44-inch wide fabric in contrasting print
⅜ yd of ¾-inch wide elastic
One pair of decorative clips
Two jumbo snaps
Matching sewing thread

TO MAKE

1 Position one pair of pocket pieces with right sides together. Sew across top edge, then match shaped edges and stitch, leaving a 1¼ inch opening in one edge. Trim seam allowances, clip across corners and turn right side out. Slipstitch opening. Repeat for remaining pockets.

2 Center the front pocket on the front of main bib piece and stitch close to edge, forming a triangle of stitching at top corners. Position back pocket pieces on back pants pieces following markings, and stitch as for bib pocket.

3 Position contrasting bib piece on main piece with right sides facing. Stitch around sides and across top. Clip into seamline and trim seams. Turn right side out and press. Topstitch if desired.

4 On front pants pieces, fold tucks toward center front and baste in place along marked lines. Stitch center front seam. Press seam allowances to one side and topstitch 1¼ inch from seamline to give a strong seam and prevent edges from fraying. Repeat for center back seam.

5 Join inside pant leg seam and press and stitch seam allowances as before. (Leave side seams open at this stage.)

6 Pin main part of bib to pants front with right sides facing and stitch, without catching contrasting

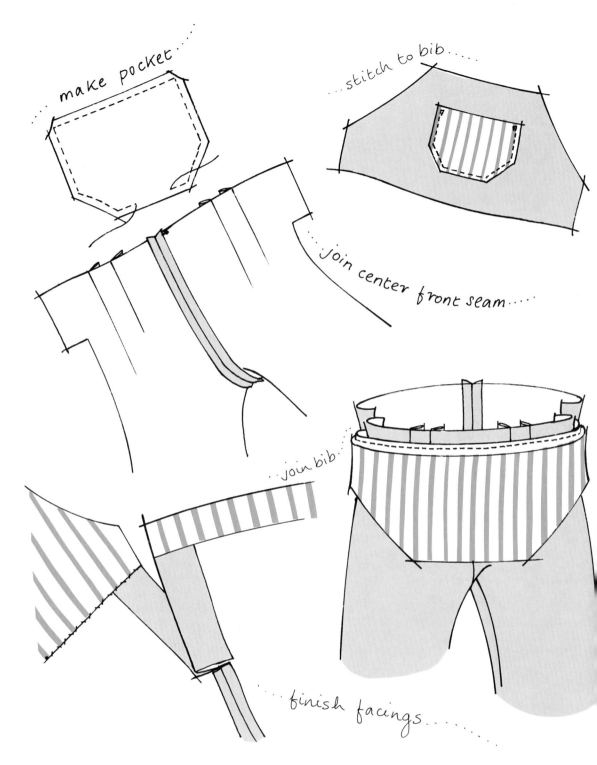

fabric in seam. Turn under seam allowance along free edge of bib and slipstitch to inside of pants front, enclosing seam allowances.

7 Position waistband pieces together, right sides facing, and stitch along top edge. Trim seam allowances and turn right side out.

Press. Stitch main part of waistband to top of pants back, turn under free edge of contrasting fabric and slipstitch in place enclosing raw edges, leaving ends open.

8 Turn pants inside out and stitch outside leg seams from lower edge of waist opening to hem. Press

seams open and finish raw edges. Turn under and press front facings in line with seam. Finish raw edge.

9 To finish back facing, clip into seam allowance level with lower edge of facing. Fold facing in half, folding it back on itself, and finish raw edge. Position back facing

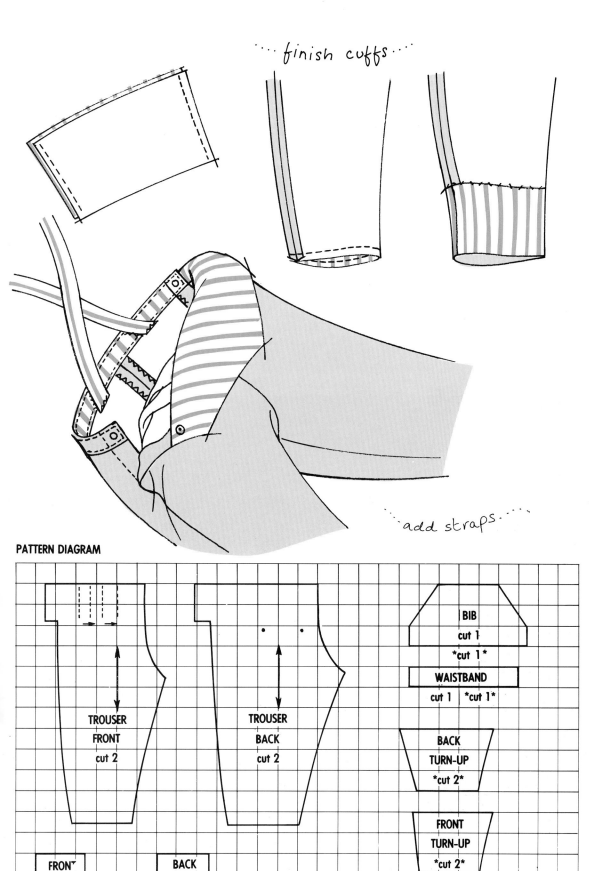

····finish cuffs····

····add straps····

PATTERN DIAGRAM

behind front facing and stitch together from seamline to edge of front facing.

10 Topstitch close to each edge of waistband to form a casing. Thread elastic through and check fit, then stitch ends of elastic in place 1 inch from seamlines at each end of waistband. Turn in seam allowances and slipstitch by hand. Attach snaps on each side of opening, following the instructions.

11 Position front cuffs on back cuffs and stitch side seams. Press. Slip cuffs over ankles of pants and stitch together around lower edge. Turn right side out and press. With cuffs fitting inside pant legs, turn under a narrow hem and topstitch or slipstitch in place.

12 Position pairs of shoulder strap pieces together, right sides facing, and stitch all around edges, leaving slanted edge open. Turn right side out and press. Topstitch all around if desired. Position straps on inside of waistband, so they cross over. Check length, adjust if necessary, and stitch securely by hand. Attach decorative clips to square ends.

TO MAKE PATTERN
Following diagram, in which each square represents 2 inches, enlarge pattern to full size. Trace the pattern.

NOTE
Seam allowances throughout are ⅝ inch unless otherwise stated.

TO CUT OUT
Cut out in main fabric:
2 pants fronts
2 pants backs
1 bib
1 waistband
2 straps
Cut out in contrasting fabric:
2 front and 2 back cuffs
1 bib
2 front pockets
4 back pockets
1 waistband
2 straps

Cut in contrast fabric where indicated: *cut 1*

177

7 Sewing for the home

Home decorating is a satisfying and rewarding pastime – and if you can create your own home furnishings you will not only be able to save money; you will also find you can add your own distinctive finishing touches to a room.

PLANNING STYLES AND SCHEMES
Before embarking on any home sewing project, it is important to collect inspiration and ideas from books and magazines. Fashions change, so be sure you will not tire of the scheme before the furnishings wear out. Bear in mind that well-made draperies in good fabrics should last a lifetime, while other decorations (paint and wallpaper) need attention every few years, so if you choose adaptable colors and patterns you will be able to give a room a new look without having to make new draperies. On the other hand, slipcovers will not have such a long life as carpets, so plan colors accordingly.

COLORS, SHADES, AND TINTS
It is useful to understand some of the principles of color scheming when planning home furnishings. Careful selection of color helps to set the atmosphere of the room: bright primary colors for busy kitchens, warm earthy tones of terracotta and cream for a quiet living room, restful combinations of colors for bedrooms, and so on.

The primary colors, red, blue, and yellow, are pure colors which cannot be produced by mixing other colors. However, mixtures of these colors, combined with black, gray or white, create the subtle tones of paints and furnishing fabrics. Deep-

Choose practical colors and fabrics for home decorating: pale, flat colors soon look tired in a busy family home – choose darker colors with a slight fleck or gentle pattern to disguise wear and tear.

er shades of a color are produced by adding black or gray, while paler tints result from adding white.

When the colors are arranged in a wheel, it is easy to see how the different combinations are created: violet as a mixture of red and blue, green as a mixture of blue and yellow, and orange as a mixture of yellow and red. Of course, mixing the three colors together in controlled amounts creates the tones of peach and beige which are so popular for soft furnishings.

WARM AND COOL COLORS

Colors can be divided into warm and cool tones: the warm colors are red, orange and yellow, and cool colors are blue and tones with a high proportion of blue in them. (For example, aquamarine – green with a high proportion of blue – is a cool color, while sunny yellowy green is warmer.)

Besides setting the feeling of a room (for exam-ple, rich warm reds creating a welcoming glow), color can be used to alter the proportions of a room. Deep shades and warm colors tend to make things seem larger, advancing towards you, while pale tints and cool colors behave in the opposite way, diminishing the apparent size of an object so that it seems farther away and the room feels more spacious.

The neutral colors – white, cream, gray, and beige – are particularly useful in decorative schemes, providing a backdrop for bolder colors and patterns.

CHOOSING COLORS

Color harmony is the art of grouping colors pleasingly in a room. Many ideas on color com-binations can be gleaned from nature: look at a sunset or a seashore scene: in a sunset the colors blend gently together, whereas the clear blue of sea

COLOR AND MOOD
Warm, mellow tones create a welcoming atmosphere in this formal living room (below left) while a predominantly blue color scheme brings a light, spacious feeling to a slightly more informal living room (below).

179

Manufacturers of furnishing materials take great care to co-ordinate the patterns and colors, so that it has become easy to mix and match different elements of the room. You need not stick to one particular manufacturer's range, but the color schemes they suggest are a useful starting point for developing your own individual style in decorating.

and strong yellow of the sand create a much harsher color scheme, which needs strong sunlight to make it effective. The scale on which colors are used is also carefully controlled in nature: think of the size and color of a peacock compared with those of an elephant.

Think of the strength and balance of colors when you plan a scheme – concentrating strong, dark colors in one corner of a room and pale colors in the rest of the room upsets the balance and does not achieve the harmony you should be seeking.

The aspect of a room (whether it faces toward or away from the sun) can also affect the choice of colors. Most decorators advocate warm colors for north- and east-facing rooms, which do not have the benefit of the warmth of sunlight, while cool colors can be used happily in bright, sunny rooms. Of course, in the southern hemisphere, it is the south- and west-facing rooms that may not get adequate sunshine. In hot climates, however, you may prefer to use cool colors in such rooms to create a quiet retreat from the heat of the day.

The final consideration is the style and function of the room: romantic bedrooms demand soft pastel tints, while deep, strong colors set the style of masculine studies.

Prints and florals, whether they are in fabrics, rugs, or wallcoverings, should be used with care. Too many contrasting patterns will create a feeling of confusion. Family habits also affect the choice: bright, busy patterns are useful for disguising the wear and tear, but a single person's apartment can take plainer, paler colors, which might show the dirt in other households.

It is useful to choose a dominant color in a room, using shades or tints of that color around the room to give different amounts of interest. Select a diffe-rent color to give accent and contrast. Repetition of a color can be monotonous, but picking out an accent color from a print creates a coordinated effect. For example, if you use a floral print which is predominantly cream and peach with touches of green, use the neutral tones for large areas, like walls and carpet, but cover chairs or cushions in the same green which appears in the print. Manufactur-ers also make the job of co-ordination easier by producing ranges of fabrics which are designed to be used together, often with wallpapers to comple-te the effect. For example, a simple, striped wall-paper could form the backdrop to a room, with cotton sateen or chintz draperies which have the same stripe, plus a floral motif. Other fabric acces-sories could be made from a matching fabric which uses only the floral element of the pattern, for

example.

The textures and weaves of fabrics are also important in creating a harmonious scheme. In an almost monochromatic scheme, different textures provide the variation that gives visual interest to the room. Consider simple dobby weaves – with small geometric patterns – or more elaborate damasks and brocades. The woven patterns may be geometric or floral. You can also achieve some interesting effects with fairly loosely woven fabrics in a range of natural and neutral colors.

SELECTING FABRICS

The fabrics you choose for home decorating de-pend on the item you are making. Slipcovers take the most wear and tear, so choose heavier fabrics – particularly for items in daily use. Linen-blends and corduroy are good choices for busy living rooms: reserve chintz and cotton sateen for side chairs. The firmer the weave the more durable the fabric will be. When choosing fabrics for draperies, con-sider how they will drape: use more loosely woven fabrics, or fabrics with a rich sheen, such as sateen velvet, and brocade.

The use and style of the room also affect the choice of fabric. For formal, traditional rooms consider damask, brocade, taffeta, furnishing satin, velvet, and traditional floral prints. Informal, country-style rooms look good with small floral prints, gingham, linen-cotton blends, glazed cotton, or canvas. Modern, sleek rooms demand leather, corduroy, canvas, neutral cottons and linens, or splashes of color in glazed cotton.

Other home furnishing accessories require diffe-rent qualities. Lampshades should be made from firmly woven, translucent fabrics. Use vinyl for tough shopping bags and efficient aprons, and fine linens for embroidered pillows and table-cloths. The range is almost endless.

Fibers may be natural or synthetic. Natural fibers have returned to fashion in recent years – but for some items a proportion of synthetic fiber makes for easy care and extra durability.

Select needles and thread as for dressmaking, using cotton-wrapped polyester, mercerized cot-ton, or 100 percent polyester, as appropriate. Some synthetic threads are suitable for the whole range of fabrics. Normally, a size 90 (13) needle is suit-able, with stitch length varying from 15 to 20 for fine fabrics to 12 for heavier fabrics. For very heavy fabrics you may need a size 100 (16) needle.

Bedroom furnishings

Many fabric furnishings can be introduced into the bedroom – either an adult room or a child's room – to create a feminine, romantic atmosphere. Bedspreads can be made in fabrics to match other furnishings in the room, and are a great money-saver, since tailored bedspreads in luxurious finishes can be expensive.

The headboard is often the focal point of a room, so it is particularly appropriate to add drapes or make a padded headboard to attract the eye.

MAKING YOUR OWN BEDSPREADS

Whether austerely tailored or frivolously feminine, bedspreads are a dominant feature in a bedroom. Choose a style to suit the style of your room and your own needs. When choosing fabrics, bear in mind that the bedspread covers an article not easily overlooked, so plain colors and soft patterns may be easier on the eye than strong patterns.

FABRICS AND LININGS

Many fabrics are suitable for bedspreads, including rayon or silk taffeta, chintz, faille, or polished cotton, velveteen, firmly-woven furnishing cottons, and linens. A lining is often included, either under the complete bedspread, or just the top panel on a bedspread with a flounce. Choose lining of the same width as the main fabric, so that seams coincide. Note the position of seams for double beds on the measuring diagrams: this ensures that there is not an ugly seam down the central, focal point of the bed.

Calculate the amount of fabric you need by drawing a cutting layout on graph paper, or use the Fabric Estimates on page 252.

Plain bedspreads may be made up in ordinary or quilted fabric. Flat fabric should be lined, and may be interlined, if desired, to give it extra body. The edges may be hemmed or bound. Plan the size of the bedspread to suit the room: arrange it so it hangs halfway down the bed, showing off a dust ruffle over the base and legs of the base, or make it floor length.

For fitted bedspreads, the skirt should hang to floor level. Join widths of fabric to make up the top and side panels, taking ⅝ inch seams and pressing them open. Finish raw edges, or make a flat fell seam, if the bedspread is unlined. Then make them and attach skirt.

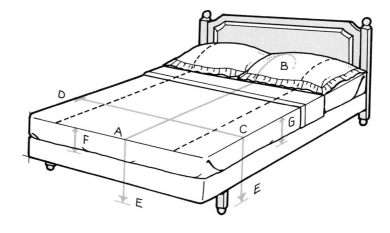

MEASURING
Fitted bedspread.

Main panel. LENGTH: A-B, measuring over pillow to foot of bed. Add 15 inches for pillow tuck-in allowance, ⅝ inch seam allowance at foot and 1 inch for hem at top edge.
WIDTH: C-D plus 2½ inches seam allowance for double bed, 1¼ inch seam allowance for twin bed.

Skirt. DEPTH: C-E plus ⅝ inch for seam allowance and 1½ inches for hem.
LENGTH: twice A-B including 15 inches for pillow tuck-in, plus C-D, plus allowances for pleats or gathers:
For box skirt allow 16 inches for each of two inverted pleats, plus 2½ inches for seam

allowances, plus 2 inches for hems at the headboard end.
For gathered skirt, multiply by 2½ to 3 for fullness, and include at least 8 inches for seam allowances and hems at the headboard end.

Plain. LENGTH: A-B plus A-E, plus ⅝ inch seam allowance and 1½ inch hem allowance.
WIDTH: D-C plus twice C-E plus 3 inches hem allowance.
LINING: cut lining 1 inch shorter and 2 inches narrower than main fabric.

Average measurements for plain bedspreads are:
DOUBLE: 94 × 110 inches.
TWIN: 74 × 110 inches.
KING-SIZE: 100 × 120 inches.

Before measuring, make up the bed with your usual bed linen and pillows.

CRISPLY COVERED
Cool blues and warm pinks complement each other in this fresh, feminine bedroom. The draperies, bedcovers, tablecloth, and generous pile of pillows add up to give a soft but crisp effect.

join widths

bind edges

QUILTED PLAIN BEDSPREAD

Join widths of quilted fabric to make up a single panel, using flat seams. Unpick the lines of quilting stitch and trim batting from seams to eliminate bulk. Join the top layers of fabric and press seams open. Turn under seam allowance on backing and slipstitch by hand.

Cut a strip of binding to go across top edge, and cut and join strips to fit all around sides and lower edge: this should be cut on the bias, and should be fairly wide, about 6–8 inches for a bold finish. See pages 66–68 for instructions on cutting, joining and applying binding.

SKIRT WITH INVERTED PLEATS

Make up center panel (for double beds) with a full width of fabric down center and narrow strips down each side. Trim selvages from seam allowances to prevent puckering. Lay center panel over bed and check fit. Mark curved seamline around lower corners if necessary. Allow ⅝ inch seam allowance. Make up cording and pin and stitch in place down sides and across lower edge of center panel.

For the skirt, cut one end section with 12½ inch pleat and seam allowance. Cut two side sections, adding 9¼ inches for hem, seams and pleat. For the length of the skirt, include the allowances on page 181. To avoid unnecessary seams, cut the side skirt panels on the lengthwise grain and the end skirt across the fabric. Seam the end section to match the top panel. Join the three sections of the skirt, taking ⅝ inch seams. Hem the lower edge, turning under ⅝ inch then 1 inch, and press. Slipstitch or machine stitch in place.

Place a pin at the center of each side and lower edge of center panel. Pin mark the skirt at the same points. Position center panel of skirt across lower edge of center panel of bedspread, and pin, matching pin marks and working out to the corners. Fold inverted pleats, making each fold 4 inches deep. Then pin side panels of skirt down

side edges of center panel, right sides facing and raw edges matching. Stitch in place, using the cording or zipper foot.

Finish top of center panel and ends of the skirt with a ½ inch double hem.

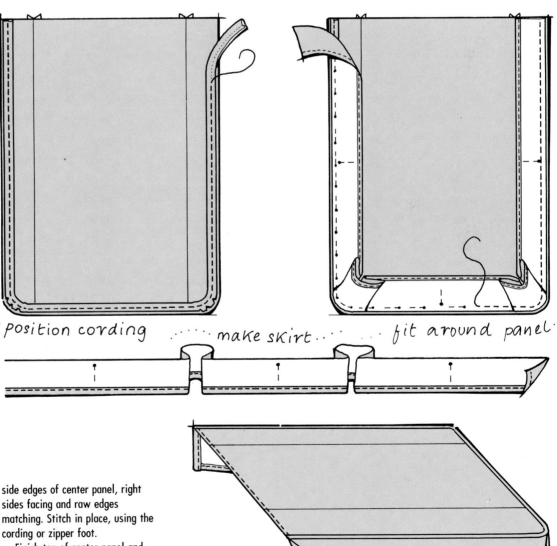

position cording   make skirt   fit around panel

Bedlinen and draperies

There is an enormous variety of bed linens from which to choose these days, in both solid colors and prints. However, you may sometimes wish to make your own – to get a perfect match with other fabric furnishings in the bedroom, for example, or to create something special, such as real linen pillowcases, for example, perhaps monogrammed as a wedding present.

PILLOWCASES

Pillowcases take on more importance if you choose to cover your bed with a down comforter, or duvet, in the European way, since they are on full view all the time. For a neat effect, make "housewife"-style pillowcases, as shown here. These have a tuck-in flap on the underside, so that the pillow is completely enclosed. The basic pillowcase design can be varied by the addition of a flat border or a ruffle. Machine or hand embroidery can also be used for decorative effects.

DUVET COVERS

Because duvets are still something of a novelty in the United States, covers for them are available only in a somewhat limited range of patterns and colors. However, you can easily make your own cover from lightweight fabric, decorating it in any num-

ber of different ways – appliqué, embroidery, or a ruffle around the edge are some of the possibilities. And, of course, patchwork is a "natural" for a duvet cover.

If you are making the cover from plain fabric (as opposed to patchwork) and must join widths, place a full width at the center and partial widths on either side of it. Duvet covers are normally fastened with snaps; for convenience choose those that come already attached to woven tape. You can use buttons instead, fastening them with either buttonholes or thread loops. Position the opening across the foot of the cover, making it about 20 inches less than the width of the duvet. If you make the opening any shorter than this, it will be difficult to get the duvet in when you change the cover (a difficult enough task at the best of times!).

WAYS WITH SHEETS

If you prefer the traditional type of bed linen, you may wish sometimes to give the top sheet an individual touch, perhaps by applying narrow cord to the top hem or binding it with fabric to match the bedspread. Remember, too, that readymade sheets can be used in all sorts of imaginative ways – made into curtains or skirts for dressing tables or covers for throw pillows.

BASIC ENGLISH PILLOWCASES

This pillowcase is made from a single strip of fabric. Allow 7 inches for tuck-in and turning at one end, and 4½ inches for border and hem at the other end. Allow ⅝ inch seam allowance along each long edge.

Turn under and stitch a ½ inch wide double hem at one end, which will be the tuck-in end. At the other end, turn and press ½ inch to the right side, then turn over another 4 inches to form the border. Topstitch in place, adding decorative cording if desired. Press under 6 inches at the tuck-in end, and fold the strip in half, wrong sides inward. Make a French seam along top and lower edges. Press and turn right side out.

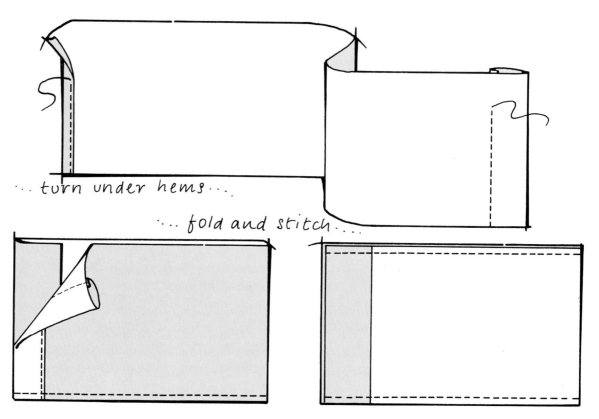

... turn under hems ...

.... fold and stitch ....

... stitch ruffle ...

... add back ...

RUFFLED PILLOWCASE

Cut a panel of fabric for the front of the pillowcase, allowing ½ inch seam allowance all around. For the back of the pillowcase, cut one panel the same as the front panel, and a second panel 7½ inches wide and the same depth as the main panel, to form the tuck-in.

Turn under and stitch a ½ inch double hem along one end of the back panel, and one side of the tuck-in. Position the tuck-in behind the main panel, so that the ½ inch seam allowance extends beyond the finished edge of the main panel. Baste together along side edges of tuck-in.

Cut a double ruffle to fit all around pillowcase, and gather. Position on top of main panel of fabric, right sides facing and raw edges matching, allowing extra fullness at corners. Stitch in place. Lay the pieced back panel on top of the ruffled main panel, right sides facing, and stitch together all around outer edge, taking ½ inch seams. Do not catch the finished edge of the back panel in the end seam. Zig-zag stitch raw edges together, press, turn right side out, and press again.

FLAT-BORDERED PILLOWCASE

Cut main fabric and back panels the same size as for a ruffled pillowcase. Position tuck-in and back panel on wrong side of main panel of fabric, so that raw edges match all around, with the tuck-in behind the main back panel. Baste and stitch all around, taking care not to catch the finished edge of the back panel in the seam.

Cut a 4-inch wide border on the straight grain, and fit it all around outer edge of pillowcase, mitering corners (see page 68).

... position back panels ...

... add border ...

... turn over top hem ...

TRIMMING A SHEET

Your sewing machine can be used to work decorative stitching along the top hem of a sheet. A particularly attractive touch is to apply a narrow filler cord along the stitching line. Use the braiding foot and contrasting thread, and work over the cord with machine satin stitch.

For a contrasting edge, trim off the top hem of the sheet and bind the edge, using a 9-inch wide strip of fabric cut on the straight grain. Allow ½ inch for turnings at each end. Press under a ½ inch turning down each long edge and across ends. Fold binding in half, wrong sides together, and fit it over the top raw edge of the sheet. Stitch in place by hand or machine, slipstitching folded ends of the binding together for a neat finish.

... add cord ...

... or bind edge ...

MAKING A DUVET COVER

Cut two panels of fabric for the cover, allowing 1 inch for seams all around edges.

Press under the 1 inch seam allowance across lower edge and zig-zag raw edges to finish them. Make 5 inch long flat seams at each side of the lower edge of the cover. Stitch lengths of nylon snap tape to the seam allowance along the opening. Stitch seam allowances together across ends of tape.

With wrong sides facing, stitch narrow, ½ inch wide seams around sides and lower edge, then trim seam allowances, clip across corners, and turn inside out. Stitch another seam, ½ inch inside the previous one, so that raw edges are enclosed. Turn right side out and press.

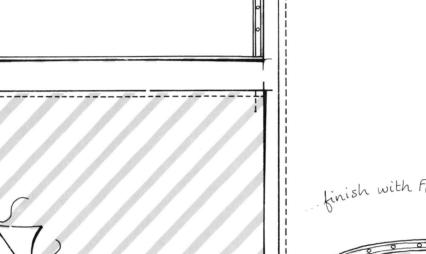

...position tape...

...finish with French seam...

THE ROMANTIC TOUCH

Embroidered white linen pillow covers, and sheets with antique lace trims, combine with softly draped curtains at the head of the bed to set a romantic mood in this country-style bedroom (opposite).

TRIMS FOR DUVET COVERS

Most of these ideas for trims should be applied to the top panel of fabric before making up the duvet cover.

- A corded trim, to match pillowcases, can be stitched across the top of the cover, about 6 inches from the seamline. A double row of cording gives extra emphasis (see page 185 for hints on applying cording).
- A ruffle can be topstitched in place, positioning the line of stitching about 4 inches inside the seamline, all around the main panel of the duvet cover (see page 85 for making and fitting a topstitched ruffle).
- Bands of ribbon or lace can be topstitched in place, using straight or decorative stitches over the edge of the trim (see page 58).
- For a contrasting border, cut the main panels of fabric smaller than the finished cover, and cut a border of fabric to fit all around the edges. Join the border to the main fabric, mitering the corners and zig-zag stitching raw edges together and pressing them toward the border. Check that the resulting panels of fabric include the seam allowances given for a plain duvet cover, and assemble as usual.
- Appliqué motifs can be stitched to the top panel of fabric before assembling: use a single, large motif in the center, or a row of smaller motifs close to the top edge, with groups of motifs in the lower corners.
- Make lines of pin tucks down the main panel of the cover: these are particularly effective when combined with eyelet lace trims and ruffles.

- For a ruffle set into the seams of the cover, reduce seam allowances around sides and top edge to ½ inch. Make up a ruffle to fit around sides and lower edge, allowing at least 1½ times the fullness. (A ruffle is not normally inserted along the top edge of the cover, as it can be uncomfortable.) You can also use deep, eylet lace trims as gathered ruffles. Position ruffle around sides and lower edge of main panel, with right sides facing and raw edges matching, and baste in place, distributing fullness evenly. Along lower edge, the raw edge of the ruffle should be ½ inch in from the raw edge of the panel. Center one half of the snap tape along the seam allowance, over the gathered edge of the ruffle. Topstitch in place. Fit the opposite half of the snap tape to the opposite seam allowance. Assemble the duvet cover, stitching the two panels together, with right sides facing, taking a ½ inch seam – 1 inch along short seams on either side of opening at lower edge. Press, then zig-zag stitch raw edges of cover and ruffle together. Zig-zag stitch to finish raw edges along bottom of cover, then topstitch across seam allowances at ends of fastening tape.
- For a child's bedroom, you can go to town with appliqué motifs, perhaps taking your inspiration from favorite fairy tales or comic strip characters. Or make a dramatic patchwork effect, using blocks of bold primary colors – a particularly useful idea if the bedspread is wider than the fabric available.

DUST RUFFLES

A dust ruffle is a skirt that is fitted under the mattress, over the box springs. Occasionally, a dust ruffle may be fitted over the mattress, to replace a fitted sheet – but this is not particularly practical, since it creates a bulky, flounced sheet which is difficult to launder.

Dust ruffles may be made from medium-weight cotton, or from heavier, furnishing fabric to match other items in the room. In a feminine setting lace trims and ruffles are appropriate, or you may prefer to add simple ribbon trims, or bound edges to coordinate with other furnishings.

For economy, the central panel, under the mattress, can be made in unbleached muslin or other economical fabric. Check that the fabric (together with any trims) can be laundered in the same way as the fabric used for the skirt section.

MAKING A DUST RUFFLE

Cut and join fabric widths for top panel. Cut strips for ruffle across grain, and join; use a French seam on fine fabrics. Hem lower edge, and finish ends of flounce with ½ inch double hem. Run lines of gathering stitch along raw edge of flounce. Pin mark the edge of the top panel to divide into four or six equal parts, and pin mark top edge of flounce to match. Pin flounce to top section, matching pins. Each end of the dust ruffle should extend 6 inches around top edge. Draw up gathering threads to distribute fullness evenly, allowing a little extra fullness at corners. Stitch in place, then finish top edge of center panel by turning under and stitching.

Attach trims, such as lace, ribbon, or binding, before fitting the skirt to the main panel. As an alternative, you could make up the skirt with crisp box pleats, in which case allow up to three times the finished pleated measurement of the skirt when cutting out the fabric.

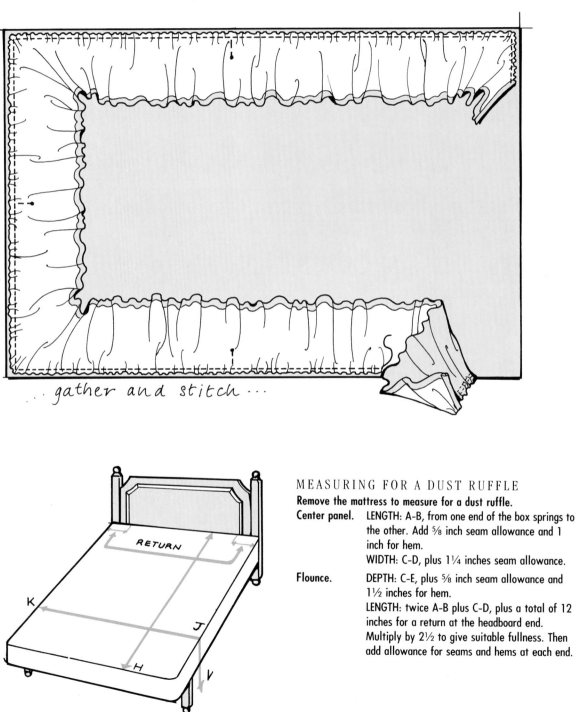

... gather and stitch ...

MEASURING FOR A DUST RUFFLE

Remove the mattress to measure for a dust ruffle.

Center panel.	LENGTH: A-B, from one end of the box springs to the other. Add ⅝ inch seam allowance and 1 inch for hem.
	WIDTH: C-D, plus 1¼ inches seam allowance.
Flounce.	DEPTH: C-E, plus ⅝ inch seam allowance and 1½ inches for hem.
	LENGTH: twice A-B plus C-D, plus a total of 12 inches for a return at the headboard end. Multiply by 2½ to give suitable fullness. Then add allowance for seams and hems at each end.

TRIMS FOR THROW PILLOWS

In the bedroom, throw pillows are particularly effective at the head of the bed, breaking up the expanse of bed. You can achieve this effect in a number of ways, but lacy trims are very effective in creating a romantic mood. You can add touches of color, using sheeting to co-ordinate with sheets, or ribbon trims, for example. You can use eyelet lace, or nylon or cotton lace, either applied to the front of the pillow, or inserted in the seam around the sides of the pillow.

Mix shapes as well as trims: square, circular, bolster shapes – even heart-shaped pillows can be attractive; by adding ribbon trims to heart-shaped pillows you can hang them on the wall as you would a picture.

Synthetic stuffings are usually appropriate: they are lightweight and maintain their shape well. You can add an extra dimension to your decorative scheme by inserting sachets of pot-pourri into the pillows. Use lawn or organdy for the sachet, and make it relatively large and flat to disperse the scent.

OPENINGS AND FASTENINGS

Of course, you can set zippers into pillows, but it may be more appropriate to finish openings with more lightweight fastenings: touch-and-close (Velcro) is useful, or simple covered buttons. You can also use simple tapes or ribbons to tie openings. With all these methods, allow a good overlap down the sides of the opening. You can make a tuck-in in the same way as the pillowcase tuck-in (see page 184) or center it across the back of the pillow.

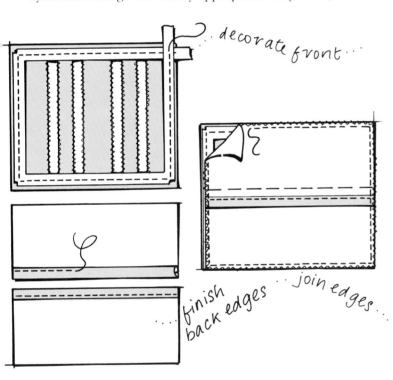

...decorate front...

...finish back edges · ·join edges...

MAKING LACY PILLOW COVERS

Start by measuring the pillow carefully: if it is circular or shaped, cut a template the exact size of the finished pillow. When cutting out, add ½ inch seams all around.

Decorate the front panel before trimming to size. (For suggested finishes, see below.) Any ruffles, cording or other trim should also be applied to the front panel.

For the back panel cut two pieces of fabric, allowing 2 inches plus 1 inch for overlap and turning down each center edge; the panels can be the same size, or you can offset the overlap, so that the opening is exactly centered, or to one side of the back of the pillow.

Turn under ½ inch double hems down the center edge of the two back panels and overlap them by twice the overlap allowance included. Baste the layers together, then treat the two panels as one.

Make the cover in the usual way, stitching the front to the back with right sides facing, and then finish seam allowances together. Press. Turn right side out and press.

To hold the opening edges together, make simple machine buttonholes (see page 91) in the overlapping edge, positioning them about 6 inches apart. Cover button forms with fabric to match the pillow, and sew them to the underlap to match the buttonholes.

Alternatively, stitch tapes to each side of the opening, or use nylon touch-and-close tape.

IDEAS FOR DECORATIVE TRIMS

- Topstitch ribbon or lace strips to the front of the pillow. If you work around each side of the pillow, miter the corners for a neat finish. To avoid mitering, lay all the trims in one direction across the front of the pillow. For a decorative corner finish without mitering, where there are several parallel trims, weave the ends of the trims into a trellis at each corner.
- Combine different trims for extra interest: ribbon alternated with lace or eyelet lace is very effective, and you can insert ribbon into special slotted eyelet lace or real lace for an extra decorative touch. Add a ruffle in the same type of lace as you applied to the front of the pillow.
- Pin tucks give a crisp finish with a Victorian air: run them only one way across the pillow to avoid awkward finishes at the corners.
- Add a contrasting center panel, or a matching panel, surrounded by a wide, lacy border. You can use lace fabrics, stitched over pastel-colored backgrounds to produce interesting effects. Stitch the lace and panel as for appliqué, either turning under the edge of the center panel or finishing it with a decorative zig-zag stitch. By using a panel of lace the same shape and size as the pillow, you avoid having to cut strips and do not need to miter corners on square pillows. It is also a good finish for circular or shaped pillows, as the trim can follow the curved outline of the cover, which would not be possible with straight ribbon or lace trims.

BED DRAPERIES

For a touch of real luxury in the bedroom, you can add full-length draperies around the head of the bed. There are any number of ways of doing this: your choice depends on the shape and size of the room and the effect you are after.

Some beds come with a frame for hanging draperies from – four-posters, or what was traditionally known as a "half tester", a canopy over the head of the bed, with draperies hanging on either side.

You can make your own supports for bed draperies: a simple rod above the head of the bed can be fitted with a curtain with a cased heading, or you can fit a drapery rod to the top of the wall, near the ceiling. For a more decorative effect, you can fit a small, semicircular shelf above the center of the headboard, and trim it with fabric, to form a decorative cornice. Hang the drapery below the shelf, drawing it out to the sides of the bed and fixing it in place on either side.

FABRICS AND FIXTURES

You can use a wide range of fabrics, depending on the effect you are after: don't skimp on quantities,

as a full effect adds to the sumptuousness of the draperies. However, you can use fabrics that are less expensive, and which might not be suitable for window treatments. Except in very sunny rooms, light resistance is not such an important consideration as with curtains and window draperies.

Go to town with trailing lengths of muslin, with a simple cased heading or just wrapped and tied over the supporting rails. Or choose plain cottons, which are reversible, to give a fresh, airy effect. The fabric should be translucent, diffusing light around the headboard.

Many styles of drapery are seen from both sides, so it may be appropriate to line the draperies in matching or contrasting fabric. Combinations of prints and gentle broken color effects, or plain glazed chintz are particularly appropriate. You can fit such draperies from a rod with a tape heading, like a window drapery, or make an easing to go over a rod around the head of the bed.

On a four-poster, it may be necessary to fit a drapery rod inside the top frame: make sure that you arrange the draperies so that the fixture cannot be seen from inside or outside the bed.

MOCK FOUR-POSTER

Fit four lightweight wooden curtain rods to the ceiling, over the head, sides and foot of the bed. Fit the poles at the head and foot of the bed on longer brackets than those at the sides, arranging them so they overlap at the corners. Make a full, unlined curtain with a deep, cased heading, to fit over the pole at the head of the bed. Make six narrow curtains with cased headings (you need use only half a width of fabric), and fit them to each end of the remaining three poles. Make tie-backs, or use ribbon to draw the curtains to the corners: at either side of the head of the bed, fit hooks to the wall to fit the tie-backs to.

...fit drapery rods...

...make cased headings...

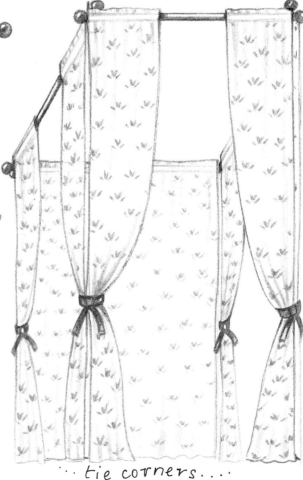

...tie corners....

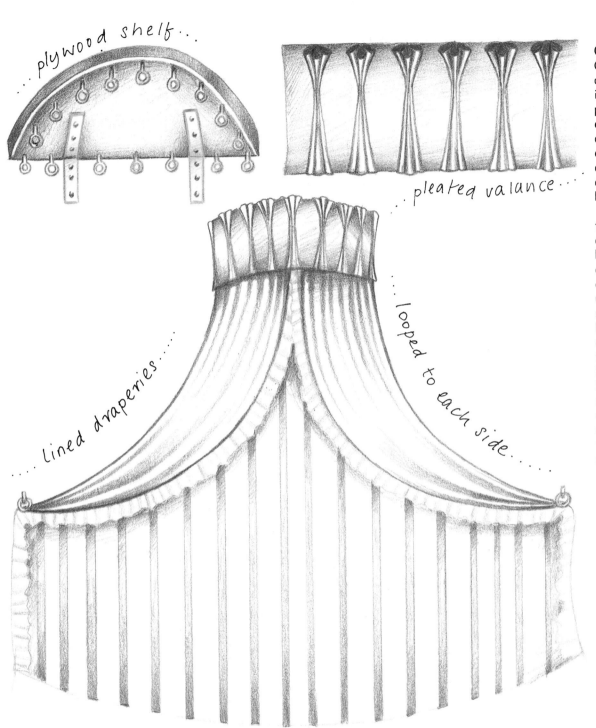

...plywood shelf...

...pleated valance...

...Lined draperies...

...looped to each side...

CORONET

Cut a semicircle of plywood, with a radius of about 12 inches. Cover it with fabric, sticking the fabric in place with fabric glue. Fit screw eyes along the back edge and all around the lower side of the curved edge, spacing them about 2 inches apart. Fit the shelf to the wall above the bed with a pair of simple brackets.

Make a valance, and fit it around the curved edge of the shelf. Make a lined drapery with a shirred heading (using shirring tape), allowing maximum fullness. Use a decorative fabric for the lining. The ungathered width of the drapery should be at least as wide as the head of the bed. The edges of the drapery look best if they are finished with a ruffle, cording or binding. Fit the drapery, with the lining to the inside, so that the edges of the drapery are at the center of the shelf, then draw the sides open, and loop them back to the wall with hooks and curtain rings.

For an alternative finish, make large bound buttonholes (see page 92), positioning them horizontally near the edge of the drapery, and fit them over large decorative knobs fixed to the wall on either side of the headboard.

IDEAS FOR BED DRAPERIES

- Fit a slim brass rod across the head of the bed, and hang a large lace panel: it may be hung flat against the wall or gently gathered. Make a cased heading, or use shirring tape to gather the lace in soft folds.
- To complement the clean lines of a modern pine four-poster, cut simple, rectangular panels of fabric. Finish the edges and fit simple ribbons to the top of the panel to tie over the top bars of the four-poster.

- For a simple canopy, fit wooden curtain rods to the ceiling at the head and foot of the bed. Make up a flat panel of double-thickness fabric, seaming the edges, and hang it so that it runs from the head of the bed, up over the pole, then loops to the second pole and down to the foot of the bed (or half way down to the foot). If necessary, use touch-and-close fastening to hold the drape in place, glueing the hooked side of the fastening to the top of the poles.

SLIP-ON HEADBOARD COVER

Use ready-quilted fabric, and bind the edges with 2-inch wide bias binding.

Measure the board the cover is to fit. If it is shaped, cut a paper template. If the board is not more than 1 inch thick, add up to 1¼ inches for ease, and ⅝ inch seam allowance all around. Cut out two panels of quilted fabric to these dimensions. If the headboard is wider than 1 inch reduce the ease allowance slightly, and cut a gusset the width of the board, plus ⅝ seam allowance down long edges, and long enough to fit around the sides and top of the headboard.

Position a strip of bias binding all around sides and top edge of front panel of cover. Position with right sides facing, and fold of binding along seamline of cover. Stitch in place. Position back panel of cover on wrong side of front panel, wrong sides facing, and stitch together along seamline all round sides and top edge. Trim bulk from seam and press, then press binding over raw edges of seam allowance. Slipstitch folded edge of binding along seamline.

If there is a gusset, fit binding around both front and back panels, then join to the gusset using the same seam finish.

Fit cover and check length: the lower edges should butt neatly under the headboard. Bind lower edge of cover, catching tape or ties made from binding into the seam to hold cover in place.

For a corded cover, cut out in the same way. Position cording all around right side of front panel (and back panel if there is a gusset) then join fabric, right sides facing. Press and trim seam allowances, then turn right side out and press. Finish lower edge as before.

join and bind edges ...

... or insert a gusset ...

... finish with ties ...

HEADBOARDS

If you do not want to go to the expense of full draperies at the head of the bed, you can still add a luxurious touch with a padded headboard. Of course, you can buy fully upholstered headboards, often shaped and with deep buttoning, but there is a limited range available, and there are many alternative ways to make your own cover.

Simple Hollywood beds are usually fitted with bolts or brackets to hold headboards in place, and you can either make your own panel to fit to the top of the bed, or use a simple wooden one – in either case you can make a removable, fitted cover, decorated in any number of different ways.

As an alternative to a covered headboard, you can fit panels of fabric-covered foam as backrests at the head of the bed. The simplest method is to make gusseted cushions, and fit them to a wooden rail above the head of the bed.

FABRIC AND FINISHES

Quilted fabrics are a particularly appropriate choice for headboard covers, adding padded comfort for those who like to sit up and read in bed. If you do not use quilted fabric, it is still essential to add some form of padding: polyester batting is easy to handle, or you could use layers of heavy interfacing of the kind used for interlining draperies and bedspreads.

Choose fabrics to match other furnishings in the room – draperies or upholstery, or the bedspread.

For a smart, tailored effect, for example, you could make a fitted bedspread with inverted pleats at the corners, and a matching headboard cover in quilted fabric, corded in the same way as the bedspread. A more feminine, ruffled duvet cover, perhaps with an appliqué motif, can be matched with a simple slip-on headboard cover, with similar appliqué motifs.

For a removable cover, the simplest finish is to bind the lower edge and attach ties to hold the cover in place under the edge of the board. For a fixed, tailored cover, turn under the lower edge and baste or staple it to the board. With fixed covers, it is a good idea to make extra panels to cover the area behind the head: by attaching them with touch-and-close fastening, you can remove them for regular washing.

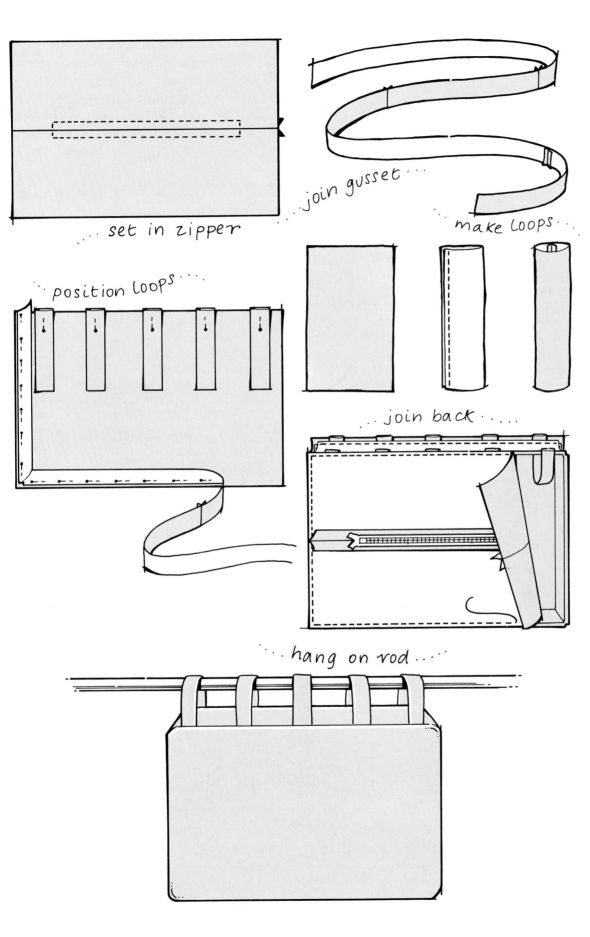

...set in zipper

join gusset...

make loops...

position loops...

...join back...

...hang on rod...

BACKREST CUSHION

Cut a piece of foam, at least 2 inches thick, to make a rectangular cushion large enough to suit the size of the bed. (For double beds it is easier to make two backrests.)

Measure the cushion and make and fit a tight unbleached muslin cover. Cut a front and back panel allowing ⅝ inch seam allowance all around. The back panel may be made from two pieces of fabric, with a zipper set between them so the cover can be removed for washing. Cut a gusset long enough to fit all around the cushion, positioning seams to coincide with the corners of the cushion, including the same seam allowance.

For the straps, cut four or five pieces of fabric, at least 12 inches long and 9¼ inches wide. Make up into tubes at least 12 inches long and 4 inches wide, positioning the seam down the center back of the strap.

Mark the positions of the straps on the top edge of the front and back panels, spacing them evenly apart: position one close to each end, but not within the seam allowance. Pin ends of straps to front panel, then pin gusset in place all around. Baste in place. Pin free ends of straps to back panel, checking that they are not twisted, then pin and baste gusset in place. Stitch seams to make up cushion cover, enclosing ends of straps in seams. If you did not insert a zipper into the back panel, leave an opening in the lower edge. Press, trim seam allowances, and press toward gusset. Turn right side out and press.

Insert the cushion, slip-stitching opening if necessary. Slot the straps onto a curtain rod fitted above the head of the bed.

Ways with windows

Windows bring light and air into your home. When you look at them with a homemaker's eye, your first thoughts are to ensure privacy without obstructing the sunlight or the view if it is a pleasant one. When you look at them with a decorator's eye, your concern is to create a window treatment that is in harmony with the other furnishings of the room and still captures the light and the view. The window treatment you decide on depends mainly on your plans for the room. The style of the window may suggest or even dictate the treatment, but even that can be changed by the clever use of curtains or draperies or by simple carpentry tricks that alter inside window proportions.

There are many types of window treatment from which to choose: classsic draw draperies, with or without glass curtains underneath; stationary draperies framing the window, perhaps combined with Venetian blinds, louvers, or roller shades; frothy Austrian shades in sheer fabric; tailored, crisp Roman shades; perky café curtains; and superbly elegant swags and cascades, hung alone or over full-length draperies. The permutations are endless, although the need to harmonize with the style of the room may restrict your choice.

IDEAS FOR WINDOW TREATMENTS

There are various factors to consider when choosing a window treatment. The shape and size of the window is the first consideration, followed perhaps by the style of the décor. The height of the ceiling is an important element; if the ceiling is low, it is usually best to avoid cornices or valances, which tend to make it appear even lower; in this case, straight draperies with a simple pleated heading, hung from a conventional traverse rod placed close to the ceiling, might be the best choice. With a higher ceiling, you could opt for a decorative pole, or a cornice or valance to match the draperies. If the ceiling is very high, you could go for a dramatic effect with a contrasting cornice or an elaborate swag.

Remember also to consider how much light you want to admit. An Austrian or balloon shade is fairly bulky when pulled up, so these styles are best suited to bedrooms, where you are less likely to require full sunlight during the daytime.

To admit as daylight, lined draperies should normally be designed so that when opened they will clear the window. Remember to allow for this "stackback" when buying hardware and fabric.

TOP DRESSING

A shaped valance with layered ruffles frames this delightful square bay window (opposite). The topstitched ruffles are also used down the outer edge of the draperies to complete the picture. Simple roller shades provide an instant screen when necessary.

PICTURE WINDOWS

Full-length windows, patio doors and "window walls" need full length curtains or draperies. The rod is mounted on the wall above the window, as close to the ceiling as possible, so that when the draperies are closed the whole wall becomes a single drop of fabric. If the window does not extend to the end of the wall, it is often advisable to fit the rod so that the draperies extend to the end: this gives plenty of "stackback" for draperies during the day, so that they can be pulled clear of the window.

BAYS AND BOWS

It is important to choose the right kind of rod for bay and bow windows, which can be curved to fit around the alcove. In some cases, you can fit a rod on the outside of the bay, so that the bay is closed off at night when the draperies are closed. Another alternative is to fit stationary draperies (draperies for show, which are not large enough to draw across the window) on the outside of the recess, and use shades, hung close to the windows, to screen the room at night.

ASSYMETRIC STYLES

An unusual form of window dressing, which rose to popularity over 150 years ago, has been enjoying a revival: this is the idea of dressing a window asymmetrically. The treatment often consists of a sheer curtain — perhaps made of voile — on one side and a stationary drapery, of rich velour or brocade on the other, but you can adapt the style to many other fabrics. The treatment may also include elaborate swags and cascades, cord ties, and tassels. (A more modern asymmetric treatment is a single drapery, which stacks at the side of the window when it is drawn open.) With these elaborately draped styles, it is often best to fit a plain roller shade against the window to screen the room at night, rather than complicating the arrangement — and spoiling the effect — with a traverse rod.

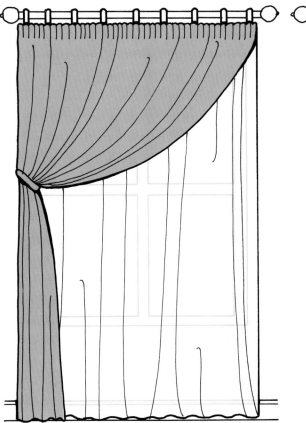

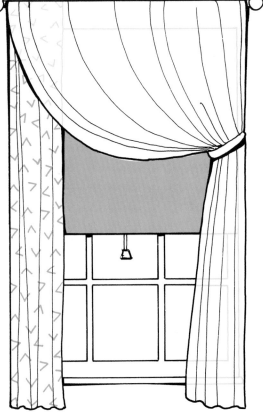

196

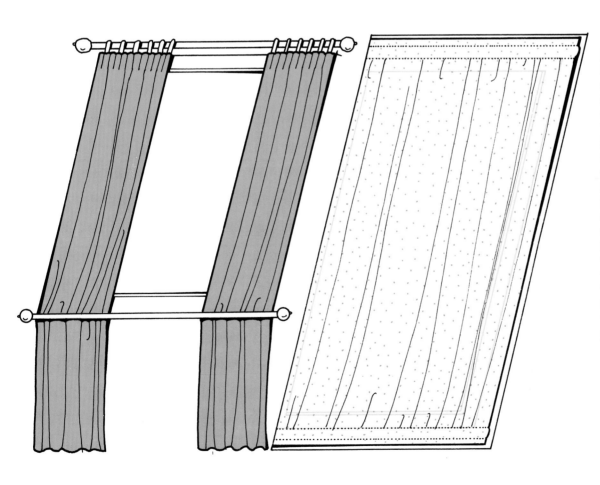

DORMER WINDOWS

Dormer windows, set into the sloping roof of a house, usually demand small, informal curtains, fitted into the dormer recess. A tension rod, which fits inside the window recess, is a convenient type of rod for dormers. Another good window treatment is a single roller shade or Roman shade.

ROOF WINDOWS

In some homes, particularly where rooms have been converted from attics and lofts, sloping roof windows are set into the ceiling. The choice of window treatment is limited, since normal "hangings" would be useless. The solution is either to fit narrow curtain rods at the top and bottom of the window frame or to fit substantial decorative rods, one at the top and one at the angle where the roof meets the wall. Then you can hang the curtains or draperies from the top rod and drape the lower end of the curtains over the lower rod. You may need to add extra weights to the hem to hold the drapery in place.

CORNER WINDOWS

Where a window runs around the
corner of a room, fit two one-way
traverse rods so that the draperies
can be drawn away from the corner.
You can also buy cut-to-measure
traverse rods that will go around
curves and corners and draw
draperies to one side only.

GLAZED DOORS

You may sometimes want to hang
sheer curtains on glazed doors – the
back door, for example – to give
privacy. To prevent the curtains
from blowing around, and catching
in the door as you open or close it,
fit curtain rods at both the top and
bottom of the door, and make casings
so that the curtains are held in
place. The same technique is useful
for pivot windows, and casement
windows that open inward.

CAFÉ CURTAINS

In some situations, particularly in
kitchens that are overlooked, you
may want to screen only the lower
half of the window. In this case,
hang café curtains from a rod fixed
across the middle of the window.
You can make them with a heading
casing and with a pleated heading
using pleater tape or with a
scalloped heading, either with
hand-made pleats between scallops
or with decorative loops for hanging
over the rod.

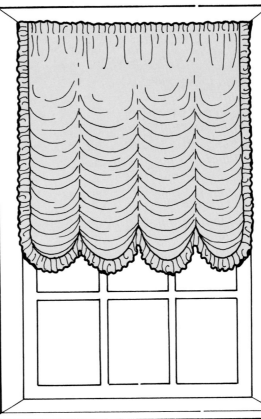

BALLOON SHADES

Balloon shades can be made in a way similar to a curtain, with a casing that fits over a rod; or they can be headed with drawstring-type tape. They may be lined or unlined. Extra tapes are fitted vertically down the shade, with cords running through them, so that they can be drawn up during the day.

AUSTRIAN SHADES

Similar to balloon shades, these are made without lining, with extra length. The vertical tapes are fitted so that they permanently gather the fabric at regular intervals across the shade. Again, cords are fitted to draw up the shades during the day. Austrian shades may also be made up in sheer fabrics as an alternative to glass.

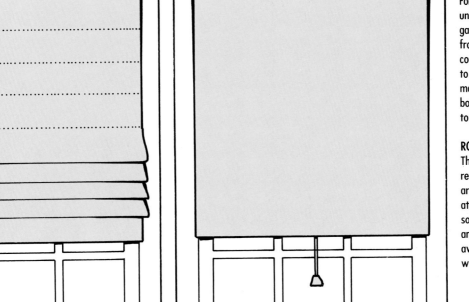

ROMAN SHADES

For a more tailored effect, lined or unlined Roman shades have no gathers or flounces. They are made from a flat panel of fabric, and cords run up the back of the shade to draw it up into deep folds. They may be trimmed with braid, or bound at the sides and lower edge, to add extra interest.

ROLLER SHADES

These are the simplest shades, and require a minimum of sewing. They are made from stiffened fabric, attached to a special sprung roller, so that they can be pulled down to any level at the window. Kits are available for making roller shades with your own choice of fabric.

Measure for shades in the same way as draperies: where the window is in a recess, the shades are more often hung inside the frame.

CURTAIN AND DRAPERY HARDWARE

There are basically three types of rod from which curtains and draperies are hung: flat curtain rods, which are used for curtains made with a casing, or rod pocket; decorative rods or poles, for hanging café curtains and stationary draperies; and traverse rods. The latter are constructed with a system of cords and pulleys. The cord operates one or two master slides, to which the leading edge of each panel is attached; by pulling on the cord you move the master slide back and forth along the rod, the other slides – and the rest of the drapery – following.

Traverse rods are available in a great range of sizes, styles, and types, with both one-way and two-way draws. Some are fitted with flat curtain rods, so that you can easily combine the draperies with glass curtains or a valance. Decorative traverse rods resemble simple poles with rings, but are cunningly constructed with a pulley system to give you traditional elegance with modern convenience. To fit unusual or distinctively shaped windows – such as bow windows – you can have traverse rods cut and shaped to order.

Decide on the type of rod you wish to use, and fix it in place (or mark the fixing position) before measuring the window for the draperies or curtains. The fixture can be placed inside the window recess (tension rods for lightweight curtains will fit neatly into awkward spots), on the wall just above the window frame, or at ceiling height.

CALCULATING FABRIC QUANTITIES

Once you have decided where to fit the rod, and how long it should be, the next step is to calculate how much fabric you will need. Decide on the fullness of the curtains or draperies; in the latter case this is normally dictated by the heading tape. Aim to use an exact number of widths of fabric, to avoid wastage. With hand-pleated draperies, the fullness can be adjusted to suit the length of the rod, by altering the size and spacing of the pleats, so that you use an exact number of widths of fabric for the pair of draperies.

When joining widths of fabric, it is important to match the pattern across the widths of fabric used: check the length of the pattern repeat on the fabric before calculating how much you need. You should also check whether the pattern repeat runs straight across the width or whether it is a "drop" repeat, with the pattern match staggered.

CUTTING OUT AND STARTING TO SEW

When cutting out curtain or drapery fabric it is important to be able to lay out the full width of the fabric and the full length required totally flat on the cutting surface. Few of us have tables which are large enough: if you have a cutting table, this may be sufficient, but in many cases you will have to resort to the floor. Cover the floor with a sheet, which can be washed easily, to avoid getting the new curtain fabric dirty.

Unroll the first length of fabric with the top of the pattern at the raw edge. Check that the end is cut straight across the grain (and the pattern). See page 32 for notes on straightening the grain and squaring the end. If there is a bold motif on the pattern, position it just below the bottom of the heading. Trim the top of the fabric appropriately.

Count the appropriate number of pattern repeats (as calculated when estimating fabric amounts) and mark the fabric on each selvage. Cut straight across the fabric, following the pattern. (With solid-color fabrics, mark a chalk line across the fabric to use as a cutting guide.)

Unroll the next length of fabric on top of the first aligning the pattern for either a straight match or a drop match. Cut the fabric at the same point in the pattern as before. Continue until all the lengths have been cut.

If the pair of draperies is made from an uneven number of widths of fabric, cut one length in half down the center. The extra half width should be positioned down the outer side of each panel.

Join fabric widths using flat seams. If there is a difficult pattern match, slip-baste from the right side to ensure a good match. After stitching the seams, clip into the selvages to prevent puckering.

MAKING THE CALCULATIONS

- Multiply the length of the rod by the fullness required, and add seam and hem allowances to get the total width of fabric required for the two panels.
- Divide the total width by the width of fabric you plan to use and round up the the nearest whole number. This gives the total number of widths of fabric required.
- Take the total finished length of the curtains or draperies and add appropriate allowances for hems (these are given on the following pages, varying according to the method of making the curtains or draperies).
- Divide the total length of fabric required by the pattern repeat, and round up to the nearest whole number (or the nearet half number with drop repeats). This gives the total number of pattern repeats which will run down each width of fabric.
- Multiply the number of pattern repeats by the length of the pattern repeat, and then by number of widths of fabric, to give the total amount of fabric required.

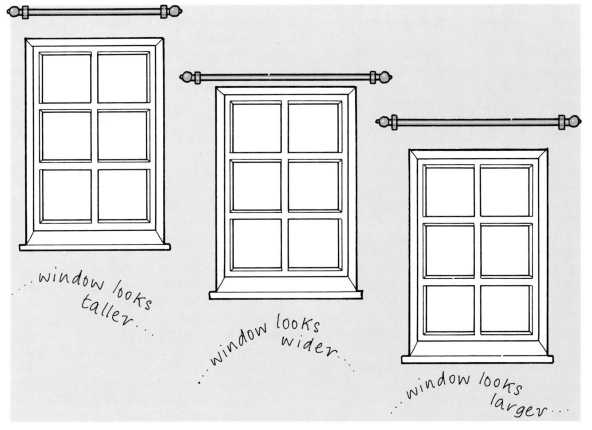

... *window looks taller* ...

... *window looks wider* ...

... *window looks larger* ...

WINDOW PROPORTIONS

The way you hang the curtains can create illusions, making the window appear taller, wider or larger than it really is.

To increase height fit the rod above the window, without extending it beyond the window.

To increase width extend the track for 4–8 inches beyond the window. With bulky draperies, increase this amount, to ensure that the draperies can be stacked clear of the windows during the day.

To increase both height and width, mount the fixture above the window, and extend it on either side.

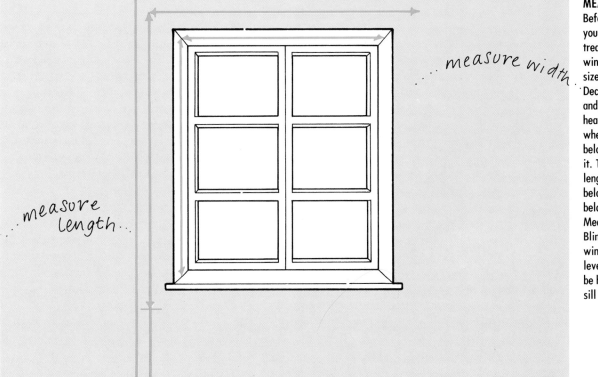

... *measure width* ...

... *measure length* ...

MEASURING YOUR WINDOWS

Before calculating how much fabric you need for your window treatment, you must measure the window to determine the finished size of the drapery (for example). Decide on the position of the rod, and, depending on the type of heading you are making, decide whether the drapery should hang below the rod, or so that it covers it. Then measure for the finished length of the draperies: to sill level, below sill level – about 6 inches below the sill – or floor level. Measure the width of the rod. Blinds are normally hung inside the window frame, dropping to sill level, although balloon shades may be hung outside the frame, to below sill level.

Sheers

Curtains and draperies made of sheer fabric can be used to provide privacy or screen out an ugly view, while admitting soft daylight. Some of the heavier sheer fabrics lend themselves to being made as unlined draperies with pleated headings (see page 207), and are hung from traverse rods so that they can be opened and closed. Lightweight sheer fabrics, such as marquisette, are normally used for stationary glass curtains, made with a casing and hung from a curtain rod under draperies. Another use for lightweight sheers is as ruffled curtains – a pretty window treatment for a bedroom.

SHEER DELIGHT
Soft, synthetic fibers in a variety of patterns create a translucent screen for windows.

FABRICS

Plain sheers are generally made from polyester or similar synthetic fabrics. These have the advantage of being economical, easy to hang, and quick to wash. However, there are also many fabrics for sheer curtains made from cotton or mixed fibers, and there is a choice of patterned fabrics and lace effects. Some fabrics for sheer curtains are made with a ready-stitched slotted heading running down one edge of the fabric, and a finished, decorative, or plain edge down the other side. With this type, the width of the fabric corresponds to the length of the curtains, and you simply have to make narrow hems down the sides of the curtains, where the fabric was cut off the roll.

CASED HEADING

If you are making your own cased heading, measure the finished length of the curtains, allowing ½ inch clearance at floor level: bear in mind that the top of the casing will extend for 1 inch above the curtain rod. Add 2¼ inches for the heading and 6 inches for a double 3 inch deep hem. Measure the width of the rod and multiply by two to three to give the required amount of fullness. If this measurement is more than the finished width of the fabric you plan to use, divide it by the width of the fabric and multiply the number of widths by the total length for each drop of fabric, to give the total fabric requirement. Include an extra allowance if there is a pattern repeat and a small allowance for straightening the fabric at each end.

To cut out, first straighten the ends (see page 32), then cut each drop straight across the fabric. It is important that the lengthwise grain of the fabric hang straight down the curtains. Join widths of fabric with a narrow French seam (see page 49). Turn under side hems, make the heading and casing and finish the hem following the diagrams.

RUFFLED SHEER CURTAINS

Ruffled sheers give an informal, fresh dressing to a window. For the style described here, they are made up in two panels, which may meet in the center of the window, overlap slightly, or overlap across the whole width of the window. Measure for each panel, in the same way as for curtains with a cased heading, but subtract the depth of the ruffle from the hem, and add ⅜ inch for turning. For the ruffle, measure around the leading (or center) edges and hem, where the ruffle is to be applied, and multiply by 1½ to 3, depending on the fullness required. The ruffle is usually cut across the width of the fabric: divide the width of the fabric you plan to use into the total length of ruffle required to find how many strips you will have to join to make up the required length. Decide on the depth of the ruffle – this is usually from 4 to 8 inches – and add ¾ inch for upper and lower hems. For a topstitched ruffle, the total depth of fabric is the overall depth of the ruffle, including a ½ inch heading, and a total of ½ inch for ⅛ inch double hems down the long edges of the ruffle. Multiply the total depth required for the ruffle by the number of strips required to give the amount of fabric for the ruffle. Allow extra fabric for a casing, to hold the curtains in position, and tie-backs if desired. You may also want to include a valance across the top of the curtains.

Cut out the total number of strips required for the ruffle on each curtain, and join them with narrow French seams. Cut out the required number of lengths for each curtain, and join them in the same way. Finish the ruffle as shown, then join it to the curtain using the topstitched method shown on page 85 or the over-edge method shown here. Stitch the side hems and finish the heading as for cased headings.

If you want to add a valance, make it in the same way as the ruffle, hemming both edges. Top-stitch in place as shown.

It is advisable to use a cord, fitted into a casing, to hold the curtains back from the center of the window, as these curtains never need to be closed. Hang the curtains, and drape each side back, holding them in place with a tape measure. Pin the inner and outer edges of the curtain to mark each end of the casing position. Topstitch a narrow casing across the curtain and thread a cord through. At the inner edge of the curtain, stitch across the end of the casing, to hold the cord firmly in place, and tie the other end of the cord to a hook, fixed to the window frame.

OTHER IDEAS FOR SHEERS

You need not restrict yourself to curtain styles for screening or dressing the window. Roman, Austrian, and balloon shades can be made up in sheer fabrics and there are many ways of draping lengths of muslin or lace around drapery rods to give a light dressing to a window that is not overlooked.

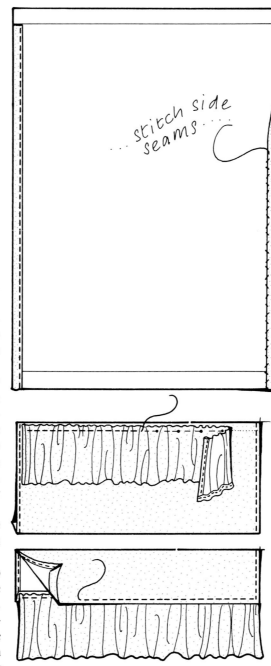

TIE-BACKS

For ruffled tie-backs, measure total length, using a tape measure looped around the curtains. Cut a band to this length, plus ½ inch for seam allowances, 2½ inches wide. Decide on the finished depth of the ruffle, and add a ¼ inch hem and ¼ inch seam allowance. Allow 1½ times fullness for the tie-back ruffle. Finish ends and long edge of ruffle with a ⅛ inch double hem. Gather the ruffle. Turn under ⅛ inch at each end of band and stitch.

WIDTH-FOR-LENGTH CURTAINS

If you use extra-wide fabric, designed to be hung widthwise, you can avoid seaming entirely. Check the widths available before positioning the curtain rod. Some of these fabrics are as wide (or deep) as 118 inches, ample for a very high window, but in other cases the fabric might fall a bit short. It may be possible, however, to lower the position, however, to lower the position of the rod slightly to compensate for this.

The amount of fabric you require is a length equivalent to 2 to 3 times the width of the window, depending on the fullness required.

To make up the curtains, simply turn under a double, ⅜ inch hem down each edge of the fabric. Press, baste, and stitch in place by machine, or slipstitch by hand if the edges of the curtains are visible once they are hung.

If you want to be able to open the curtains, cut the fabric in half down the center and make two separate curtains.

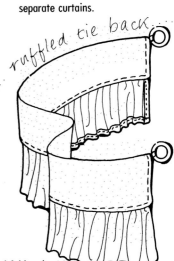

Fold band in half, and fold under ¼ inch along each long edge. Position one raw edge of band along raw edge of ruffle, with right side of band facing right side of ruffle. Pin in place, distributing fullness evenly. Stitch. Press, then turn band away from ruffle and press. Fold band over to right side of ruffle and pin folded edge of band over line of stitching. Pin in place then stitch close to foldline. Attach a ring to each corner of the band.

SHEERS WITH A CASED HEADING

Side hems. Turn under a 1 inch double hem down each side of the curtain. Pin in place and press. Stitch close to the fold.

Heading and casing. Turn under ¼ inches and press. Turn under another 2 inches, press, and pin in place. Stitch close to the folded inner edge; reverse stitching at each end. Place a row of pins half-way between stitching and top edge of the curtain. Check that the casing will fit over the curtain rod or wire you are using, and adjust position if necessary. Stitch along line of pins.

Lower hem. Hang the curtains to check the length. Turn up and pin a 3 inch double hem, or more if necessary. Stitch in place close to the folded edge of the hem.

Weights. To help the curtains hang evenly, and prevent them from billowing, insert weighted tape into the hem of the curtain. Use the lightest weight, covered in polyester. Slot into the hem, and sew at each end to enclose tape.

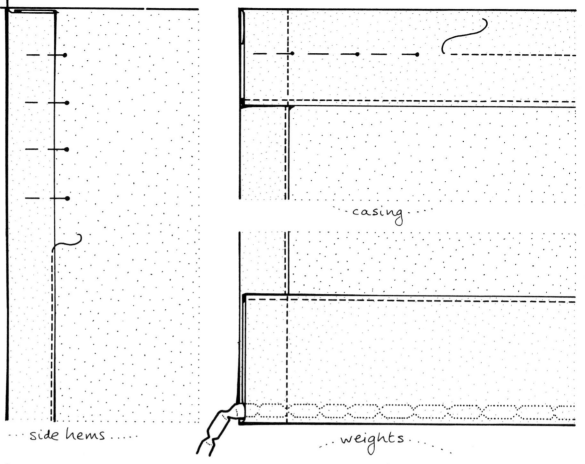

··· side hems ·····

casing ···

··· weights ···

SHEER AUSTRIAN SHADES

Austrian shades are often made of sheer fabric. The top edge may be finished with a casing or rod pocket and gathered over a curtain rod or given a drapery-type heading with special tape. Shirr tape is used to gather the fabric up vertically.

You will need a panel of fabric two and a half to three times the depth of the window, and one and a half times the width of the rod. If you have to join widths of fabric, make flat fell seams: French seams would create unnecessary bulk. Never join widths in the middle of a scallop – only where tape will be placed.

Turn under and baste 1¼ inches down each side edge. The raw edges and top and bottom edges are finished later. Decide on the spacing of the vertical tapes: allow 1 inch at each edge of the finished panel, then divide the fabric into scallops 8 to 12 inches wide. Remember that you need one more tape than

there are scallops: for seven scallops, you will need eight tapes.

Mark the tape positions with pins or dressmaker's chalk, then position the tape along each vertical line, and along each side hem, leaving 1 inch to form a ruffle at each edge. The side tapes should cover the raw edges of the side hem. Stitch across the lower edge of the tape so that the cord is firmly held in place. At the top edge, turn under a narrow hem, and fit a drawstring heading tape (see page 206). Or, if you prefer, make a cased heading, as described above. At the lower edge, turn up a double hem, enclosing the ends of the tape. Topstitch in place. The lower edge may be fitted with a topstitched ruffle (see page 85).

Draw up the vertical cords and tie in place so that gathers are evenly formed. Draw up the heading tape and hang the curtain from a drapery or curtain rod.

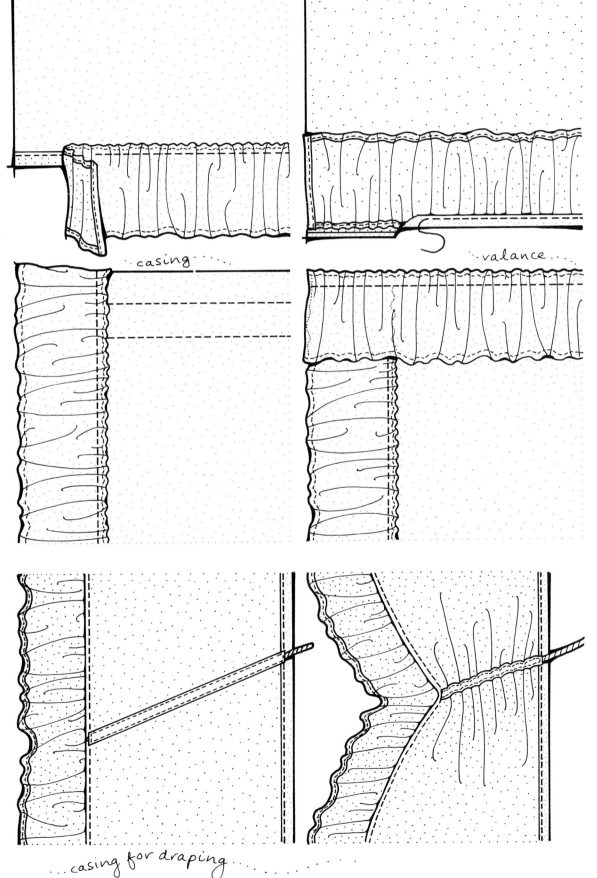

RUFFLED SHEERS

Making the ruffle. Turn under a narrow, double ¼ inch wide hem, and stitch. Alternatively, use a decorative zig-zag stitch to edge the ruffle, then trim away the fabric close to the stitching. For a topstitched ruffle, finish both edges in the same way. Turn under a ⅛ inch double hem at each end. Gather the ruffle, positioning stitches ½ inch from one edge on a topstitched ruffle, or ¼ inch from the raw edge.

Attaching ruffle with heading. Turn over ⅛ inch, then ¼ inch to the right side of the curtain down the center and lower edge. Pin and stitch. Position ruffle over edge of curtain on right side, and pin and topstitch in place.

Ruffle without a heading. Pin the ruffle to the wrong side of the curtain, so that raw edge of ruffle is ⅜ inch from the raw edge of the curtain. Distribute fullness evenly. Turn over ¼ inch then ⅜ inch down edge of curtain, over edge of ruffle. Stitch near edge of fold, over gathering stitches.

Side hems. Turn under a ⅜ inch double hem down each side of curtain. Pin and stitch.

Cased heading. Lay out the curtain panels, overlapping them the desired amount. Pin together across top. Turn under ¼ inch, then 2 inches across top of both curtains, and make a cased heading as for plain cased curtains.

Valance. To add a valance, make the valance in the same way as a topstitched ruffle, and gather with a line of stitching 1 inch from the top edge. Gather up to fit across the top of the curtain. Pin so that line of gathering matches top line of casing stitching. Stitch.

Casing for draping. Cut a strip of fabric on the lengthwise grain, 1 inch wide and the length of the diagonal line marked on the curtain between the pin marks, plus ½ inch for turning. Fold under ¼ inch all around casing. Pin to wrong side of curtain along marked line, and stitch along each long edge. Thread the cord through the casing and stitch across ends of casing to hold cord in place.

...ruffle with heading... *or without...*

casing

valance

casing for draping

Making draperies

Many people take up sewing in order to make their own draperies. Although ready-made draperies are relatively inexpensive, they are seldom completely satisfactory, since they are available only in a limited range of sizes – and you may not find any in exactly the kind of fabric you have in mind. With custom-made draperies you can have just what you want – but at a hefty price. The solution is to make your own. Making draperies does not demand any advanced sewing skills; all that it necessary is plenty of space in which to work and a patient, methodical approach.

LINED DRAPERIES

Draperies can be made without a lining, but it is generally worthwhile including a lining, to give a more luxurious effect and make the draperies hang better. A lining will also increase the life of the face fabric, protecting it from dirt and fading.

Linings can be stitched into the drapery by machine or by hand. If a drapery panel includes two or more widths of fabric, it is advisable to attach the lining to the drapery with lines of lock-stitch at intervals across the panel, in order to prevent it from sagging; this will also improve the appearance of the draperies. The side seams joining lining to drapery will then need to be stitched by hand, rather than machine.

Many people prefer to finish the side seams by hand even if the lining is not locked in, to make sure that the draperies will hang well.

CHOOSING FABRICS

The choice of suitable fabrics for draperies is very wide, ranging from textured sheers to brocades and velvets. The fabric you choose should drape well, so that the draperies will hang in balanced, graceful folds. It is also a good idea to check whether the fabric has been treated in any way to withstand fading and sun rot, or to make it flame-resistant.

Drapery fabric is not cheap, so before you invest a lot of money in it, make sure you will be happy living with it for years to come. If you are at all uncertain, buy a yard of the fabric and take it home, where you can evaluate its suitability in your room, along with other furnishings.

Lining fabrics intended especially for draperies are available in various weights and are most often made of cotton or rayon. Sateen linings come in white or cream; but you may prefer to use a colored lining to harmonize with your fabric. If you wish to use colored lining, check it against the face fabric in bright sunlight to make sure that the color of the lining does not affect the color of the draperies when they are hung together.

DRAPERY HEADINGS

In order to hang well, draperies must be pleated in regular folds across the top. Pinch pleats are by far the most often-used style. These groups of three pleats, separated by flat spaces about 4 inches wide, give draperies a neat, elegant appearance and are suitable for both modern and traditional interiors. There are, however, some other styles from which to choose, which you will find illustrated in these pages, along with various methods of achieving these effects.

Pleater tape This stiffened heading tape is made with narrow pockets, into which four-pronged hooks are inserted to form pinch pleats. The hooks help to hold the pleats in shape and are inserted directly into the slides of the drapery rod.

Drawstring tapes are made with narrow horizontal casings containing cords, which are drawn up to form the pleats. Although not so widely available as the standard pleater tape, they come in

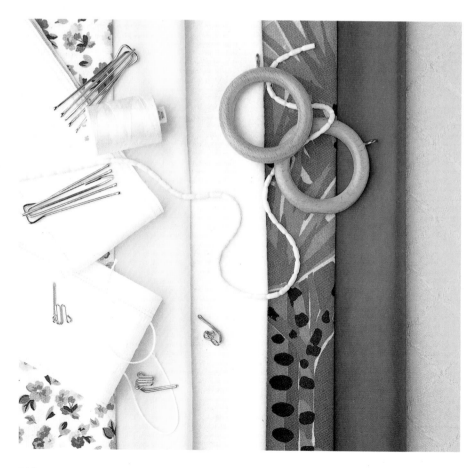

INGREDIENTS FOR DRAPERIES
Just some of the items essential for a professional finish: slotted and drawstring tapes, hooks, rings, weights for drapery hems and fabrics (including colored linings and soft, white interlining).

several different styles including pinch pleats and shirred and "smocking"-type headings.

Hand-made headings give the professional touch to draperies. The top of the drapery is interfaced, and the size and spacing of the pleats must be carefully arranged to suit the window and width of fabric.

You can buy a special tape marked with stitching and fold lines for pinch pleats, which simplifies the process, although it does not allow the flexibility you have when planning the pleats yourself.

ESTIMATING FABRIC AMOUNTS

Measure the window as described on page 201. Add 3 inches for hem at the top and 3½ inches for the lower hem. If you are using a heading tape that is narrower than 3 inches, reduce the allowance accordingly. For the width, take the finished width (pleated) of each drapery panel and allow the appropriate fullness for the type of heading you choose.

Details of fullness for hand-pleated headings are given on page 212. Divide the total width of fabric for the two panels by the width of the fabric you intend to use, to find the total number of fabric widths you will need, rounding up to the nearest width. Multiply the total length of fabric for the draperies by the number of widths of fabric to give the total amount of fabric, adding an allowance for pattern matching if necessary. It is important that the pattern should match across both panels, as well as at seams within the panel.

For lining, the total length required is the same as the finished length of the curtain. Calculate the amount of fabric in the same way as for curtains.

CUTTING OUT

Straighten the grain of the fabric (see page 32). Cut out lengths of fabric, so that the top raw edge falls on the same part of the pattern for each drop of fabric. Join widths with a flat seam, and press open. Finish raw edges of seams if the drapery is unlined. Slip-baste seams from the right side if there is a pattern to match.

TRIMS AND FINISHES

Normally, draperies are simply hemmed down the sides and across the lower edge, but you can, if you like, add ruffles of fabric or lace, broad bands of binding, in strong, solid colors, or topstitched braids or other trims. Of course, your choice will depend on the style of the room: trims such as these are an ideal way to link your draperies visually with other fabric furnishings.

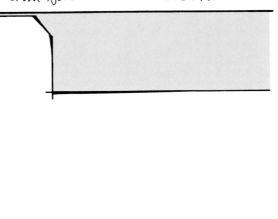

··trim fabric at corners·······

··· slipstitch side hem·······

··· add tape·····

···turn up lower hem·······

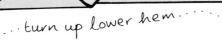

MAKING UNLINED DRAPERIES

Turn the heading. Press under 3 inches across top of drapery. To remove bulk from hem at top corner, trim into hem allowance for 2½ inches positioning cut 2½ inches from side edge. Clip along the top foldline for 1½ inches from outside edge, then cut off fabric diagonally.

Side hems. Turn ⅜ inch to underside and press. Turn under a 2 inch hem and press. Slipstitch in place, or machine blindstitch.

USING DRAWSTRING HEADING TAPE

Cut a length of tape to the same measurement as the width of each drapery panel. Turn under ¼ inch at each end. Position tape on drapery, ¼ inch from top fold, and pin in place. Topstitch ⅛ to ¼ inch from edge of tape, double stitching across ends to make sure that drawstrings are held firmly.

Lower hem. Check length of draperies at each side edge, and trim level if necessary. Turn under ½ inch then 3 inches, and pin in place. Miter the corners, and ease the hem down slightly at the point to allow for the thickness of the fabric.

Pleater tape. It is important to plan the pleating carefully to suit the window. Most draperies have a "return": the rod is hung slightly away from the wall, and the ends of the drapery wrap back to the wall. You should also arrange the pleating so that there are no pleats on the overlapping sections at the center.

Reduce top hem allowance to ½ inch. Attach heading tape as follows. Cut lengths of pleater tape 5 inches shorter than the total width of the panel of fabric for each drapery. Position tape across top of drapery with right side of tape facing right side of fabric, with ends of tape 2½ inches from raw edges at sides of drapery and top of tape just under ¼ inch from top raw edge of drapery. Pin in place and stitch across top, ¼ inch from top of tape. Turn drapery back over tape at stitching line, fold tape to wrong side of drapery and press. Pin lower edge of tape to drapery and stitch ¼ inch from edge of tape.

TRIMS FOR UNLINED DRAPERIES

Add a topstitched ruffle around the side edges, remembering to reduce the finished length of the drapery to allow for the depth of the ruffle which extends along the lower edge. You can finish the sides and lower edge with a single ⅝ inch hem, machine stitched in place, since the line of stitching will be covered by the ruffle.

Edges may also be finished with a deep binding, mitered at the corners. Omit hem allowances when assembling the main panel of fabric.

A pleated ruffle is another tailored touch: make and pleat the ruffle, then stitch all around the sides and lower edge, on the right side of the drapery with raw edges matching. You will have to allow extra fullness at corners so that the pleats lie flat. Finish the raw edges and press toward the drapery.

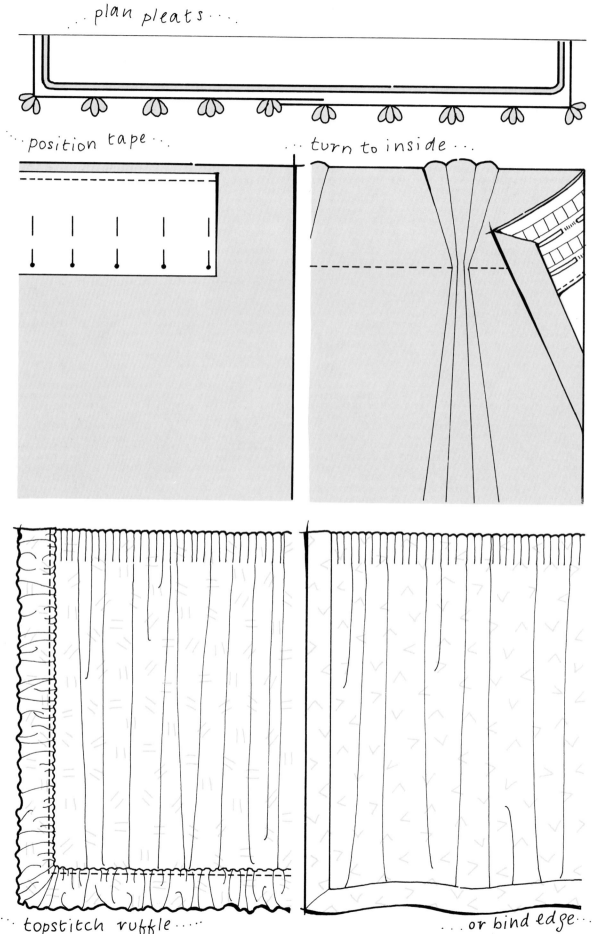

... plan pleats ...

... position tape ..

... turn to inside ...

... topstitch ruffle ....

... or bind edge ...

...join lining...

press to form a border...

...turn down top allowance...

MACHINE-STITCHED LININGS

Cut lining and join seams if necessary, to make a panel of lining fabric 6½ inches shorter and 8 inches narrower than the unfinished drapery panel. Turn up a 1½ inch double hem across lower edge of lining. Turn under and press a ½ inch seam allowance down side edges of curtain and lining. Turn under and press a ½ inch hem across top of lining for a hand-made heading, or trim 1 inch for a drawstring heading. Position lining on right side of drapery, right sides facing, so that top edge of lining is 3½ to 4 inches from raw edge of fabric. Adjust drapery so that you can pin the side edges together. Baste, if necessary, then stitch along pressed seamline. If the selvages form the seam allowance, clip into them to prevent puckering. Press, then press both seam allowances toward the lining. Turn right side out and center lining on the drapery. Press creases down side of drapery. This should give a 2 inch border of fabric down each side of the drapery.

To finish heading, turn the top allowance to the underside, tucking it inside the side hem, and trim bulk at corners. For hand-stitched pleats, slipstitch the fold of lining to the top hem. For a pleater tape heading or a drawstring tape heading, topstitch the tape in place over the raw edges, as for an unlined drapery with a tape heading.

Finish the hem as for an unlined drapery, arranging the lining loose over the drapery hem. If the draperies are large, the hems may be held together with bar tacks. These are made in the same way as belt carriers (see page 139), but the initial stitches are taken between the drapery hem and the lining hem. Position the tacks at seamlines.

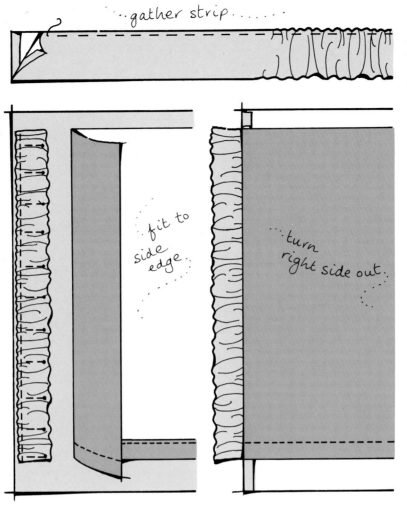

gather strip

fit to side edge

turn right side out

TRIMS FOR LINED DRAPERIES

Gathered double ruffles can be set into the seam between the lining and the fabric, down the leading edges of the drapery (the edges toward the center of the window). Allow a ⅝ inch hem down the center edge of both the fabric and the lining. Cut a strip of fabric for the ruffle twice the width of the finished ruffle plus 1¼ inches for seam allowance. Make up a double gathered ruffle by folding the strip of fabric in half, wrong sides out, and stitching a seam across each end. Trim seam allowances, and turn right side out, then run a line of gathering stitches through the seam allowance down the raw edges. Lay out the fabric and lining, right sides together, and position the ruffle between the two layers so that raw edges match. Leave the seam allowance across top of drapery and hem allowance at lower edge free, with no ruffle. Pin in place, distributing fullness evenly, then stitch through all layers of fabric, ⅝ inch from raw

edge. Press. Finish the outer edge as for plain draperies, then turn right side out. Press the drapery so that the ruffle sits neatly down the outer edge, and the fabric turns to the back of the drapery down the opposite edge. Apply heading and hem lower edge of drapery in the usual way.

For a broad, firm binding around the sides and lower edge of the drapery, cut the panels of lining and face fabric to the exact size of the finished (unpleated) drapery. Cut the binding four times the width of the finished border. This allows for a deep seam allowance, to give extra body to the bound edge. Fold and press binding. Position fabric on lining, wrong sides together, and pin and baste binding all around sides and lower edge of drapery, with right side of binding matching right side of drapery, forming neat miters at the corners. Machine stitch in place, then turn binding to wrong side and slipstitch folded edge to previous line of stitching.

HAND-MADE HEADINGS

Hand-made headings enable you to tailor the heading and pleats to suit the style of the window. The size and position of pleats has to be planned carefully, before working out the quantity of fabric you need.

If the window has a return (the rod stands away from the wall, and wraps around the end of the window) position the first pleats at the outer edge of the draperies on the corner of the return. If there is an overlap at the center of the draperies, do not position any pleats on the underlapping section of drapery. The draperies are made as described for lined draperies, and the pleating is done once the drapery has been made.

Interfacing. To stiffen the top of the heading, use buckram. Crinoline can also be used. This is available in 4 inch wide rolls, from furnishing fabric departments.

INTERLINED DRAPERIES

In houses where heat loss is a problem, it is a good idea to interline draperies for extra insulation. A layer of thick fabric is sewn into the draperies

between the face fabric and the lining. It can be sewn in only by hand, and pleats must be hand sewn also, using one of the methods given on page 213. A soft, thick fabric, such as flannelette or thin polyester batting, should be chosen. Avoid fabrics that are very dense and would add proportionately too much weight to the draperies.

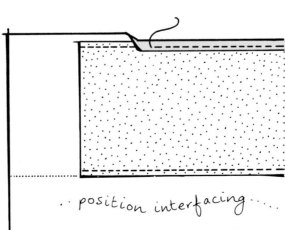

position interfacing

LINED AND INTERLINED

Full draw draperies (opposite) take on an extra touch of luxury with a thick interlining. Bound ruffles and a shaped tie-back trimmed with an elegant bow hold the draperies clear of the window.

INTERFACING HEADINGS

To interface a heading for a hand-finished drapery, turn under and press the allowance across the top of the drapery. Cut interfacing to match the width of the finished (unpleated) drapery. Position interfacing on wrong side of drapery, with lower edge of interfacing matching crease line. Leave 2½ inches clear for side hems. Stitch in place ¼ inch from edge of interfacing. Turn raw edge of drapery over top edge of interfacing and stitch again.

Finish lining and side hems, and pin lower hem as described for lined draperies.

HAND-STITCHED LININGS

For hand-sewn headings, interface the heading allowance (see page 211). Turn under heading allowance – normally 3 inches across top drapery – and press. Cut out top corner to remove bulk. Turn under and press side seam allowances down each side of drapery – normally 2½ inches – and seam allowance down lining – ½ inch. Turn under ½ inch across top edge for hand-pleated draperies. Turn under 1½ inch double hem across lower edge of lining, and stitch. Lay out drapery, right side down, on a flat surface, and position lining on top of it, centering the lining on the fabric, with the top edge ½ inch from top of drapery. Catch the lining to the drapery down the length of the drapery, at 24 inch intervals across the curtain, following the straight grain. Turn the lining back to make the stitch, catching only one or two threads of face fabric in each stitch. The stitches should be about 6 inches apart.

Slipstitch the lining to the hem allowance down the side edges of the drapery – and across the top, if this is to have handmade pleats. Finish hems as usual, adding weights at corners and seamlines if desired.

catch lining to drapery...

INTERLININGS

To interline draperies, cut interlining to same measurement as finished (unpleated) drapery. Center interlining on wrong side of fabric, leaving the usual hem allowances all around. Lockstitch the interlining to the drapery fabric, then turn top and side edges over interlining. Turn under hem allowances on lining, and turn up hem. Lockstitch lining to interlining, and finish as described on page 209.

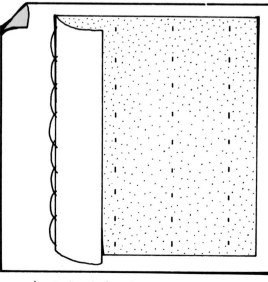

... lock in interlining ......

ALLOWANCES FOR HAND-MADE HEADINGS

- For pinch pleats and French pleats, allow 5 to 6 inches for each pleat, and about 4 inches between them.
- For box pleats, decide on the finished width of each pleat – for example, 2 inches – and double this for the pleat allowance – 4 inches. Allow 4 inches of fabric between pleats.
- For cartridge pleats, allow about 2 inches for each pleat and about 2 inches between them.
- For side hems, allow 2½ inches at each side of each drapery panel.
- For the top hem, allow 4½ inches for 4 inch wide buckram.
- For hems, allow 3½ inches.

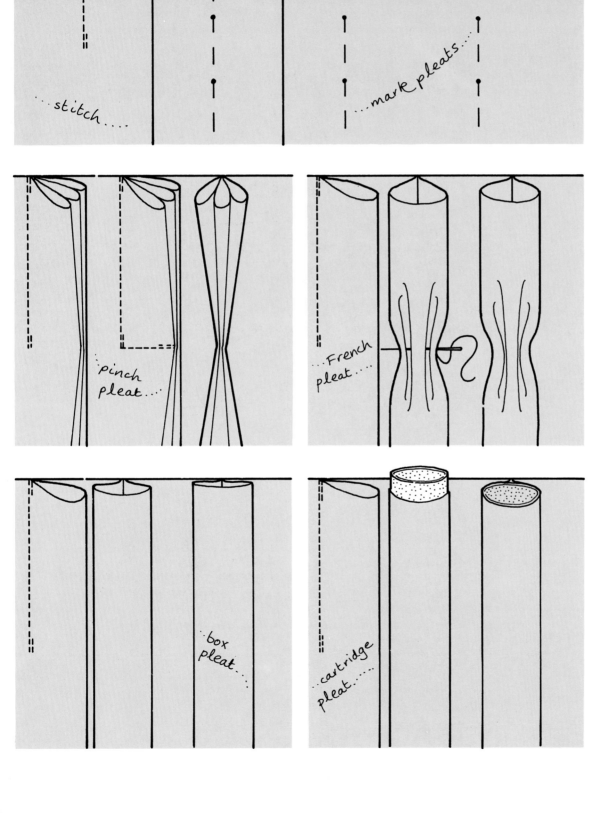

...stitch....

...mark pleats....

pinch pleat....

...French pleat....

box pleat....

cartridge pleat....

FORMING THE PLEATS

After making the drapery, measure and mark the pleat positions with pins. Check that the pleated length of the drapery fits the rod. Pin pleats in place, then stitch from the top edge to ½ inch below the interfaced heading; reverse stitching at each end.

PINCH PLEATS

Divide each pleat evenly into three smaller pleats, and crease the length of the pleat. At the lower edge, stitch through the pleats by hand or machine.

FRENCH PLEATS

At the lower edge of the heading, divide the pleat into three smaller folds, but do not press. Hand sew through the pleats several times, then finish threads on underside of drapery.

BOX PLEATS

Slip two fingers inside the pleat and finger-press it open. Then press flat, keeping the folds an equal distance from the stitching line. Baste the top and bottom corners of the pleat to the drapery, placing the stitches under the pleat.

CARTRIDGE PLEAT

Form small, round pleats and slip a tube of buckram or non-woven interfacing into the cylinder. You can add extra stuffing to hold them crisply if necessary.

Making shades

Balloon shades are similar to a curtain, made in a single panel with a drawstring tape or box-pleated heading. There is often a ruffle or lace trim across the lower edge. Vertical tapes run down the shade with cords running through them to pull up the shade. The tapes may be standard cotton tapes, with curtain rings to hold the cords in place, or special shirr tapes, which have loops woven into them to thread the pull-cord through.

Austrian shades are similar to balloon shades, but extra fullness is included in the length. The tapes running down the back of the shade have drawstrings running through them so that the extra fullness is permanently drawn up. Cords can be fitted through the tapes to pull up the shade, but with sheer Austrian shades these are usually omitted (see page 204).

Roman and roller shades give a more tailored effect at the window. Roller shades are easy to make from kits, but you can add your own trims to suit the style of the room.

Roman shades may be made in many different ways: the most important factor for a crisp finish is to use an evenly woven fabric with a true grain. And any pattern must be printed true to the grain, so that it appears right when hanging. Geometric patterns are more appropriate for this style.

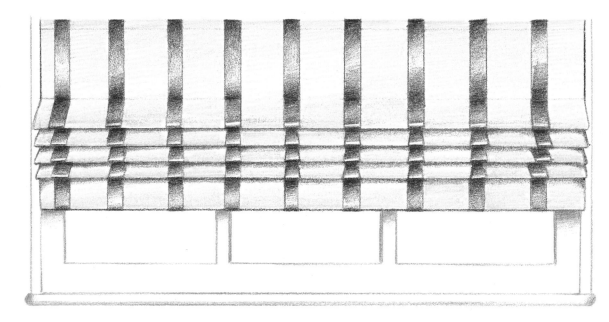

SOFTER STYLES

Choose lightweight fabrics – glazed cotton, lightweight chintz, and soft silks are all suitable. If the shade is to be lined, choose a plain cotton lining in white, off white, or a suitable color.

Balloon shades. Allow twice the fullness across the shade, to suit chosen heading. Allow 1½ inches for side hems on either side and ⅝ inch for hems top and bottom. Cut lining to the same width as the shade, with ⅝ inch seam allowance at the lower edge.

For a shirred heading, cut heading tape to width of finished (ungathered) shade plus ½ inch for turning under. Decide how many vertical tapes you will need: position one at each outer edge, and one at each seamline. Space remaining tapes evenly between these points, about 12 to 14 inches apart. Multiply the number of tapes by the length of finished shade to give the total amount of tape required. Calculate amount of cord, allowing for cords to run up the shade and across to one side, then half-way down to lower edge of shade.

Austrian shades. The main panel should be cut so that it is about half again as long as the area the shade is to cover, and 1½ to 2 times the width. A topstitched ruffle makes an effective trim for the shade. Decide on a suitable spacing for the vertical tapes between 8 and 16 inches and calculate the number of lengths of tape required. Calculate heading tape in the usual way.

SHADES – PLAIN AND FANCY
Balloon shades, gathered across the heading, draw up in soft folds, while Austrian shades are permanently gathered for a ruched effect. Crisp Roman shades, which can be edged with a plain border and stiffened with battens, give a tailored effect, while simple roller shades are an instant cover-up for any window.

UNLINED BALLOON SHADE

Turn under hem of ruffle and gather long raw edge. Fit to lower edge of shade, right sides facing and raw edges matching. Draw up fullness and distribute gathers evenly. Pin, baste and stitch in place, taking ⅝ inch seams. Press raw edges upwards and finish together. Turn under ⅝ inch then 1 inch down side edges, to lower edge of ruffle and stitch in place. Turn under and press ⅝ inch across top edge of shade. Pin vertical tapes down shade, turning under ⅜ inch at lower end, and matching fold to seamline of ruffle. Turn under ¼ inch at each end of heading tape and pin in place ¼ inch from top fold, to cover raw edge at top of shade and top raw

LINED BALLOON SHADE

Position lining on shade, right sides together with lower raw edges matching. Adjust face fabric so that raw edges match down side edges. Stitch, taking ⅝ inch seams. Press seams toward lining. Adjust shade so that lining is centered on shade. Make up ruffle, finishing lower and side edges. Gather long free edge. Position ruffle between shade and lining, with right side of ruffle facing right side of shade. Draw up fullness so that ruffle matches lower edge of shade. Stitch in place and finish raw edges together. Turn shade right side out. Position heading tape and vertical tapes and finish as usual.

AUSTRIAN SHADE

Turn under a ¾ inch double hem down sides and topstitch by machine or slipstitch in place by hand. Mark positions for vertical tapes with pins or dressmaker's chalk, so that outer tapes are level with finished side edges. Pin tapes down back of shade and stitch in place. Turn up a ¾ inch double hem across lower edge, enclosing raw ends of tape. Stitch firmly across ends of tape to hold cords securely. Make a topstitched ruffle and fit along lower edge. It may also extend up the sides of the shade — in which case allow extra fullness

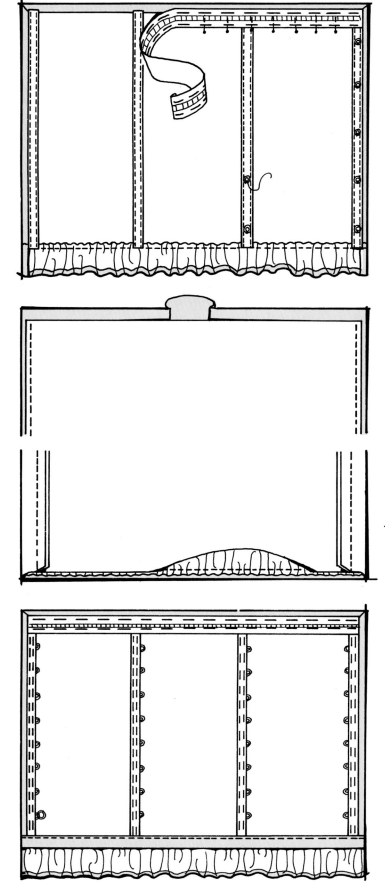

edge at top of shade and top raw edges of vertical tapes. Topstitch all tapes in place. Hand sew curtain rings to back of tape up the length of the shade, spacing the rings 6 to 8 inches apart. Cut lengths of cord, and tie ends to lowest loop or ring in tape. Thread up through vertical tapes. Hang the shade and fit a screw eye into the window surround or cornice board at the top of each vertical tape. Thread cords through screw eyes and across to one side of the window. Knot together near side of shade and braid ends together. Fit cleat at side of window to wrap pull cord around.

at the corners. Turn over seam allowance at top of shade, and turn under raw ends of heading tape. Position heading tape across top of shade, over raw edge of top hem and stitch in place by machine. Pull up drawstrings in both vertical tapes and heading tape to gather up fullness. Fit a ring to the bottom of each vertical tape, and tie a length of cord to it. Thread the cord up through the loops in the vertical tapes, through every third or fourth loop, and carry the cords across the top of the shade to one side. Hang the shade in the same way as a balloon shade.

216

ROLLERS AND ROMANS

Roller shades should be made from firmly woven fabric, although translucent fabrics and even lace may be used if you want a sheer effect and will not have to raise and lower the shade too often. They can be made with a simple casing along the lower edge, or finished with a faced edge, shaped in scallops or formal curves. An attractive finish is to make loops along the lower edge and slot a brass rod through it. In this case, the shade can be raised and lowered by pulling the rod, and you need not add a shade pull. Since the shade fabric is stiffened, the fabric cannot fray, and no seams are necessary down the side of the shade. In fact, seams and hems could create problems in raising and lowering the shade due to the extra bulk.

Special tapes are available for Roman shades, with rings to guide the cords straight up the back of the shade. A simple bound edge creates a bold outline which suits the style, or you can topstitch a border, spacing it an inch or two in from the edge of the shade.

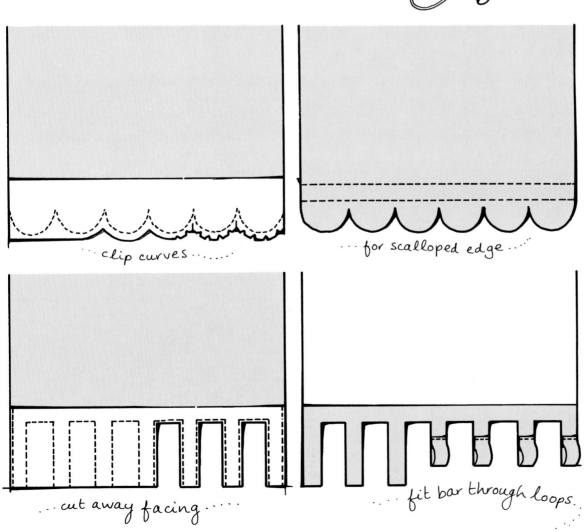

...make casing...

...tack to roller...

...add pull cord...

...clip curves...

...for scalloped edge...

...cut away facing...

...fit bar through loops...

MAKING A ROLLER SHADE

Buy a roller shade kit to fit the window: if you cannot find one exactly the right size, choose one a size larger than you need, and trim it to fit. Fit the brackets on either side of the window, checking that the slotted and round brackets are on the appropriate sides. Measure the distance between the brackets, then trim the roller and slat to fit. Stiffen the fabric using a special fabric spray, then trim it to the width and length required, allowing a total of 4 inches for hems. (The fabric may shrink slightly when sprayed, so it is important not to trim it before it has been stiffened.) Turn up 3 inches across lower edge of shade, and make two lines of stitching, close to the lower edge, about 1¼ inches apart, to form a casing for the slat. Fit the slat, then fit the pull cord holder and pull cord to the back of the casing. Turn over 1 inch across top of shade and fit it to the roller, following the maker's instructions.

FINISHES FOR ROLLER SHADES

Faced edges. Cut the fabric an extra 2 inches in length after stiffening the shade. Fold up a 5 inch hem to right side of shade across lower edge. Mark the pattern for the shaped lower edge and stitch along line. Trim seam allowance and clip and notch curves (see page 51). Turn facing right side out and finger-press to give a crisp edge. Stitch a casing for the slat about ⅜ inch from the raw edge. Loops and bar. Turn up the lower edge of the shade twice the depth of the loops plus 4 inches to wrap around pole and form facing. Fold up on right side of shade, and mark deep rectangular panels, twice the depth of the loop plus 2½ inches or so to wrap around bar. These areas will be cut out to form the loops. Stitch along marked lines, then trim seams. Turn loops right side out and press. Turn up and stitch loops to form a series of slots to hold the bar. Fit bar through slots. Fit shade to roller.

UNLINED ROMAN SHADE

Suitable fabrics for this style of shade include plain, heavy cottons and linens; solid colors and stripes are most appropriate. Cut the fabric to the size of the finished shade plus 2 inches for side hems, 5 inches for hem across lower edge, and 8 inches for attaching at top edge.

Turn under a 1 inch double hem along side edges and topstitch in place. Position Roman shade tapes across width of shade, spacing them up to 20 inches apart. The lower ends of the tape should be 8 inches from the lower raw edge. Make sure that the loops are aligned across the shade. Stitch tapes in place.

Turn up ¾ inch and then 4 inches across lower edge of shade and press. Stitch hem by hand or machine, mitering corners. Tie a brass or plastic curtain ring to the lowest loop of each tape. Tie a cord to each ring, and run the cord up through every second or third loop in the tape (depending on how deep

you want the folds of the shade to be). Carry the cords across the top of the shade and a third of the way down one side. Draw up the cords and arrange the folds of the shade, then press them in place. This helps the shade to fold neatly.

Cut a wooden batten the width of the shade, and tack or staple the top of the shade over the wood. Screw the wood to the top of the window recess or to the wall above the window. Fit screw eyes to the lower side of the batten, and thread the cords through, and knot. Fit a cleat at the side of the window.

LINED AND BOUND ROMAN SHADE

Cut fabric and lining to the same size: the only allowance needed is 8 inches at the top edge for attaching the shade. Cut a broad binding to fit around the sides and lower edge of the shade. The binding should be twice the width of the desired border, plus ½ inch for turning under on each long edge. Fold binding in half and press, and press under seam allowances.

Lay out fabric, wrong side up, and position lining on top of it, right side up. Decide on a suitable spacing for the tapes: the outer ones should be just inside the border, with the remainder spaced evenly – up to 20 inches apart. Position tapes so that rings are aligned, extending the lower edge into the border area. Topstitch in place through fabric and lining. Bind the edges of the shade, mitering the corners. Thread up cords and hang shade as usual.

... position tapes ...

... fold binding ...

... stitch tapes ...   ... finish edges ...

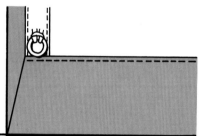

Café curtains

Café curtains are used at windows where you want to screen only the bottom part of the window – in kitchens, for example. Fit the rod across the window before measuring for the curtains.

The curtains can be made with a simple casing, as for glass curtains. Or they can be created like draperies and given a pleated heading. Looped and scalloped headings are other attractive options.

LOOPED HEADINGS

Make the curtain, allowing one and a half times the width of the window for fullness. If the curtain is lined, fold the top of the lining over, and pin it to the top hem. On unlined curtains, turn under the raw edge and slipstitch in place before turning in side hems. Calculate the number of loops required, allowing about 1½ inches for each loop and twice that between loops.

For 1½ inch wide loops, cut strips of fabric 3½ inches wide and long enough to loop around the rod, plus 2½ inches for seams. Make the loops by folding in half down length, right sides together, and stitching down one long edge, taking ¼ inch seams. Turn loop right side out and center the seam at back. Press. Attach to top of curtain as shown.

SCALLOPED HEADING

For a softer finish, a popular heading for café curtains combines scallops and pleats. Fit the rod, and measure for length and width of the curtain. Allow 4½ inches for the heading, and the usual lower and side hem allowances. For fullness, decide on the spacing and size of each pleat: allow about 4½ inches for each pleat, spacing them about 4 inches apart. Position a pleat at each outer edge of the curtains. The heading must be interfaced and faced to give a neat finish.

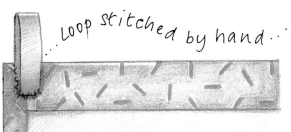

…loop stitched by hand…

ATTACHING LOOPS
Fold strip in half, and turn in ¼ inch at each end. Press. Machine stitch or slipstitch loops in place at back of curtain heading.

FACED SCALLOPS
Turn under ½ inch across top of curtain. Turn under and press side hems. Cut a strip of medium-weight interfacing, 4 inches wide, and the width of the flat curtain. Mark the position of the pleats, and the shape of the scallops, on the interfacing and position across top of curtain, 4 inches from finished top edge. Turn top hem of curtain over to right side of fabric and pin, so that the fold is barely above the edge of the interfacing. Stitch the scallops, following the pattern, using a short stitch. Cut away the interfacing close to the stitching, trim fabric ¼ inch from stitching, and clip into seam allowance. Press and turn heading right side out. Finish side hems and lower hem by hand, then stitch French or pinch pleats between scallops (see page 213).

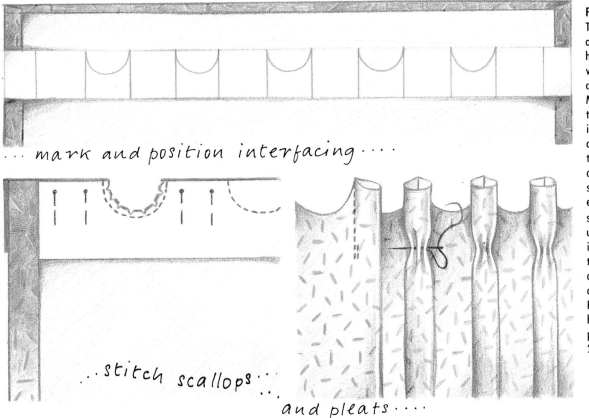

…mark and position interfacing…

…stitch scallops…

…and pleats…

219

Valances and cornices

Many styles of curtains and drapery need no further embellishment at the top – especially if they are hung from decorative rods. In other cases, however, a cornice or valance will provide a suitable finishing touch, perhaps hiding unattractive drapery hardware in the process.

A cornice is a firm, shaped structure. Some are made entirely of wood, then painted or padded and covered with fabric. Others consist simply of a cornice board – a kind of shelf – to which stiffened fabric is attached. A cornice board can also be used as the support for swags and cascades – a luxurious style which is enjoying a revival in popularity.

A valance is essentially a very short curtain or drapery, normally made of the same fabric, and in the same style, as the curtains or draperies themselves and hung from a separate rod.

PLANNING AND MEASURING

A shaped fabric cornice involves the minimum of carpentry and is just as effective as a box cornice. Begin by fixing the cornice board to the wall with angle irons, then experiment with stiff cardboard or unbleached muslin to judge the best shape and depth for the cornice. The fabric can be fixed to the board with Velcro or upholstery tacks.

For swags and cascades it is essential to make a preliminary version in unbleached muslin and then use this pattern (called a *toile*), adjusted as necessary, for cutting the main fabric and lining.

Swags and cascades may look more luxurious if they are interlined. Cut interlining to same size as muslin pattern, and lock to fabric before stitching lining (or facing) in place.

SHAPED FABRIC CORNICE
Cut a paper pattern. Cut buckram to the exact measurement of the pattern. Cut interlining, adding ½ inch all round. Cut the drapery fabric, allowing 1 inch all round. Cut lining ¼ inch larger all around.

Lay out fabric, wrong side up, and position interlining on top of it. Center buckram on top of interlining. Press seam allowance of interlining and fabric over buckram, clipping and notching seam allowances. Herringbone stitch raw edge of fabric to buckram. Turn under and press ½ inch all around lining. Slipstitch lining to underside of face fabric.

PLEATED VALANCE
Make a pleated valance in the same way as the draperies. For a crisply tailored effect, position handsewn pleats across the valance, to match pleats across top of drapery.

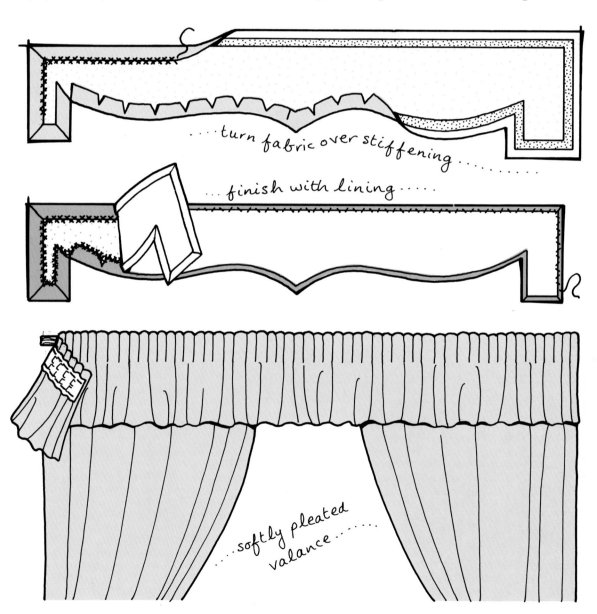

... turn fabric over stiffening ...

... finish with lining ...

...softly pleated valance...

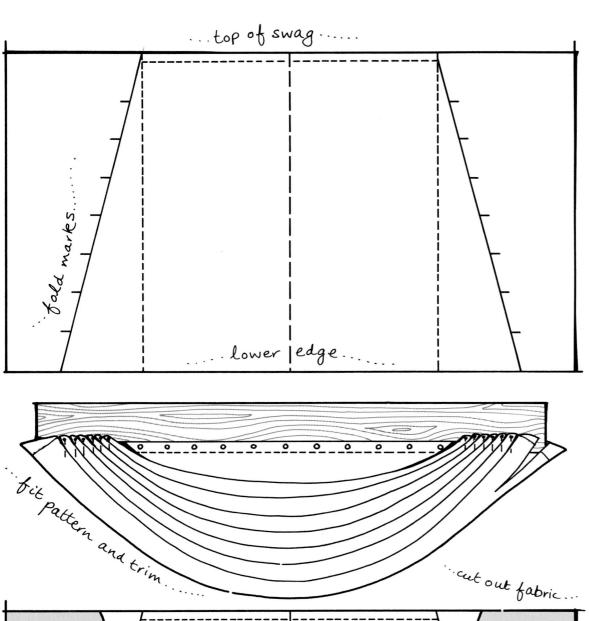

... top of swag .....

... fold marks ....

..... lower edge .....

fit pattern and trim ....

...cut out fabric...

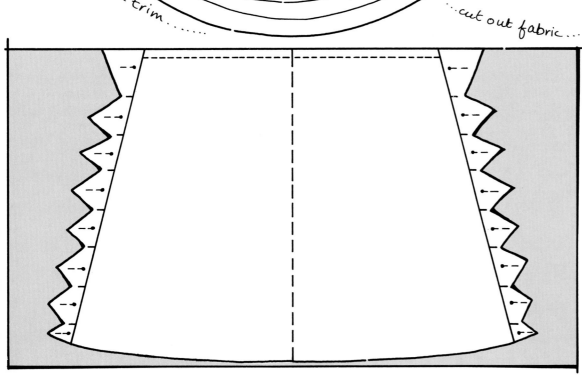

SWAGS

Make a pattern from a piece of unbleached muslin: the depth of the swag should be about 36 inches. Measure the length of the cornice board. For the top edge of the swag, subtract about 10 inches from this measurement and mark on the top edge of a piece of muslin. For the lower edge of the swag, add about 16 inches and mark this on the lower edge. Divide the fabric horizontally into eight equal parts, leaving a 1 inch overlap at the top, to give seven folds in the swag. Use thumbtacks to pin the overlap at the top of the swag to the cornice board. Fold up the swag at the marked points, and pin it in place, to check the fit of the swag. Trim excess fabric at one end, along the top of the cornice board, and taper the lower edge slightly.

Remove muslin from board and open it out. Fold it in half down center line, and use cut end as a guide to cut the other end, to give a complete pattern. Cut out fabric, allowing ½ inch for turning under at lower edge. Cut out lining, making it ¼ inch shorter along lower edge.

Turn under and press ½ inch along lower edge of lining and swag. Lay lining on swag, wrong sides facing. Zig-zag stitch together around top and side edges. Slipstitch fold of lining to turning of swag along lower edge. Nail the swag to the cornice board, as for the muslin pattern.

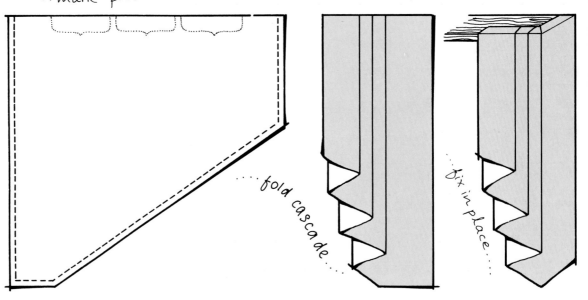

CASCADES

Decide on the finished length of the cascades at outer and inner edges, and on the number and width of the pleats. Make a calico pattern for cascades, shaping it as shown in the diagram. Allow a 1 inch overlap for fixing at the top. Cut out fabric and facing allowing ½ inch down sides and across lower edge. Position facing on fabric, right sides together, and pin. Stitch around edges, taking ½ inch seams. Trim seam allowances and clip across corners. Press. Turn right side out and press, then zig-zag stitch raw edges of fabric together across top of cascades. Nail to top of cornice board.

BRAIDED TIE-BACK

Measure for the tie-back with a tape measure, and make three lengths of tubular cording (see page 95), one and a half times the length of the finished tie-back. Leave the ends open.

Arrange the three pieces of cording so that they overlap slightly, and stitch together across the end. Braid the cords, and when the tie-back is the appropriate length, arrange the cords to match the opposite end of the braid and topstitch together. When you are happy with the shape and length of the braid, trim the ends of the cords just outside the lines of stitching. Use short strips of matching or contrasting fabric to bind the ends, turning in ends of binding neatly. Fit rings, and make another matching tie-back.

TIE-BACKS

Tie-backs are both practical and decorative, holding curtains or draperies clear of the window to let in extra light and adding interest lower down the window, to balance a decorative heading, cornice or valance.

They can be made in many ways: tailored, shaped tie-backs, made in a similar way to a fabric cornice, suit formal settings, with or without a matching cornice. Twisted or braided tubes of fabric are particularly attractive; or, in a more romantic setting you may prefer a ruffled tie-back, made in a similar way to the sheer tie-back on page 203. You can also use ready-made tie-backs, or make them from ribbon or tasseled cords thus eliminating all, or nearly all, sewing. Pre-gathered eyelet lace can also be used for minimum-sew tie-backs.

Plan the position of tie-backs carefully: this is usually easier after you have made the curtains or draperies, since you can hold them in place to see how they drape. It is also easier to measure for the length of the tie-back after the drapery has been made, by holding a tape measure in position where the tie-back is to be placed.

The ends of the tie-back are usually held in place with small brass rings, slipped over a small brass hook in line with the outer edge of the curtain. Stationary draperies, which do not close across the window, are particularly effective if they are tied back, and since they do not have to be closed, the folds can be carefully arranged to show off the fabric, and will not be crushed by repeated opening and closing.

TAILORED TIE-BACKS

Measure the length and decide on a suitable depth for the tie-back. Draw a paper template to represent the size of the finished tie-back, making it slightly curved or banana-shaped. Make the pattern symmetrical by drawing it on a folded piece of paper with the center of the tie-back at the fold. This foldline should be placed on the straight grain of the fabric when you cut it out.

Cut out a piece of lightweight batting or heavy interfacing, and a piece of iron-on buckram the same size and shape as the paper pattern. **For corded tie-backs,** cut out a piece of main fabric and a piece of lining using the pattern as a guide, adding ⅝ inch seam allowance all around. Make up enough cording to fit all around the finished tie-back. Fix the iron-on buckram to the lining, and position the batting or interfacing on the main fabric, leaving the seam allowance free all around. Herringbone stitch in place all around outer edge.

Fit cording around outer edge of main fabric, with right sides facing and raw edges matching, and stitch in place, overlapping ends at one inner corner. Press seam allowances

to wrong side of fabric piece. Press under seam allowance all around edge of lining piece, and slipstitch to cording following the previous line of stitching.

Attach a curtain ring to each end of the tie-back. Make a second one in the same way, to make a pair. Fit hooks to window frame to hold tie-backs.

For bound tie-backs, cut main fabric, lining, buckram, and interfacing to the same size as the paper pattern. Cut a strip of binding on the bias, about 2 inches wide and long enough to go all around the tie-back, plus ½ inch turning at each end. Position and press iron-on buckram to lining. Baste interfacing to main fabric piece all around edge. Stitch binding to fabric piece all around edge, taking ⅜ inch seam in binding and ⅝ inch seam in fabric. Position stiffened lining on interfaced fabric and baste in place all around edge. Fold binding over tie-back, and press under ⅜ inch along raw edge. Slipstitch folded edge of binding to back of tie-back, just inside previous line of stitching. Fit rings, and make a second, matching tie-back.

..... cut pattern .....

..... interface tie-back .....

..... add cording .....

..... and lining .....

..... or join lining and bind edge .....

223

Pillow and cushion covers

Pillow covers are a good starting point as an introduction to making more intricate fabric furnishings, such as slipcovers. They involve many similar techniques – fitting fabric and cording around square corners, for example – but are on a smaller scale, and usually more simply shaped so they are much easier to handle.

There is no limit to the range of styles and different finishes for pillows: some detailed instructions involving simple techniques are given on pages 226–228.

FABRICS AND TRIMMINGS

Avoid choosing too many different fabrics and finishes for pillows that are to go in the same room. Although you can usefully use up remnants of fabric, too many contrasts are confusing to the eye and restless.

Firmly woven furnishing cottons are the easiest to handle when making pillow and cushion covers, but you may want to use richer fabrics – velvets and brocades – to suit the style of the room. Boxy cushions, for dining chairs, window seats, and so on (known as welted cushions) can be backed with firm canvas rather than fabric if they are not reversible – for example if the top panel is made from needlepoint.

Choose trimmings according to the type of fabric you are using. Ribbons and ruffles would be quite out of place on formal, velvet pillows, for example: upholstery braid is a more suitable choice.

You can use a wide range of decorative sewing techniques to trim pillows, and since they are small projects they are a good way to practice and perfect your sewing skills. Appliqué is a popular choice, or pin tucks on fine fabrics. Quilting and machine embroidery can also be used, and needle is a traditional choice.

PILLOW FORMS AND SHAPES

For the pillow itself, you can buy a ready-made pillow form; these are usually stuffed with polyester fiberfill, though you may also find some filled with foam chips or feathers. Solid pads made of foam are also available; if you choose one of these, you should make an inner cover for it, using cheap cotton or polyester. The foam breaks down in time, and when this happens you can dispose of the whole pillow, without leaving messy crumbs in the good outer cover.

Pillow forms come in various shapes and sizes; however, if you need an unusual size or shape, you can easily make one yourself. The fabric should be firmly woven, to keep the filling well contained. Unbleached muslin is a good choice; cambric is another. The most luxurious filling is feather and down; however this is expensive and not very widely available. Avoid using it for pillows you plan to sit on, as it doesn't hold its shape well. Polyester fiberfill is more buoyant and is soft and lightweight; it can be purchased in many craft shops and notions departments. It is also non-flammable – an important consideration. Kapok, a natural fiber previously often used for stuffing toys and throw pillows, is flammable and is therefore not recommended.

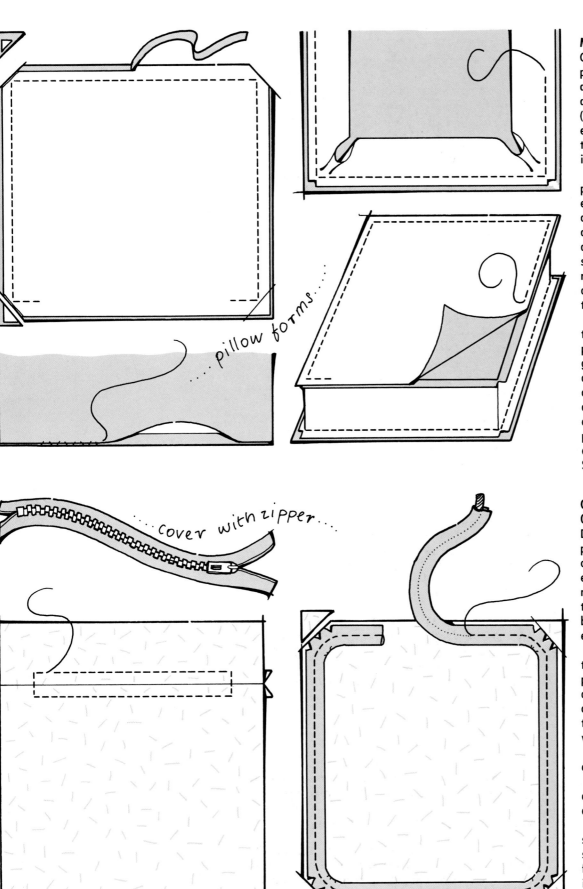

....pillow forms....

....cover with zipper....

MAKING PILLOW FORMS

Cut one panel for the top of the pillow and one for the back, allowing ⅜ inch seam allowance all around. If the pad has sides (welted), cut a strip of fabric long enough to go all around, joining it at the corners if necessary. Allow ⅜ inch for seams.

For a simple pillow, join the two pieces of fabric all around the edges, leaving a 12 inch opening down one edge. Trim seam allowances (except along opening) and clip into corners. Press under seam allowance along opening. Turn right side out. Insert the stuffing and slipstitch opening edges together.

For a box pillow, join the sides to the top, taking ⅜ inch seams, then position back against free edge of gusset and stitch in place, leaving an opening as before. Trim seam allowances, clip into seam allowance of gusset at corners, and clip across corners of top and back panel, then press. Turn right side out and insert stuffing or foam. Slipstitch opening to close.

CUSHION COVER WITH ZIPPER OPENING

Decide where the zipper should be positioned: along one side (the back) of a welted pillow; close to the edge of a square pillow (to make it more or less reversible), or across the back of a circular pillow. On a bolster pillow, it may go across one end, or along the side of the pillow.

When cutting out the fabric for the panel where the zipper is to be positioned, cut it in two pieces, allowing the usual seam allowance all around and a ⅝ inch seam along the edges which will be joined when the zipper is set in.

Set the zipper in, using the centered method (see page 99).

Make the pillow, trimming seam allowances and clipping corners and curves.

Cording may be inserted into the seams, in which case you should stitch the cording in place to the front of the pillow, and to the back if it is a welted pillow. Then join the panels in the usual way.

225

Scatter pillows

These four pillow covers use a wide range of basic sewing techniques. Make them in coordinating fabrics, to pile at a headboard, or add a welcoming touch to a sofa, or choose one style and a distinctive fabric, to add a dramatic touch. Choose fabrics and colors to suit the style of the room.

Besides illustrating different sewing techniques, the pillows use two different fastenings: one is sewn up after the pillow form has been inserted, and the others have zipper plackets – the ruffle-trimmed pillows have zippers in the back panel, while the buttoned pillow has a zipper in the gusset.

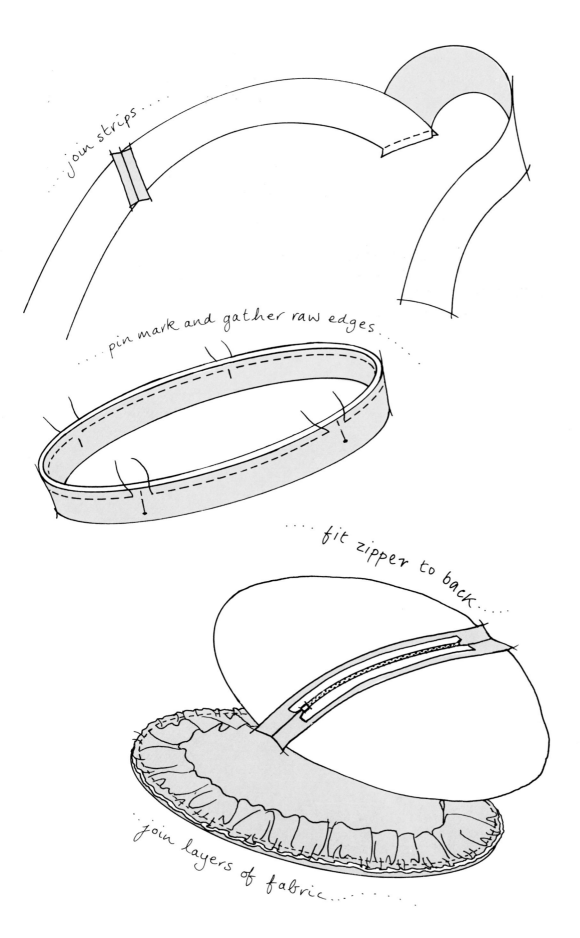

join strips....

....pin mark and gather raw edges........

....fit zipper to back.....

...join layers of fabric.........

RUFFLE-TRIMMED PILLOW

FINISHED SIZE
15 inches in diameter.

YOU WILL NEED
15-inch round pillow form
¾ yd of 48-inch wide printed furnishing cotton fabric (extra fabric will be needed for double ruffle)
14-inch zipper
Matching sewing thread

TO CUT OUT
For cover, cut one piece of fabric 16¼ inches in diameter for front; cut two semicircles, each 16¼ inches in diameter, adding ⅝ inch seam allowance across straight edge of each. For a double ruffle, measure around the outer edge of one cover piece and double the measurement – 3¼ yds – and decide on a frill depth, about 3¼ inches. Double the finished width measurement, adding 1¼ inches for seams.

TO MAKE
1 For a double ruffle, join all the strips with right sides together and plain seams to form a ring. Fold ruffle in half lengthwise, wrong sides together, and press.
2 Work two rows of gathering stitches along raw edges: divide the edge into four equal sections, and mark with pins. Begin and end each set of gathering stitches inside each marked section of ruffle.
3 Divide front cover piece evenly into four sections, and mark with pins. Position ruffle on right side of front cover piece, matching marking pins together. Pull up gathers evenly in each section in turn, and pin to hold. Pin, baste, and stitch all around outer edge.
4 Place back cover pieces with right sides together; pin and baste across straight edges. Stitch in from each side for 1½ inches. Press seam open. Fit zipper (see page 99).
5 Place back on front with right sides together, sandwiching ruffle. Pin, baste, and stitch all around. Trim and turn to right side.

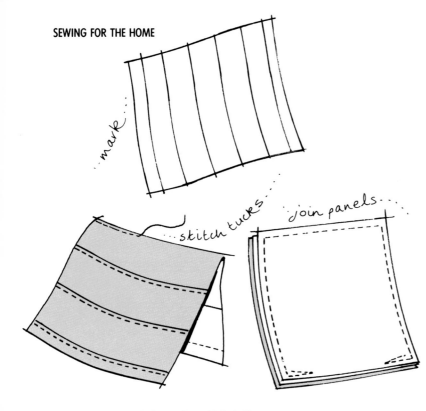

mark

stitch tucks

join panels

PIN-TUCKED PILLOW COVER

FINISHED SIZE
15 inches square.

YOU WILL NEED
15-inch square pillow form
¾ yd of 48-inch wide satin fabric
1⅞ yds of medium-thick piping cord
Matching sewing threads

TO CUT OUT
From satin fabric cut out one piece 16¾ × 16¼ inches for front; cut one piece 16¼ inches square for back.

TO MAKE
1 Make up a length of cording as before.
2 To form pin tucks, mark ⅝ inch in from outer edge on each side. Divide the area in between into five equal sections. These will be the positions for the tucks.
3 Fold the fabric along each marked line, with wrong sides together. Pin, baste, and stitch down each fold, close to the edge.
4 Pin, baste, and stitch cording round cover front, joining ends together in the same way as before, snipping into cording fabric at each corner.
5 Place cover front on back with right sides together; pin, baste, and stitch together all around, leaving an opening for turning. Trim and turn right side out, insert pillow form and slipstitch opening.

fit cording

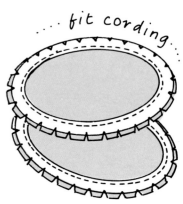

ROUND BUTTONED PILLOW

FINISHED SIZE
15 inches in diameter.

YOU WILL NEED
15-inch diameter pillow form with 2 inch gusset
¾ yd of 48-inch wide glazed cotton
⅝ yd of 48-inch wide glazed cotton in contrasting color
2⅝ yds of medium-thick filler cord
18-inch zipper
Two 1½ inch diameter self-covered buttons
Matching sewing threads

TO CUT OUT
From fabric cut out two 16¼ diameter circles for pillow front and back. Measure around one cover piece to find length of gusset, about 48 inches. Cut out one piece to half this length, plus 1¼ inches all around for seams. Cut another piece to the same length but 1¼ inches wider. Cut this gusset section in half lengthwise.

TO MAKE
1 Make up two 50 inch lengths of cording in contrasting fabric as follows. From contrasting fabric cut out 2-inch wide bias strips. Join with right sides together to make up the correct length. Fold strip evenly in half around filler cord and baste along length; stitch down each length of cording, close to cord, using zipper foot on the machine.
2 Position a length of cording around each cover piece, with cord lying inward and raw edges matching outer edge of cover. Clip into the fabric edges at ¾ inch intervals all around cover. Where cording meets, trim cord so that ends butt together. Trim fabric, so that edges overlap for ¾ inch. Turn under one edge for ⅜ inch and overlap opposite raw edge. Pin and baste cording in place.
3 Match one long raw edge of each of the narrow gusset sections. Pin and baste with right sides together; stitch in from each end for 3½ inches. Place zipper right side up behind basted section of seam; pin and stitch zipper in place. Open zipper.
4 Place gusset ends with right sides together; pin and stitch to form a ring. Trim and turn to right side. Press.
5 Position gusset on cover front with right sides facing and raw edges matching. Pin, baste, and stitch in place. Repeat, to stitch opposite half of gusset to cover back in the same way. Trim and turn cover right side out through zipper.

5 Place cover front on back with right sides together; pin, baste, and stitch together all around, leaving an opening for turning. Trim and turn right side out, insert pillow form and slipstitch opening.

set in zipper

join gusset

Slipcovers

Slipcovers are an effective way to bring new life into a room. Professionally tailored slipcovers are expensive, so you can save yourself a considerable outlay by making your own. By making two sets of covers, you can change the mood of the room with the seasons.

Covers should fit snugly over the chair or sofa you are covering: during construction they have to be fitted to the chair, rather like a pin fitting in dressmaking. However, the trick is to work with the fabric wrong side out, so that you can adjust the seams easily. Then seamlines are marked, and you can cut the panels of fabric to shape, before assembling them. You can make it in muslin first, but this is necessary only when you are using very expensive fabrics, and fabrics that will show pin marks (some glazed cottons, for example).

FABRICS AND PATTERNS

Choose closely woven fabric that will hold its shape, to give prolonged wear and a crisp effect. Linen, chintz, velveteen, and many synthetic fabrics are available. Your furnishing fabric retailer will be able to advise on suitability. Plain colors are the easiest to work with, since there is no pattern matching. Small patterns, which may not need matching, help to disguise marks, so are a practical choice in a family home. Bold floral patterns are also popular, but these need extra care when cutting out, as motifs must be centered on sections of the chair or sofa, and matched carefully.

THE BASIC PRINCIPLES

To make slipcovers, start by dividing the chair into sections, following the seamlines of the existing covering. Measure carefully, measuring at the widest point of each section and adding seam allowances. You must also include an allowance for tucking in around the seat and down each side of the back of the chair. Shaped or square cushions should be measured separately.

The next stage is to work out how much fabric you will need, using the measured panels as a guide. The simplest way to do this is to make a scale diagram, marking the width of the fabric and sketching in the position of the pattern pieces, to make sure they will all fit. Include an extra allowance for pattern positioning, depending on the scale of the pattern.

After buying the fabric, cut out rectangles for each section of the chair or sofa (you usually have to join widths of fabric when covering sofas). Cut all panels on the straight grain of the fabric. These panels are then positioned over the chair, with the wrong side outwards, and pinned to fit around the edges. When you are happy with the fit (only one side needs to be fitted) mark the seamlines. Remove the fabric from the chair, remove pins, and trim, leaving a 1 inch seam allowance.

Stitch the seams in the same order as the seams are pinned and fitted, checking and re-pinning seams at each stage in construction – before moving on to stitch the next section.

A FITTING FINISH
Smart striped fabric to coordinate with floral draperies give a crisp finish to the cover on this sofa (overleaf). Notice how the stripes align on the back and seat cushions, front section and skirt of the cover.

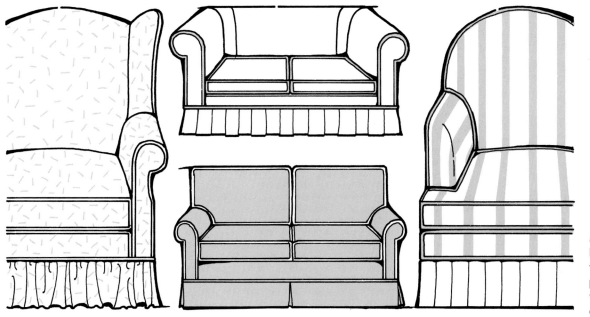

MEASURING UP
Before measuring up, decide where to position seams. This is particularly important on sofas, where seams may be positioned to coincide with seat cushions.

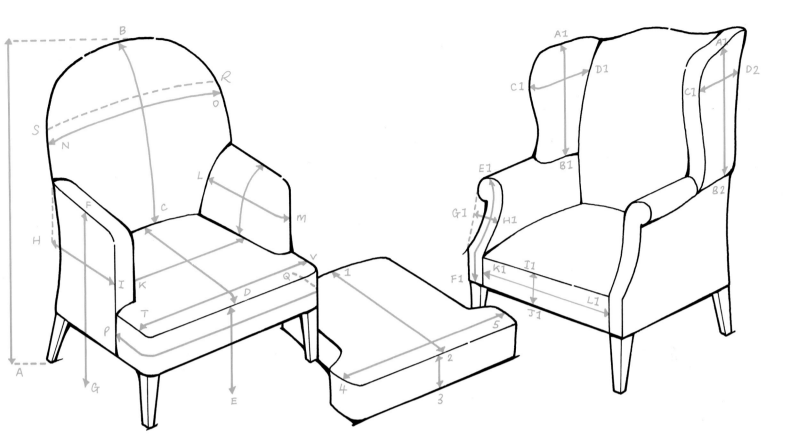

MEASURING

Outside back. LENGTH: A-B plus 1 inch seam allowance.
WIDTH: S-R plus 2 inches seam allowance

Inside back. LENGTH: B-C plus 2 inches seam allowance and
3 inches tuck-in allowance.
WIDTH: N-O plus 2 inches seam allowance.
(Check that this gives sufficient tuck-in
allowance across lower part of back.)

Seat. DEPTH: C-D plus 2 inches seam allowance and
3 inches tuck-in allowance.
WIDTH: J-K plus 2 inches seam allowance and
6 inches tuck-in allowance. *OR:*
WIDTH: T-U plus 2 inches seam allowance.
(Use whichever is the greater.)

Front. LENGTH: D-E plus 1 inch seam allowance.
WIDTH: P-Q plus 2 inches seam allowance.

Outside arm. LENGTH: F-G plus 1 inch seam allowance.
(Cut 2) WIDTH: H-I plus 2 inches seam allowance.

Inside arm. LENGTH: F-J plus 2 inches seam allowance and
(Cut 2) 3 inches tuck-in allowance.
WIDTH: L-M plus 2 inches seam allowance and
3 inches tuck-in allowance.

Cushion. LENGTH: 1-2 plus 2 inches seam allowance.
WIDTH: 4-5 plus 2 inches seam allowance.
DEPTH: 2-3 plus 2 inches seam allowance.

ADDITIONAL MEASUREMENTS FOR A WING CHAIR

Inside wing. LENGTH: A1-B1 plus 2 inches seam allowance.
(Cut 2) WIDTH: C1-D1 plus 2 inches seam allowance
and 3 inches tuck-in allowance.

Outside wing. LENGTH: A1-B2 plus 2 inches seam allowance.
(Cut 2) WIDTH: C1-D2 plus 2 inches seam allowance.

Front arm. LENGTH: E1-F1 plus 2 inches seam allowance.
WIDTH: G1-H1 plus 2 inches seam allowance.

Front seat. LENGTH: I1-J1 plus 2 inches seam allowance.
WIDTH: K1-L1 plus 2 inches seam allowance.

There may be extra panels of fabric,
or different-shaped panels,
depending on the shape of the chair.
Make a list to suit your needs, and
measure, following the existing
seams on the tight cover.

Add allowances for pleated or
gathered skirts and for cording as
necessary.

PIN FITTING CORNERS

With some styles, extra fitting is needed at the top corner or around the arms of the chair. Either stitch darts or run a line of gathering stitches along the seamline to control fullness.

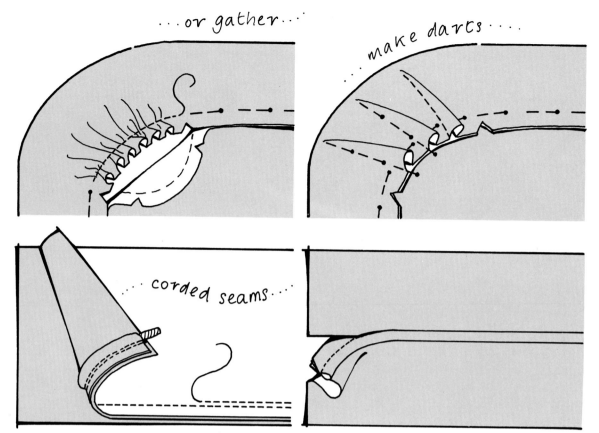

...or gather...

...make darts...

ACCENTING SEAMS

Cording is used to emphasize seams. Measure the total length of all the seams to be corded, and make up sufficient cording before starting to sew the seams. Cut bias strips three times the width of the filler cord, plus 2 inches. Cover the cord, and stitch, using the cording foot, then stitch cording to one side of seam. Sandwich cording in place as you stitch the seam.

...corded seams...

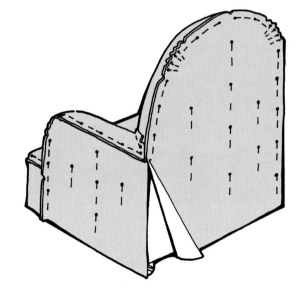

On wing chairs and chairs with front arm sections there are extra seams. Pin sections to seat and back cushions in the same way.

SEQUENCE OF CONSTRUCTION

Follow this sequence for pin fitting the fabric and for constructing the seams of the cover. Pin fabric panels to chair, centering the panel and ensuring that the crosswise grain is parallel to the floor. Then pin seams.

1 Pin inside back and inside arm sections together, with seam fitting snugly over the arm and tapering to the full tuck-in allowance at the seat. Clip into seam allowance at curve.

2 Pin inside and outside arm together along top of arm.

3 Pin front section to front edge of seat, wrapping around corners if necessary.

4 Pin seat to inside arm along side of seat, fitting at outer edge, but tapering to full tuck-in allowance at back of seat.

5 Pin outside arm to front section below arm.

6 Join the seat to inside back section, allowing full tuck-in allowance.

7 Pin outside back to inside back, starting from the center and working outward. Continue pinning down outside arm section. Mark position for opening (usually down back corner) and check that you have made it long enough to fit the cover over the chair.

FINISHING THE LOWER EDGE

Around the lower edge of the chair, there is a choice of finishes. The raw edges may be turned under to form a casing, and the cover drawn tightly under the chair with a drawstring tape. Or a pleated skirt or gathered flounce can be added, hanging to floor level.

For a skirt or flounce decide on the finished depth of the trim. Measure around the chair at the appropriate height to find the finished length of the skirt.

For box pleats, plan pleat size and space between pleats so that a box pleat falls at the center of the front of the chair, and the space between the pleats falls at the corners. Divide finished length of skirt by the desired space between the pleats to give the number of pleats. Add pleat allowance and space allowance together, and multiply by the number of pleats to give the total length required.

For knife pleats, allow three times the finished (pleated) length.

For a gathered ruffle, allow 1½ to 2½ times the finished (gathered) length, according to the weight of the fabric and the effect desired.

Add seam allowance at ends and top edge, and hem allowance at lower edge.

Cut the strips across the fabric on the straight grain, and join with flat seams. Finish raw edges, press, then press seams open. Turn up hems and stitch by hand or machine.

For a straight skirt with inverted pleats at corners, measure the length of each side of chair and add 10 inches for pleat, seam, and ease. Allow 1½ inches for seams along top and bottom edges. Cut four underlays for the pleats, each the depth of the skirt plus seam allowances, and 10 inches wide. Cut

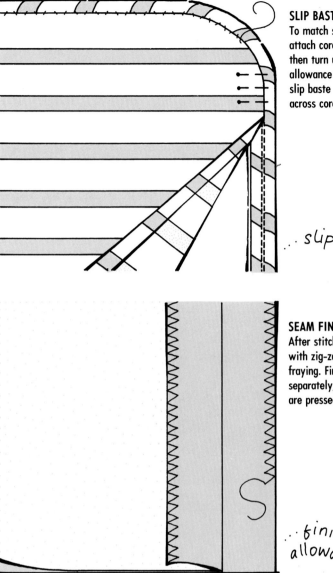

... slip basting...

... box pleats ...

... knife pleats ...

SLIP BASTING CORDED SEAMS
To match striped and plaid fabrics, attach cording to one side of seam, then turn under and press seam allowance on opposite edge. Pin and slip baste so that pattern matches across cording.

SEAM FINISHES
After stitching seams, finish edges with zig-zag stitch to prevent fraying. Finish each edge separately, even if seam allowances are pressed in the same direction.

.. finish seam allowances ....

PLEATED SKIRTS
Pin mark the pleats across the top of the skirt. Fold and press pleats, then baste in place. Stitch cording across top of skirt, along seamline, before attaching skirt to cover.

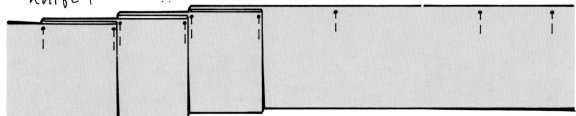

OPEN INVERTED PLEATS

Place lining over skirt sections and underlays, right sides facing. Pin along lower edge and stitch, taking ½ inch seam allowance. Press, then press seam allowance toward lining. Trim seam allowances to ¼ inch. With right sides together, fold top fabric ¼ inch from stitching line and pin lining in place across ends. Stitch. Trim seam allowances and clip bulk from corners. Turn to right side and press. Turn under 4 inches at each end of long skirt sections. Bring folds together, wrong side up, and place underlay over folds, wrong side up. Position the underlays so that they extend slightly above pleat at top seamline. Pin and stitch in place, stitching cording around top of skirt at seamline if desired. At opening corner, stitch underlay to one side of the pleat only. Finish top raw edges of underlay. Set in zipper. Attach a snap fastener to the corner of the underlay.

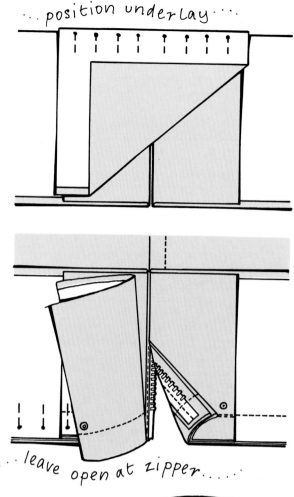

...position underlay...

...leave open at zipper.....

ATTACHING SKIRTS AND FLOUNCES

Trim away excess fabric around lower edge of cover, leaving a 1 inch seam allowance. Position skirt or flounce around cover, with right sides facing and raw edges matching. Stitch in place, taking 1 inch seams. Trim and grade seam allowances. Press, then press seam allowances toward cover.

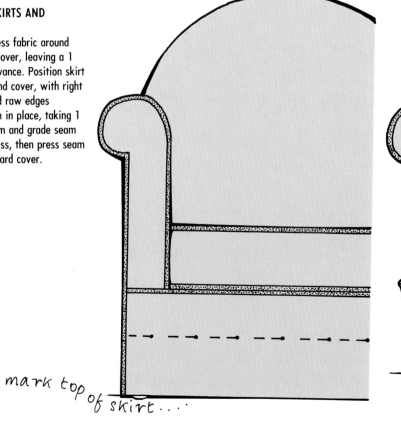

...mark top of skirt....

panels of lining to the same widths, but ¼ inch shorter than top fabric.

For a drawstring finish check that there is at least 3 or 4 inches for turning under around the lower edge of the cover. Make up the cover and fit it on the chair, then trim away fabric at legs, leaving a ½ inch seam allowance. Fit the zipper, then finish the raw edges around the legs before making the casing.

FINISHES FOR OPENINGS

Openings are needed to slip the covers onto the chair. Measure and mark the opening at the fitting stage. Leave the opening unstitched, but pin it closed at each fitting stage.

The opening may be finished with a zipper, or there are special hook-and-eye tape fastenings which can be stitched to the seam allowances.

For pleated or gathered skirts, the zipper pull tab should be about 2 inches from the lower edge; with inverted pleats it is level with the top of the skirt, and for drawstring casings it is level with the top of the legs of the chair.

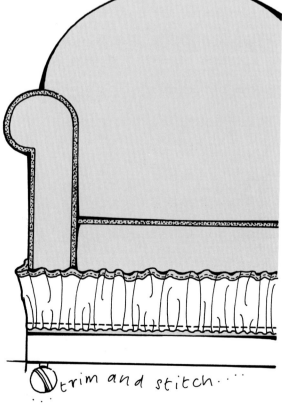

...trim and stitch....

INSERTING A ZIPPER

Pull out and trim cord from cording within the seam allowance. For a zipper down the left back corner of a cover, fold seam allowance under ¼ inch from the seamline, down opening to lower edge of flounce (except on skirts with inverted pleats). Close the zipper. Pin and baste folded edge of seam allowance to right side of zipper tape, ⅛ inch from teeth. Position pull tab about 2 inches from lower edge of skirt (or level with top of skirt with inverted pleats). Adjust zipper foot to left of needle and

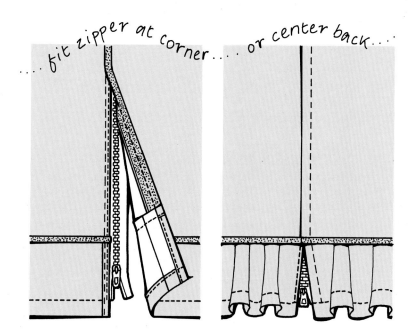

...fit zipper at corner... ...or center back...

stitch near the fold from the top of the opening to the lower edge of the flounce. On the opposite side of the opening, fold the seam allowance under on the seamline, carrying fold to lower edge of flounce. Lap the folded edge over the zipper, to meet the seamline down the opposite side, and pin. Baste through all thicknesses, ⅝ inch from the fold. Adjust the zipper foot to the right of the needle, and stitch across the top end and down the side of the zipper to the hem of the flounce, following basted line. Tie threads on underside.

HOOK-AND-EYE TAPE

Pin eye side of tape to seam allowance down left-hand side of opening, so that the outer edge is a small fraction of an inch inside the seamline. Turn under lower end of tape. Topstitch in place down long edges and across lower edge. Fold back seam allowance down opposite side of opening. Pin opposite part of of tape to seam allowance through

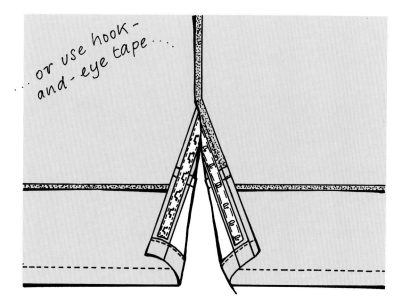

...or use hook- and-eye tape...

both layers of fabric, positioning outer edge just in from seamline to match first side. Baste in place all around edge of tape, checking that hooks and eyes match. Topstitch across top of opening, through top fabric, both halves of tape, and both seam allowances. Stitch hook part of tape in place from outside of cover, following basting stitches.

DRAWSTRING FINISH

Cut 1½ inch wide bias strips, and pin and stitch to edge of fabric around legs, taking ½ inch seams. Slash into the corners, almost to the stitching. Press. Turn bias strip to underside and turn under ½ inch down long raw edge. Slipstitch to inside of cover. (At opening, finish edges on each side of opening before inserting zip.)

Turn under ½ inch then 1 inch all round raw edge of cover. Stitch close to foldline to form a casing. Thread tape through casing and fit cover. Fasten zipper and pull tape up and tie tightly.

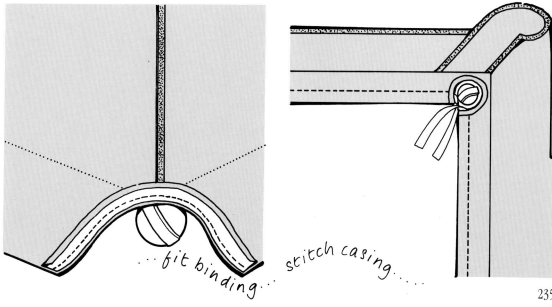

...fit binding... stitch casing...

Making lampshades

Lighting is an important element in the decoration of a room. Besides being functional, it creates a distinctive atmosphere in a room; lamps produce pools of light and serve as focal points in their own right, and lampshades play an important role in tempering and directing the light produced.

Although there is a great variety of lampshades on the market, you may sometimes have difficulty finding exactly the style you want in the appropriate color. Or you may already have a lampshade which, though still usable, will not harmonize with a new decorating scheme. In such cases, a good option is to remove the existing fabric from the frame and re-cover it with suitable fabric.

If you have never made a lampshade before, it is wise to start with a simple style, such as the gathered conical shade, rather than a fitted, shaped shade, which entails stretching the fabric on the bias. In this way you can become familiar with some of the materials and techniques involved before attempting a more difficult project.

For most styles of shade it is advisable to bind the frame with cotton tape, which enables you to stitch the cover firmly in place. It is important that the tape be firmly fixed, so follow the method described here carefully.

TAPING THE FRAME

Use ¼-inch wide cotton tape. Wrap it into a bundle and tie it with a rubber band so that you can hold it in the palm of your hand and grip it tightly as you work.

Start by binding the struts. Lay one end of the tape down the last couple of inches of the first strut, wrap it over the bottom ring in a figure-eight, then wrap it tightly around the strut, working upward, covering the free end of the tape to hold it firmly. Work up to the top ring, then wrap the tape around in a figure-eight. Slip the end of the tape under the last loop, and pull tight, then trim end.

Repeat for all the struts. Starting at a strut, bind the top and bottom rings in the same way, wrapping the tape around each strut in a figure-eight to anchor the ends firmly. When the rings are bound, turn under the ends and stitch in place.

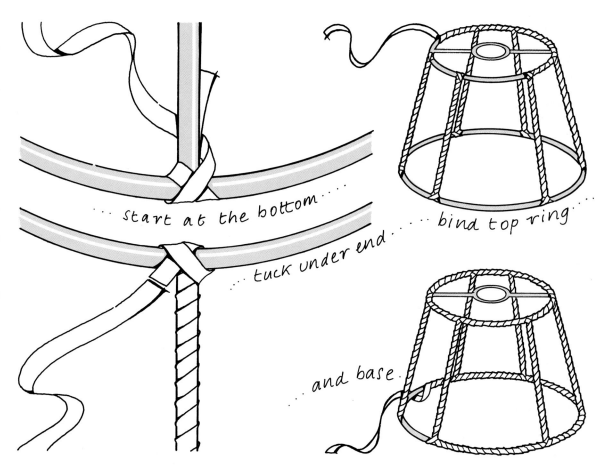

... start at the bottom
... tuck under end
... bind top ring
... and base

FABRICS AND TRIMS

Lightweight furnishing fabrics should be used for lampshades. When choosing, think of the overall color of the fabric, and check how it will diffuse the light. A white lining may help to give a brighter effect. For a simple gathered shade, a firmly woven cotton is suitable, but for more tailored styles, silks and satins, in synthetic or natural fiber, are more appropriate – again, they must be firmly woven.

Avoid fabrics that fray easily.

Fitted shades may be finished with self-fabric binding, contrasting binding stitched in place, or ribbon or braid glued around the upper and lower rings of the shade after it has been stitched in place.

For simple bell or balloon pendant covers, use lightweight cotton – eyelet lace can look particularly effective in a bedroom setting or use gingham for a country kitchen.

GATHERED CONICAL SHADE

Measure the distance around the lower, larger ring and allow a fullness of 1½. Measure the height of the shade along one of the struts and allow a hem of 1 inch. Cut a piece of fabric to these measurements. Join the sides of the shade, right sides together, and finish raw edges (or make a lining to match and insert inside main fabric, wrong sides facing).

Run lines of gathering stitch through upper and lower edges of fabric, 1¼ inches from raw edges. Slip fabric over taped frame and draw up fullness, distributing gathers evenly. Fasten ends of gathering threads, then pin fabric in place to upper and lower bound rings. From right side, stitch fabric to binding along the pinned line, holding the gathers firmly in place. Trim away fabric close to stitching.

Cut bias binding to fit around upper and lower rings, and stitch over the raw edge and ring by hand.

FITTED SHAPED SHADE

For a fitted shade, cut a rectangle of fabric on the bias, long enough to wrap around the largest ring of the shade and deep enough to fit the height of the shade, allowing 2 inches all around. Fold the fabric in half, and baste the two layers together across the center in both directions. Pin the fabric to the frame down the outer side struts and around rings, stretching it to fit tightly as you work. Mark stitching lines with dressmaker's chalk all along pinned struts and rings.

Remove the fabric from the shade, and stitch together down marked side seamlines. Remove basting. Trim away fabric from seam and finish raw edges. Wrap a strip of folded fabric around the joint between the struts holding the lamp fitting in place and the lower ring and stitch to ring. This gives a neat edge to the joints when the shade is in place. Slip the shade over the frame and re-pin along marked ring stitching lines. Overcast fabric to binding along marked lines, then trim away fabric close to stitching.

To make the lining, cut and fit a rectangle of lining in the same way as for main shade. After fitting the main fabric, slip the lining inside the frame. Stretch and fit it inside the frame, wrapping over the upper and lower rings. Clip into the trimming allowance of the lining in line with the struts that hold the lamp fitting in place, so you can stretch the lining tightly over the lower ring. Pin along outside of upper and lower rings, then stitch in place just outside previous row of stitching. Trim lining close to stitching. At the joints around the lower ring, tuck the lining under the folded fabric strips for a neat finish.

Finish the lampshade by binding or gluing velvet ribbon or braid over stitching.

gather fabric

stitch to frame

bind edges

mark and stitch seams

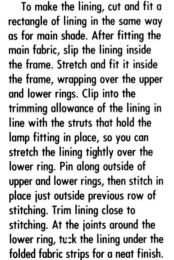

finish struts

stitch to frame

bind edges

237

SIMPLE DRAPED SHADES

For a simple fabric cover for a conical shade, cut a square of fabric so that each edge is about twice the diameter of the shade. Cut a hole in the center of the shade, about 1½ inches in diameter. Fit a strip of ½ inch wide bias binding around the hole, right sides together and with foldline of binding ¼ inch from raw edge of opening. Clip into seam allowance around hole, press and then turn the binding and seam allowance to the inside. Topstitch the free folded edge of binding to the shade to finish the edge of the fabric and form a casing. Thread elastic through casing.

Finish the raw edges of the fabric square with satin stitch, making it scalloped or following the lines of a pattern if appropriate. (To do this, apply an underlay of stitch-and-tear interfacing, then mark position of stitching. Stitch with a closed-up zig-zag stitch, then trim away fabric close to stitching and remove underlay.) For extra

decorative effect you can add topstitched trimming, decorative machine stitching, or appliqué, for example.

Fit the cover over a paper shade, and use over a low wattage bulb. Make sure that there is plenty of ventilation at the top of the shade.

... bind central hole ...

LIGHTWEIGHT BALLOON SHADE

Measure the distance around the frame at its maximum diameter. Add 2 inches for seams and ease. Measure the height of the frame along one of the struts, and add 4 inches for turning and casings. Cut a piece of fabric to these dimensions, and stitch and finish the side seam taking ½ inch seams. Make casings around the top and lower edges, turning over ¼ inch then ½ inch and stitching close to the folded edge. Thread elastic through casings, and fit shade on frame. The top casing should fit tightly around the top ring, leaving a good hole for ventilation. Tighten the elastic in the lower casing so it draws the lower edge of the cover under the bottom of the frame. Trim and join ends of elastic.

A ruffle may be added around the lower part of the shade, to hang below the lower ring.

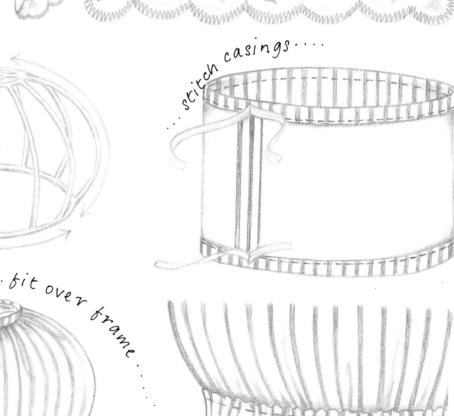

... stitch casings ....

... fit over frame ....

add ruffle ......

Bags and purses

Useful home accessories or stylish fashion accessories – bags and purses are economical to make, and practical. Tough vinyl shopping bags or shoulder bags are long lasting and simple to make. Small fabric bags (with shoulder straps as a practical touch) can be made in quilted fabric; or choose elegant taffeta or silky fabrics for evening use.

BEADS AND SEQUINS

Beads and sequins add a glamorous touch to evening bags. They can be sewn on by hand or machine, onto a number of different fabrics: velvets and heavy silks are particularly appropriate. Plan the work carefully, and do a test sample on a scrap of matching fabric to check the combination of beads, fabric, and thread give the effect you want.

There are two methods of hand beading. Choose the method of hand beading to suit the fabric and the type of beads you wish to use. Mark out the design with chalk or lines of basting, on the right side of the fabric. For plain beading, use a needle fine enough to slide through the beads easily.

Alternatively, the beads may be held on another length of thread and stitched in place by couching.

Sequins may be used to produce outline designs, or to fill in an area outlined by a row of beads or sequins. They should be sewn on by hand.

Machine beading is similar to the couched method of hand beading. The beads are held on a strong thread, and a small zig-zag stitch is used to hold the beads in place. The work must be planned so that there is always room to fit the narrow zipper foot between the rows of beading. The method is suitable for small, round beads.

HAND BEADING

Fasten the thread on the underside of the fabric with two tiny backstitches. Bring the needle up through the fabric, slip a bead over the needle, and take a backstitch, bringing the needle out exactly a bead length from where the thread came out. Start each successive backstitch against the previous bead, to hold the beads close together. Control the tension of each stitch so that the beads lie flat.

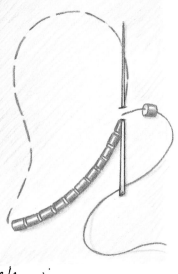

..use backstitch...

COUCHED BEADING

Fasten a thread at start and thread beads onto it. Use a fine needle, with matching thread, to couch the beads: fasten the thread on the underside with two tiny backstitches. Hold the beads in position, and bring the needle up through the fabric on the left of the beading thread. Bring the thread to the right, between the beads, and take a stitch over the thread holding the beads. Bring the needle up to the left of the beading thread again, sliding the next bead up to the stitch. At the end, fasten the couching stitch with backstitches. Remove beads and fasten beading thread on the underside.

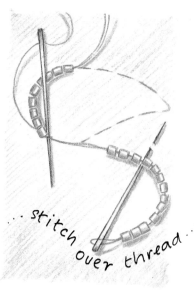

..stitch over thread...

MACHINE BEADING

Position an underlay of organdy or tear-off backing behind the area to be embroidered. Mark the pattern on the backing, then machine stitch along the outline to transfer the pattern to the right side of the fabric and form a firm backing for the stitching.

Thread the beads onto a double strand of matching fine cotton-polyester thread, tying the first knot a short distance — about 4 inches — from the end of the thread. Arrange the beads evenly on the thread, and anchor the last bead by passing the needle through it a second time. Adjust the machine for a medium-width zig-zag stitch, with the needle in the central position, and a 15 stitch length. Place the beads directly over the line of the design and adjust the zipper foot so that it can follow the edge of the string of beads. Zig-zag stitch over the line of beads, adjusting the position of each bead with the index finger of your left hand (or a pair of tweezers) so that the stitches fall between the beads. Adjust the spacing of the beads to suit the length of the stitch.

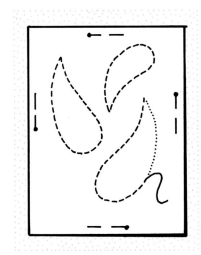

...mark outline......

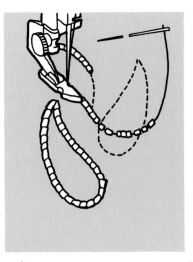

...stitch over thread...

SEWING ON SEQUINS

Use a fine needle and a thread to match the sequins. Fasten thread on the underside of the fabric, then bring the needle up through the fabric and through a sequin. Hold the sequin flat against the fabric, right side up, and take a stitch in front of it. Pass the needle up through the next sequin from the right side, then take a backstitch from the edge of the first sequin to the same distance beyond the previous stitch. As you tighten the stitch, arrange the sequin right side up over the thread holding the first sequin.

To hold single sequins in place with a small bead, choose a bead that is larger than the hole in the sequin. Bring the needle up through the fabric, and through the sequin and bead. Then carry the needle back through the sequin and into the fabric at the same point.

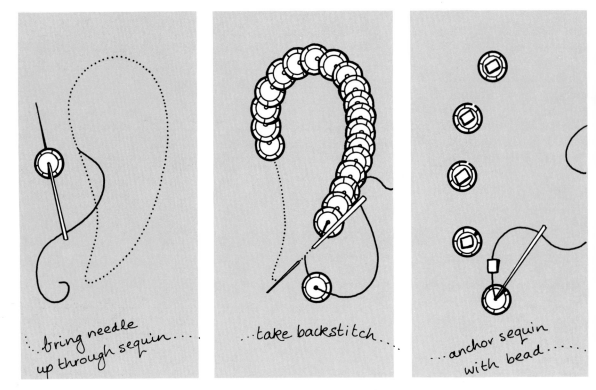

...bring needle up through sequin....

...take backstitch....

...anchor sequin with bead......

FUN IDEAS FOR CHILDREN'S BAGS

For a child's purse, you can cut the front panel to almost any shape. Make up the back panel from two pieces of fabric, and insert a zipper between them. Topstitch a strap to the back panel at each end of the zipper before making the bag.

- For a cat purse, use black fake fur fabric, and cut the purse as a circle. Appliqué the front panel with felt patches for eyes and cheeks, and add pipe cleaners for whiskers. Cut felt triangles for ears, and fit them into the seam as you stitch around the edge.

- For a fish-shaped purse, embroider the front of the purse using a metallic thread and a selection of machine embroidery stitches, to make scales and fins.
- For a strawberry purse, cut the purse from satin fabric (adding a lining). Embroider the front of the purse with yellow beads to represent the seeds, and add appliqué leaves at the top.
- For a down purse, appliqué bold features and add yellow yarn for hair.

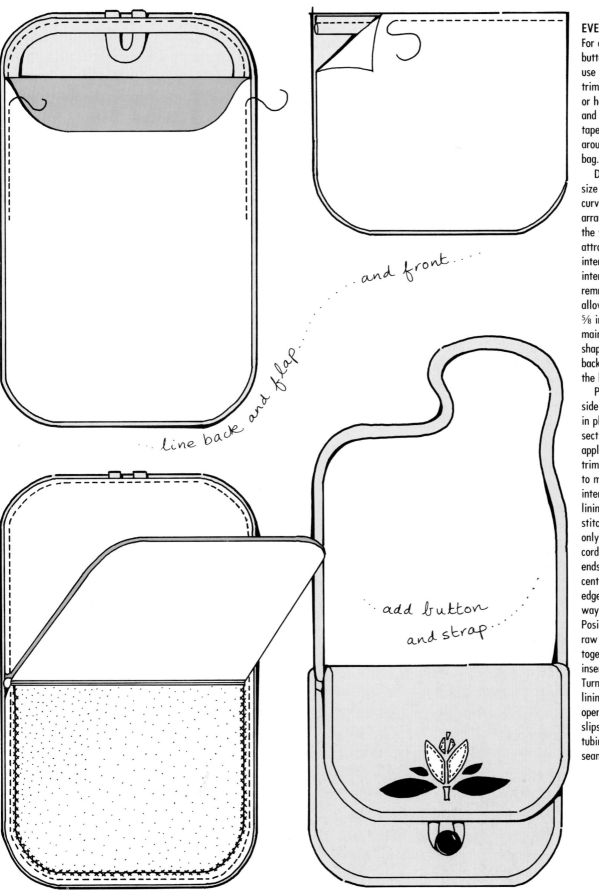

...and front...

...line back and flap...

add button and strap...

...join front to back...

EVENING BAG

For a simple evening bag with a button-over flap and shoulder strap, use a silky fabric with a corded trim, tubing button loop and strap, or heavier velvet with a cord trim and strap. Insertion cord, with a tape edge, can be used like cording around the flap and sides of the bag.

Decide on an overall shape and size for the bag: a rectangle with curved corners, with the top flap arranged to button three-quarters of the way down the front, is attractive. The bag should be interlined with heavyweight interfacing and lined with a remnant of fabric. Omit seam allowance for interlining, but add ⅝ inch seam allowance for the main fabric and lining. Cut and shape rectangles of fabric for the back and flap and for the front of the bag.

Position interfacing on wrong side of bag, and herringbone stitch in place. Decorate the front flap section of the bag with beads, appliqué, or another appropriate trim. Cut a length of cord or tubing to make a button loop. Position interfaced back and flap panel on lining, right sides together, and stitch together around flap section only, inserting cording or insertion cord into the seam and catching ends of button loop into seam at the center of the flap. Stitch the top edge of the front panel in the same way. Turn right side out and press. Position front panel on back so that raw edges match all around. Stitch together, through main fabric only, inserting trim, if desired, in seam. Turn bag so that you can stitch the lining together, leaving a 4 inch opening. Turn bag right side out and slipstitch opening. Attach cord or tubing strap to top of each side seam.

VINYL BAG

A simple vinyl shopping or shoulder bag can be made to almost any shape or size. Choose good quality vinyl that will hold its shape.

Decide on the finished measurement of the bag: for an upright shopping bag, make it about 18 inches deep and 14 inches wide, with a 2 inch gusset all around. For a shoulder bag, make it wider than it is deep, since this is more manageable in use.

Cut out panels of fabric for the front and back of the bag, allowing ½ inch seam allowance around sides and lower edge and a 2 inch hem along upper edge.

Cut out a strip for the gusset (joining lengths to coincide with corners of bag if necessary) allowing ½ inch seam allowance down sides of strip and 2 inches for turning under at each end. Fit gusset around sides and lower edge of front and back of back, right sides facing and raw edges matching. Stitch, pivoting fabric on needle at corners, taking ½ inch seam. Press seam open with fingers, and clip across corners. Turn bag right side out. Turn under 2 inches across top edge. Cut handles or shoulder straps, making the straps three times the finished width. Fold strips into three and topstitch down each edge to make handles. Divide the top edge of each side of the bag into three

and mark. Position ends of handles under top hem on bag, at the marked points. Topstitch hem in place, stitching over ends of handles, making two lines of stitching, close to the folded edge and the raw edge of the hem. Overlap rows of stitching at each end for a firm finish.

...stitch gusset...

...add straps...

SHOULDER BAGS

Cut a single panel for sides and base of bag, allowing 1 inch top hem and ½ inch for side seams. Cut two side gusset pieces, with top hem as before and seam allowance all around. Cut two straps, 3 inches wide; the length should be twice the height plus depth of the bag, plus 12 inches for a short handle or 28 inches for a shoulder strap. Turn under and stitch top hem on bag gusset. Make the straps as before, then position them so that the ends overlap on the base of the bag. Topstitch in place. Fit gussets in place, aligning top edges.

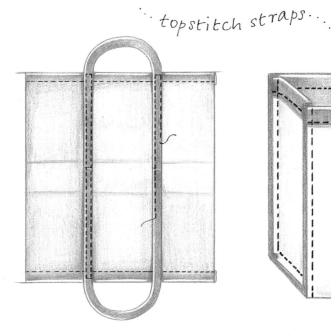

...topstitch straps...

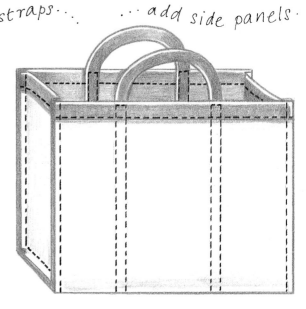

...add side panels...

The soft touch

You can use your sewing skills to introduce any number of fabric accessories to your home. Besides the obvious home furnishings – curtains, pillows, slipcovers and bedlinen – you can cover side tables and dressers with fabric ornaments. Simple and stylish, circular occasional tables make tremendous impact if they are covered with a floor-length cloth. Additional, overlaid square cloths add extra interest to the arrangement. Plain wicker baskets make practical and decorative containers for jewelry, cosmetics, or sewing accessories, for example; or you can make covers for tissue boxes or small kitchen appliances, to blend them into your decorative schemes.

KITCHEN WARES

In the kitchen or dining room, you can be more practical with your fabric accessories. Aprons and oven gloves are useful as well as decorative and make welcome gifts. Table linen and quilted table mats protect polished surfaces, or mask unsightly ones, and add a personal touch to your table.

Choose fabrics according to the type of project. Vinyl is a suitable choice for many accessories: aprons, kitchen tablecloths and covers for toasters or food processors which you want to hide away. You could also use vinyl to make a useful wall pocket bag for cleaning materials: cut a panel of fabric to hang on the back of the door, and stitch a series of pockets to it, to hold dust cloths, polishes, and so on.

Quilted fabric is also useful for making oven gloves, appliance covers, or placemats. You can use ready-quilted fabric, or quilt your own, using one of the techniques described on page 71.

Elegant tablecloths and napkins should be made in fine plain-weave linen (see page 42) or damask. For a fresh, practical look, choose simple geometric or floral prints, in bright primaries or pastel shades. Use stronger patterns for busy, family rooms, and dramatic colors and clean patterns for modern design-conscious dining.

VINYL APRON
Decide on a suitable overall size for the apron, depending on whether it is for an adult or a child: a good size for an adult is about 24 inches wide and 36 inches long. Allow ½ inch for turning under on all edges.

Cut out a panel of fabric to the desired measurements. Fold the apron in half, and mark curves to cut away fabric to form the "bib" of the apron: the line should start about two-thirds of the way across the top of the fabric and extend to about a third of the way down the side of the fabric.

Cut away fabric through both layers at the same time, to ensure that the sides match. Open out the fabric. Turn under ½ inch all around apron, pressing with your fingers. Cut away hem allowance at corners to form neat miters, and clip into curved turned-under edge so that it lies flat. Stitch hem in place by machine.

Cut lengths of 1 inch wide heavyweight tape, to make a neck strap and waist ties. Turn under ½ inch at the ends where it is to be stitched to the apron. Position on back of apron, over hem and hold in place with transparent tape. Stitch in place, all around overlap and across center for a firm finish.

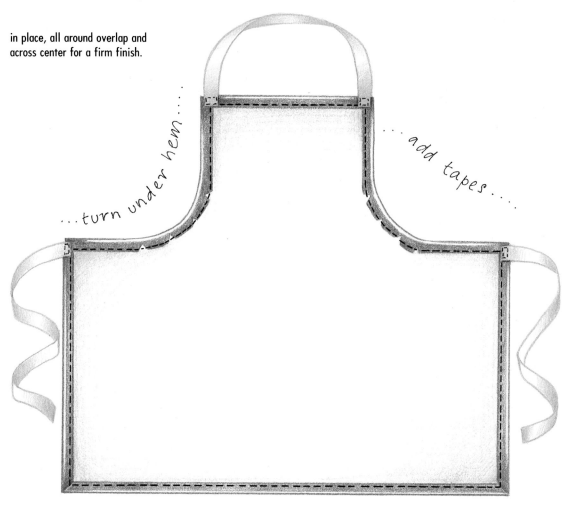

...turn under hem....

...add tapes....

QUILTED PLACEMATS

Decide on a suitable size and shape for the placemats: they can be round, oval, square, or rectangular, with square or rounded corners. If the mat is shaped, cut a paper pattern, folding it in four first to ensure that shaping matches at corners.

Cut out a panel of quilted fabric and a panel of heat reflective lining to the required size. Baste together across center. Cut a strip of bias binding (or straight binding if the mat has square corners). It should be about 2 inches wide. Turn under and press ⅜ inch down each side edge. Position binding around edge of mat, with foldline ⅝ inch from the raw edge of the mat, with right sides facing. Pin and stitch along foldline, allowing extra fullness at corners for mitering (see page 68). Turn binding to wrong side and slipstitch free folded edge of lining in place just inside first line of stitching. For a topstitched finish, stitch binding to wrong side of mat to start with. Turn over right side and topstitch in place.

For attractive children's placemats, cut them in simple animal shapes: a cat lying down, an owl or a porcupine, for example. Make the top of the mat in solid-color fabric, with a backing of batting and heat-resistant fabric. Baste the shaped layers of fabric together, then use tailor's chalk to draw in the details of the animal's features. Use a narrow, closed-up zig-zag stitch to quilt the fabric, following the marked lines. Bind the edges to match the main color.

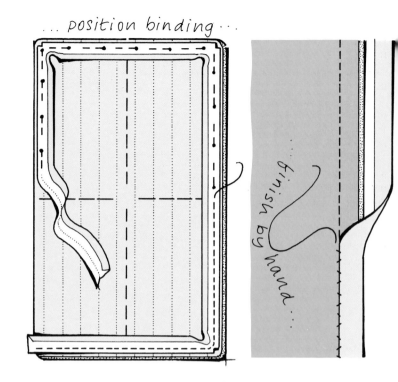

OVEN MITT

Use quilted fabric, with an interlining of heat-resistant fabric and a plain lining of reversible fabric.

Cut out a paper pattern for the glove: it should be at least 8 inches wide and 12 inches long, including a ½ inch seam allowance all around.

Cut out quilted fabric and interlining to these dimensions. Baste interlining to wrong side of quilted fabric. Position front and back of gloves together, right sides facing. Stitch together all around edges, taking ½ inch seams, and leaving lower edge open. Trim bulk from seam allowance, notch curves, and clip into angle of seam between thumb and main part of mitt. Press.

Cut out lining, using the same pattern, adding an extra 1¼ inch seam allowance around waist opening. Make up lining, taking a slightly larger seam allowance to give a good fit. Do not turn right side out. Position lining on glove and sew seam allowances together by hand. Turn main part of glove right side out, over lining. Turn up and press a ½ inch turning around lower edge of lining, then turn lining over lower edge of glove and stitch.

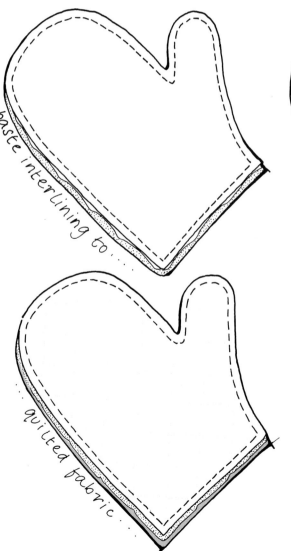

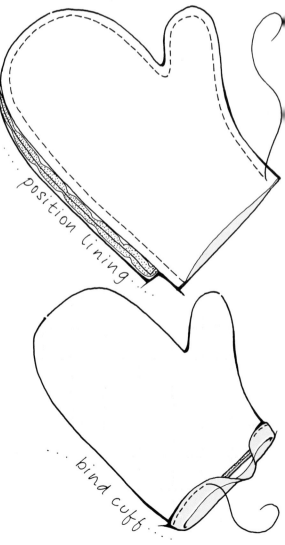

ROUND TABLECLOTH

Large round cloths can be tricky to cut out, so follow this method, using simple geometry techniques.

Decide on a suitable diameter for the cloth and add an allowance for the hem (see page 101 for details of curved hem finishes).

Cut a square of fabric to this measurement. If the width of fabric required is more than the width of the fabric you intend to use, join widths of fabric: cut a central panel using the full width of the fabric, then add another strip of fabric down each side to make up the width, joining the selvages for a neat finish. Press seams, then press open.

Fold fabric into four, and pin it together around edges. Lay it on a carpeted floor. Take a length of string, and tie it to a thumbtack and pin the fabric to the floor at the folded corner. Tie a pencil-style fabric marker to the other end of the string so that it is the same length as the radius (half the diameter) of the cloth. Draw a quarter circle on the cloth. Pin layers of fabric together just inside marked line, then cut out through all layers. Finish the cloth with a rolled hem or a faced hem, or bind the edge.

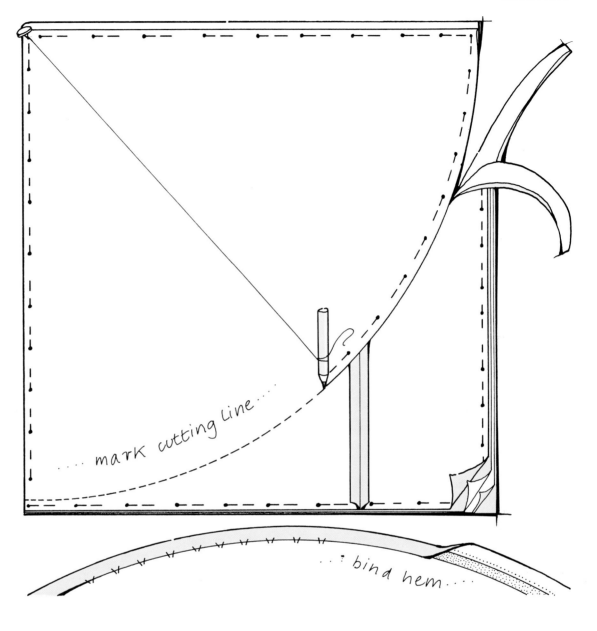

mark cutting line....

....bind hem....

FINISHES FOR TABLECLOTHS

You can add your own decorative touches to square, rectangular, or round tablecloths.

- Topstitch ribbons in place all around edge of cloth. Carry the ribbon right along each side, into the hem allowance. If you use more than one band of ribbon, you can make an attractive finish at the corners by weaving the ribbons to create a trellis effect. Topstitch ribbon in place with a straight stitch or decorative machine stitch. Press, then turn under and stitch a ½ inch double hem.
- Use the cording foot and a zig-zag stitch to fit a narrow cord trim around the edge of the cloth. On a square cloth, turn the cord and stitch neatly at each corner, pivoting the fabric on the needle.
- For a round cloth, to go on an occasional table, cut out the cloth, joining widths if necessary, following the instructions above. Cut an interlining of flannelette in the same way,

making a lapped seam. Interlock interlining to main fabric. Finish the hem with a deep bound edge. For extra luxury, add batting around the edge to make a thick rolled hem.
- Add appliqué motifs at the corners of a square cloth or around the hem of a round cloth. On solid-color fabrics, use patterned or solid-color fabric for the appliqué, but on printed cloths the effect is bolder if you use solid-color fabric for the motifs. Choose the motifs to suit the style of the room: floral motifs are appropriate in living rooms or bedrooms, but for a dining room you can achieve an amusing effect by adding motifs of fruit or vegetables.
- Hand or machine embroidery is appropriate in formal settings. Hand-rolled or hemstitched edges give a fine finish, and you could embroider a motif to match a favourite set of china, or to pick up themes used elsewhere in the room.

LINED BASKET

To line a basket, cut a panel for the base of the basket, adding ⅝ inch seam allowance all around. For the side panels, cut a strip of fabric long enough to fit around the basket by the depth of the basket plus a total of 2 inches for seams and hems. Join the ends of the strip with a flat seam, and run a line of gathering around the lower edge. Fit the sides to the base. Around the top edge, turn under a ⅝ inch double hem, and topstitch in place, leaving a 1 inch opening. Fit elastic into hem, and fit lining into basket, so that the casing wraps over the top and the elastic holds it in place.

...stitch casing...

...set in base...

...fit over basket....

FABRIC ACCESSORIES

Drawstring bags and lined wicker baskets have many different uses. Drawstring bags can be made in different sizes for different purposes: large bags to hang on the back of the bathroom door are useful for dirty linen; long, narrow bags can be used as shoe bags, to pack in your suitcase; and small bags with a waterproof finish are useful as cosmetic bags.

In the bedroom, use lined baskets for cosmetics, jewelry or hair accessories, for example. In the bathroom, use them to hold manicure tools or cotton balls. In the baby's room, lined baskets are useful for keeping together all the equipment needed at diaper-changing time: wipes, cream, tissues, diaper-liners, cotton swabs and so on. Lined baskets can also be used on the dining table to hold hot rolls, and they are useful for sewing threads or accessories, or odds and ends of stationery such as tape, scissors, string, measuring tapes, and paper clips.

DRAWSTRING BAG

Decide on the finished measurement of the bag, depending on the use it is intended for. The style shown here has a 2 inches deep hem at the top, with a ½-inch wide casing around the edge of the hem.

Cut the bag from two panels, adding ⅝ inch seam allowance around sides and lower edge and a 2¾ inch hem across top edge.

Position the panels of fabric with wrong sides together and raw edges matching. Stitch together around sides and lower edge, taking ⅜ inch seams, leaving openings on either side, 4⅜ inches from top, and the width of the casing. Reverse stitch on each side of opening to strengthen. Trim away seam allowance, trimming it level with line of stitching across opening.

Turn bag wrong side out, and stitch the second part of the French seam, leaving an opening in the stitching as before. Press and turn right side out. Turn under ¾ inch and then 2 inches across top edge, and press. Make two rows of stitching, close to first foldline, checking that casing formed is level with openings left in the side seams.

Cut two lengths of narrow

ribbon (or woven tape for a laundry bag), each twice the width of the bag plus 1 inch for turning under at each end. Thread one ribbon through each opening, then turn under 1 inch at one end, and turn the same amount to the right side at the other end. Fit folded ends inside each other and topstitch together. Draw ribbon around casing so that the joinings are inside. Pull out one loop of ribbon from each side opening in casing.

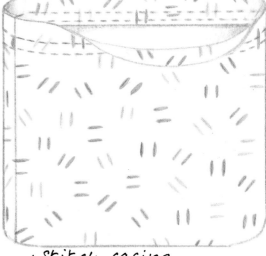

...join panels... *...stitch casing....*

...insert ribbon....

Glossary

abutted seam – Two pieces joined edge to edge with an underlay of a lightweight fabric. Usually used in interfacing and interlining.

appliqué – To sew a design of a small piece of fabric over the main fabric. The design or motif may be applied either by machine with a zigzag stitch or by hand.

armhole – The garment opening for the arm and sleeve.

backstitch – 1. The reverse stitch on the machine. Used to reinforce the stitching at the beginning and ending of seams.
2. A hand sewing stitch.

balance lines – The horizontal level on which the crosswise grain of the fabric falls at a right angle to the lengthwise grain in each dress section.

basting stitch – A long stitch made by hand or machine to hold two pieces of fabric together temporarily. Used to join garment sections before fitting and to prevent the fabric from slipping during stitching of seams.

bias – The diagonal line of fabric that is on neither the lengthwise nor the crosswise grain. A "true bias" is the diagonal line formed when the lengthwise edge of the fabric is folded to the crosswise edge.

binding – A single or double bias finish used to encase raw edges. It may be applied with or without topstitching.

blindstitch – 1. A hand stitch used for hemming and finish which is invisible, on the right side of the finished hem.
2. A zigzag machine stitch pattern used for hems. See Zigzag stitches.

block – To pin or shape and steam, rather than press – used with some kinds of embroidery and also knitted fabrics. Steam, holding iron above surface, and allow fabric to dry before handling.

bodkin – A heavy needle with a blunt point and large eye. Used to slot tape, elastic, ribbon, cord, etc., through a casing or heading.

boning – See **featherbone**.

buckram – A coarse, stiff cotton fabric used to hold the heading erect in draperies and to give body to contour belts, etc.

canopy – 1. Fabric hung or draped over a four-poster.

2. A decorative treatment above a headboard.

casing – 1. A hem or tuck through which ribbon, tape, cord, or elastic can be drawn. 2. Opening at the top of a curtain through which a rod is run.

catch – to attach one piece of fabric to another with tiny hand stitches, generally with several back-stitches over the first stitch; for example, a facing to seam allowance.

center line – The vertical center of the bodice, skirt or yoke section of a garment. It is marked on the pattern pieces and is transferred to the fabric sections with basting.

clip – To cut a short distance into a seam allowance or selvage with the point of the scissors. Used in curved seams, square corners, buttonholes, and the like, so that seams will lie flat when pressed.

crease – 1. A line or mark made by folding the fabric and pressing the fold. 2. The line or mark that may result when the manufacturer folds the fabric and rolls it on the bolt.

dart – A short fold or tuck, tapered to shape a garment.

directional stitching – Stitching of seams in the correct direction of the grain so that the fabric will not stretch during the stitching.

drape – 1. A property many fabrics have of falling easily into graceful folds; a soft silk, for example. 2. An attractive arrangement of folds in a garment, curtains, or draperies. The folds may be controlled by means of gathers, tucks or pleats.

dress form (shape) – A body shape (dummy) which is used to fit a garment. Made from various materials and often adjustable for size.

dressmaker's cutting board – A board marked in squares used for cutting fabrics where table space may not be available. Folds for storage.

dressmaker's tracing paper – A colored carbon (copying) paper used to trace a shape or pattern markings onto fabric. Usually used with a tracing wheel.

drop shoulder – Shoulder line located below the natural shoulder line.

ease – The even distribution of fullness when one section of a seam is joined to a slightly shorter section without forming gathers or tucks. Used to

Many of the terms defined here are explained more fully in the text. Consult the alphabetical index.

shape set-in sleeves, the shoulder line, and other areas.

ease allowance – The amount added to body measurements to make garments comfortable and allow for movement.

edge-stitch – 1. To stitch close to a finished edge or seam from the right side of the fabric. 2. To stitch close to the edge of a fold after the fabric edge is turned to the underside. Used to finish hems and facings.

embroidery hoop – Two narrow circles of wood, one fitting inside the other, used to hold fabric taut.

facing – The second layer of fabric used to finish necklines, front and back openings, and sleeves.

featherbone – A narrow strip of boning used to stiffen the seams and edges of closely fitted garment sections to prevent them from slipping or rolling; for example, the bodice of strapless dresses and cummerbunds.

fibers – Natural or man-made filaments from which yarns are spun.

finger-press – To press flat (as a hem or seam) using fingers and thumbnail.

finishing – The sewing techniques used in garment construction to finish seams, facings, hems, necklines, and other sections.

fly – A neatened opening that conceals the zipper or buttons. Generally used in shorts, men's pants, and topcoats.

gather – To control fullness with a running stitch or loosened machine stitch through the fabric; the thread is fastened at one end and then pulled up from the other end.

grading – Trimming all seam allowances within a seam to different widths; removes bulk so that the seam will lie flat.

grain – In woven fabrics, the lengthwise and crosswise direction of the yarn. When these lengthwise and crosswise threads or grains are at right angles, the fabric is "on the straight grain".

guidelines – Basted stitches to be followed for the final stitching (for buttonholes, pockets, etc.).

gusset – A small shaped piece of matching fabric set into a slash or seam for added width and ease. Sometimes found at the underarm and in underpants.

headboard – The upright board at the head of a bed.

heading – 1. A fabric tuck above a casing or at the top edge of curtains. 2. A narrow edge above a line of gathers that form a ruffle.

hemline – The line on which the hem is marked and turned to the underside. This line is an even distance from the floor.

hem-marker – See **skirt marker**.

interfacing – A third thickness of carefully selected fabric which is placed between the garment and facing fabrics for added body, shaping, and support.

interlining – A fabric placed between the lining and outer fabric. Used in coats, jackets, and the like to add warmth or bulk; in bedspreads to give body; in draperies to add body and to prevent light from showing through and fading the fabric.

intersecting seams – Seams that cross one another when garment sections are joined together at the waistline, shoulder line, set-in sleeve, and similar points.

"iron-on" – A term used to describe chemically treated fabric which is joined or applied to another fabric by using a warm iron.

lap – To extend or fold one piece of fabric or garment section over another.

lapel – The section of a garment that is turned back between the top button and collar.

layout – The position in which pattern pieces are laid on the fabric for cutting.

lining – A carefully selected fabric that covers the underside of another fabric, adding body to the article. 1. In dress construction, the lining is cut the same as the dress fabric and constructed separately. It adds a finished look to the inside. 2. In tailoring, the lining is constructed to fit into the jacket or coat and prevents the unfinished seam allowance from showing. 3. In home decorating, the lining is used to finish draperies and protect the top fabric. It is also used in bedspreads.

made-to-measure – Professionally made and fitted garments, slipcovers, bedspreads, curtains, and draperies.

markings – The symbols shown on the pattern for darts, buttonholes, tucks, and other construction details. They are transferred from the pattern to the fabric by means of tailor's tacks, chalk, basting, or tracing wheel.

mercerized – A finish for cotton that adds strength and luster and helps the fiber to take dyes.

miter – 1. The diagonal line formed when fabric is

joined at a square corner. After stitching, the excess fabric is generally cut away on the underside where the hems meet. Used where hems join at the corner as in a vent in a jacket, draperies and linens. 2. The diagonal fold made when applying a band, lace, or the like to square or pointed shapes.

motif – Decorative emblem or design used in embroidery, appliqué, etc.

nap – A soft fabric surface made by short fibers brushed in one direction. Should run in one direction on completed items.

notches – Outward V-shaped notches beyond the seam allowance that indicate which edges are to be seamed together. Matching notches are always joined.

notions – Small sewing needs, such as thread, needles, pins, zippers, snaps, hooks and eyes, bias binding, etc.

overwrap or overlap – The part of the garment that extends over another part, as the opening of a blouse, jacket, coat, or waistband.

pile – Raised loops or tufts on the surface of a fabric.

pinking – A serrated-edge seam finish, cut with pinking shears (used on fabrics that do not fray).

pivot – To turn the fabric on the machine needle while the needle is still in the fabric. Used when stitching square corners.

placket – A finished opening that is generally closed by means of a zipper, snaps, or other fastening. Used in dresses, skirts, shorts and other garments to make them easy to put on and to insure a good fit at the waistline, sleeve, etc.; also used in furnishings such as slipcovers and cushions.

pleats: drapery – Folds in the heading made into pleats either by hand or by using a tape with woven-in pockets.

   Cartridge pleats – A small round pleat filled with rolled fabric.

   French pleats – One large pleat divided into three at the lower edge of the heading, drawn together by hand, leaving pleats uncreased. Arranged at even intervals.

   Pencil pleats – Narrow pleats arranged close together to form a deep, firm top heading.

   Pinch pleats – One large pleat divided into two or three. Formed at intervals and fanning out at the top.

pleats: dressmaking – Folds in the fabric to give fullness, often partly stitched down.

   Accordion pleats – Fine narrow pleats made commercially.

   Box pleats – Two knife pleats that turn away from each other.

   Inverted pleat – Two knife pleats that turn toward each other.

   Kick pleat (Dior pleat) – A short pleat at the hemline of a skirt formed by an additional layer of fabric placed under an opening.

   Knife pleats – A series of pleats that are the same width and fall in the same direction.

   Release pleat – A partly stitched pleat (at top and/or bottom) in the back of a coat or jacket lining to give freedom of movement.

   Sunray pleats – Commercially pressed tapering pleats.

pleater tape – A stiffened tape with woven-in pockets or drawstrings used for draperies; forms pleats at even distances. Made from various fabrics, including nylon and polyester for sheer draperies, and in different widths.

pre-shrink – To shrink the fabric so that its dimensions will not be altered by laundering.

pressure – The force the presser foot exerts on the fabric during the machine stitching.

reinforce – To strengthen an area that will be subjected to strain. The area may be reinforced with an underlay or patch of fabric or with extra rows of stitching.

return – In drapery hardware, the distance from the curve of the track or rod to the wall. Draperies are constructed so that they extend around the return.

reversible – 1. A fabric that is woven so that either side may be used for the right side, for example damask or double-faced wool.
2. A garment finished so that it may be worn with either side out.

ruching – Several lines of stitching forming a gathered area.

seam allowance – The amount of fabric allowed for seams in joining sections of a garment or other article together – generally ⅝ inch.

seam edge – The cut edge of the seam allowance.

seamline – The line designated for stitching the seam – generally ⅝ inch from the cut edge.

selvage – The finished edges on all woven fabrics which are parallel to the lengthwise grain.

Box pleats, inverted pleats, and knife pleats are also used in soft furnishings, for loose cover flounces, bed valances and curtain pelmets, for example.

shank – The stem between the button and the garment to which the button is sewn. It can be made with thread or may be part of the button. It allows room for the buttonhole side of the garment to fit under the button.

shirring – Gathering, often elasticized, with rows of stitching, to control fullness.

skirt marker – A ruler standing from the floor (or attached to a door) with inches marked and equipped with a press bulb with chalk to mark the fabric for a hem; can be self-operated. Also available with a pin apparatus which requires a second person to operate.

snip – A small cut into the fabric (see **clip**).

stay – A small piece of fabric or tape that is sewn to an area of the garment for reinforcement. Used at the point of a slash, under bound buttonholes, and at the waistline. Also used on some seams in stretch fabrics to prevent distortion.

straight stitch – A plain straight machine stitch.

straight stretch stitch – Appears like a loose outline stitch, especially suitable for knitted and stretch fabrics.

Stitches and names may vary according to make of machine: always read your sewing machine handbook and practise zig-zag stitches before use.

tailoring – A method of sewing characterized by classic lines; in suits, coats, dresses, and pants.

tailor's tacks – Markings made of thread which are used to transfer symbols from the pattern to the fabric.

tension – The degree of looseness or tightness of the needle and bobbin threads that interlock to form the machine stitch. When the upper (needle) and lower (bobbin) tensions are balanced, both threads are drawn into the fabric to the same degree.

thread count – Number of threads (yarns) per inch in the warp and weft of woven fabric.

topstitching – A row of stitching on the right side, or top side, of a garment near the finished edge as a decorative accent. Can be made by machine or by hand.

tuck – A stitched fold of fabric which provides fullness or a decorative feature (as pin tucks); also a shrinkage or growth tuck to allow for letting out as a child grows.

underlap or underwrap – The edge of a garment that extends under another edge, as in the opening of a coat, jacket, or waistband.

underlay – 1. A strip of fabric that is placed on the underside of the main fabric for reinforcement. Used in stitching buttonholes, pockets, and similar sections; in mending; in decorative zigzag stitching.

underlining – The second thickness of a carefully selected fabric which is cut by the same pattern as the garment and is stitched in place with the garment seams. Used to give added body and shape.

understitching – A line of stitching through facing and seam allowances which helps the facing to lie flat.

vent – A lapped opening. Used in hems of tailored jackets and sleeves and in other garment sections.

waistbanding – Stiffening used as interlining or backing in a belt or inside a waistband.

warp – The threads or yarns that run lengthwise in the weaving of the fabric.

weft (old term woof) – The threads or yarns that cross the warp. Also called "filler".

zigzag stitches:

blindstitch zigzag – The stitch pattern that produces four straight stitches separated by a single sideways stitch to the left. Used in finishing seam edges, in stitching hems, and in decorative stitching.

multi-stitch zigzag – A stitch pattern that makes three stitches to the left, then four to the right in a zigzag shape. Used to finish hem and seam edges, mend, stitch darts and seams in interfacing, and sew elastic and blanket binding in place; also used for decorative stitching and other sewing.

plain zigzag stitch – A regular zigzag stitch in which all stitches are of the same width and in a straight line. The stitch length and stitch width selectors may be set for various lengths and widths.

Metric measurements are increasingly found in craft books alongside standard measurements. This table gives approximate equivalents in the two systems. It is important to remember that these (and most other) conversions are often rounded up or down to make them easy to work with, and so it is essential to work within one system or the other and never to mix the two.

EQUIVALENT MEASURES
Millimeters and Centimeters into Inches (slightly rounded)

mm	cm	inches	cm	inches
3 mm		⅛	48.5	19
6 mm		¼	51	20
10 mm or	1 cm	⅜	53.5	21
12 mm or	1.2 cm	½	56	22
15 mm or	1.5 cm	⅝	58.5	23
20 mm or	2 cm	¾	61	24
22 mm or	2.2 cm	⅞	63.5	25
25 mm or	2.5 cm	1	66	26
32 mm or	3.2 cm	1¼	68.5	27
38 mm or	3.8 cm	1½	71	28
45 mm or	4.5 cm	1¾	73.5	29
50 mm or	5 cm	2	76	30
	6.5	2½	79	31
	7.5	3	81.5	32
	9	3½	84	33
	10	4	86.5	34
	11.5	4½	89	35
	12.5	5	91.5	36
	14	5½	94	37
	15	6	96.5	38
	18	7	99	39
	20.5	8	101.5	40
	23	9	104	41
	25.5	10	106.5	42
	28	11	109	43
	30.5	12	112	44
	33	13	114.5	45
	35.5	14	117	46
	38	15	119.5	47
	40.5	16	122	48
	43	17	124.5	49
	46	18	127	50

Meters to Yards (slightly rounded)

meters	yards
0.15	⅛
0.25	¼
0.35	⅜
0.50	½
0.60	⅝
0.70	¾
0.95	1
1.40	1½
1.85	2
2.30	2½
2.75	3
3.20	3½
3.70	4
4.15	4½
4.60	5
5.05	5½
5.50	6
5.95	6½
6.40	7
6.90	7½
7.35	8
7.80	8½
8.25	9
8.70	9½
9.15	10

Available fabric widths

cm	inches
65	25
70	27
90	35/36
100	39
115	44/45
122	48
127	50
140	54/56
150	58/60
175	68/70
180	72

Available zip lengths

cm	inches
10	4
12	5
15	6
18	7
20	8
22	9
25	10
30	12
35	14
40	16
45	18
50	20
55	22
60	24
65	26
70	28
75	30

The quantities given in this chart are for 48-inch-wide fabric, unless otherwise specified. Ready-made sheets can be used in many cases to avoid piecing fabric widths.

BED DIMENSIONS AND FABRIC ESTIMATES

Standard size	Bedspread type and fabric estimates	Comforter cover and fabric estimate
Twin bed 39 × 78 inches	Plain: 7 yards Skirt with inverted pleats: 7½ yards Flounced skirt: 12½ yards	50 × 78 inches requires 9 yards of 36- or 48-inchwide fabric
Double bed 54 × 78 inches	Plain: 7 yards Skirt with inverted pleats: 8 yards Flounced skirt: 13½ yards (2½ times fullness)	78 × 78 inches requires 9 yards
Queen-size or King-size bed 60 × 80 inches 78 × 80 inches	Plain: 10½ yards Skirt with inverted pleats: 10½ yards Flounched skirt: 15½ yards	90 × 86 inches requires 10 yards of 54-inch-wide fabric

Pillow cases (with tuck-in)
Standard: 20 × 26 inches	1 yard
Queen: 20 × 30 inches	1⅛ yards
King: 20 × 40 inches	13 yards

Index

ACKNOWLEDGEMENTS

Senior editor: Camilla Simmons.
Production controller: Jenny May.
Picture research: Liz Fowler.

The editor would like to thank the following for their help in preparing the projects: Christine Jefferys, Hilary More, Beryl Miller, Wendy Crease.

Special photography: John Slater

Illustrators: Pauline Bayne, Paul Cooper, Terry Evans, Norah Fitzwater, Irwin Design, Bob Reed, Lorna Turpin.

Fabric used for curtains on front cover 'Crocodile' by Textra; fashion Poppas and Crazy Braces for children's dungarees, page 175, by Newey; fabrics on page 206 by Stiebel of Nottingham; curtain fabric on page 187 'Aimee' by Sanderson; curtain fabric, 'Rhapsody', and sofa fabric, 'Octave', on page 230 by Textra; other fabrics used in special photography from Liberty, John Lewis, Peter Jones, Laura Ashley, Dickins and Jones, and specialist fabric stores.

Special thanks to Bernina for providing the photograph of the sewing machine on page 15, and to Elna for their advice on the use of the sewing machine, used in the preparation of the text.

Photo credits: Woman's Weekly, IPC Magazines – p. 11; Elizabeth Whiting and Associates – pp 178, 179, 182, 195, 210